Erotique

Published in the United States by
THUNDER'S MOUTH PRESS
841, Broadway, Fourth Floor, New York, NY 10003

Library of Congress Catalog Card Number 98-86012

ISBN 1-56025-168-9

Managing Editor: Julian Flanders
Senior Art Editor: Diane Spender
Designer: Michael Spender
Picture Research: Lorna Ainger
Production: Alexia Turner

Printed and bound in Spain

Distributed by
Publishers Group West,
1700 Fourth Street,
Berkeley, California 94710

Erotique

MASTERPIECES OF EROTIC PHOTOGRAPHY

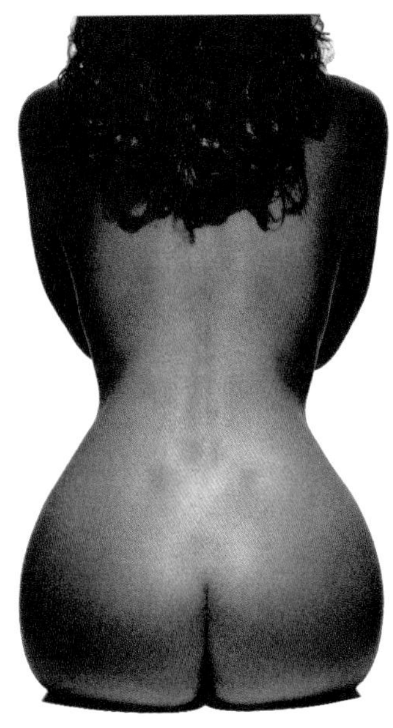

ROD ASHFORD

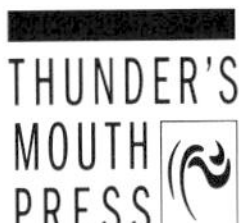

FOR MY WIFE SANDRA;
with love and thanks
for her constant
support and patience.

CONTENTS

INTRODUCTION by Rod Ashford **6**

THE PHOTOGRAPHS

Historical **19**

1950-1979 ..... **53**

1980s **73**

1990s **105**

Index, Acknowledgements and Picture Credits **221**

INTRODUCTION

THE EROTIC IMAGE

When shown a photograph, a viewer may make a number of assumptions about an apparent storyline that the picture purports to show. Assume the image of a man photographed outside a prison holding a suitcase. Is he a newly released inmate? Or is he a member of staff leaving for a trip? By picturing the same man with the same suitcase outside a railway station, a very different storyline can be constructed.

If the man with his suitcase is transported to the photographer's studio and photographed against a plain backdrop, the viewer's attention is concentrated on the man himself; perhaps his facial expression, his body language. Is he happy? Does he look friendly? The absence of any information about the man's surroundings, invites a quite different, more intimate, reaction from the viewer.

This construction of a narrative around the information within a photograph is key to the erotic genre. A photograph of a naked body is simply not enough. Detached and removed from any identifiable surroundings the body is depersonalized, reduced to its basic shape and form. If too explicit the image requires little input from the viewer and may well merely offend.

Nudity is by no means a prerequisite of the erotic. A head shot with direct eye contact can provide the viewer with an assumed intimacy with the subject, whereas a head shot of a blindfolded subject creates yet another illusion. Fabrics, and even water, accentuate and therefore eroticize the body. Undergarments, jewellery, stockings, or shoes, elicit the viewer's curiosity – how, why, where? Partially covered nakedness is, of course, by implication, partially un-covered.

By placing the subject within an identifiable surrounding, the photographer creates an allegory on behalf of the viewer. Perhaps unexpected or incongruous, as in the case of Iain McKell's Chip Shop image, or a voyeuristic peep through the keyhole during an unguarded moment typified by Charles Roff's Rue La Condamine.

THE EROTIC CONTEXT

Photographic images which provoke an emotional response from a viewer are employed in many areas and for many purposes. For instance, violent images of war are often used to justify ongoing armed conflict. However, the very same images are also used by campaigners for peace.

Given that the photograph remains the same, the difference in emotional response must therefore be governed by the circumstances in which the image is viewed. The fact that images can be cropped and retouched to fool a viewer's sensitivities is acknowledged, but variations created in this manner should not be viewed as the same image. The context in which erotic images are viewed can also have an enormous bearing on the viewer's reaction to them. However subtle the erotic motif, when viewed in an inappropriate context even images that have the power to excite can appear crude, obscene, alarming, or even bland.

A sophisticated erotic image, viewed in the testosterone bravado of an all-male environment, is more likely to be passed over in favour of something more explicit – an immediate image which requires no interpretation from the viewer, and seeks to objectify its female subject. However, in the privacy and comfort of the viewer's own chosen space, the same image might be viewed, interpreted, and enjoyed, perhaps with a loved one, as a prelude to their own passion.

THE MEDIUM OF PHOTOGRAPHY

As we stand poised at the turn of the twenty-first century, it would be fair to say that over the last 20 years or so, the computer has been responsible for revolutionizing our daily lives – certainly the production of almost everything we use, read, drive, or eat. We will enter the twenty-first century with the promise of even more technological intervention, as the way we actually conduct our lives, communicate with each other, and even think, will become ever more dependent on technology.

In much the same way as this electronics revolution shapes our perception of the world around us today, our ancestors at the turn of the nineteenth century found their lives every bit as influenced by a mechanical revolution. In a race to mechanize every area of day-to-day life, it would only be a matter of time before someone would bring about a way of mechanizing the process by which pictorial images were made.

The Development of the Photographic Process 1800-1860

The principle of projecting an image through an aperture had been known to ancient civilizations. The term 'camera obscura' means 'dark room' and describes a viewing room where pictures of the world outside were projected through a small hole in one wall on to the surface of another wall. The idea was borrowed by draughtsmen of the eighteenth century. An image was projected through a lens on to a ground-glass screen at the rear of a light-tight wooden box. By placing a sheet of paper over the viewing screen the draughtsman could trace the image and make a detailed technical drawing. Portraits were impossible using this version of the camera obscura as a lens capable of close focusing had yet to be invented.

In 1839, Louis Daguerre, a French showman, travelled to England and patented his process for automatically recording an image using a camera obscura. In Paris five days later he turned his invention over to the French Government in return for a State pension for himself and his partner.

Daguerre had not stumbled upon his process by accident – several others had almost invented the process before. Johann Schulze had recorded the effect of light on silver salts as early as 1725; Thomas Wedgwood, son of the Staffordshire potter, had made 'sun pictures' on sensitized leather around 1800, but died before perfecting a way of 'fixing' the image to stop it fading in the light; and in 1826, Frenchman Joseph Nicéphore Niépce became the first person to make a permanent picture through the action of light.

In 1839 it took at least fifteen minutes in bright sunlight to expose a daguerreotype, making it impossible to take pictures of people. However, as soon as news of Daguerre's invention became public, inventors all over Europe sought ways of refining his process. In particular, Josef Petzval of Vienna designed a lens almost ten times brighter than Daguerre's simple lens (f3.6 as opposed to f11). And by 1841, exposure times were down to a little under one minute in bright sunlight. Photographing people had become a viable reality.

Daguerre's invention resulted in a one-off image on a small sensitized copper plate. However, in England, William Henry Fox Talbot had already begun work on his own, quite different, process. Fox Talbot recorded a negative image by placing a light sensitized sheet of paper directly in the back of the camera. By using a second sheet of sensitized paper as a receptor, the negative could be reproduced again, but this time with the correct tonal values (a positive). The terms negative, positive, and photography (light drawing) are attributable to Sir John Herschel, another eminent scientist of the time.

By 1840, Fox Talbot had discovered that it was possible to remove exposed paper from the camera before the image had appeared, and accelerate development of the 'latent image' using gallic acid. In 1841 Fox Talbot was granted a patent for his calotype process (a term derived from the Greek word 'kalos', meaning both beautiful and useful).

Despite the popularity of the daguerreotype and calotype, photographers wanted a system that would combine the qualities of both: the clarity of the daguerreotype, together with the ability to make as many prints as required from one exposure (the negative). The principal requirement was for a transparent negative Although glass seemed the logical choice, chemicals that readily adhered to the fibres of paper would not stick to glass.

In 1847, excellent results were obtained using albumen (egg white) as an adhesive. But the technique was slow, requiring exposure times of up to 15 minutes. The discovery that collodion, a sticky substance previously used as a transparent dressing for open wounds, could be used as an efficient binder was to revolutionize photography. In 1851, Frederick Scott Archer discovered that if sensitized glass plates were exposed in the camera and developed before the collodion dried, the resulting negatives would be extremely sharp and contain fine detail.

The collodion or 'wet plate' process led to the development of the ambrotype, a direct positive variation, and later the ferrotype or tintype. All these processes were extensively used in portraiture between 1850 and 1860.

Although not strictly related to the process of photography itself, another device was to play a part in the evolution of the medium. On seeing the inventions by Daguerre and Fox Talbot, Sir Charles Wheatstone saw the possibility of incorporating photographic images into his own invention – the stereoscope. Two images, one as seen by the left eye, the other as seen by the right, were viewed through a series of prisms to give an impression of three dimensions. In 1849, Sir David Brewster demonstrated a much simpler stereoscope, but owing to a lack of interest from manufacturers, he took his device to Paris where optician Jules Duboscq suggested further improvements to the design.

Further Refinements 1860-1960

The photographic process as we know it today had largely been defined during the first twenty years or so since its discovery. Since then, film technology, the chemistry involved, and the designs of both cameras and lenses have undergone constant refinement.

In 1871 Richard Maddox, an English doctor, published details of his process for using gelatine as a substitute for collodion. Unlike collodion, the gelatine emulsion did not crack when dry. The discovery meant that plates could be prepared in advance of exposure and, once exposed, the plates did not have to be developed on the spot but could be carried home for processing. By 1879, dry plates were being sold ready-made, their increased sensitivity and consistency allowing exposure times as short as 1/25th second.

In America, George Eastman invented a plate-coating machine and set up the Eastman Dry Plate Company in 1880. Eastman soon saw the potential for offering photography to the mass market. In 1888 Eastman introduced the first 'Kodak' camera, a trademark invented by Eastman. The small fixed-lens camera came ready loaded with a one-hundred-shot paper roll film that had to be sent back to the factory for processing and reloading. In 1889 Kodak cameras used an emulsion-coated film, and by 1891 Kodak cameras were user-loadable.

Determining the length of time needed to make an exposure was largely a matter of guesswork until around 1890 when two British scientists, F. Hurtinger and V. C. Driffield, devised a system of rating the speed of film emulsions, making exposure tables, and later, exposure meters possible.

It has been suggested that the biggest step forward for photographic process was the ability to record natural colour. Experiments with colour photography were largely hampered by the poor sensitivity of film emulsions to all colours. However, by 1906 the first panchromatic (sensitive to all colours) film emulsions were available. A year later in France, Autochrome became the first colour film on the market. Film emulsions employing the same basic concept were continually developed into the 1950s.

However, as early as 1912 German chemists had started working on an alternative process, employing colour dye technology. In 1936, after years of extensive research in this area, Kodak launched Kodachrome. The following year, Agfa announced Agfacolour.

However, colour prints were still not viable. During the Second World War, both Kodak and Agfa introduced colour negative films, but neither were generally available before 1950. After the war, Agfa's patents were made freely available, allowing companies such as Fuji, Ilford, and Sakura to introduce their own slide films.

In 1947, almost as an aside from the development of mainstream photography, Dr Edwin Land announced the Polaroid Land process. The film technology still used gelatine and silver halide science, but held both negative and positive together in a pack that also contained the developing agent. Once exposed, the film was pulled out of the camera through a series of rollers and held for about one minute, after which the material could be peeled apart to reveal a finished print.

In 1963 Polaroid announced the first instant colour print film and ten years later introduced a single sheet instant colour film that did not have to be peeled apart.

Despite continual development of the colour process, it would be fair to say that processing and reproduction costs prohibited the widespread use of colour until the early 1970s.

Lighting

The long exposure times required by the first film emulsions relied on a good supply of bright sunlight. Indoor photography and overcast days presented early photographers with a problem. The gas lamps of the period were impractical as an artificial source of illumination as the number of jets required to produce enough light generated far too much heat.

During the 1880s, pyrotechnic flashpowder was in common use. The mixture of ground magnesium and other chemicals was usually ignited by blowing the powder into a flame, causing a brief but bright flash – as well as an unpleasant smell, smoke, and ash. Tungsten filament bulbs were also in use in 1880. However, their glow was weak and too orange which made its effects difficult to record on film.

Flash bulbs were first introduced in 1925. Contacts fitted inside the camera were connected to a battery that ignited a bulb's magnesium foil filament. Electronic flash technology became available during the 1930s – the gas-filled flash tubes and high-voltage battery packs did not initially produce as much light as flash bulbs however. During the 1960s, mains powered flash units began to offer studio photographers an alternative to their powerful tungsten filament flood and spot lights.

Although the orange glow from tungsten lamps or the predominantly blue light from flash output presented few problems for photographers working in black-and-white, as colour films became more popular the colour of the light became more critical.

Camera and Lens Design

The basic principle of a camera – a little black box with a lens on one side and a place to put light sensitive material (film) on the other – has barely changed during the last 150 years.

The opaque copper base of daguerreotype plates did not allow for viewing from the rear and therefore showed a mirror image of the subject, unless the picture was taken using a Wolcott mirror camera.

The market for stereo pairs of photographs brought about the invention of cameras that could expose both left and right images at the same time. To synchronize both exposures necessitated the use of a shutter mechanism. And as improved light sensitivity made shorter exposures possible, the recording of movement became feasible. By 1877, Eadweard Muybridge had successfully used the shutter technology of the stereoscopic camera to record moving people and animals.

Lens design remained the key to both improved image quality and shorter exposure times. Adding more glass elements to the lens improved quality, but reduced light transmission. The first anastigmatic lens was introduced by Zeiss in 1889. In 1900 an international conference in Paris agreed to standardize the sizes of lens apertures, and the series of f-stops (f2; f2.8; f4; f5.6; f8; f11, etc.) is still in use today.

During the 1920s and 1930s, the first reflex cameras, both single and twin lens varieties, became widely popular. An integral mirror allowed focusing of the image the right way round, but when the shutter was triggered, the mirror flipped out of the way and a curtain in front of the film exposed the image.

Oscar Barnack, working for Leitz in Germany, designed a miniature camera for himself in 1914. The camera used 35mm motion picture film and yielded negatives 24mm x 36mm. Ten years later, an improved version of Barnack's design was marketed under the name Leica. The small negative size required images to be enlarged when printed, which unfortunately degraded image quality due to the increase in visible grain.

Towards the end of the Second World War, Hasselblad developed a single lens reflex camera for the Swedish Air Force giving 2 1/4-inch negatives on a roll film format. After the war, professional photographers began to disregard traditional cut film sheets and plate cameras in favour of new roll film formats. From around 1950 onward film emulsions started to exhibit smaller grain structures. Both German and Japanese companies, like Nikon, began to pursue the 35mm single lens reflex (SLR) camera.

The final development in the evolution of 35mm was the addition of a pentaprism over the camera's glass focusing screen to allow eye-level focusing.

Technical Developments Since 1970

The reflex camera of the late 1950s would have very much resembled its modern counterpart. Since the 1970s, camera design has evolved much slower, although some of the modifications are significant: Automatic Exposure (AE) – an exposure meter built into the camera measures the light, and sets both lens aperture and shutter speed automatically;

Autofocus – infrared focusing devices built into the camera body, have allowed photographers to record images that previously would not have been possible.

Film technology, however, moved much more rapidly. By the end of the 1970s, colour negative films could be processed quickly and efficiently in one-hour high street outlets. Strong plastics started to replace the older acetate film bases.

Manufacturers began to experiment with ways of reducing the amount of ultra violet (blue) light produced by flash tubes. Towards the end of the 1970s flash light became much closer to daylight in its colour.

During the 1990s, rechargeable battery technology enabled manufacturers to develop portable flash units capable of delivering high light output as might be expected from a mains powered unit.

Potentially, one of the biggest advances in image capture this century is the advent of digital photography. The computer-led, desktop publishing revolution of the 1980s required a method of inputting images into a computer. Once this technology existed, it was only a short step to electronically processing the image. Photographs recorded in the traditional way can now be scanned into a computer for electronic processing or can be captured directly using a digital camera without the need for film.

Paradoxically, many of the constraints facing the early pioneers of photography have once again become relevant for those involved in the development of digital photography. While some digital camera designs can record an image in one short exposure using conventional electronic flash, others require long exposures and artificial light sources which will not flicker during the exposure. Of course, the latter designs make photographing people impossible.

THE SOCIAL IMPACT OF PHOTOGRAPHY AND ITS INFLUENCE ON THE EROTIC IMAGE

To generations who have grown up with the visual imagery afforded by the photograph playing such an important part in all areas of everyday life, it is difficult to imagine the impact the discovery had on the lives of those who viewed the first photographic images of the world around them. Previously, pictorial records of this world would have been made with a pen, pencil, or brush.

The sexual hypocrisy of the British Victorian era is well documented. What is less obvious, however, is how their legacy of shame and respectability has influenced public taste as far into the future as the sexual revolution of the 1970s, and even beyond.

The nineteenth century was a time of enormous social transition. The continuing industrial revolution had begun great economic changes, not least the emergence of a dominant social group – the middle class. Businessmen and managers whose new prosperity created a demand for products and services that had previously only been available to the very wealthy.

With this tide of change came a shift in social attitudes. Sex was seen as a base activity which, apart from drunkenness, was the only pleasure of the working class. Although the middle class privately practised birth control, publicly it was scorned – the maintenance of a pool of unskilled, uneducated workers was a prerequisite to the success of Victorian capitalism.

By contrast, it was those who publicly preached shame, demanding for instance, that piano legs should be kept covered, who openly paid to visit the Royal Academy in London to look at paintings of nudes. Nudes were held in high esteem; the artists responsible could earn as much as £10,000 a year. The classical public school education of the middle classes afforded Greek statues of the nude, and paintings depicting mythological or historical scenes great acceptability – even if they were just thinly veiled erotica, dealing with subjects such as bondage, flagellation, and necrophilia. Andromeda, painted by Lord Leighton in 1891, is viewed by many as little more than a naked woman chained to a rock. Painted nudes had to portray perfection, and subjects were neither old nor plump as had been the taste of earlier generations. Of prime importance was an absence of pubic hair.

As soon as the technical limitations involved in photographing people had been, to some extent, overcome, the public were thrilled with seeing their exact likeness recorded. In France, the commercial exploitation of the daguerreotype process was enormous. Daguerreotypist N.P. Lerebours is reputed to have been the first to open a studio in Paris in 1841, during which year he exposed over fifteen hundred portraits. It is reckoned that during 1847, in excess of two-thousand cameras and half a million plates were sold in Paris alone. In London, there were over 200 studios established by the early 1860s.

Exactly when the potential for the erotic photograph was realized is not recorded. However, it is known that a whole variety of images of a sexual nature were openly on sale in opticians' shop windows during the early 1850s.

The daguerreotype was a one off. Once exposed and developed, the metal plate became the original image, multiple copies were not possible unless multiple plates were exposed in the camera. This fact alone made the purchase of an erotic daguerreotype still only within reach of the middle and upper classes.

It is worth remembering that, at best, it could take around a minute to expose a photograph. The subject was required to remain motionless during this time. In portrait studios, subjects were usually photographed seated, and often metal clamps were used to prevent the head or body from moving. Flour was also employed to lighten skin tones. The physical discomfort that was endured by some of those models who posed for the erotic or explicitly pornographic photographs of the period is often evident in their less than relaxed facial expressions.

While the Royal Academy's nude paintings were required to closely resemble colour photographs, photographers looked to classical themes to give their erotic images credibility. Academy photographs were the acceptable face of erotic photography. Under the guise of reference material from which artists could make life drawings, academy figures often adopted classical reclined poses. This pretext of describing a photograph as art, because of its subject matter alone, and as a way of circumventing censorship has regularly been used right into the twentieth century.

The positive/negative process pioneered by Fox Talbot redefined the way in which photographs were sold and, in particular, the accessibility of the erotic image. From one negative, thousands of prints could be made. A dozen paper prints could be produced for roughly the same cost as one daguerreotype.

It was felt that such widespread distribution of erotic material demanded some action to protect the masses, specifically the feeble minded and the poor. The Society for the Suppression of Vice, which had also been referred to as 'the society for the suppression of vice in those earning less than £500 per year', campaigned against all forms of pornography. Eventually, and not without criticism, the Obscene Publications Act was passed in 1857 to 'put down pornography'. Photographs of nudes that exhibited no scientific or artistic value were deemed obscene and likely to corrupt those who viewed them.

Stereo photographs were produced by the thousand after Queen Victoria expressed an interest in a stereoscope at the Great Exhibition in 1851. An evening with the stereoscope became a family entertainment – a pastime that lasted until the popularization of television a century later. The potential for the erotic image was obvious, and thousands of nude and erotic stereo prints were produced. It has been suggested that the lifelike three-dimensional effect, and the close contact required to use the stereoscope, added to the viewer's overall erotic experience.

The fashion of collecting cartes-de-visites was popularized in France by André Disdéri during the early 1850s. Disdéri realized he could dramatically reduce his production costs if he made multiple negatives on one plate. By 1860 the collecting craze was all over Europe. The production of hand-painted backdrops and props for photographic studios became an industry in itself.

Around 1870 the popularity of the carte-de-visite was in decline. Photographers turned instead to a larger format 'cabinet' print that in turn gave way to the picture postcard. Popular subjects included royalty, music hall stars, and, naturally, erotic and pornographic images. The most popular designs were copied and re-copied by unscrupulous pirates who would re-photograph the design and print thousands of copies of the image from their own negative.

Following the upheaval of the First World War, social values were very much reassessed. The 1920s were a time of vegetarianism, gymnastics, dance, and nudism, and photographers became more aware of the aesthetics of picture-making. One criticism often levelled at photographic art was that photographers were technicians and tradesmen. Those involved in the new photographic art movement were interested in creating more painterly images, and reverted to classical themes.

Photographers began to experiment with the creative possibilities of image-making rather than simply recording detail. Photomontages, solarisation, and distorted perspectives were popularized by photographers such as Man Ray. And it also became acceptable to photograph the nude for its own sake. The naturist photographs of the late 1920s and 1930s purported to show healthy outdoor pursuits, sports, and gymnastics, but many would argue this was little more than an excuse to justify the erotic.

Prior to the emergence of the fanzine, the motion picture studios were quick to realize the erotic potential of photographs of film stars. From the 1920s onward film studios distributed millions of portraits, risqué pin-ups, and glamour images of their stars. The public's appetite for undressed celebrities has remained a socially acceptable form of erotica to the present day.

During the 1950s erotic prints were largely distributed via mail order. However, following an amendment to the Obscene Publications Act, public morality once again became an issue. The Act was rigidly enforced, shops selling magazines containing anything that might be construed salacious were raided by the police as a matter of course. The term salacious was, of course, very much open to interpretation as demonstrated by the case of photographer Roger Davis in the late 1950s – the high-heeled shoes in a photograph of a fully clothed model were deemed obscene by a policeman and Davis was arrested.

In the absence of any real guidelines, photographers and magazine sellers were largely in the hands of the authorities. It has been reported that many did not know they had broken the law, until they appeared in court and a magistrate told them. Fines were large, photographers' equipment was often confiscated, and prison sentences metered out.

Photographers such as George Harrison Marks turned to publishing their own magazines. To remain within the boundaries of the law, the images were heavily retouched to remove any trace of pubic hair and genitalia. In fact, it has been suggested that a whole generation of schoolboys grew up thinking this was what a naked female really looked like. Poses and motifs were chosen to represent art subjects, just as they had been a century before.

The early 1960s were a time of social anomaly. Sex was increasingly a theme for books and the cinema, but when a designer showed the first topless dress, fashion editors did not dare publish the photographs. During the late 1960s and early 1970s photography began to be widely accepted as an art form in its own right. It became more common for a photographer to be identified as the author of his work and magistrates and juries started to take a more liberal attitude to the nude. By the early 1970s, mens' magazines regularly published full-frontal images without the need for retouching.

Throughout the 1970s colour photography was the norm, black and white was rarely required; only a handful of photographers, among them James Wedge, kept the art alive.

Launched in 1963, the Pirelli calendar became a barometer of public taste, although its brief was to push forward boundaries. Images were blatantly erotic, but it was not until 1971 that the first nipple was exposed.

In 1971 photographs of topless models regularly appeared in daily newspapers, however, when The Times published an advertisement featuring a nude, there was a public outcry.

Social attitudes towards the nude and the erotic continued to change throughout the 1970s. Increasingly, erotic imagery was used in the cinema, advertising, fashion magazines, and books.

By the mid-1980s photographers had started to look at the creative possibilities of using black-and-white film for their images – not out of necessity, but out of choice. Thousands of black-and-white images were published as postcards and posters. The erotic images of Bob Carlos Clarke, the nudes of Charles Roff and, later, the fetish imagery of Trevor Watson were sold on the high street as framed art for the mass market.

During the late 1980s and early 1990s, designers began to exploit the fashion potential of rubber and PVC fabrics. This combination of fashion and fetish, in conjunction with public education in the need for safer sex practices, has once again changed social attitudes and allowed photographers to explore erotic imagery that would not previously have been acceptable in the mainstream.

EROTIQUE – MASTERPIECES OF EROTIC PHOTOGRAPHY

No other visual medium has the power to reach in and touch a viewer's emotions like the photographic image. Perhaps the perception of a moment, frozen in time seemingly forever, a moment, captured and recorded, true in every detail to the real life from which it was snatched, begs the metaphor of cameras and lies. But nowhere is the viewer's emotional response ever more open to manipulation than in the erotic image.

We are fascinated by each other's lives, or perhaps more often than not, what appears to be each other's lives. What better relief from the apparent monotony of one's existence than a glimpse at every last detail of someone else's? What better than a shared public interest in the life, love, or sexual preference of some minor celebrity? Or perhaps, the chance thrill of a glimpse into the private keyhole of someone else's world?

The masters of erotic photography, have, through their mind's eye, the power to realize such captured moments. Their images fulfil our fascination on our own behalf, providing each individual viewer with a visual reference around which to construct a private narrative, the effect of which is to make that image as personal as if we had witnessed the moment ourselves.

HISTORICAL

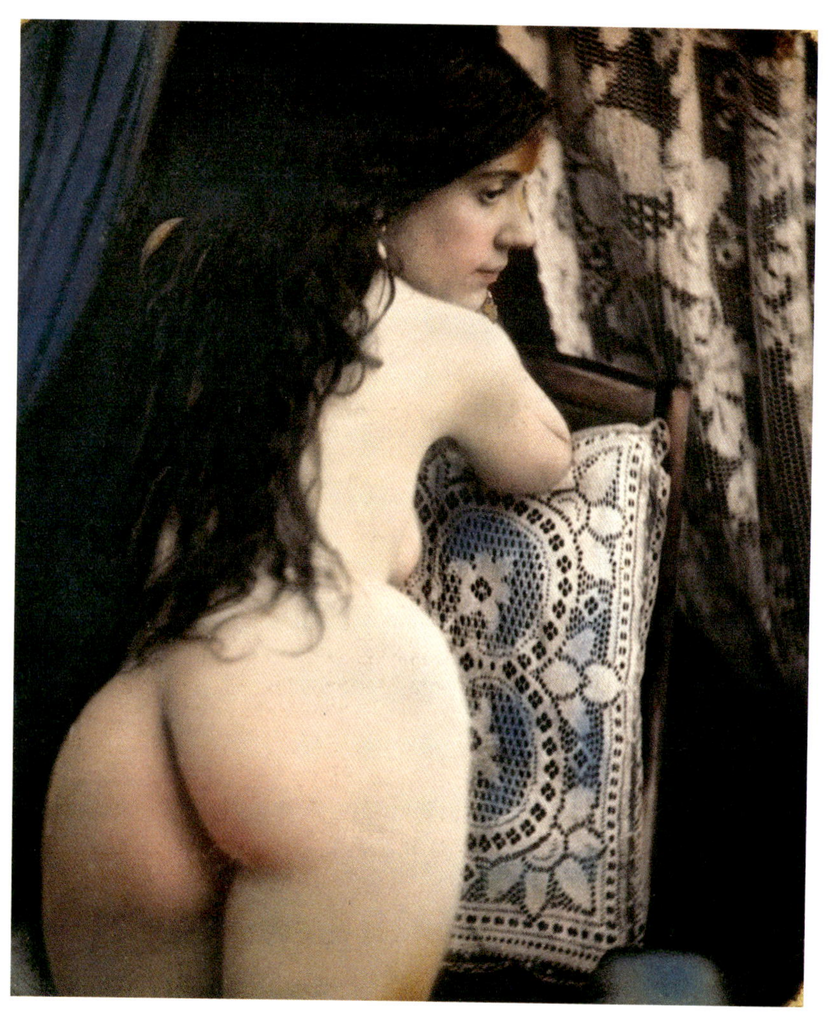

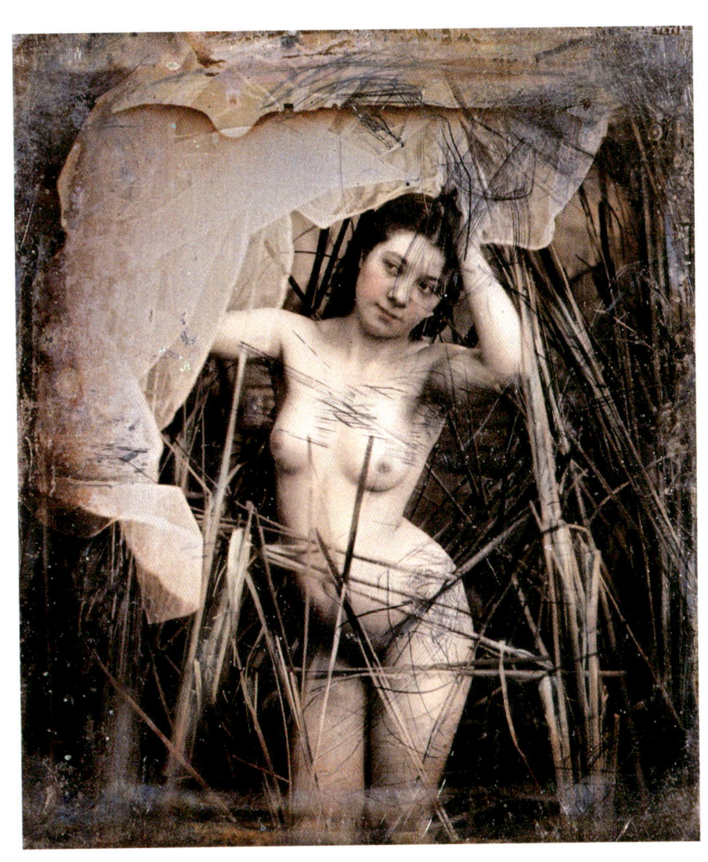

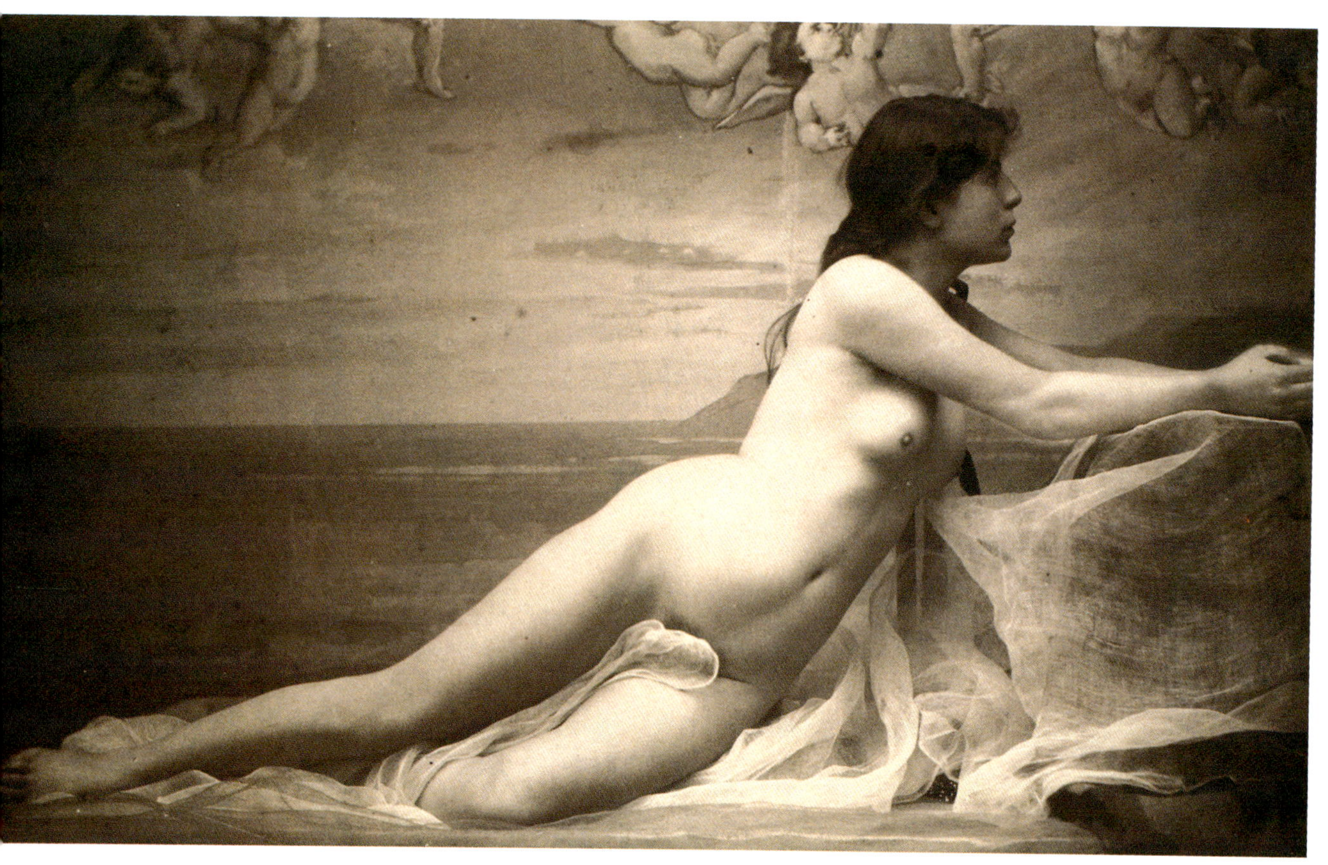

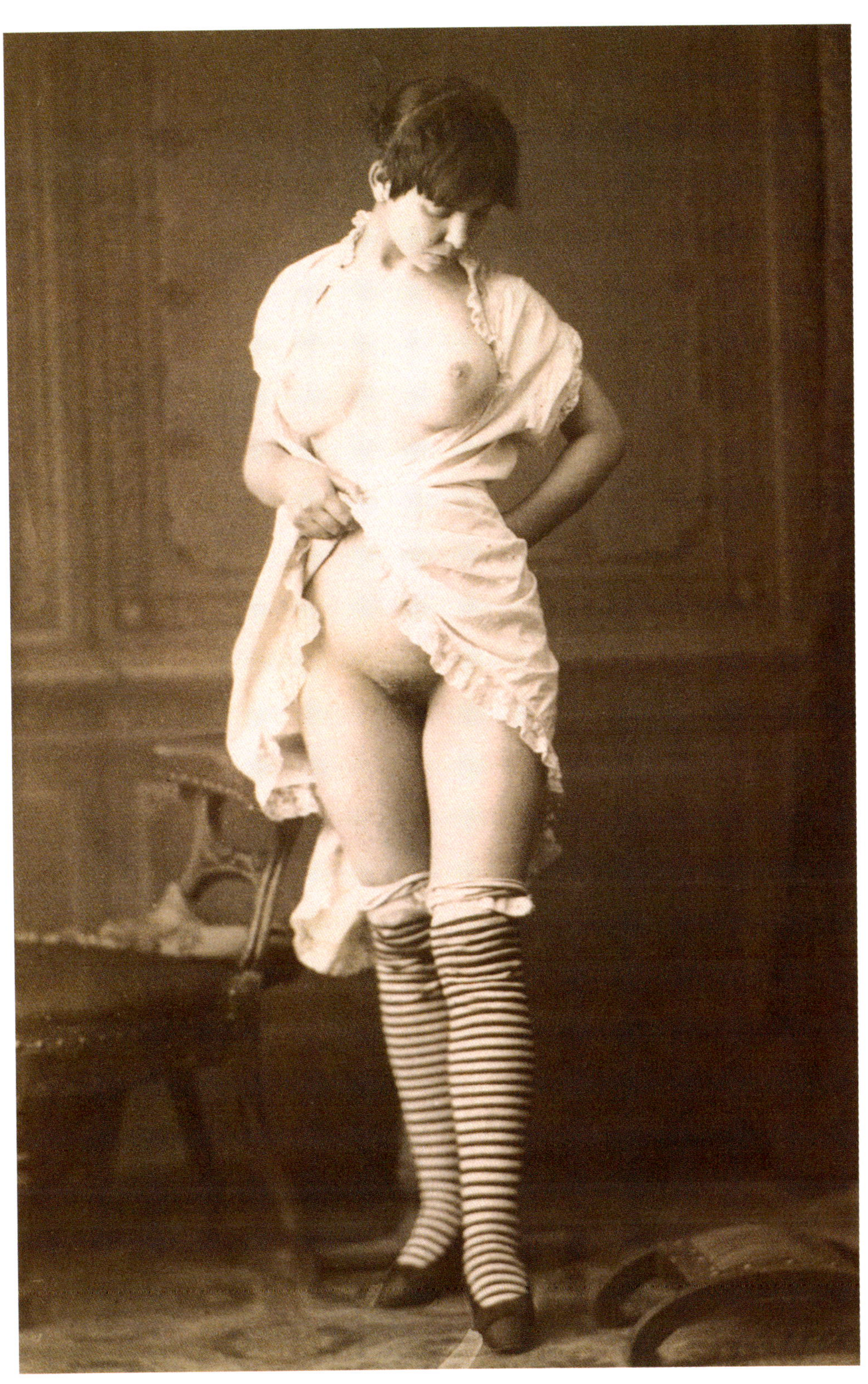

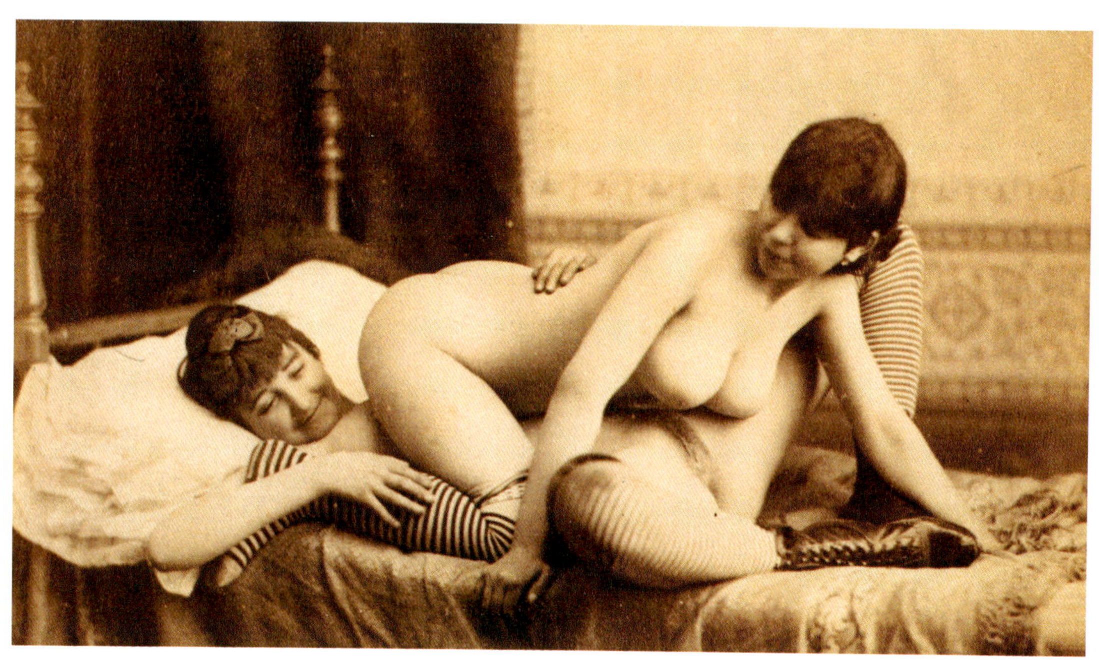

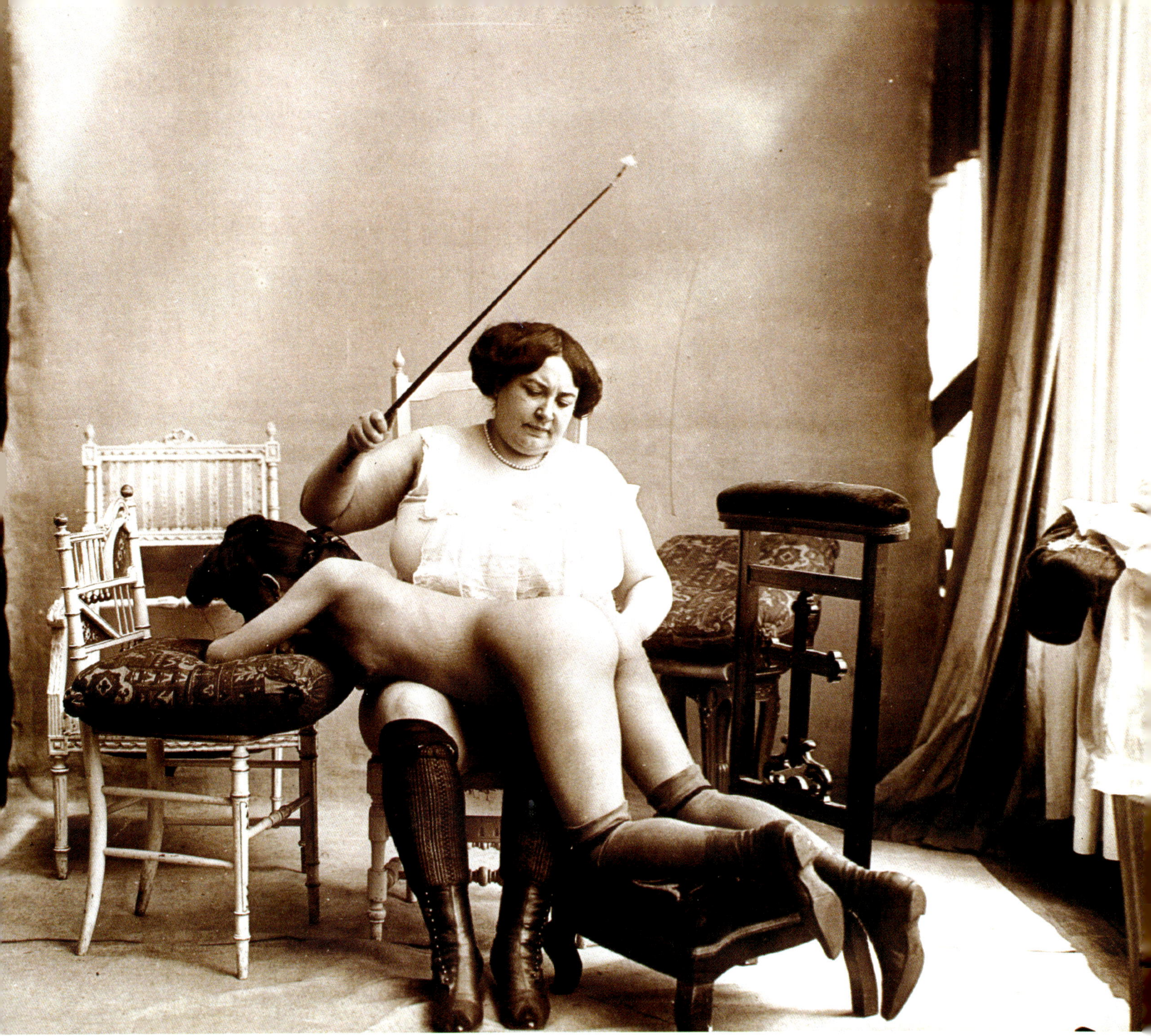

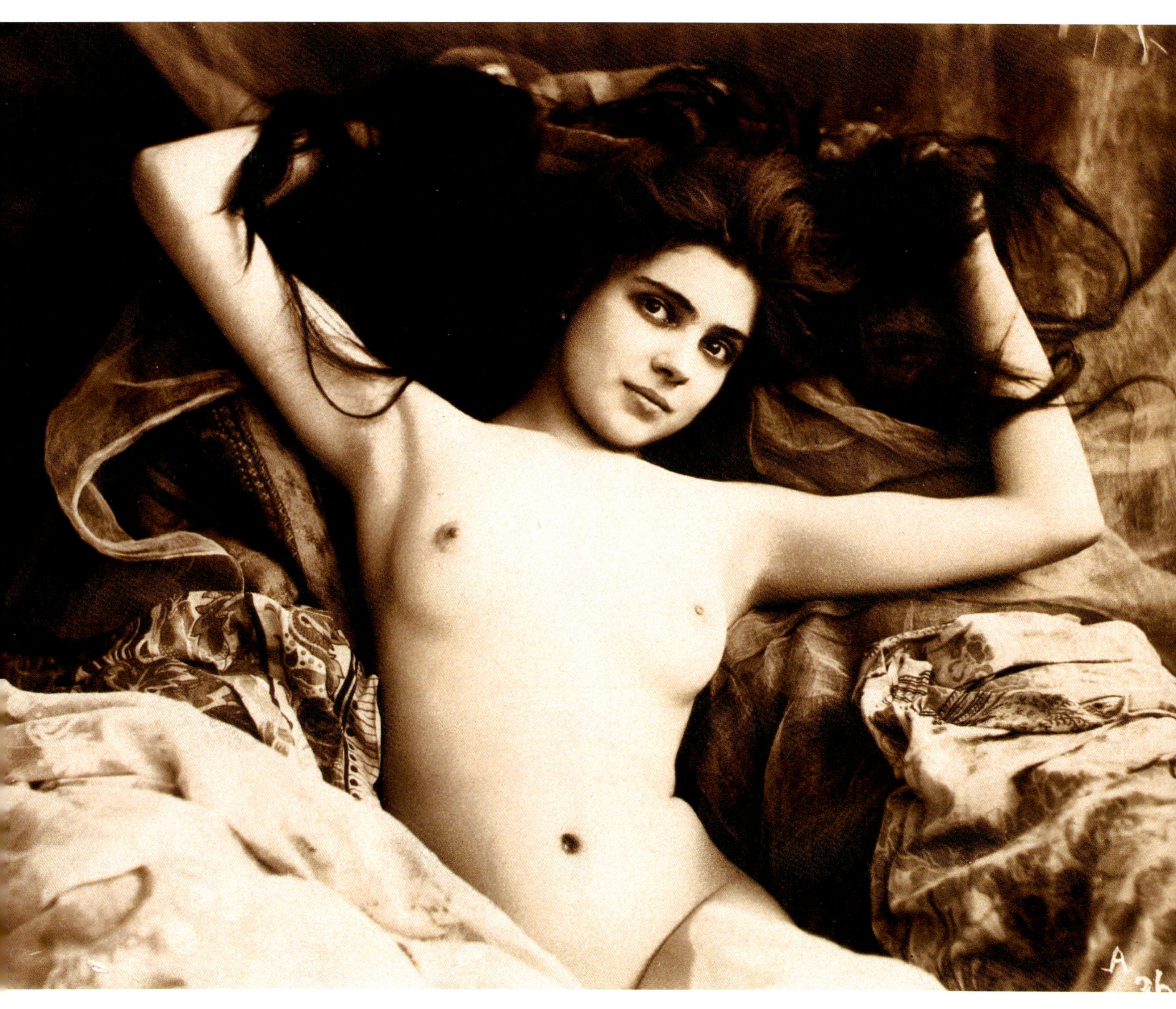

 LÉOPOLD REUTLINGER 1890

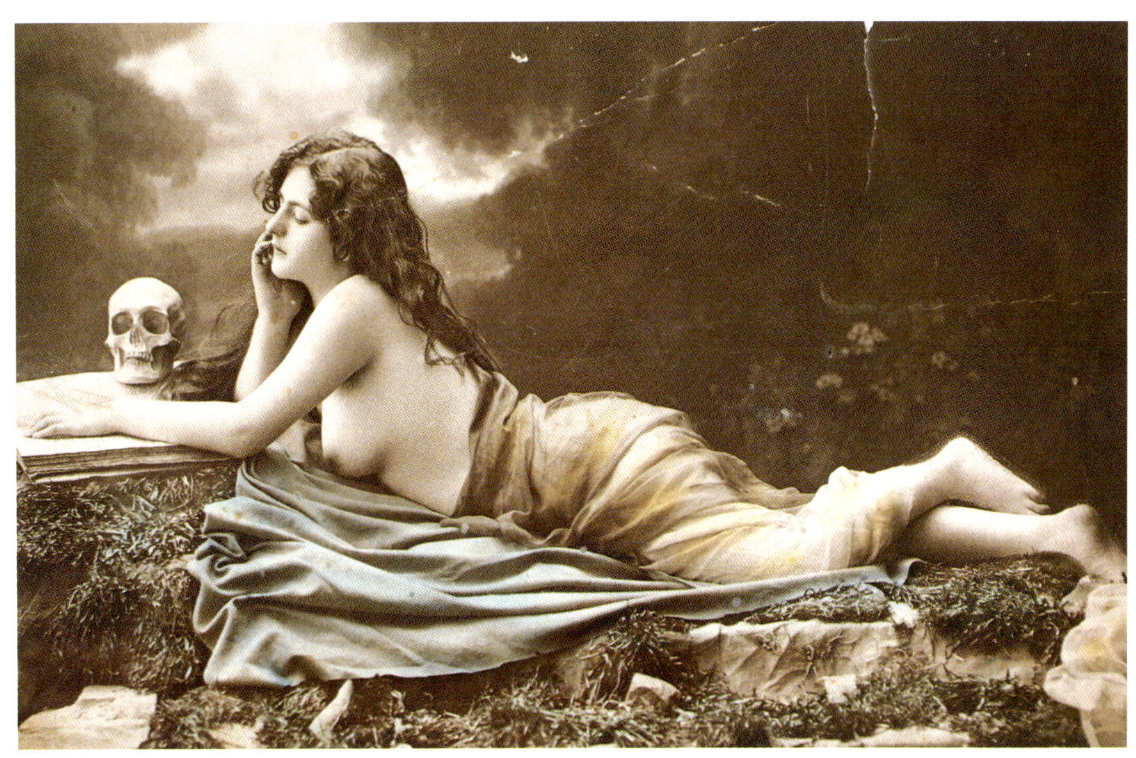

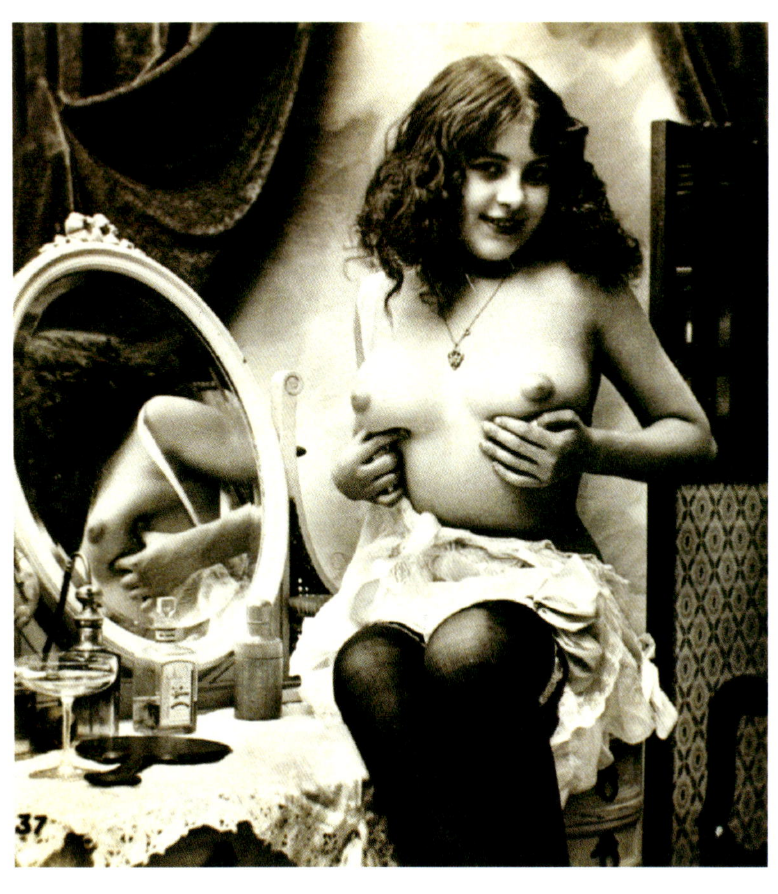
37

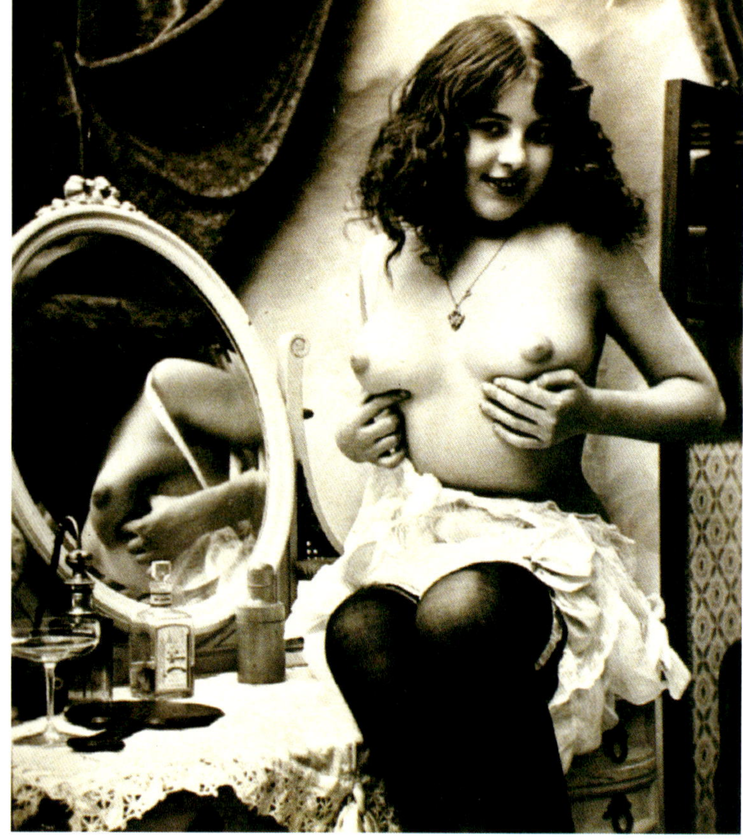

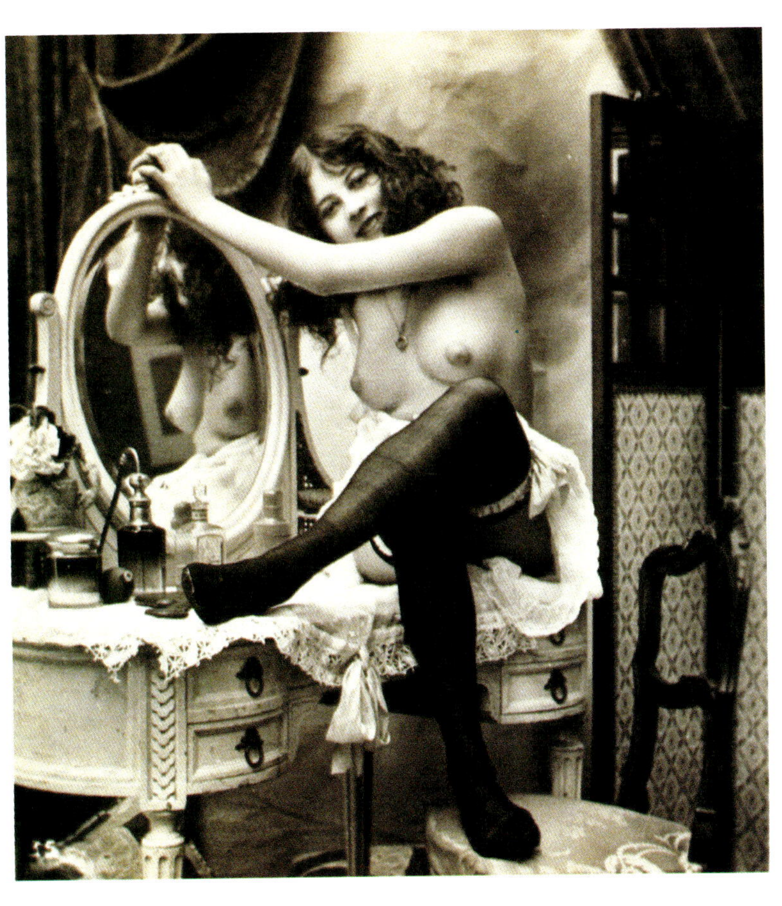

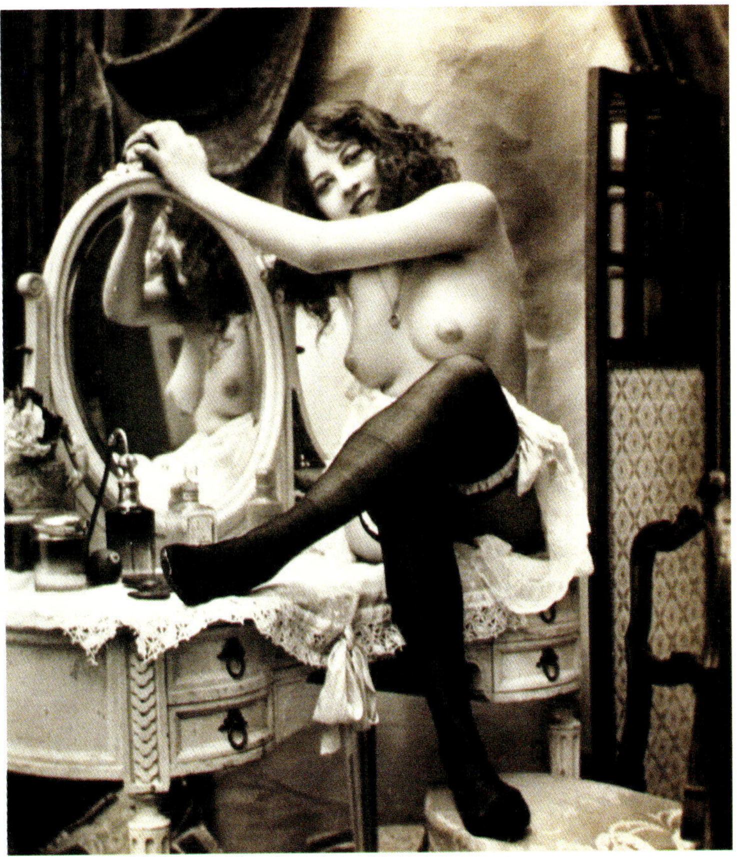

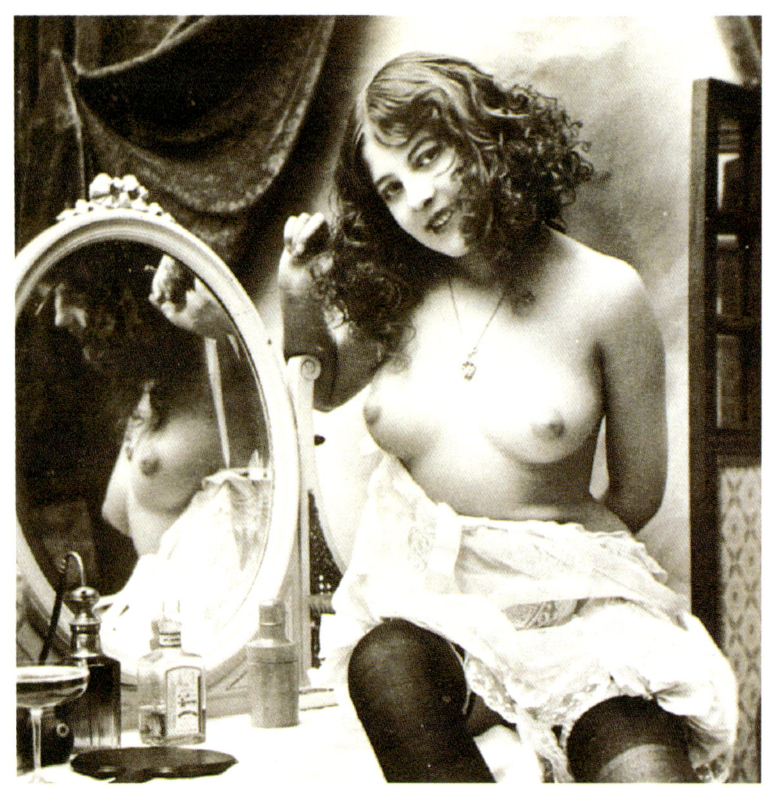

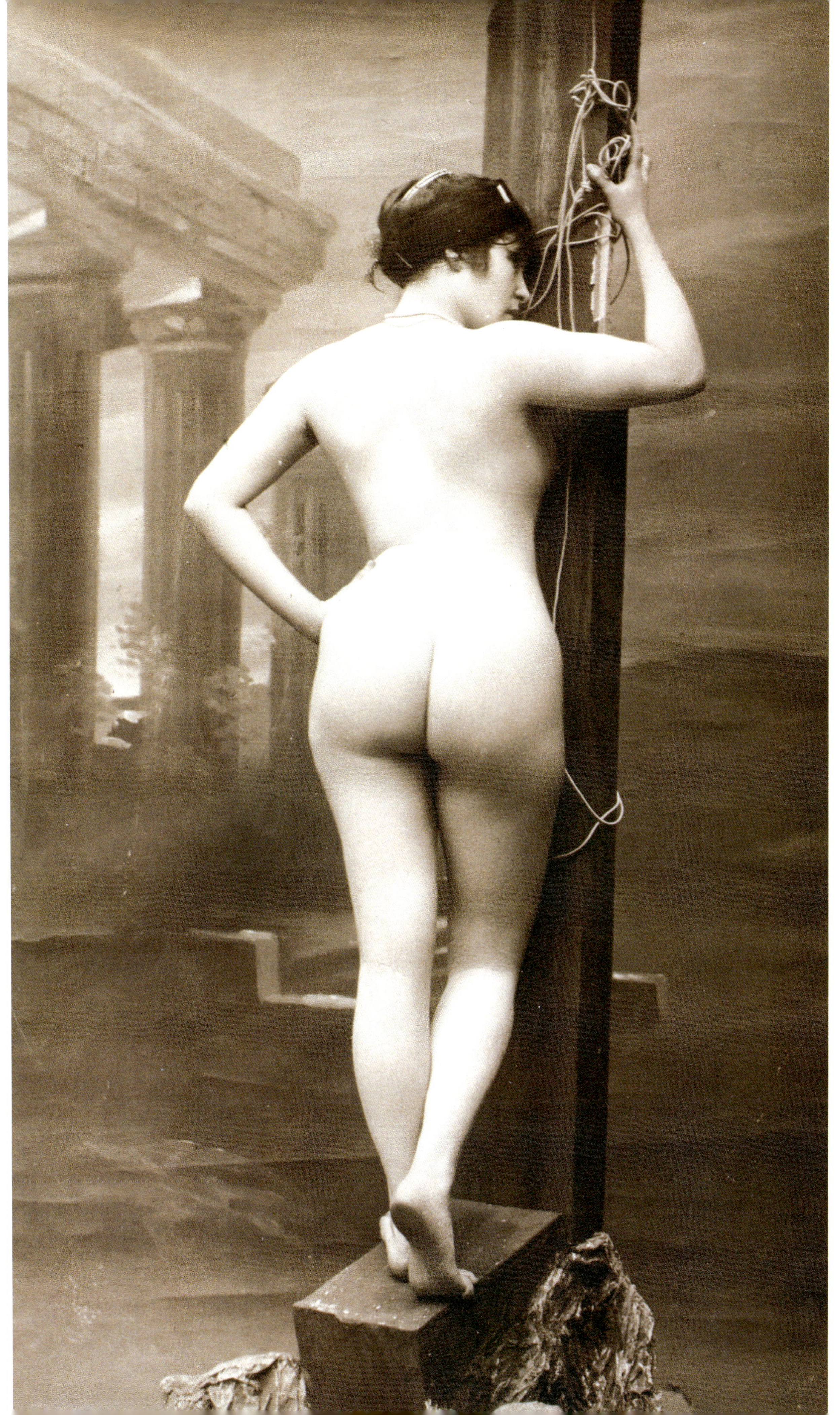

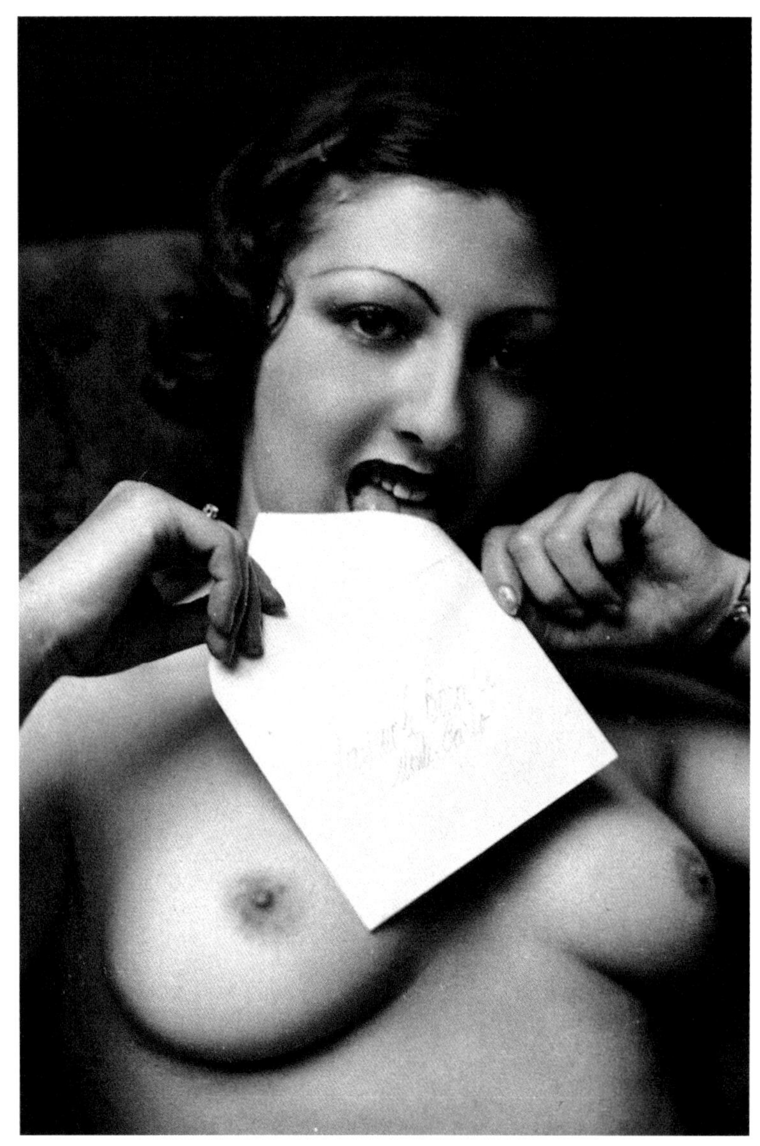

 ANONYMOUS 1910

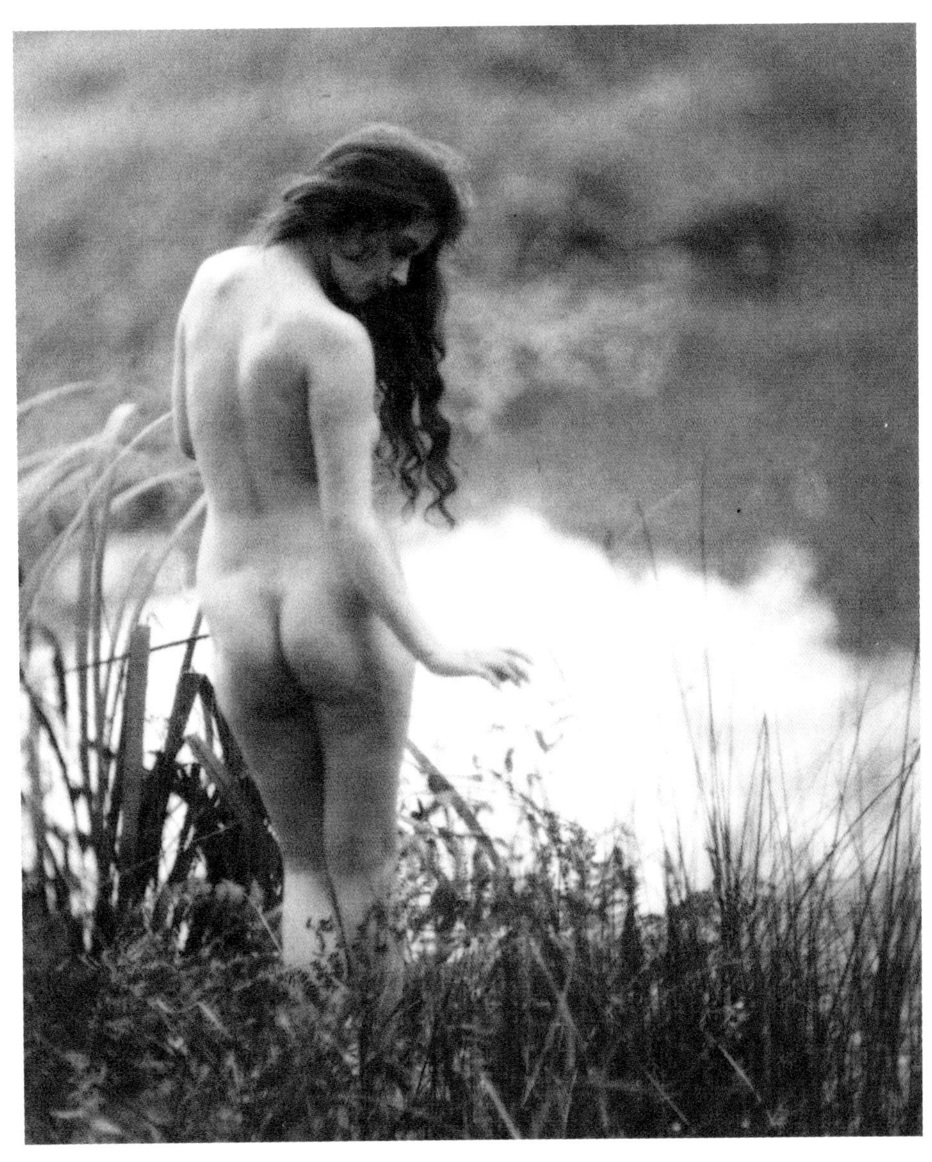

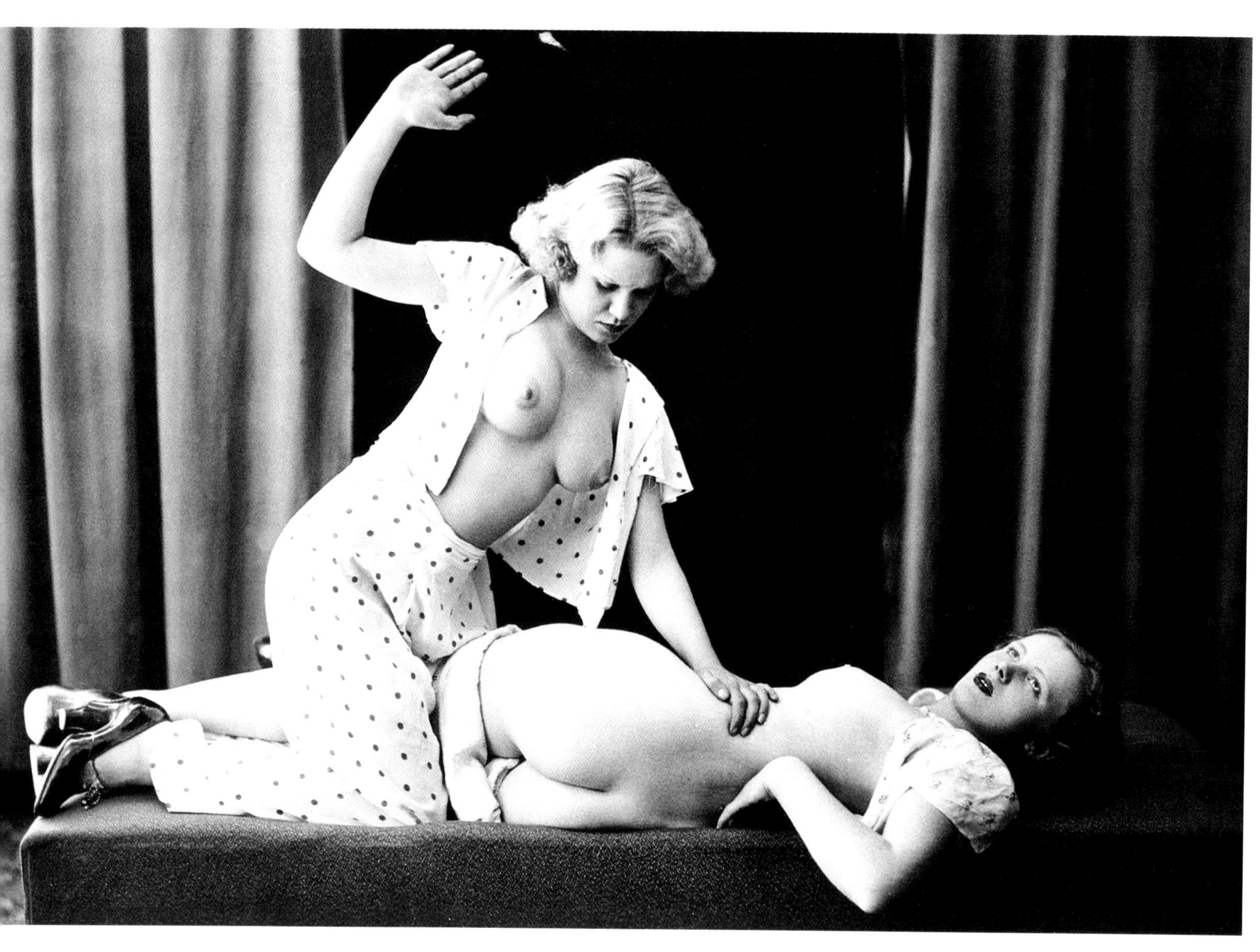

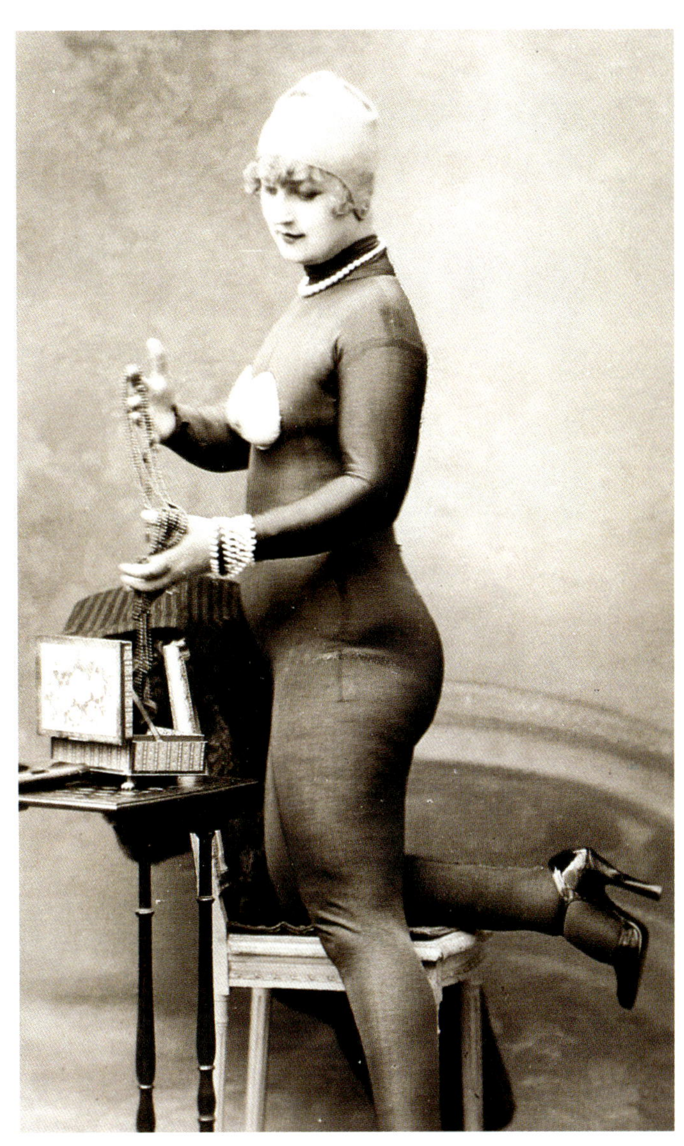

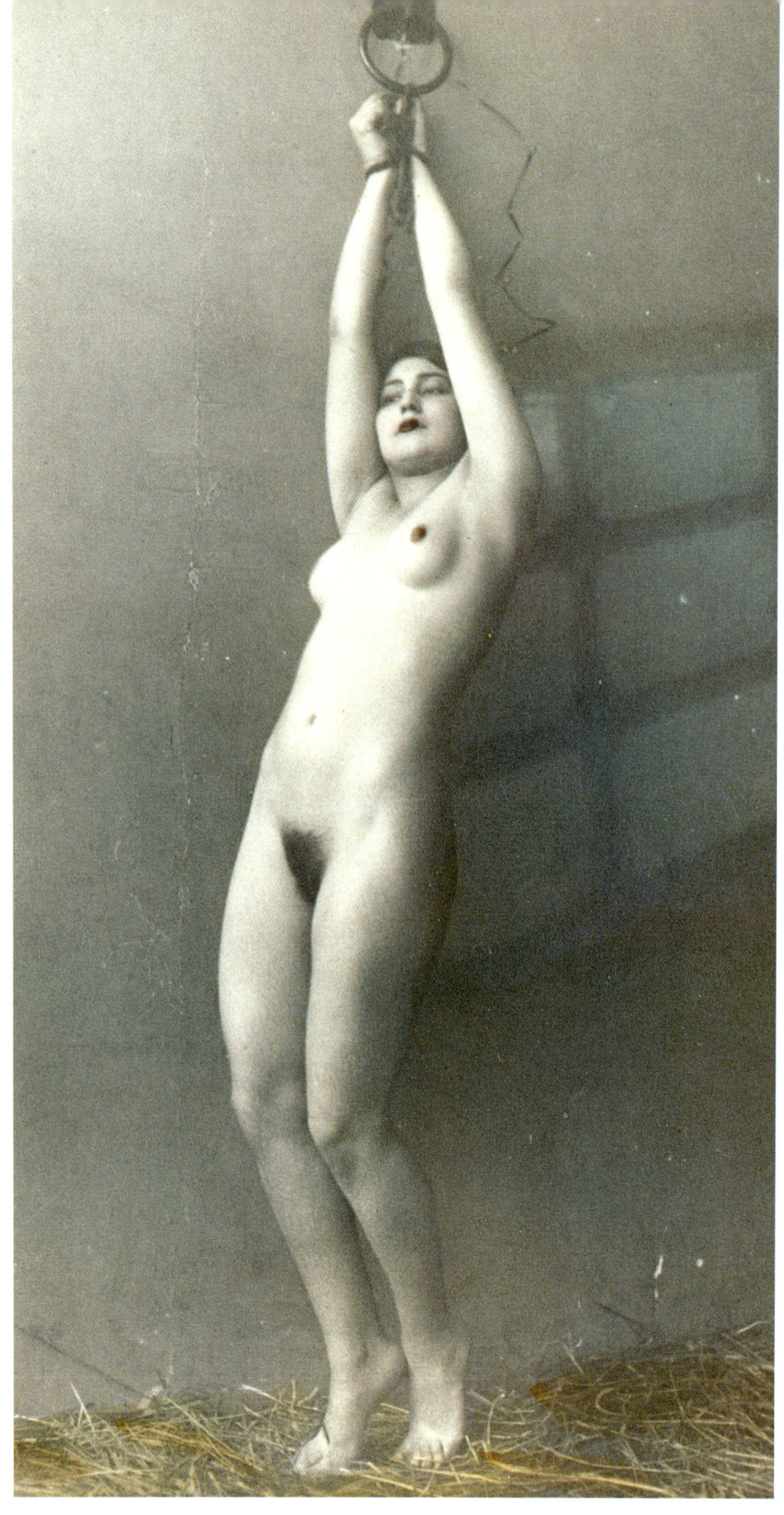

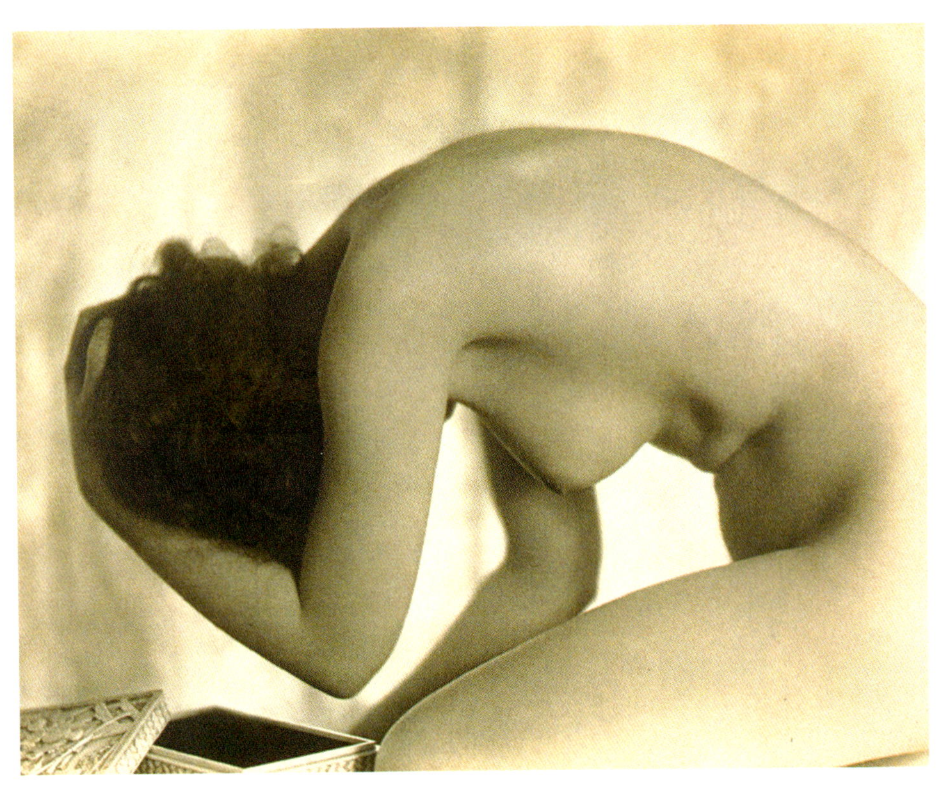

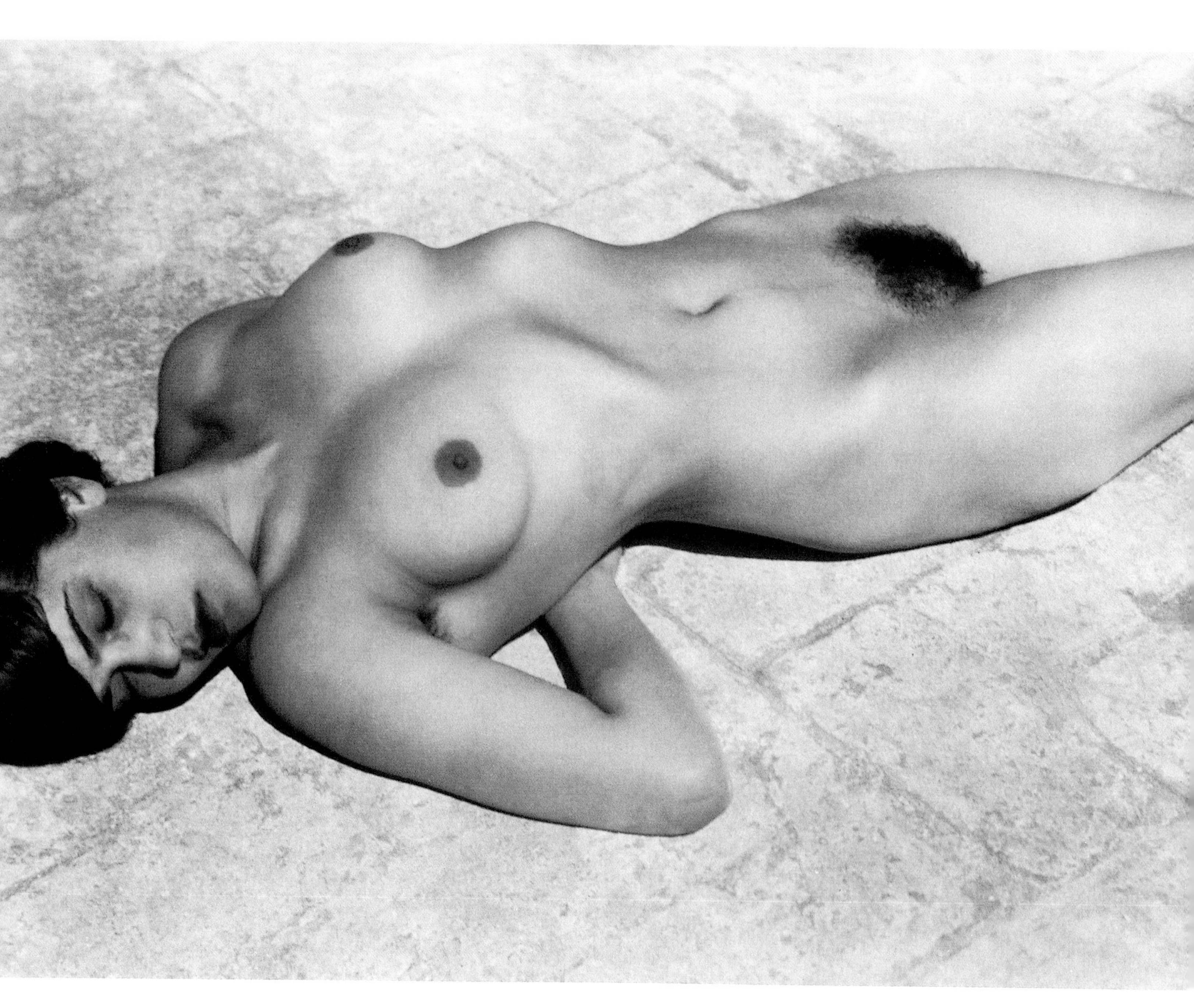

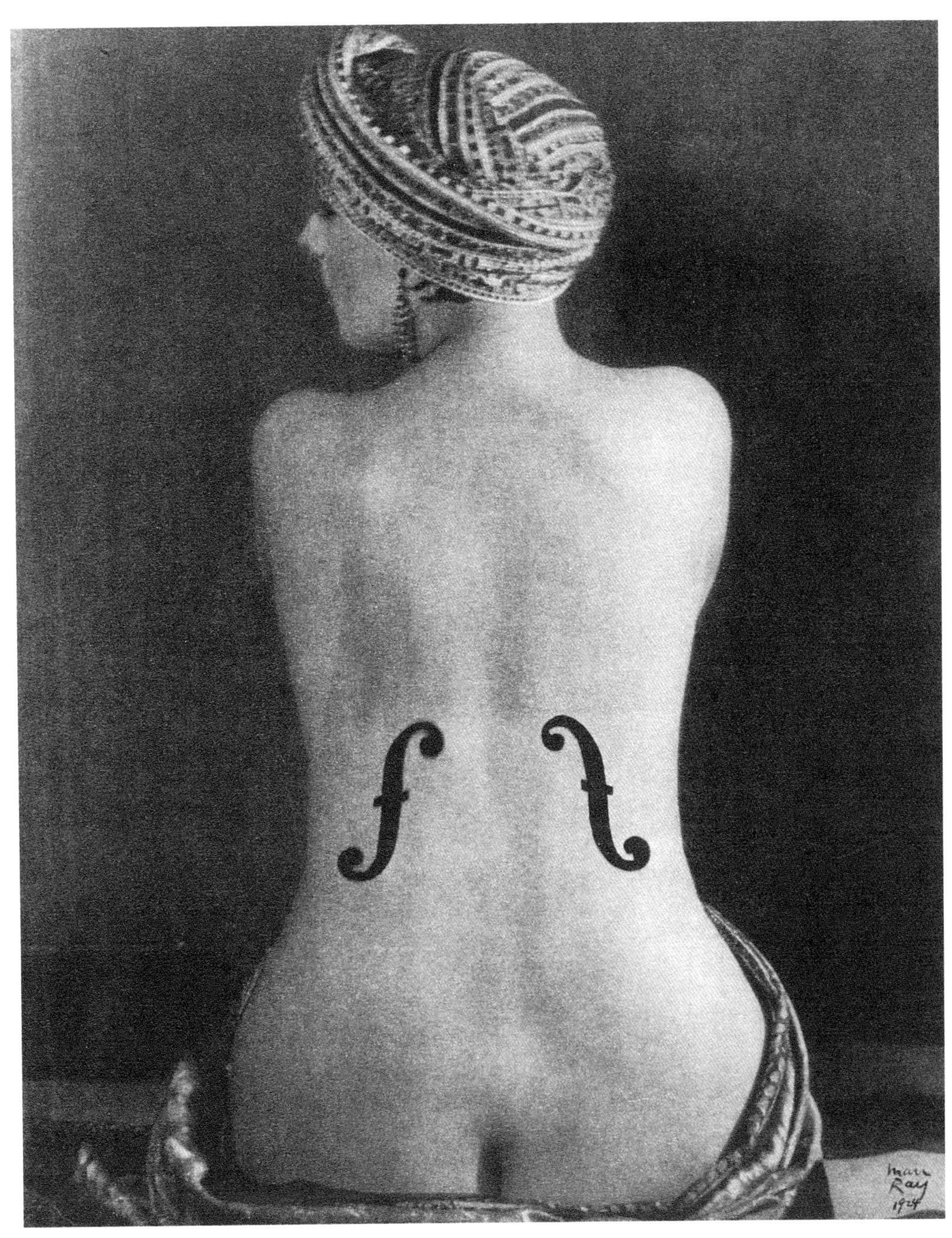
Man
Ray
1924

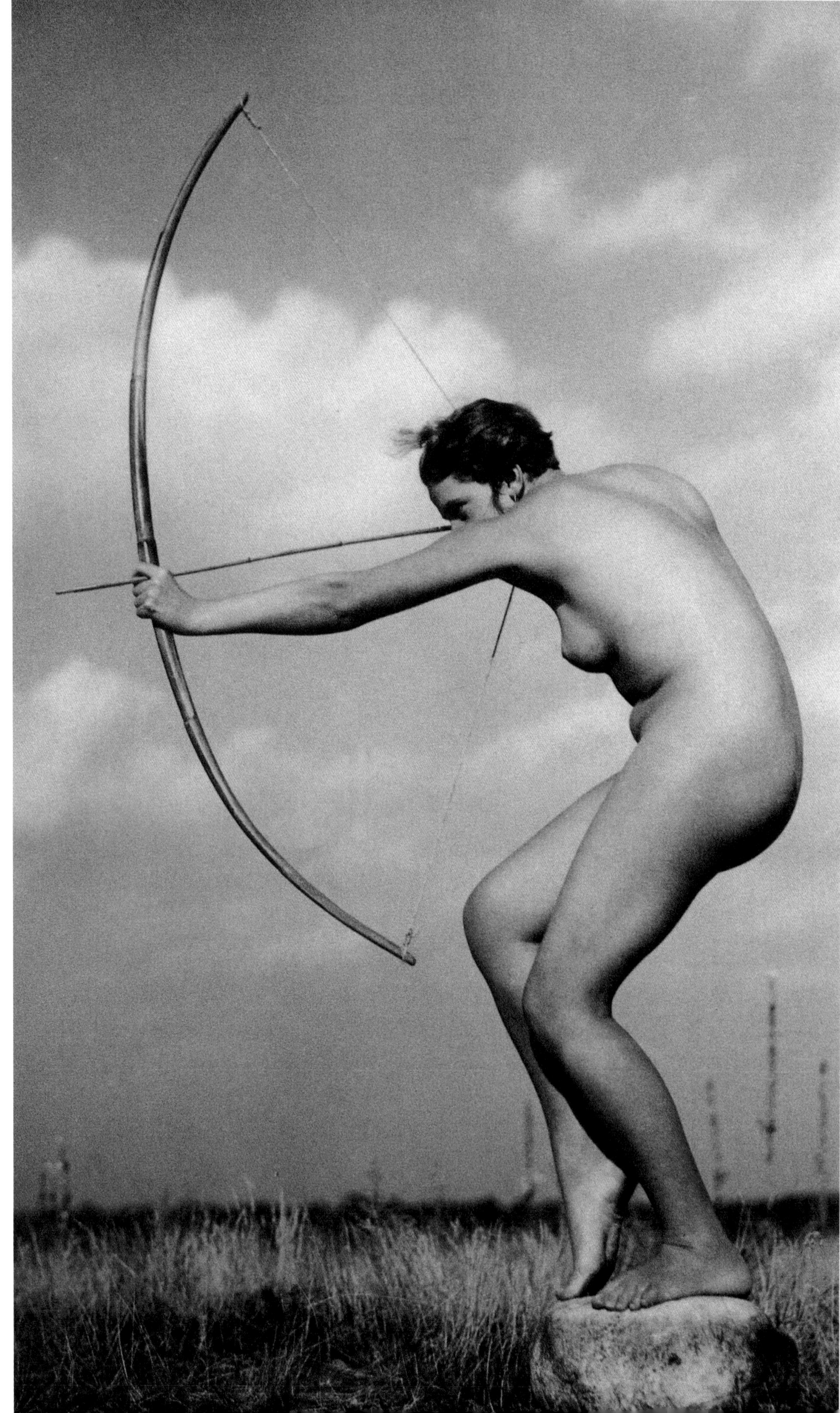

 GERHARD RIEBICKE 1925

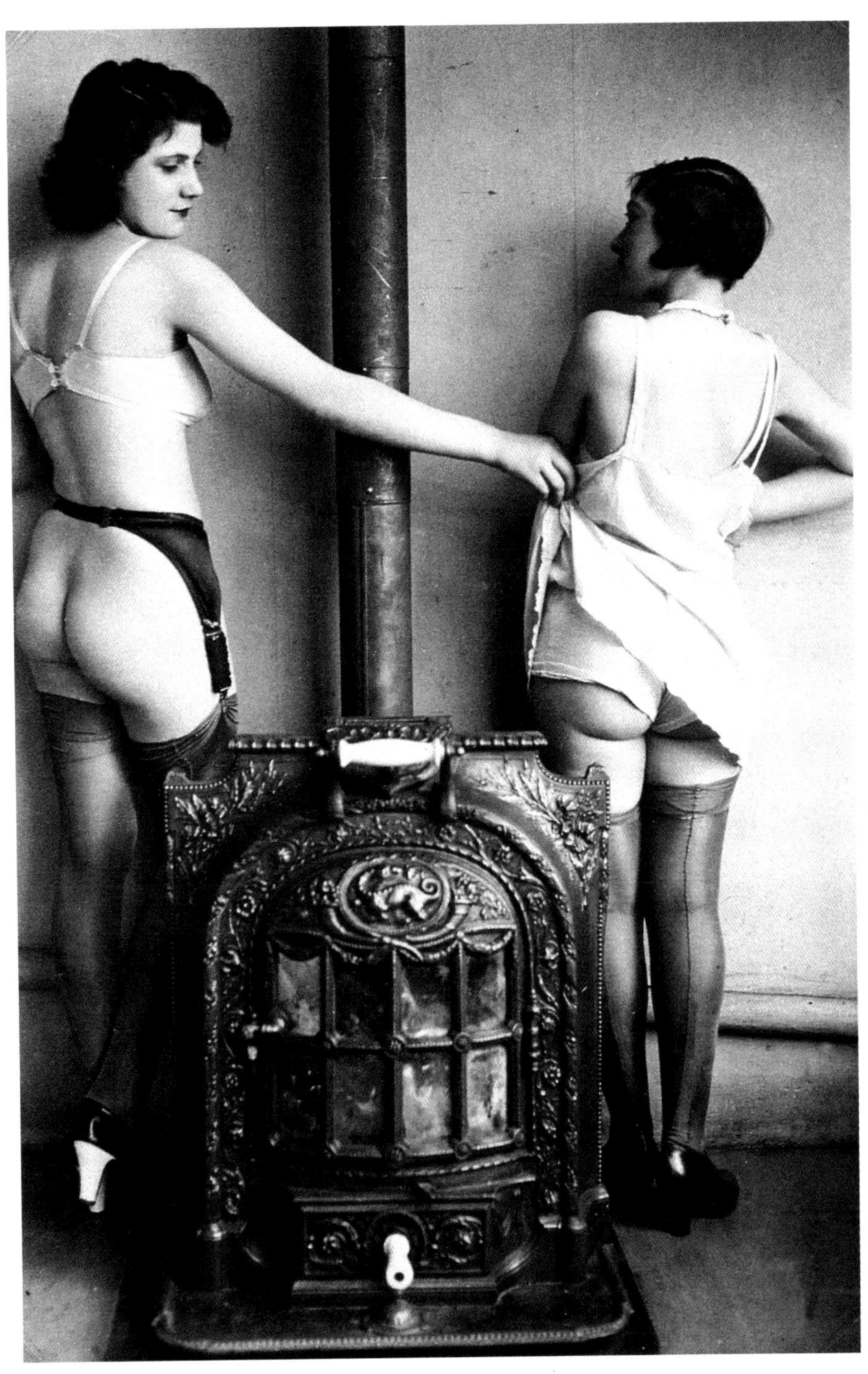

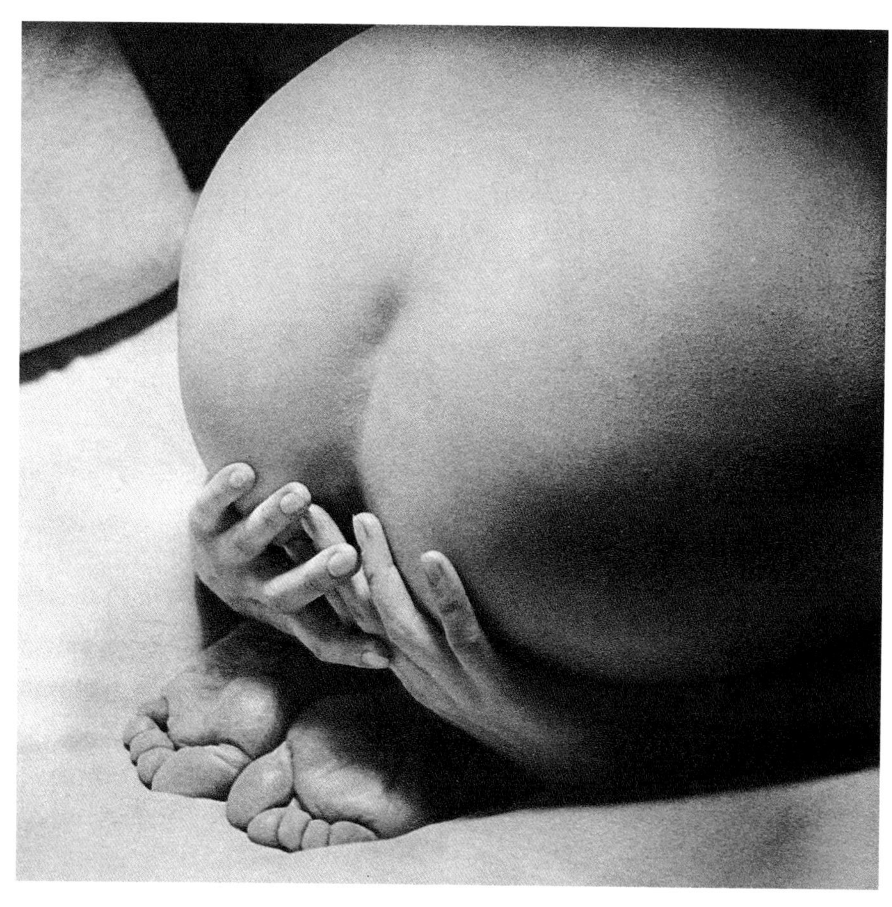

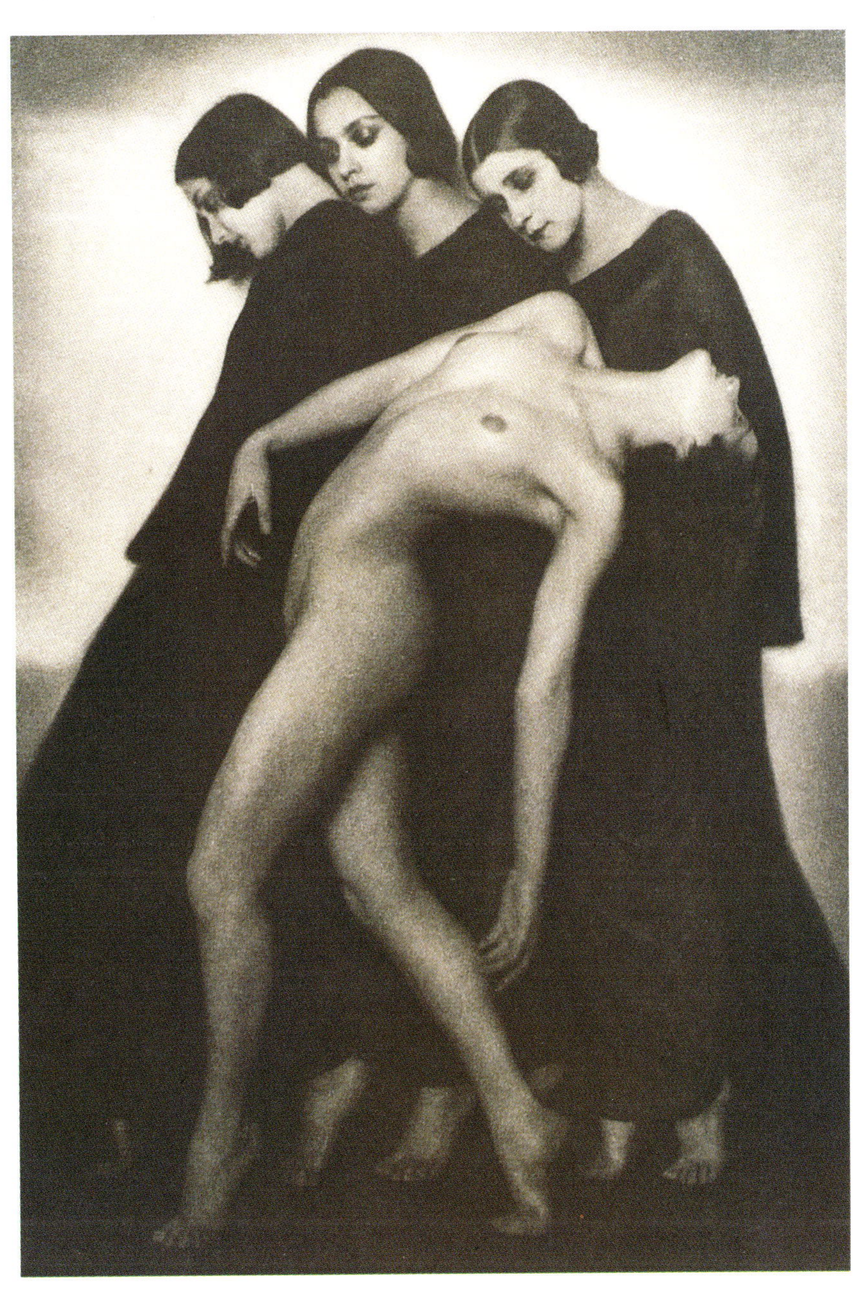

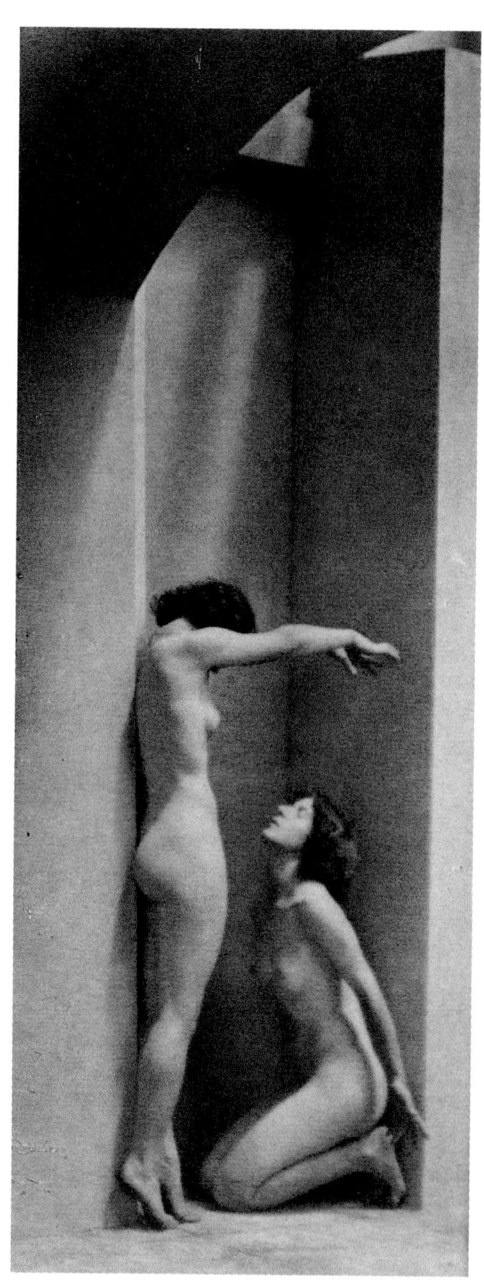

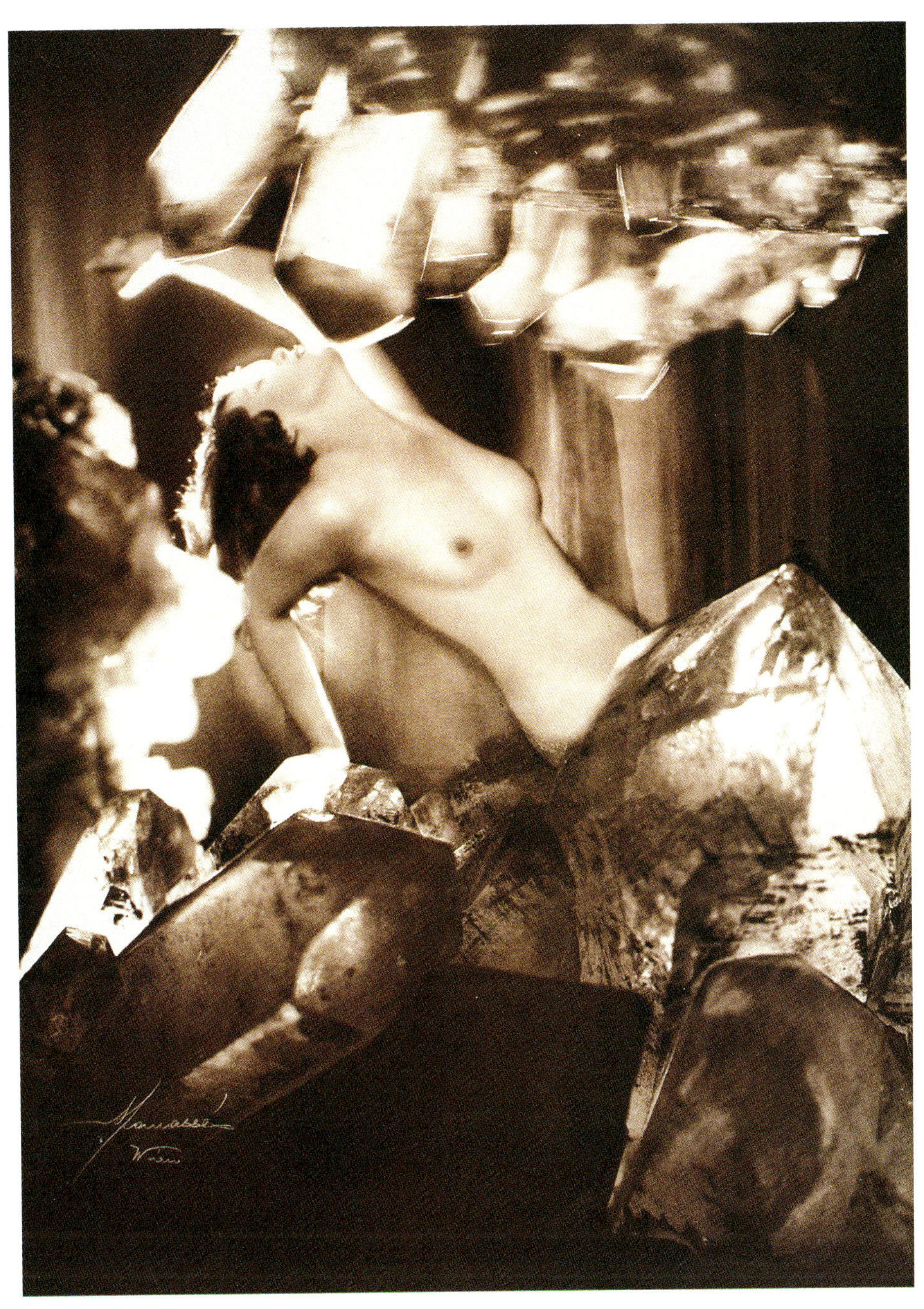

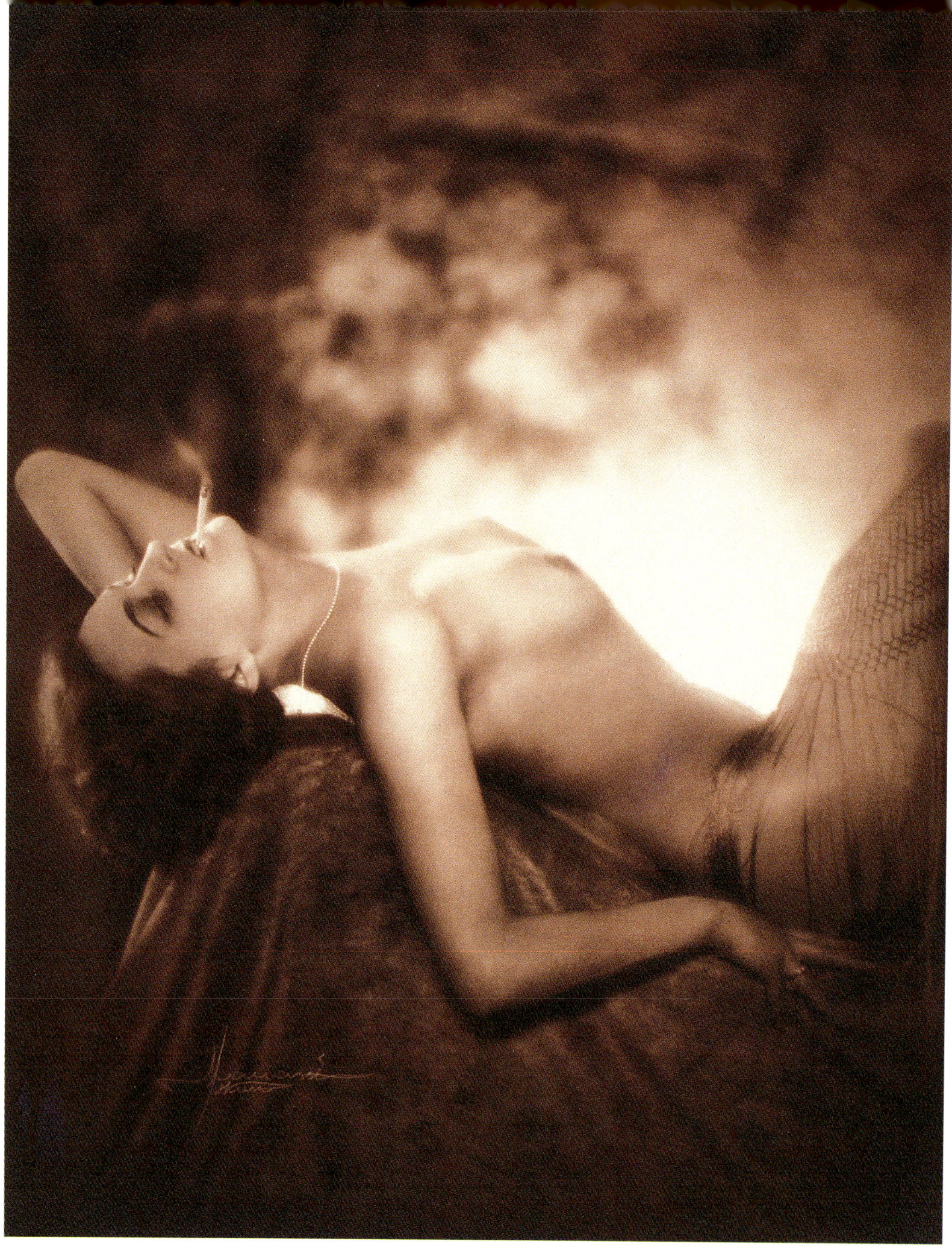

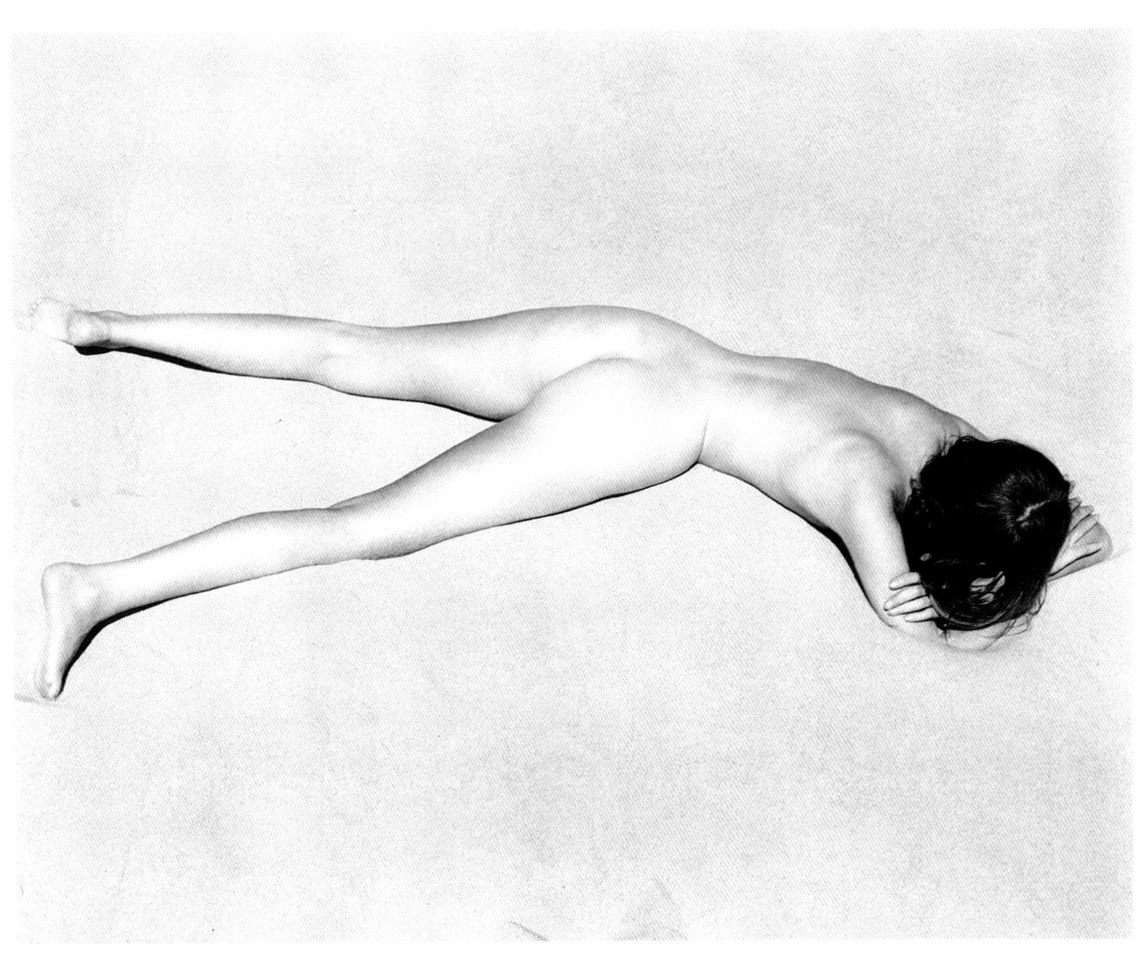

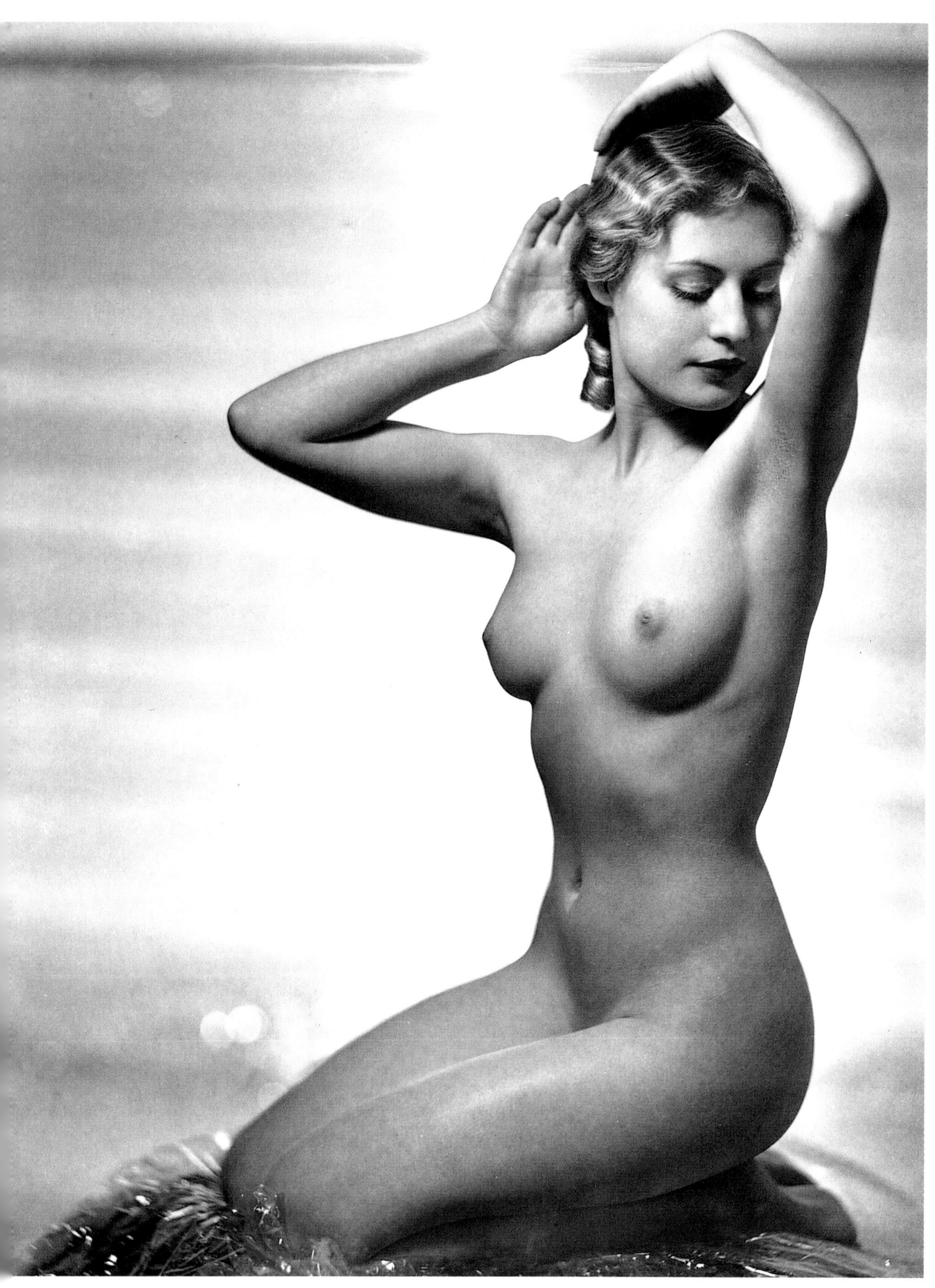

 ROSALIND MAINGOT 1936

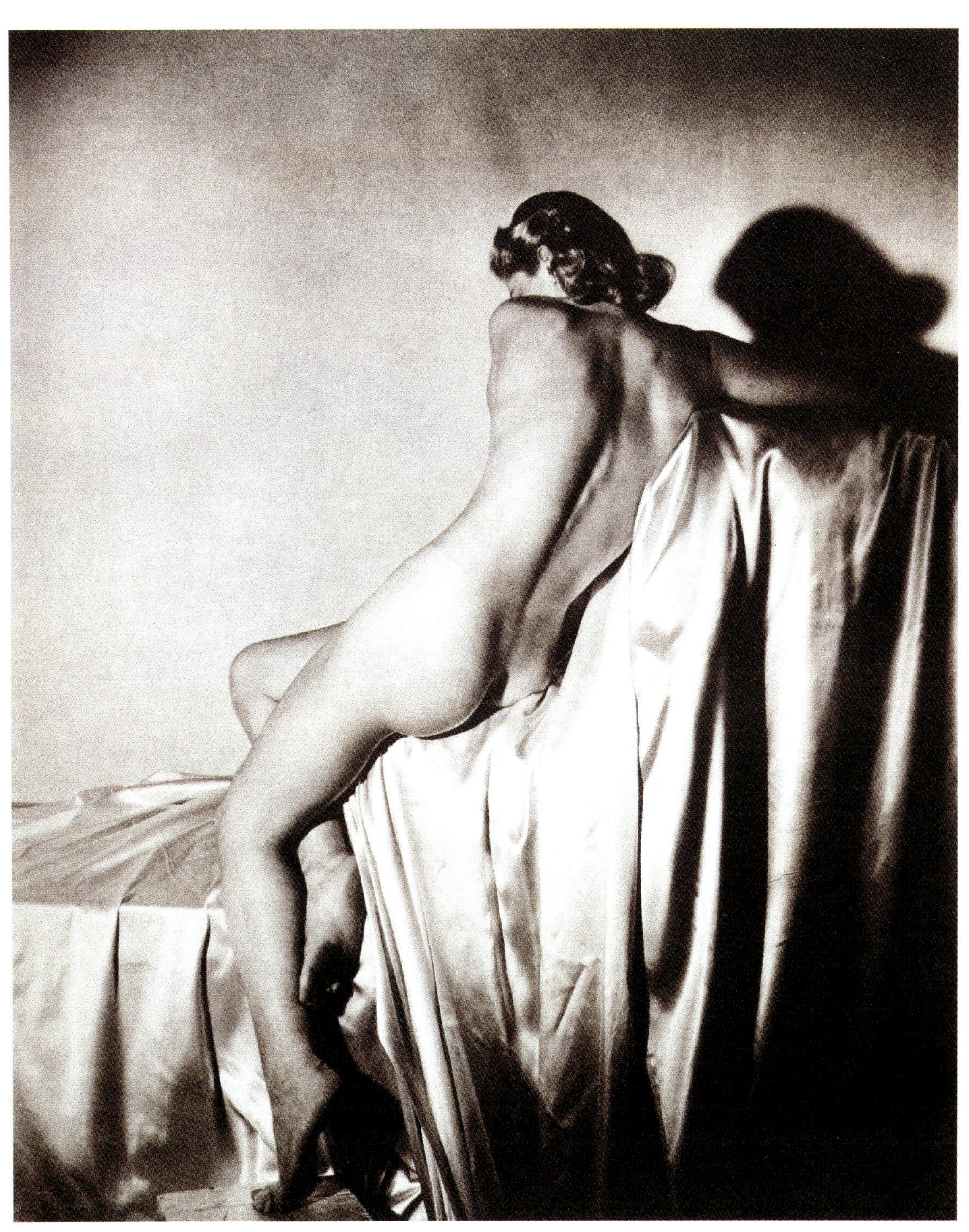

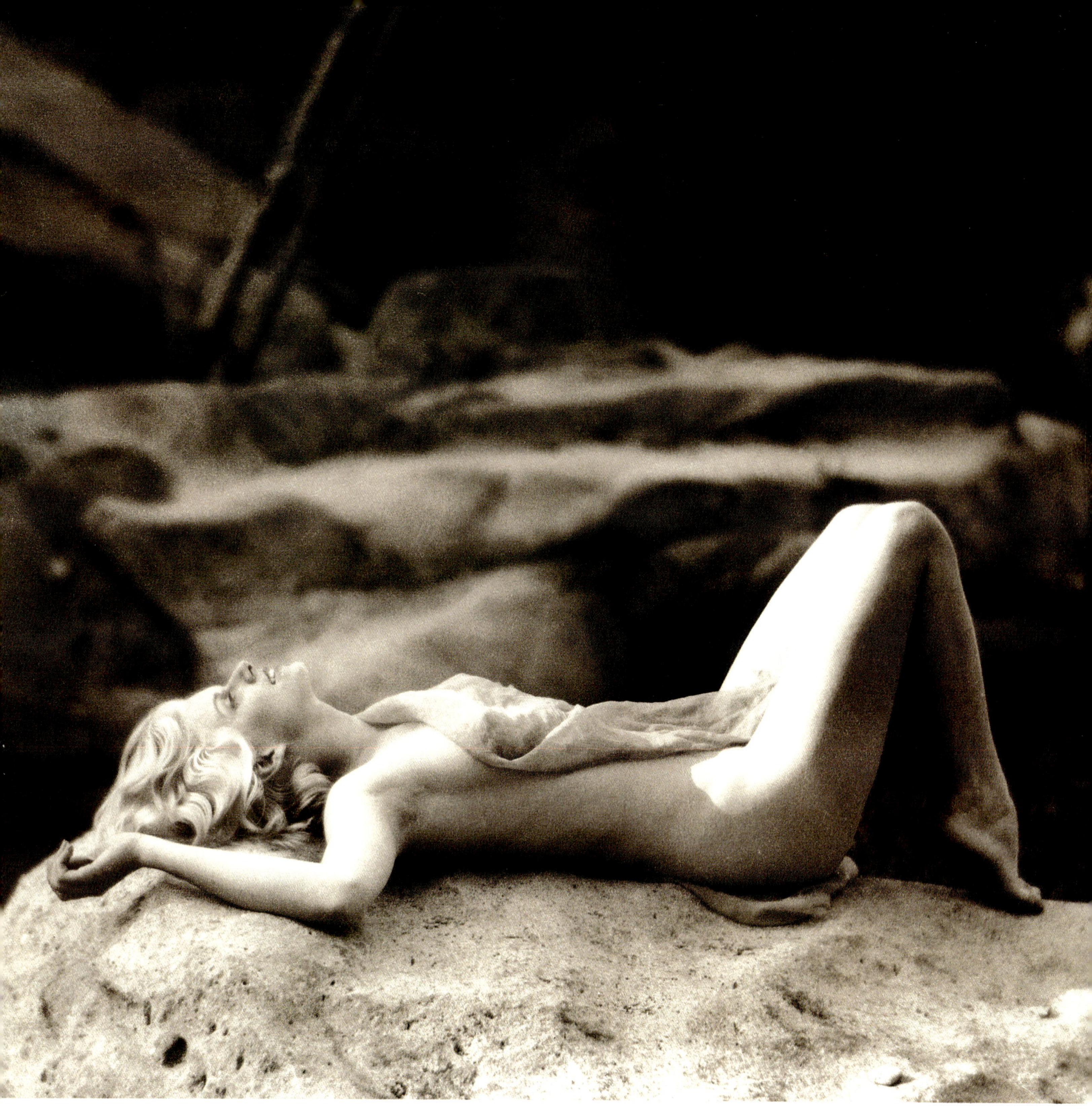

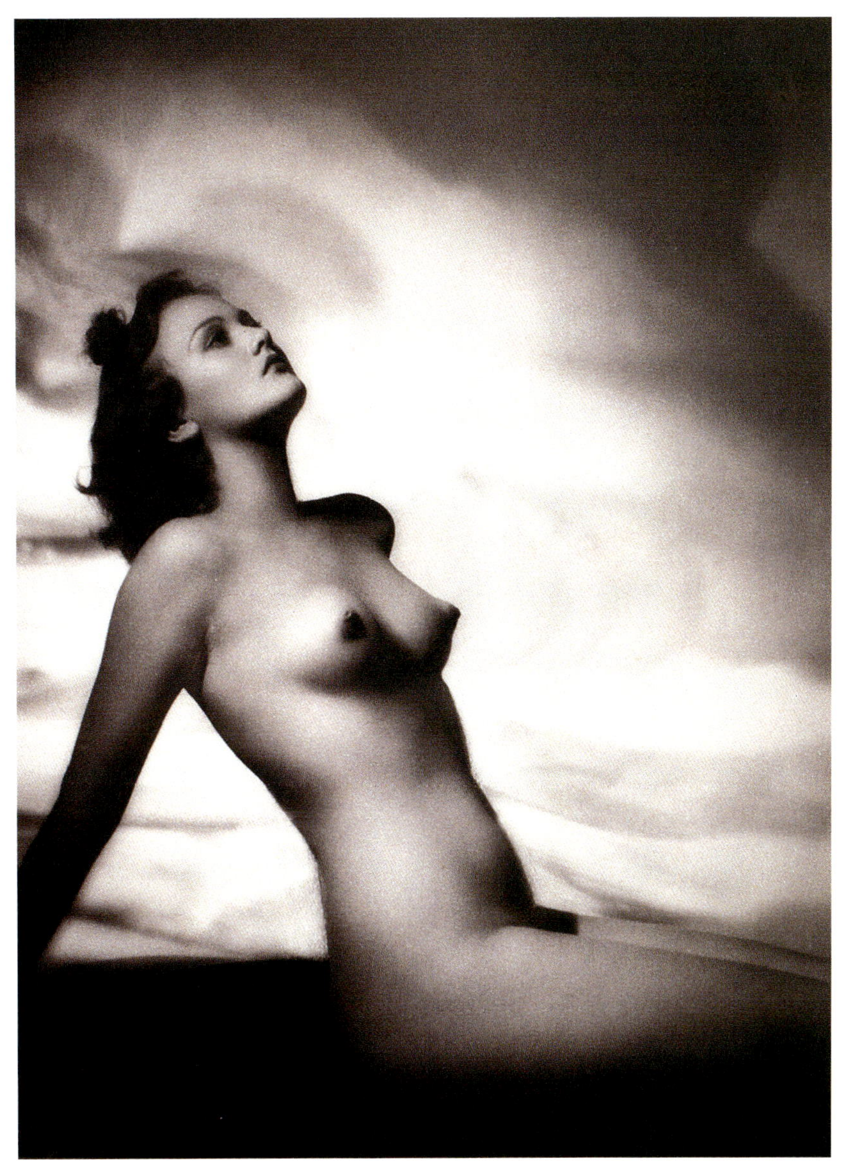

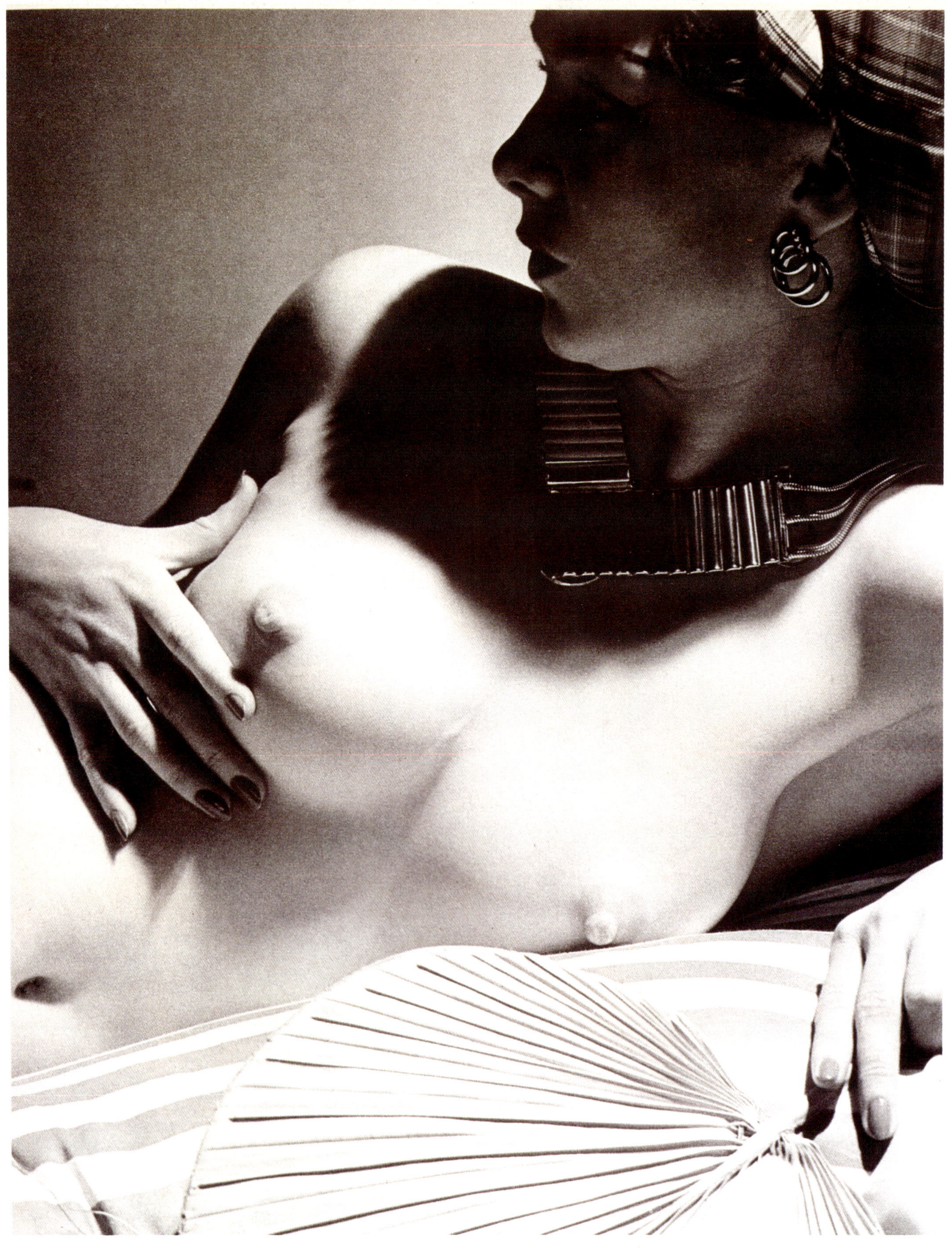

1950 - 1979

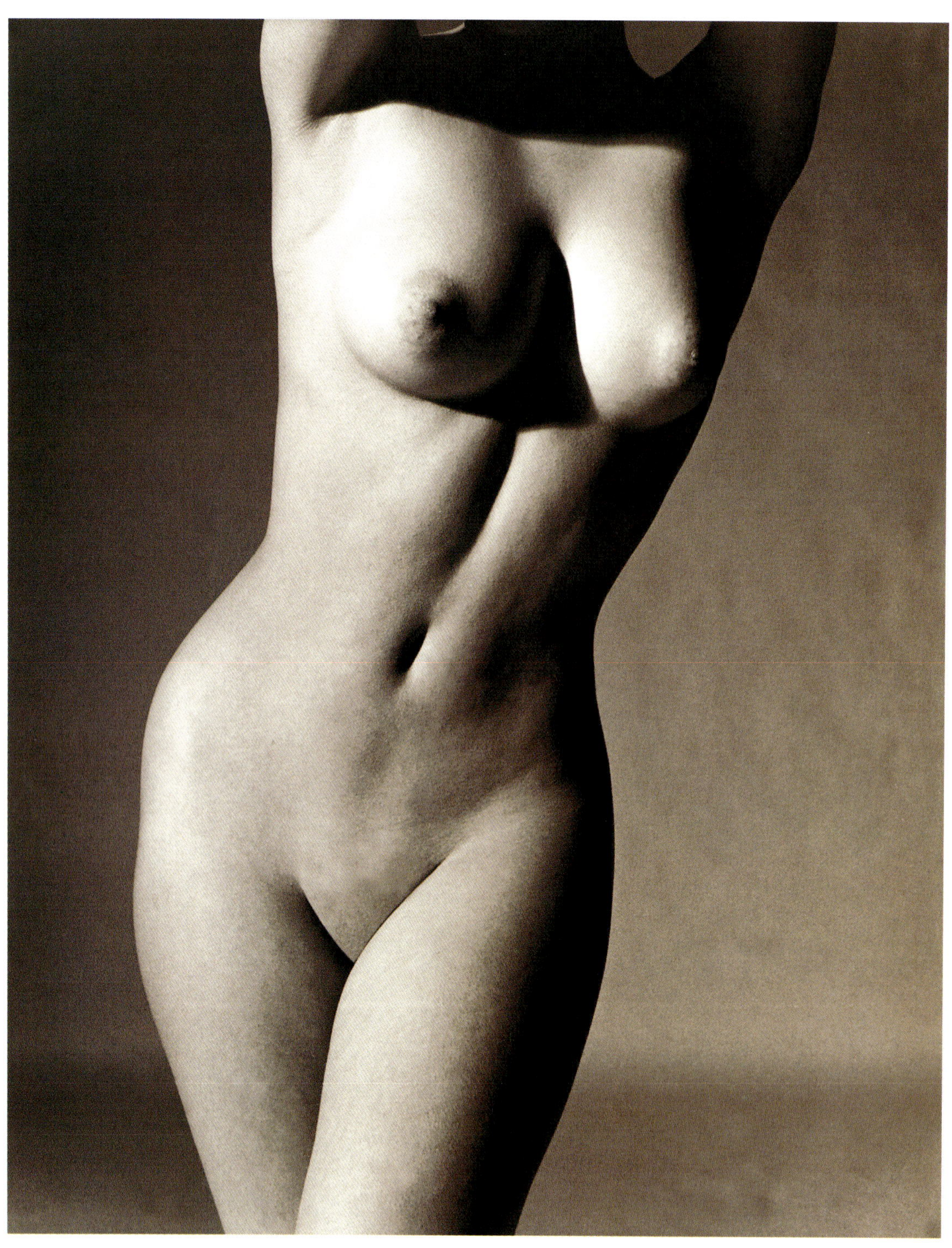

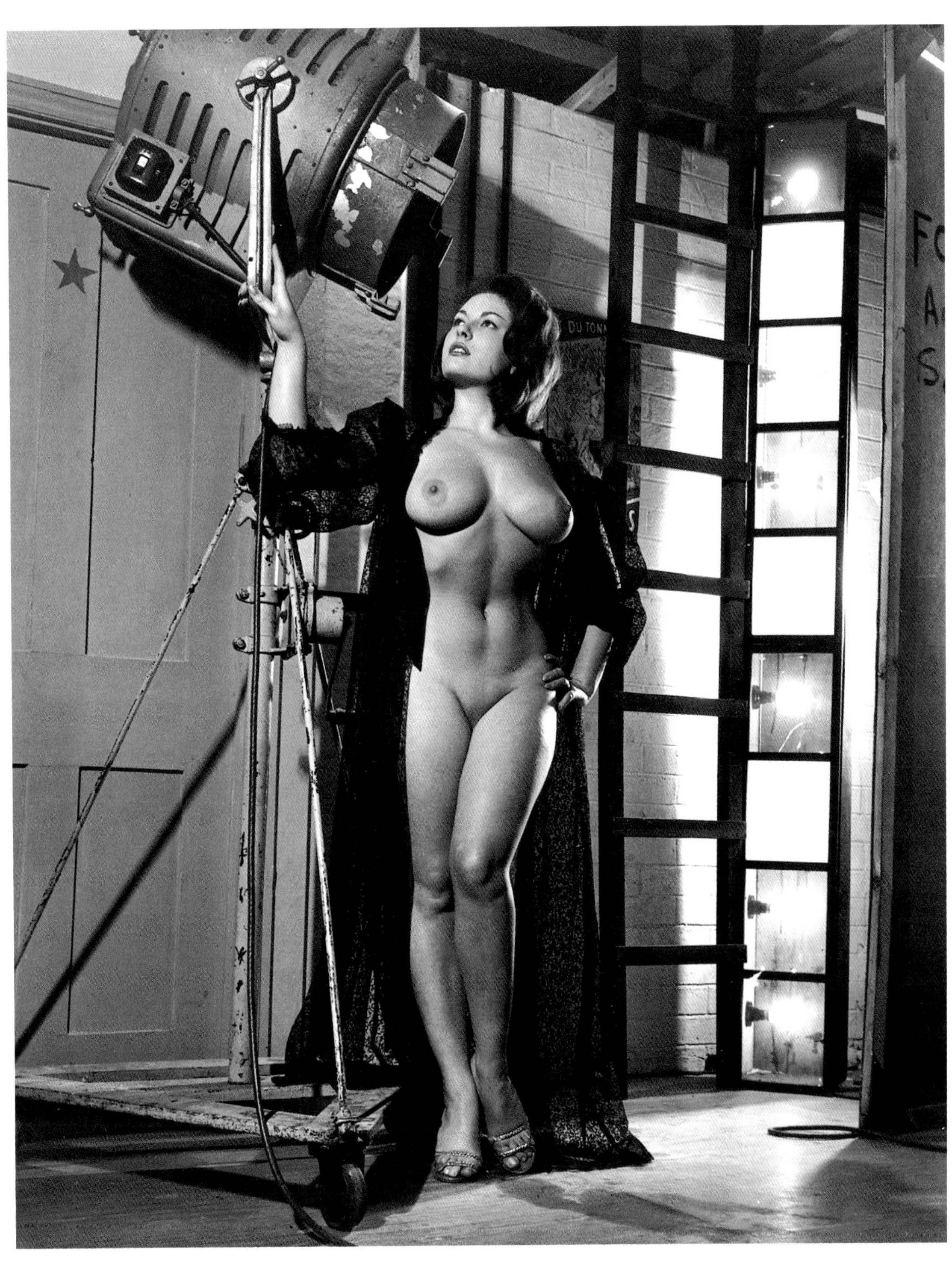

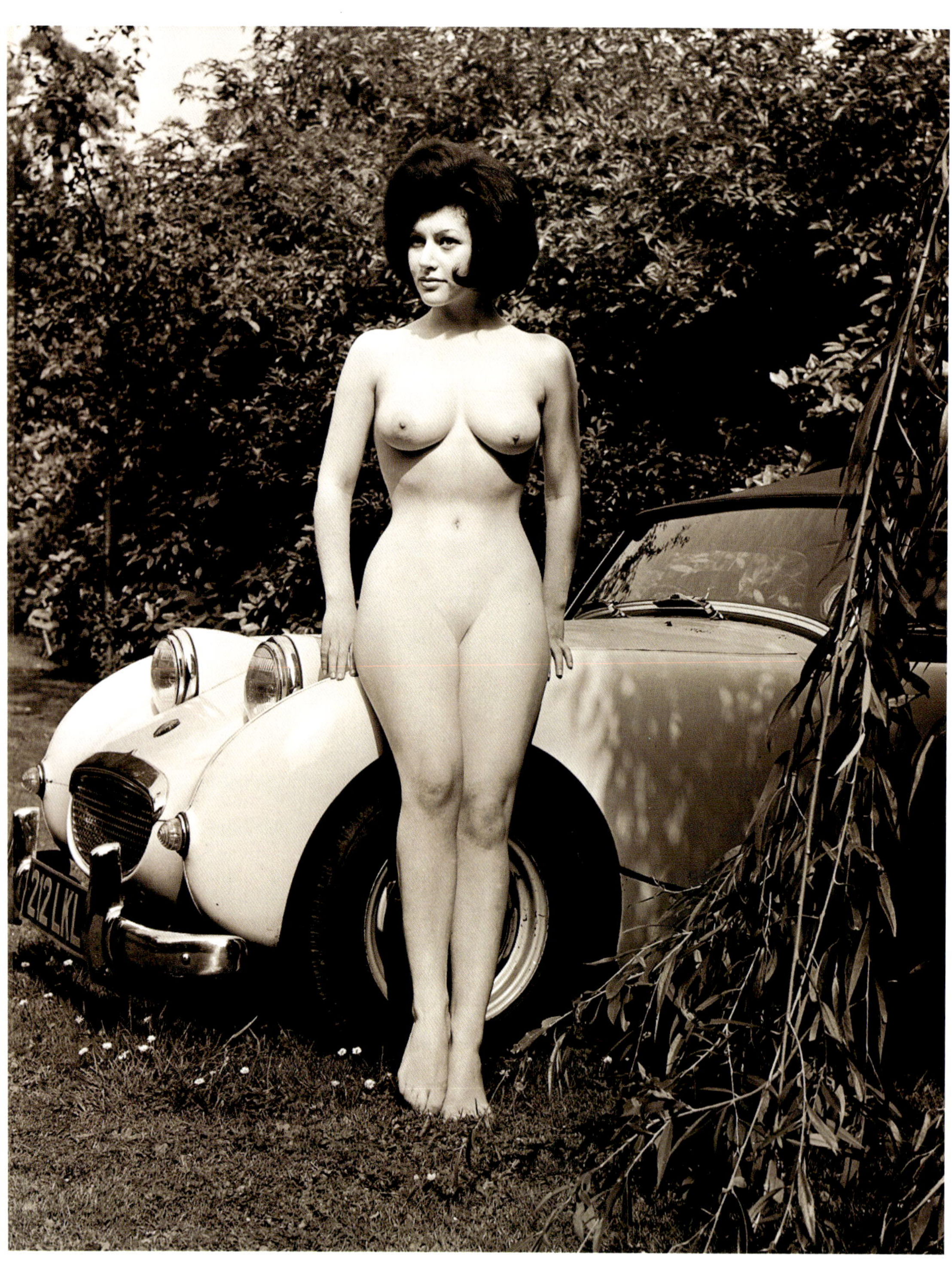
212 LKL

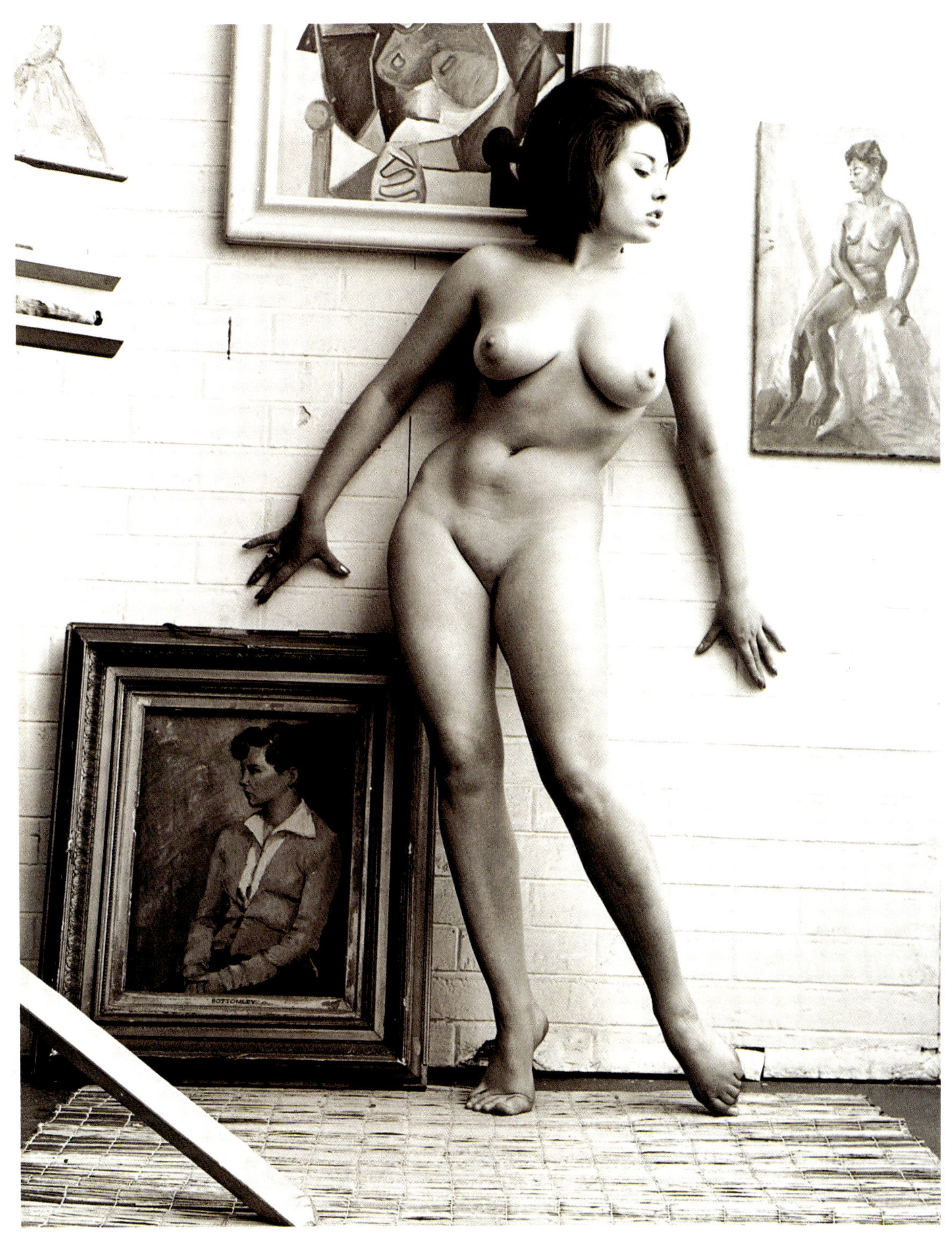
BOTTOMLEY

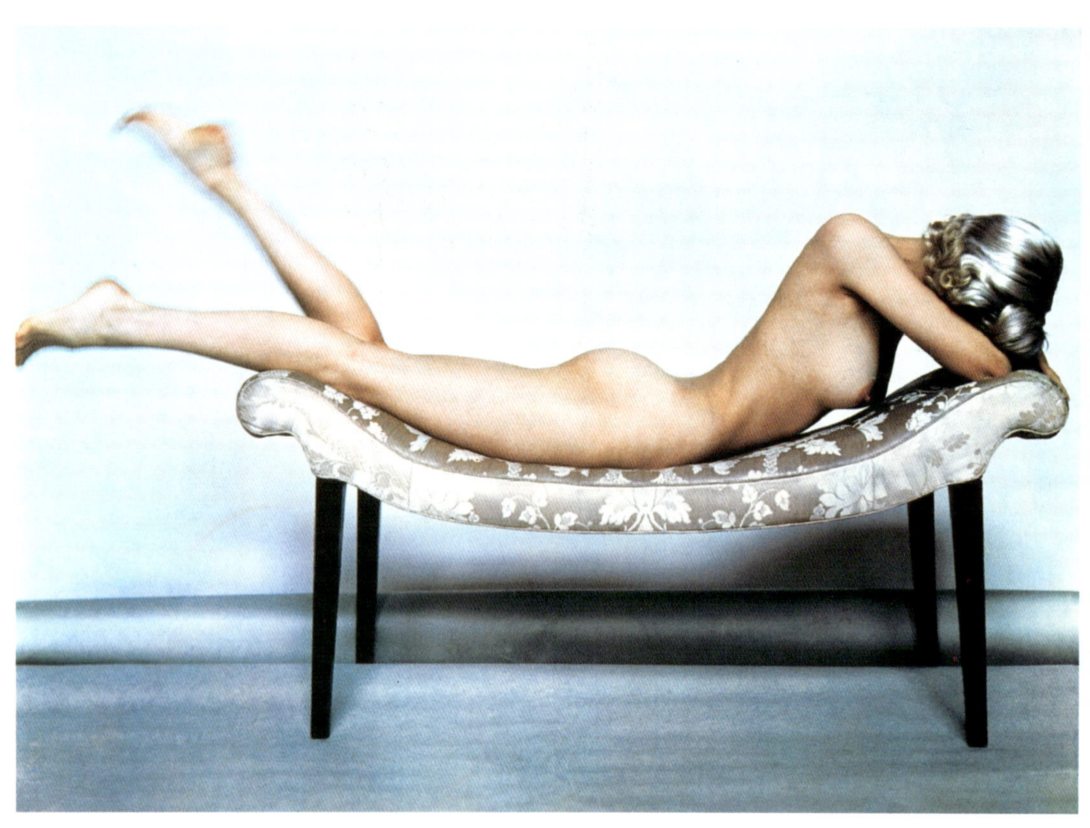

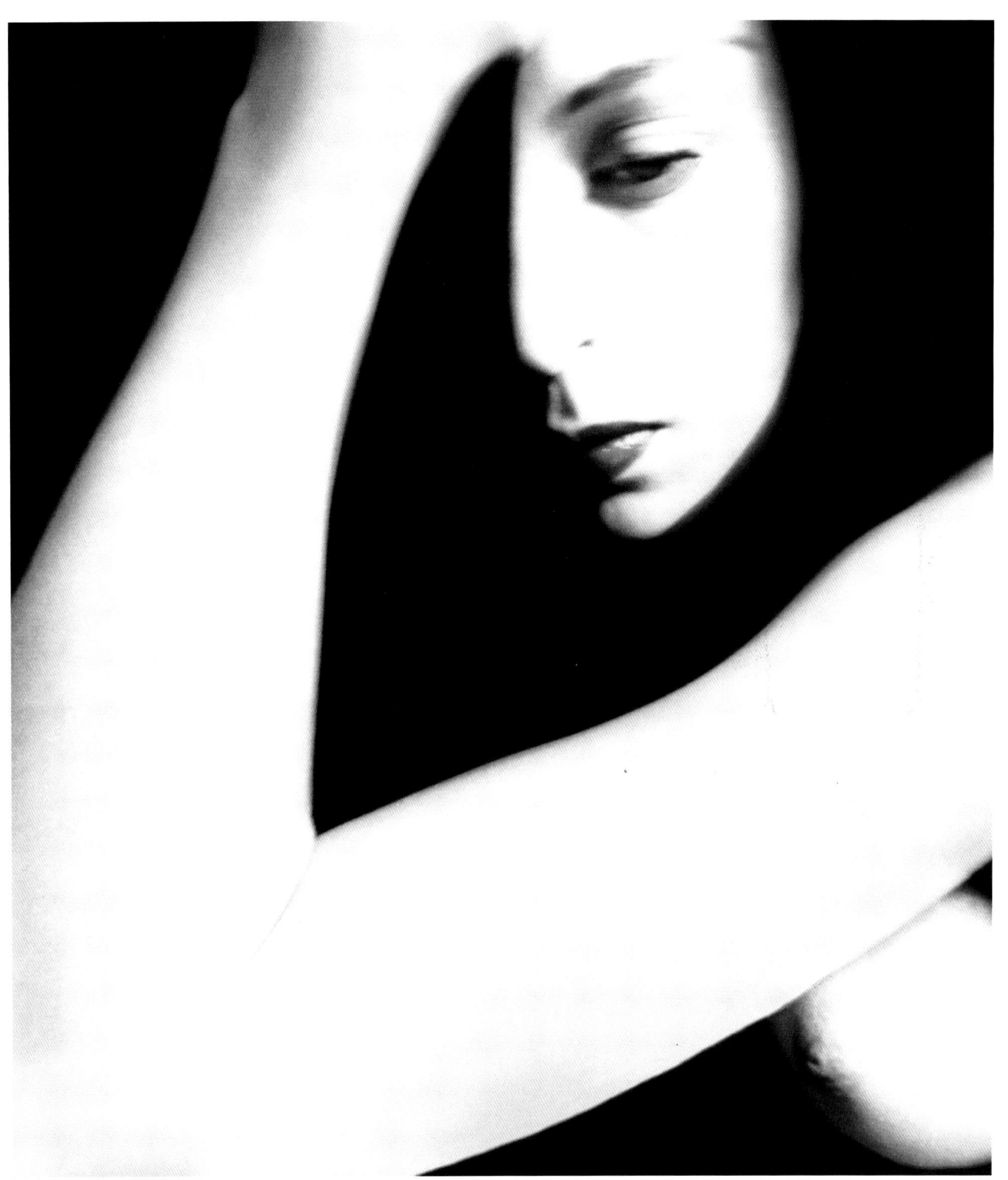

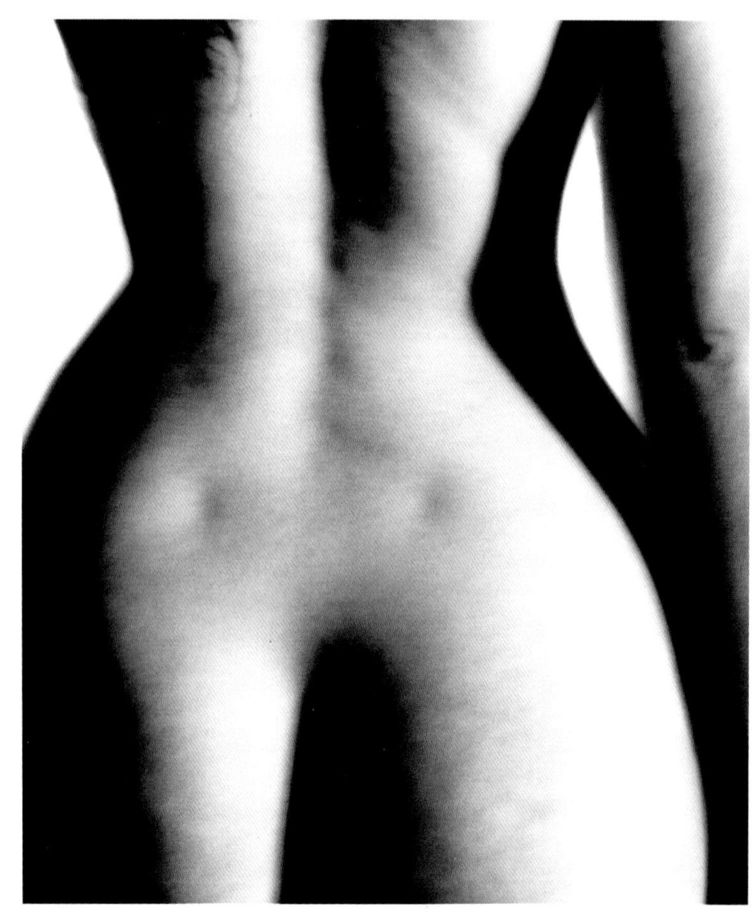

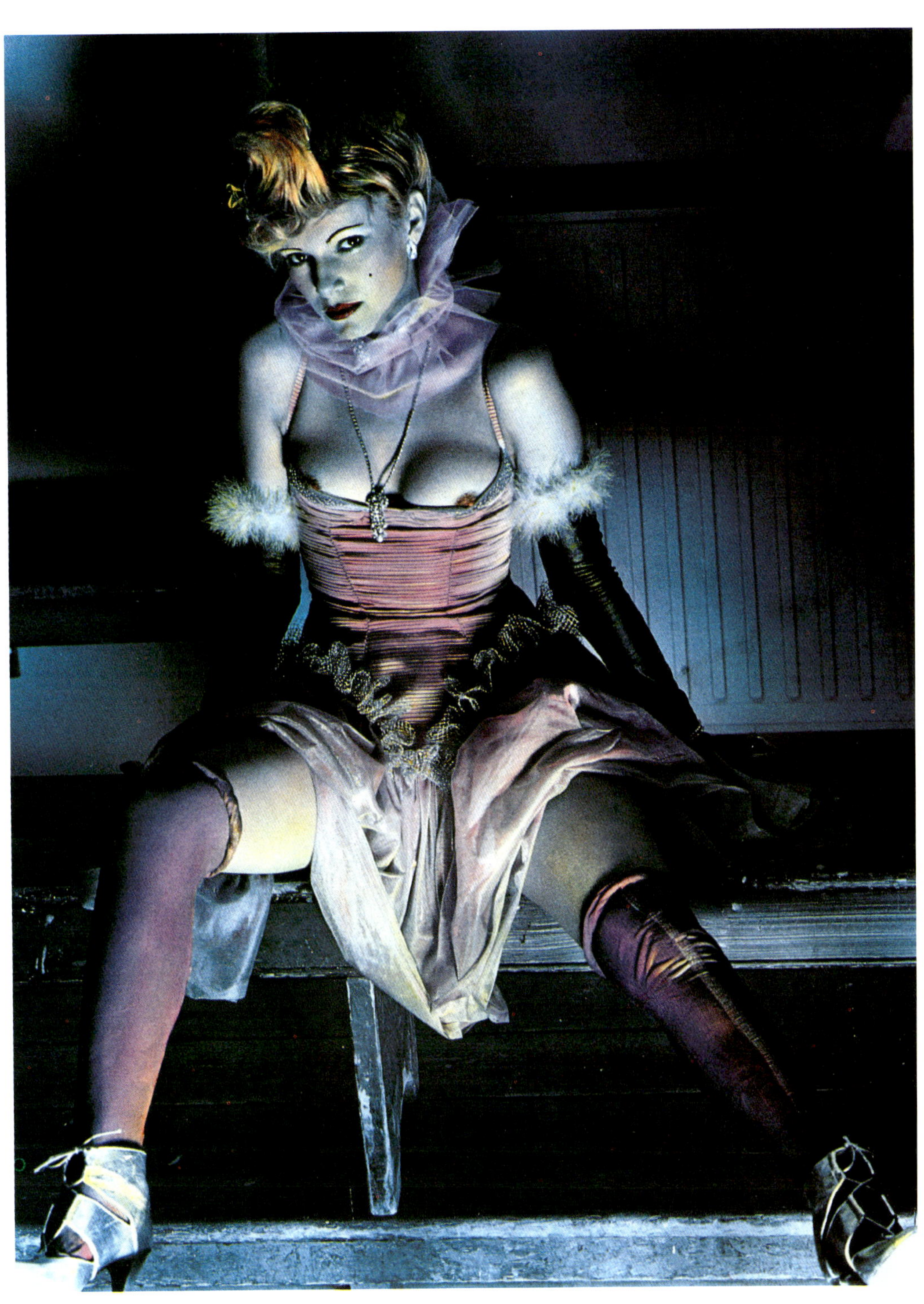

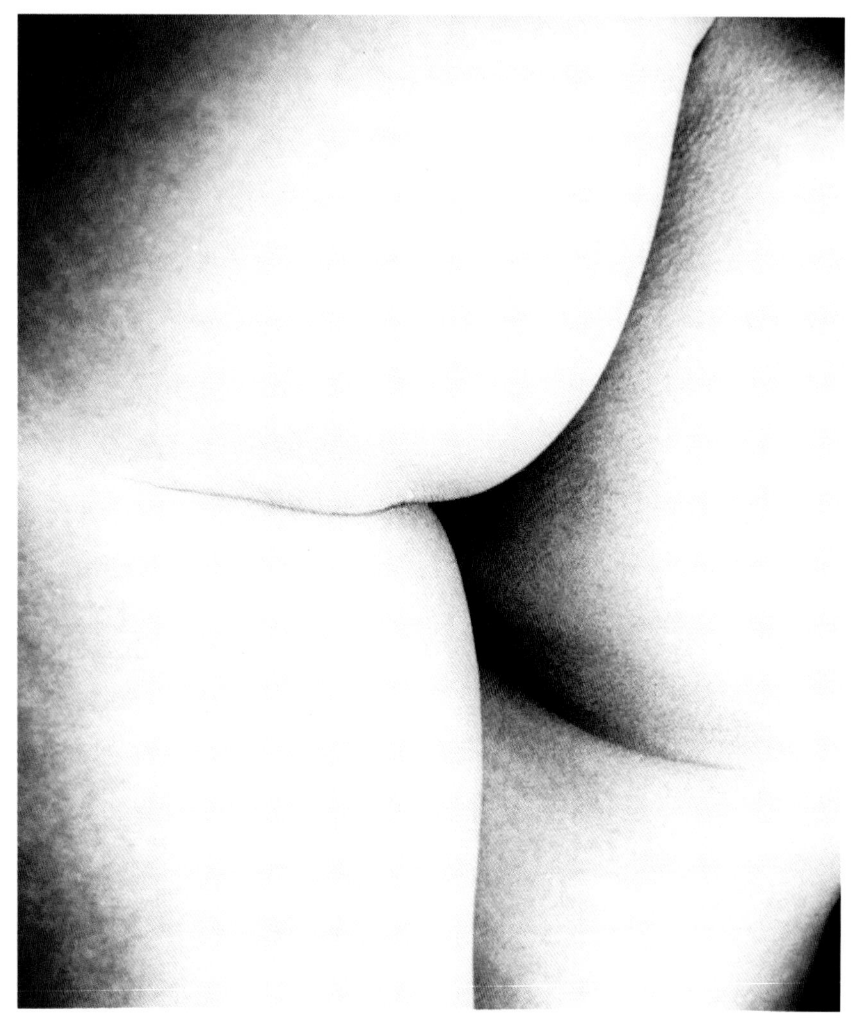

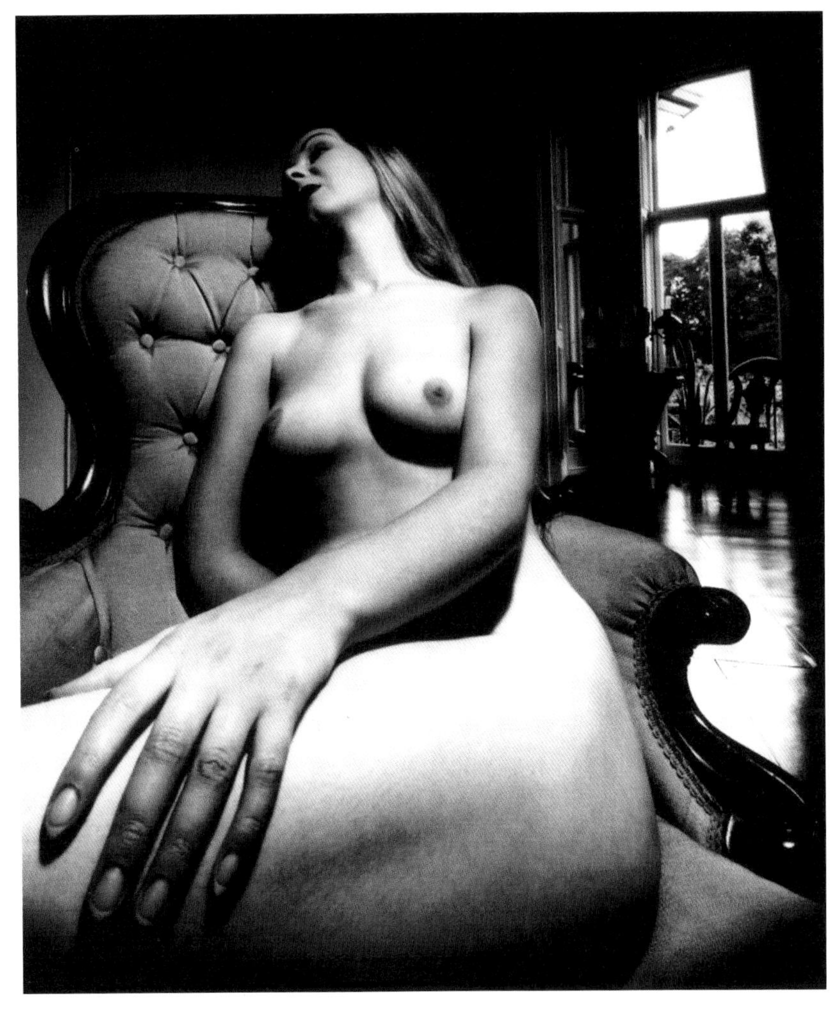

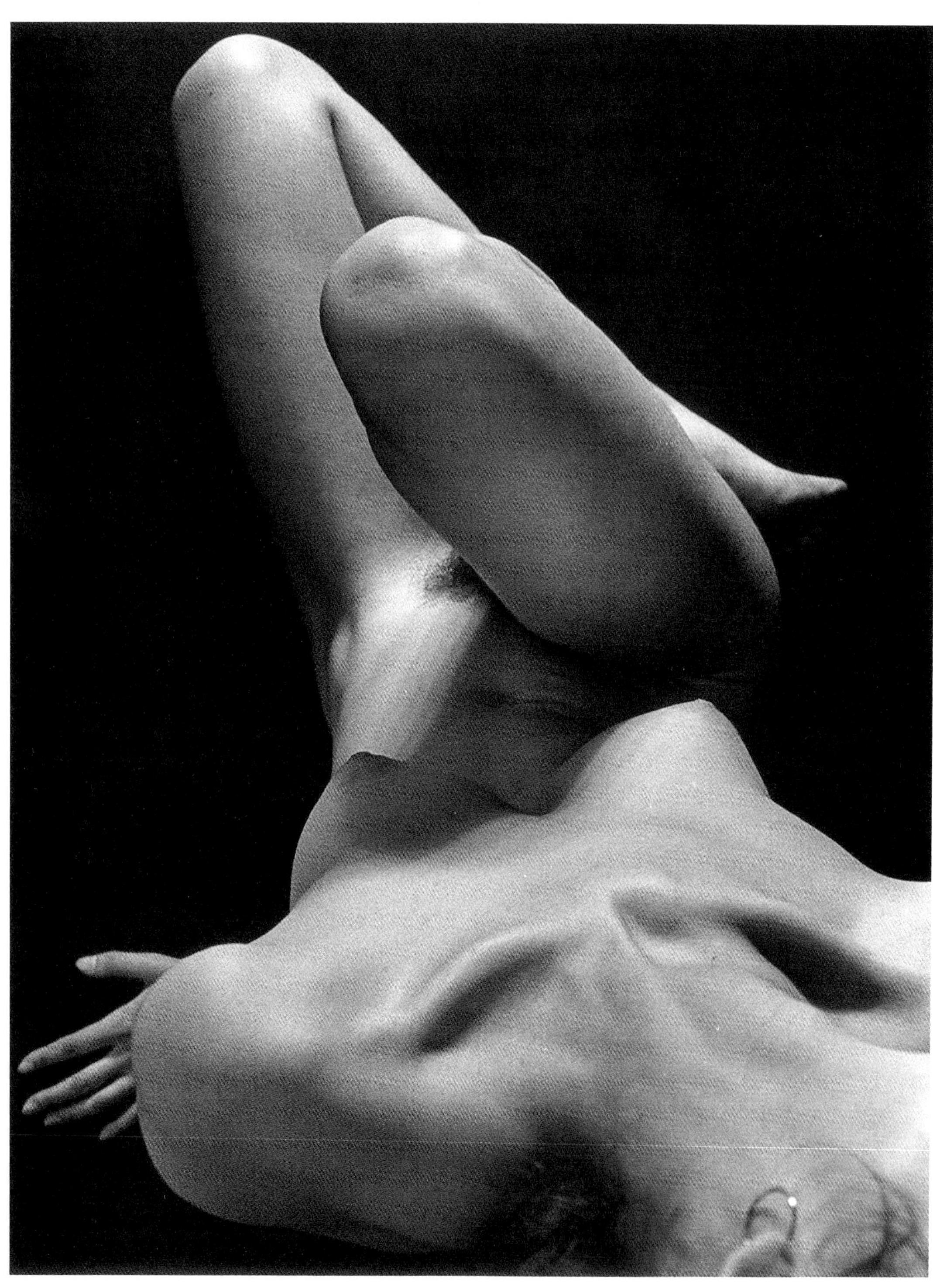

 CHARLES ROFF 1970

(right) **JAMES WEDGE** 1976

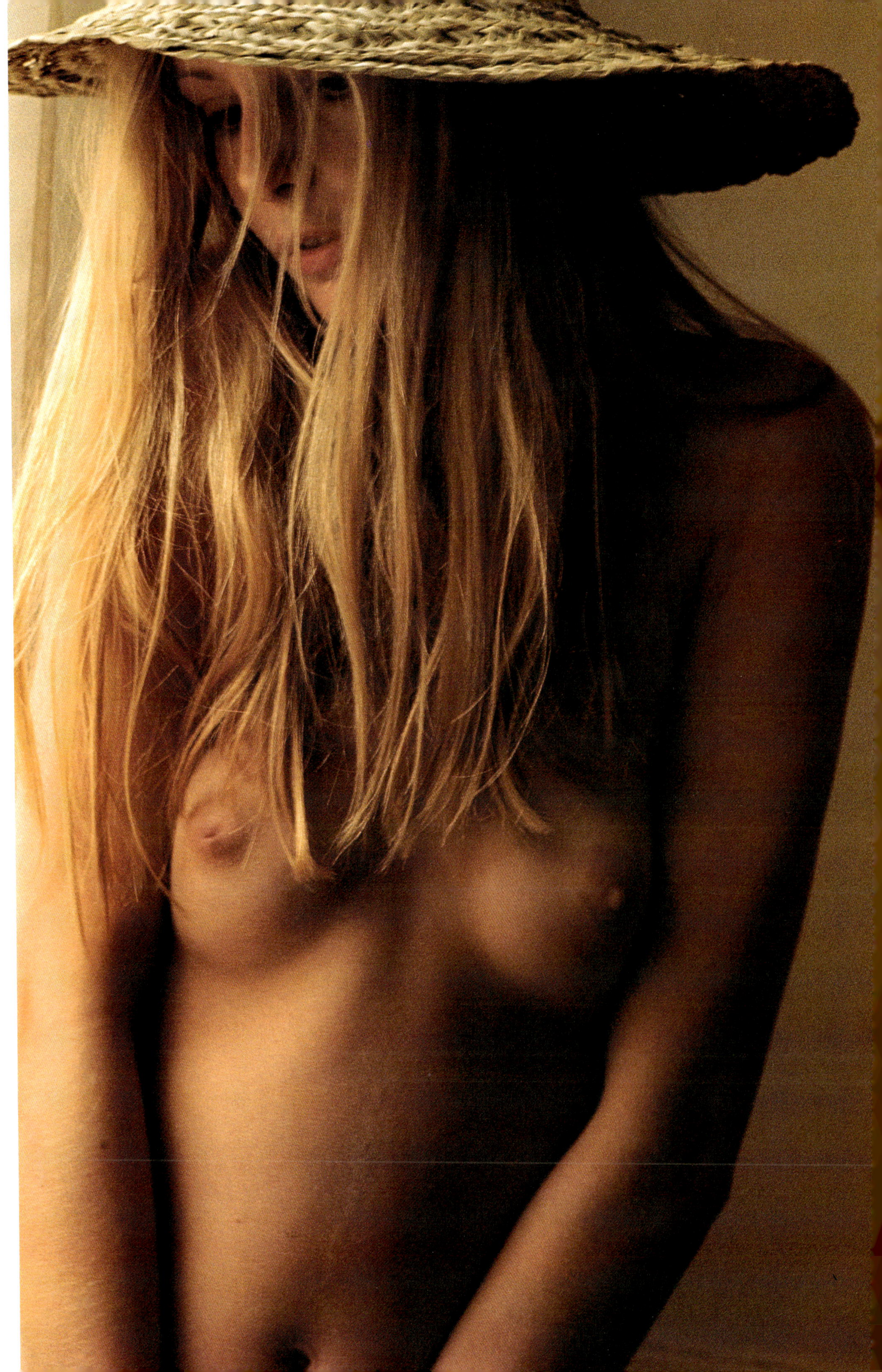

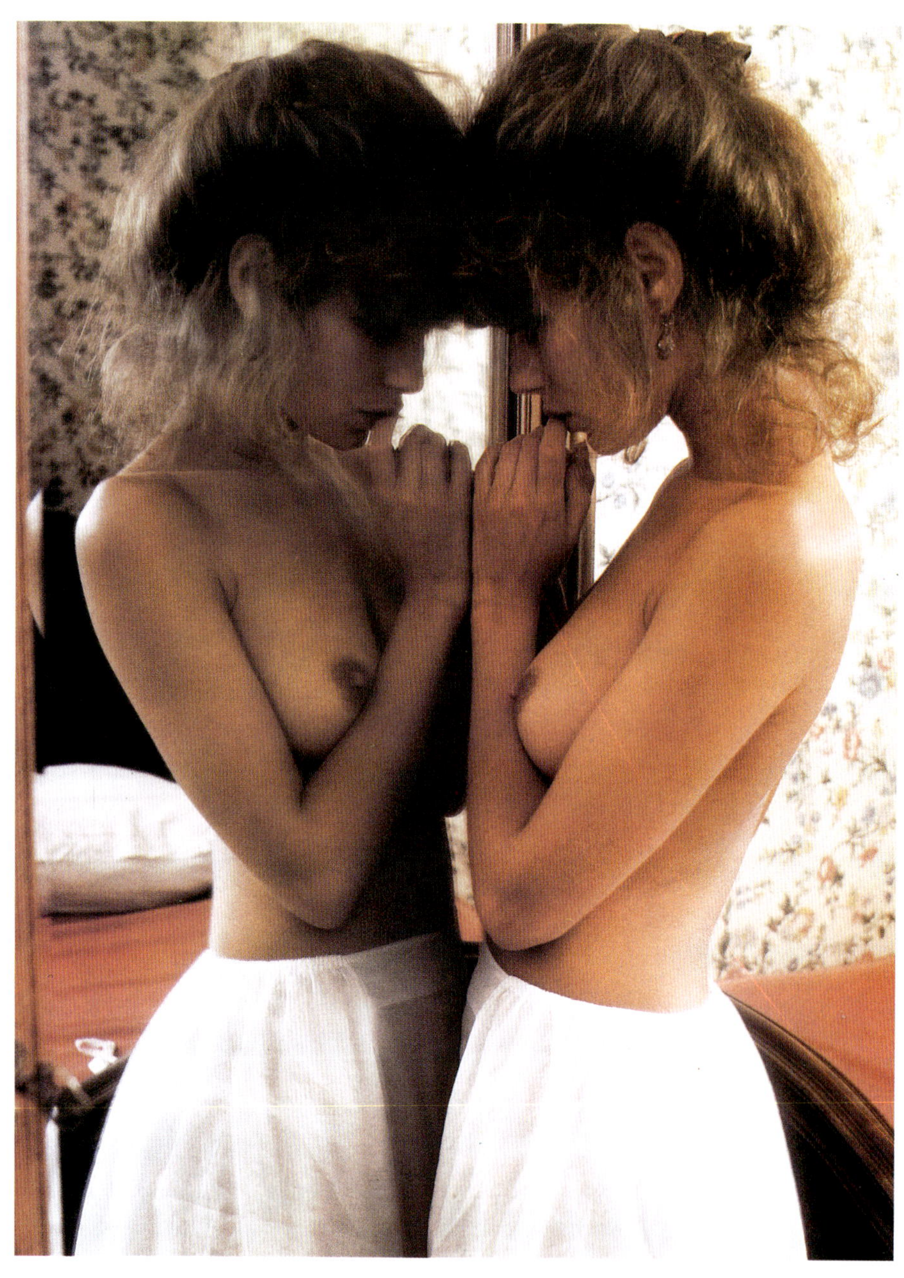

(right) **JAMES WEDGE** 1975

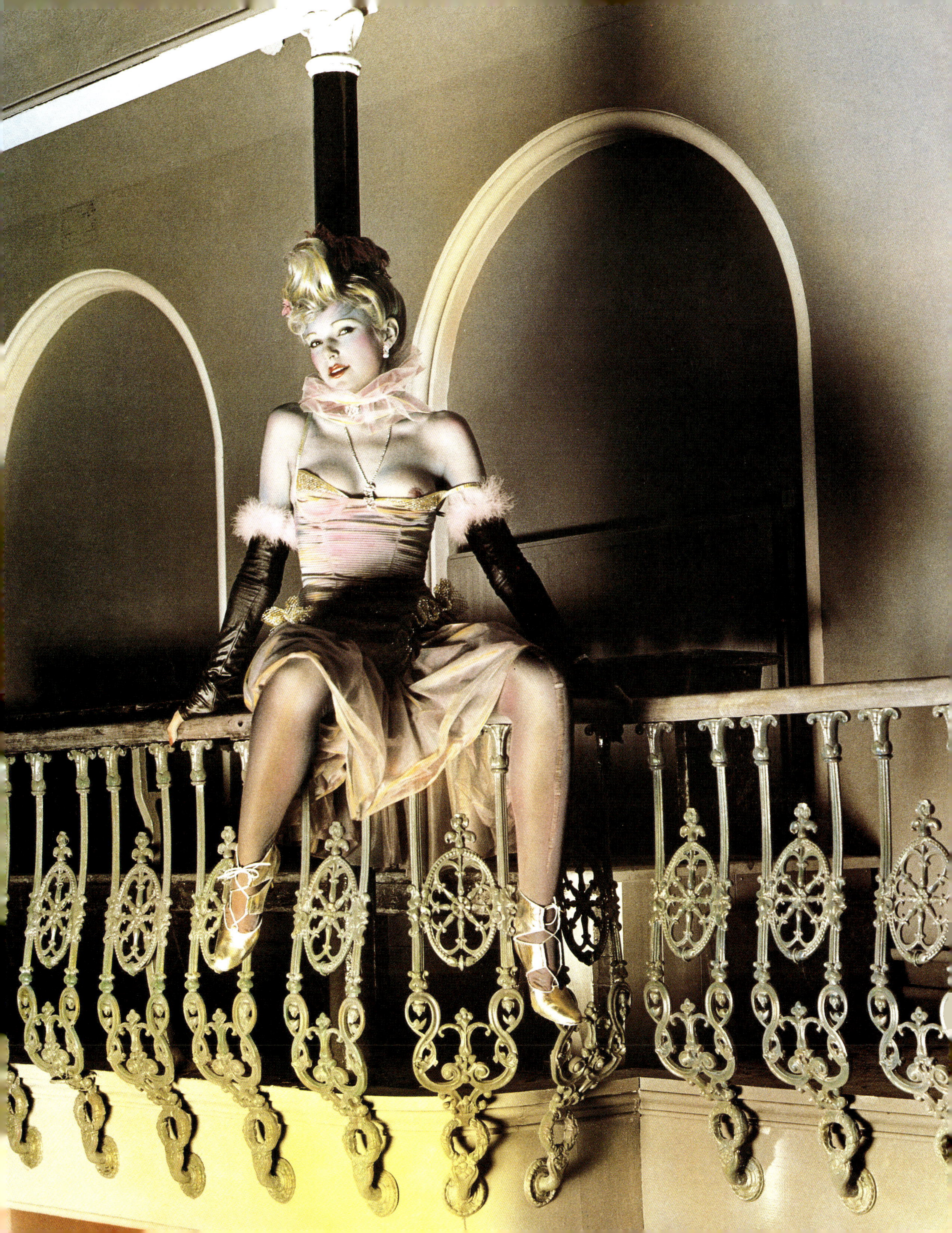

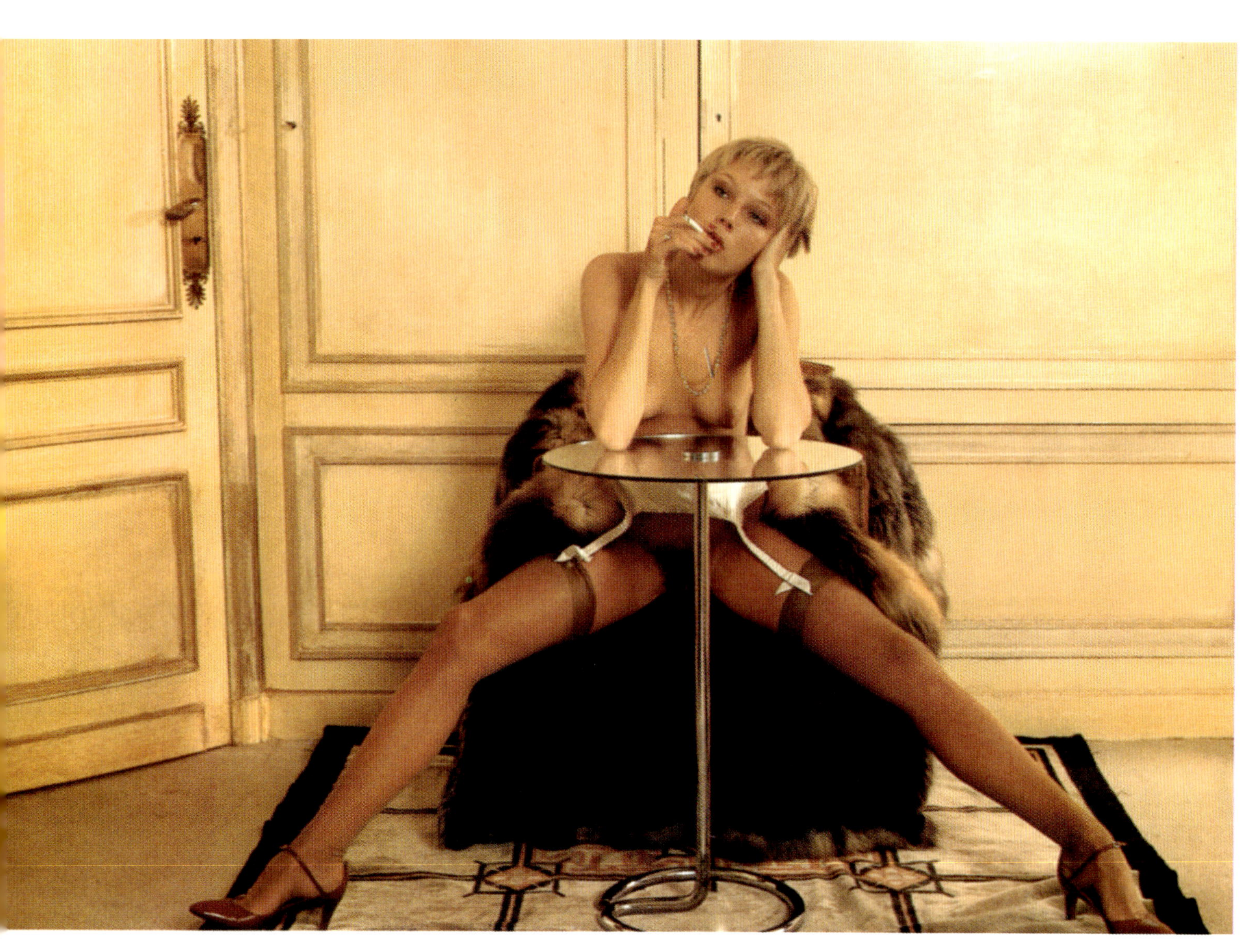

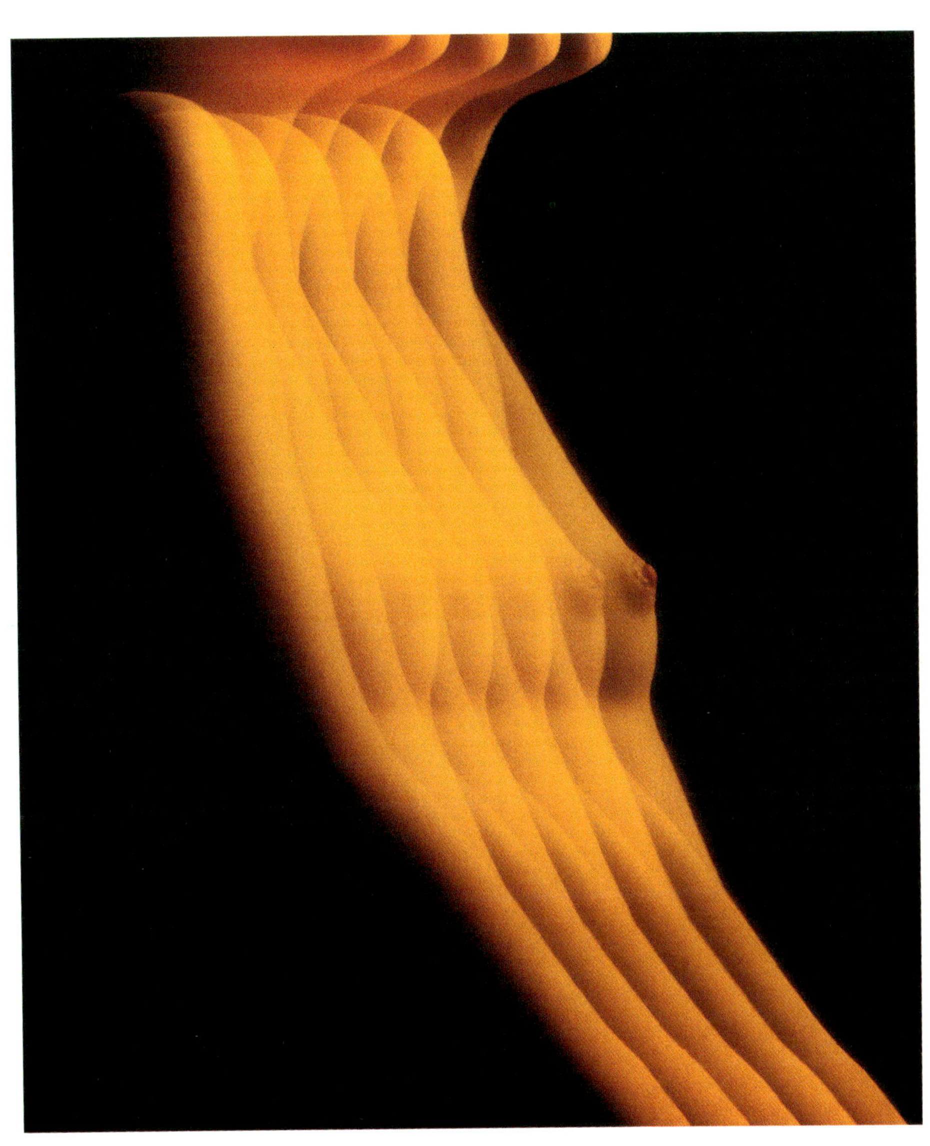

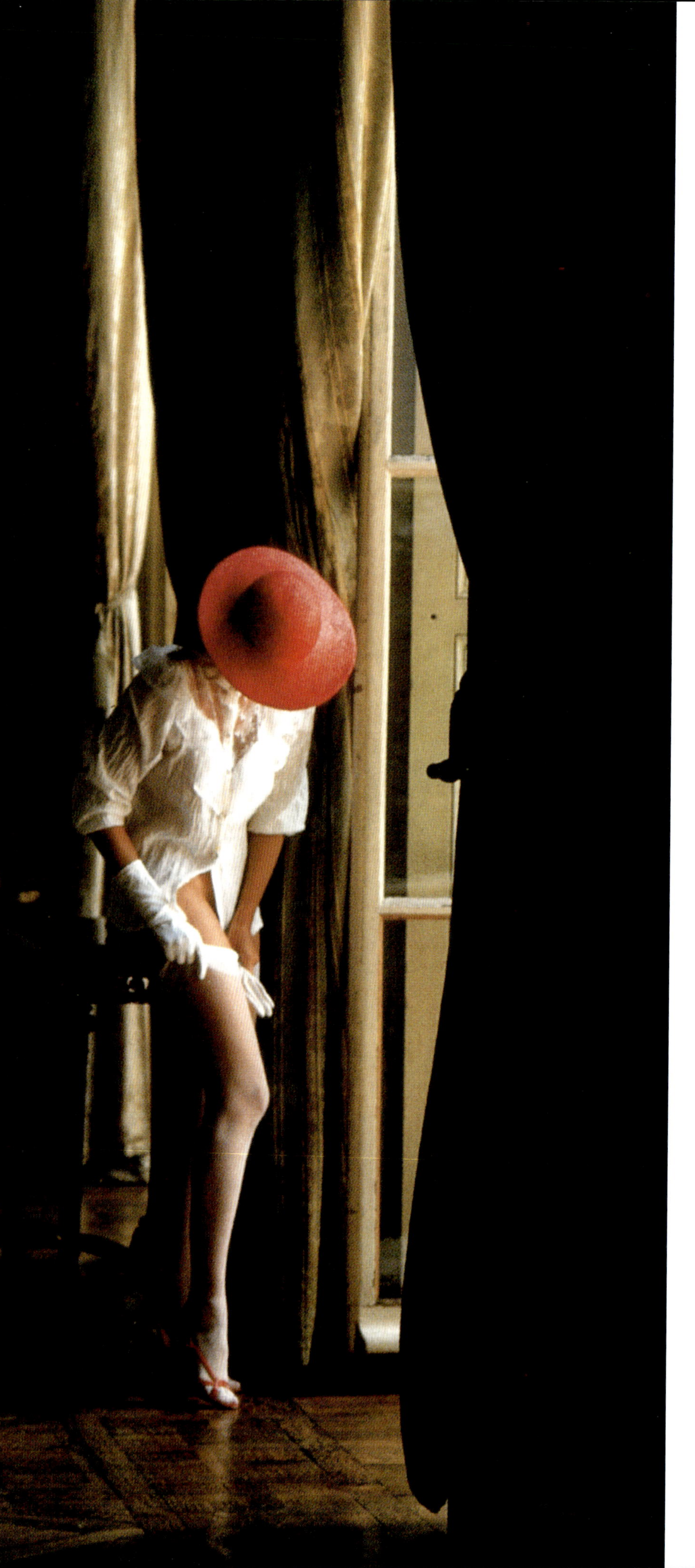

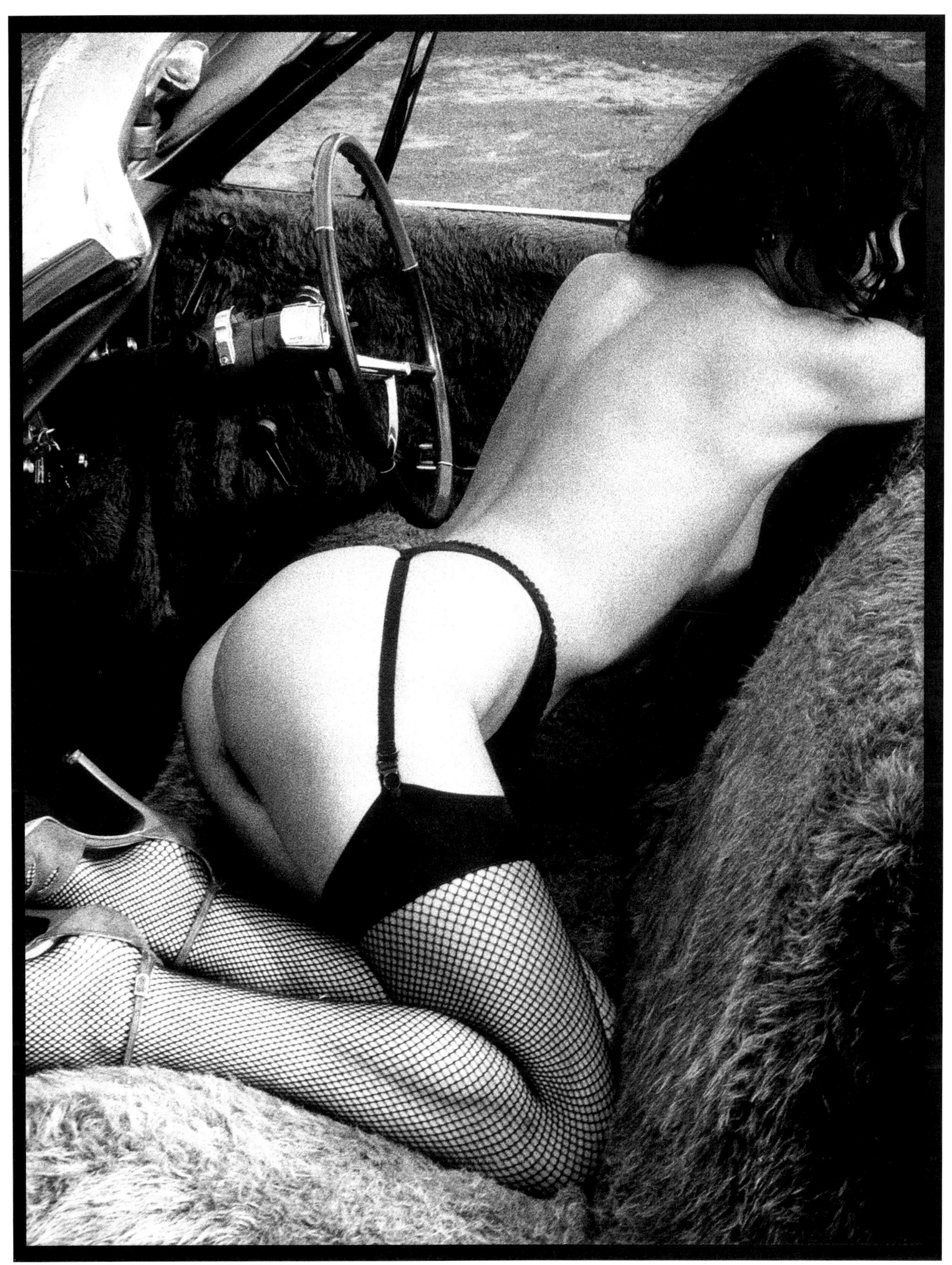

(left) **JEFF DUNAS** 1979

CHARLES ROFF 1978

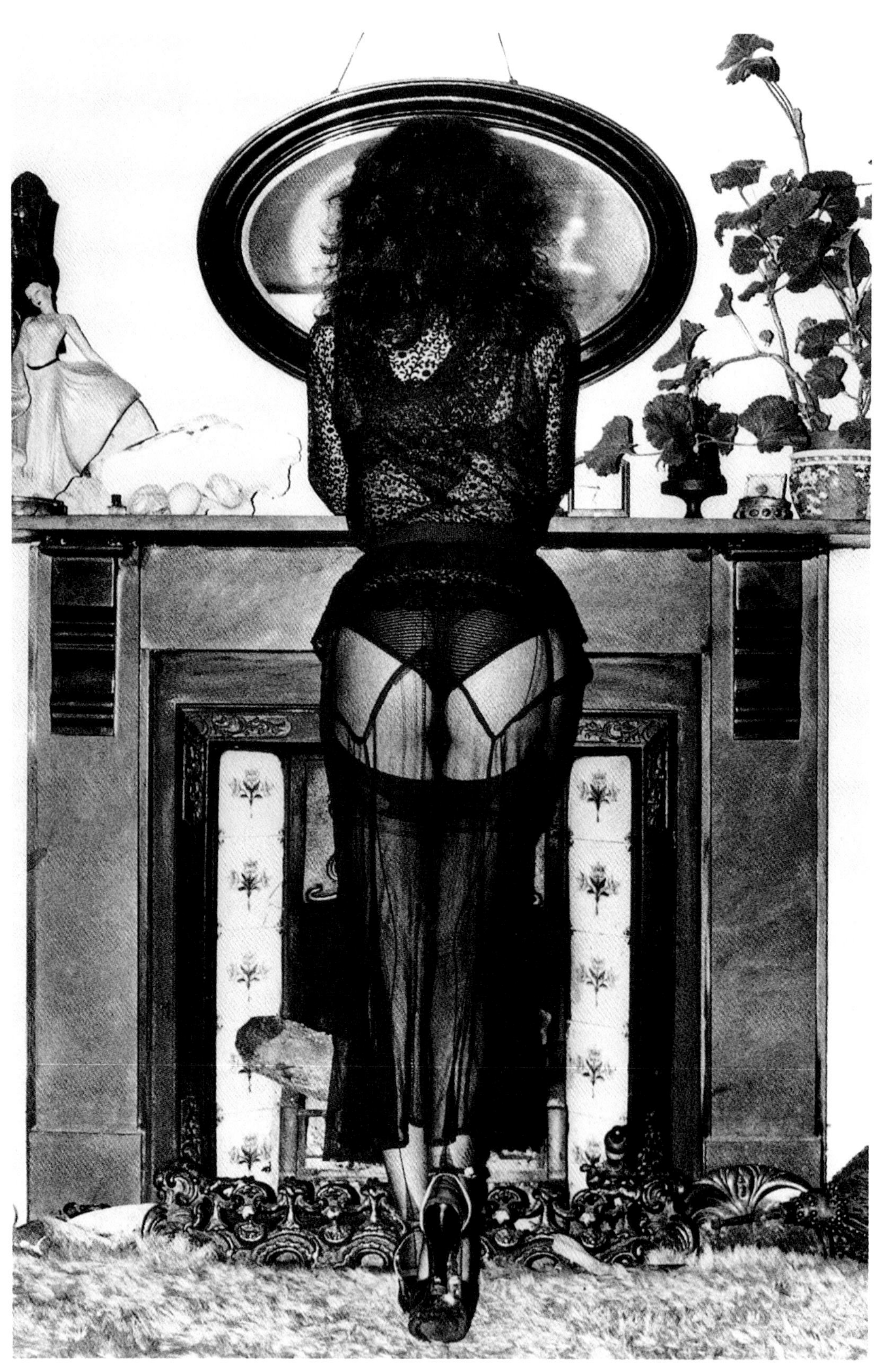

1980s

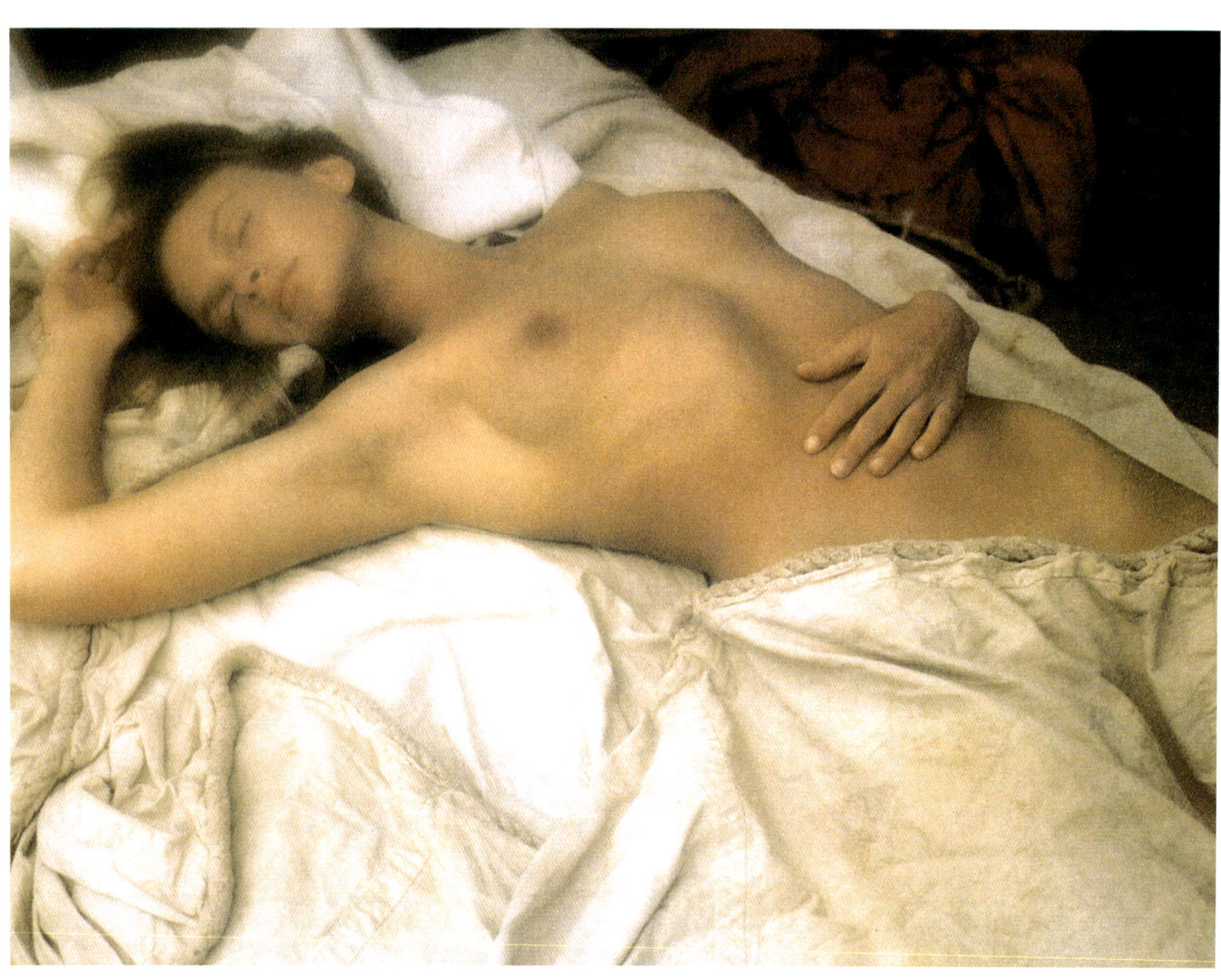

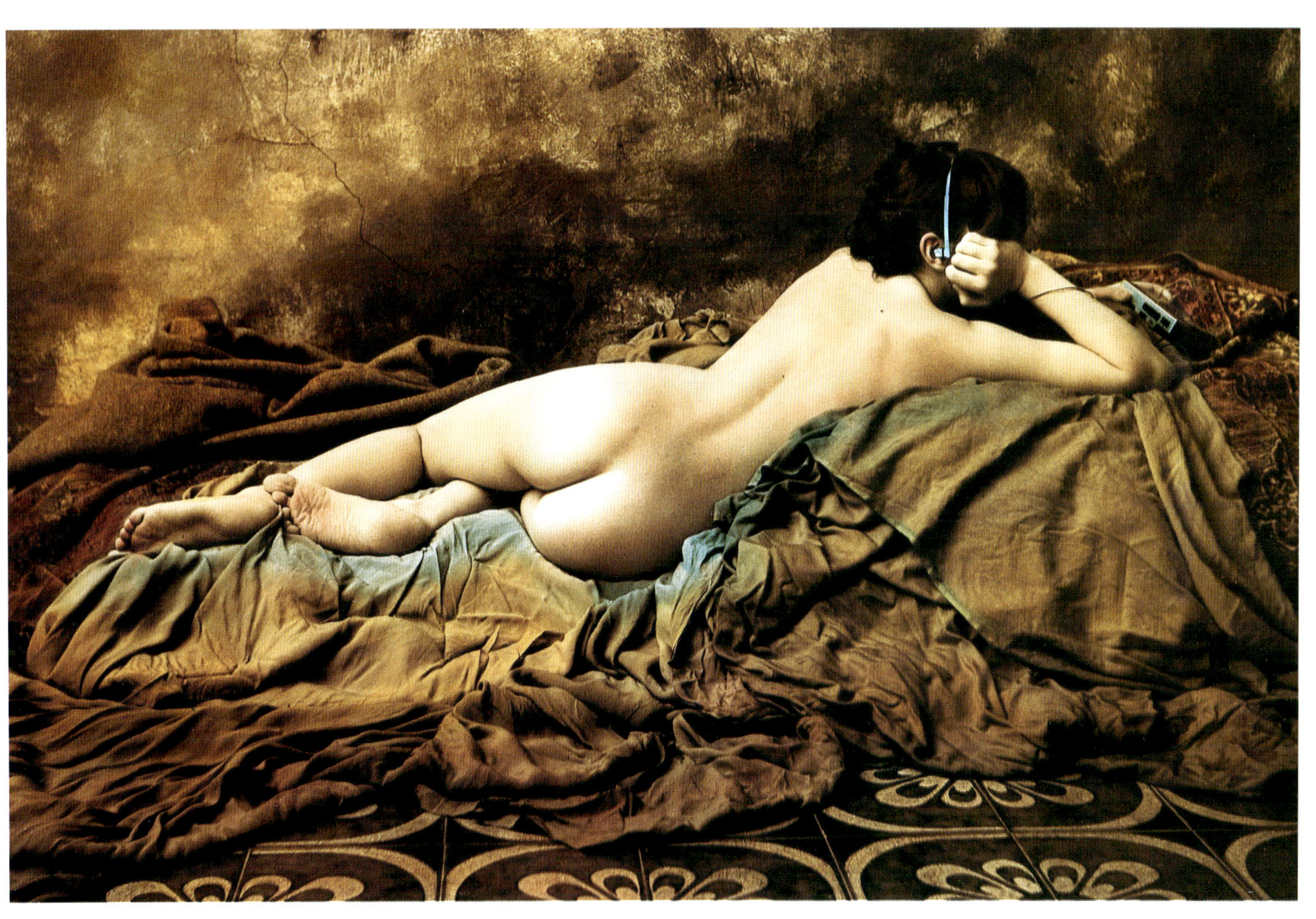

(overleaf) **NORMAN PARKINSON** 1985

JAN SAUDEK 1983 |

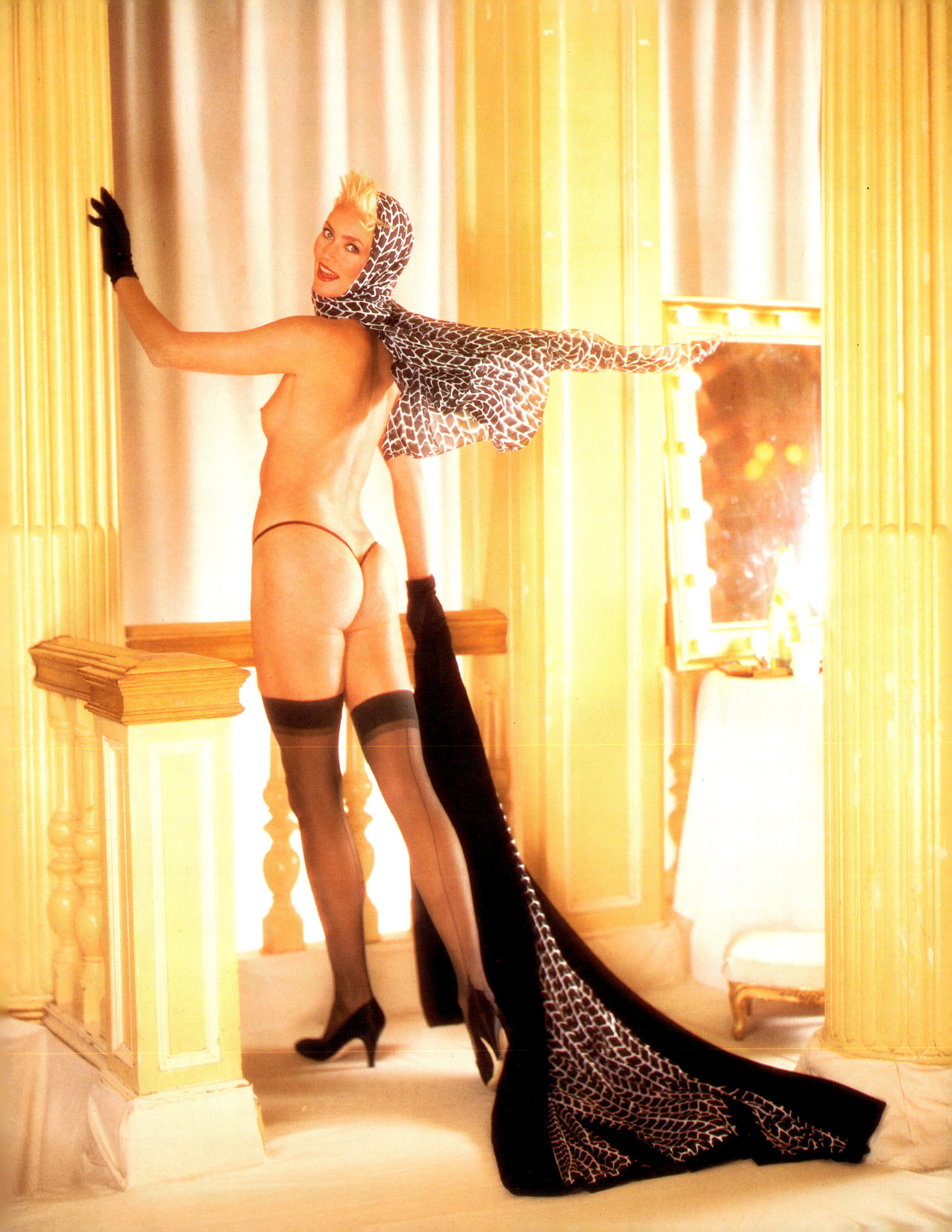

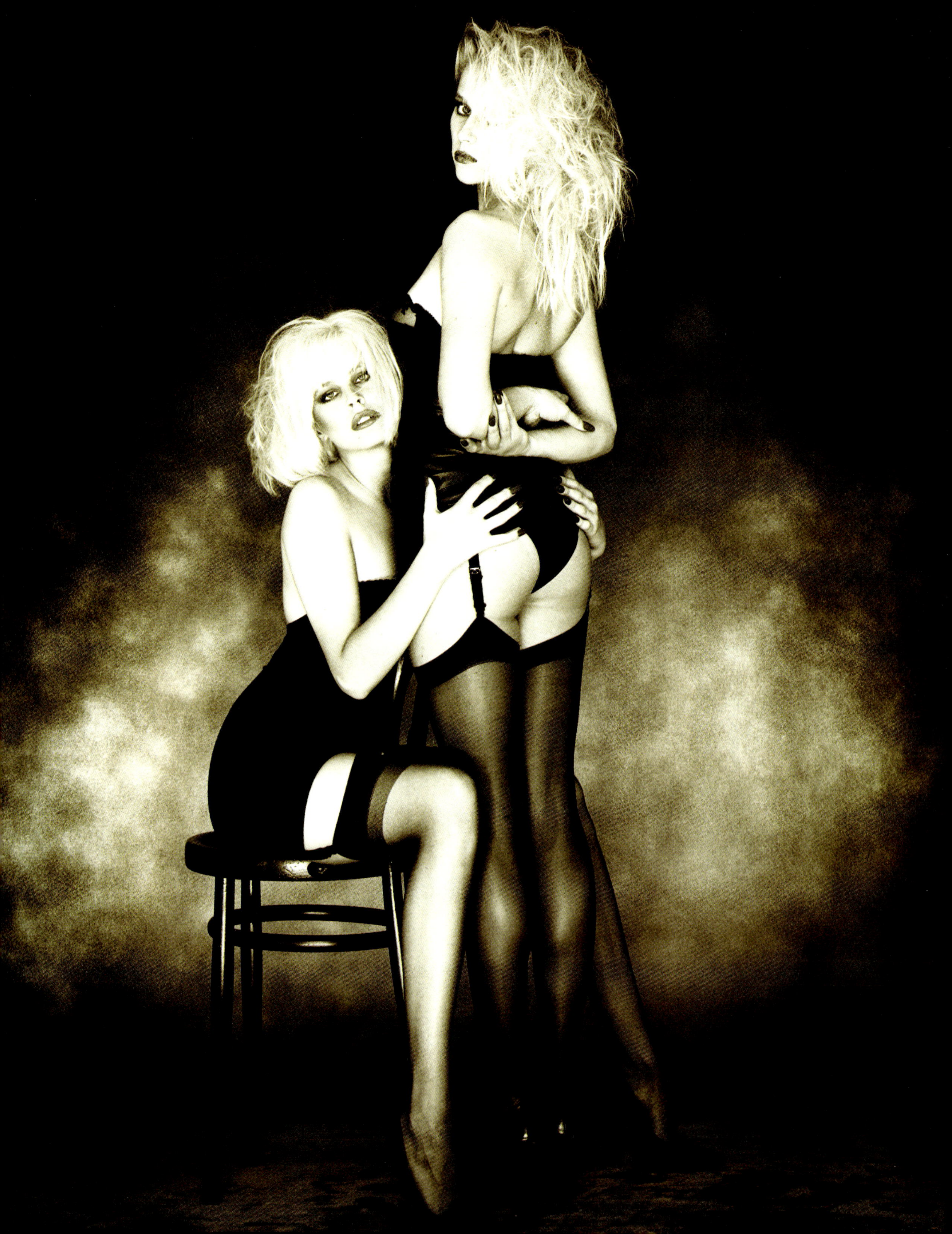

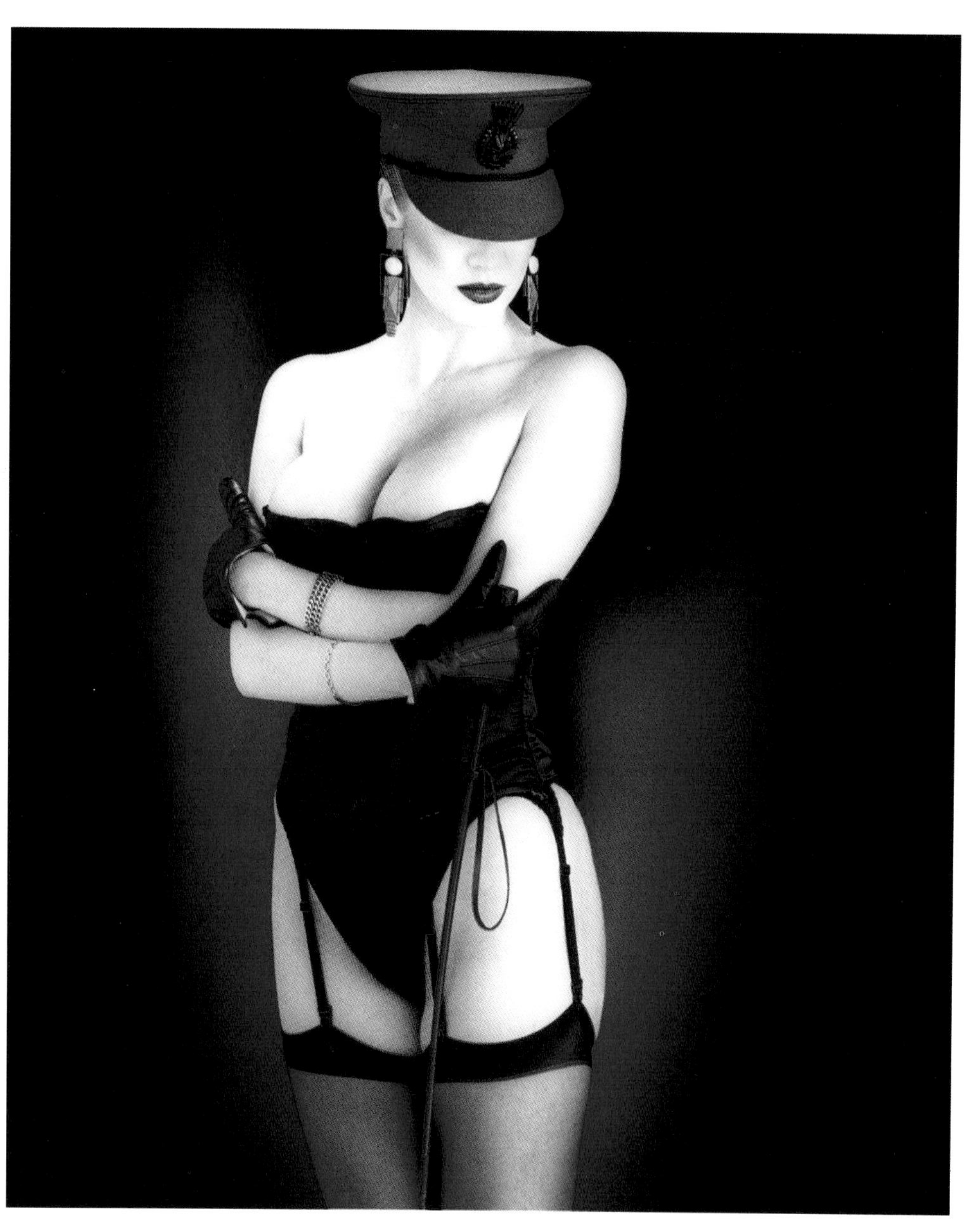

(previous page) **JOHN DIETRICH** 1989

 | **JOHN DIETRICH** 1988

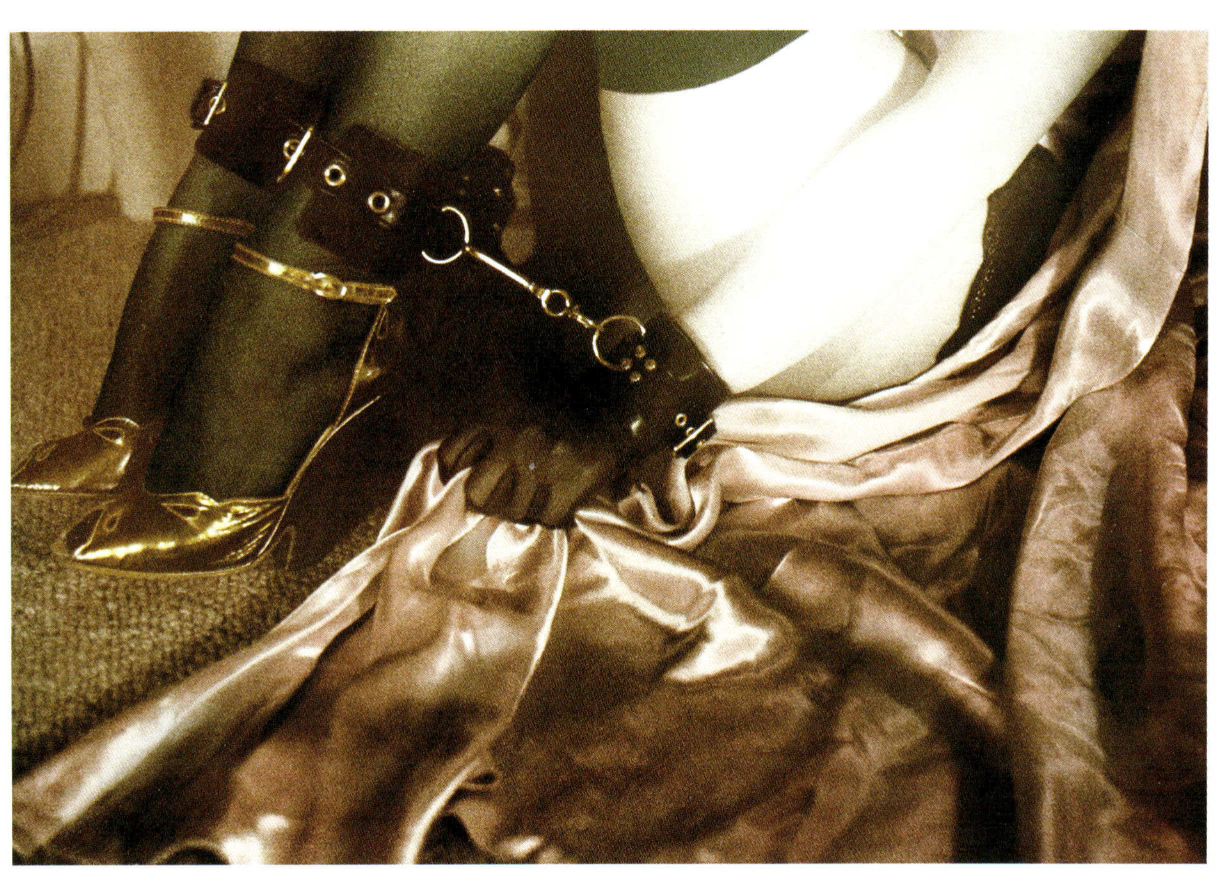

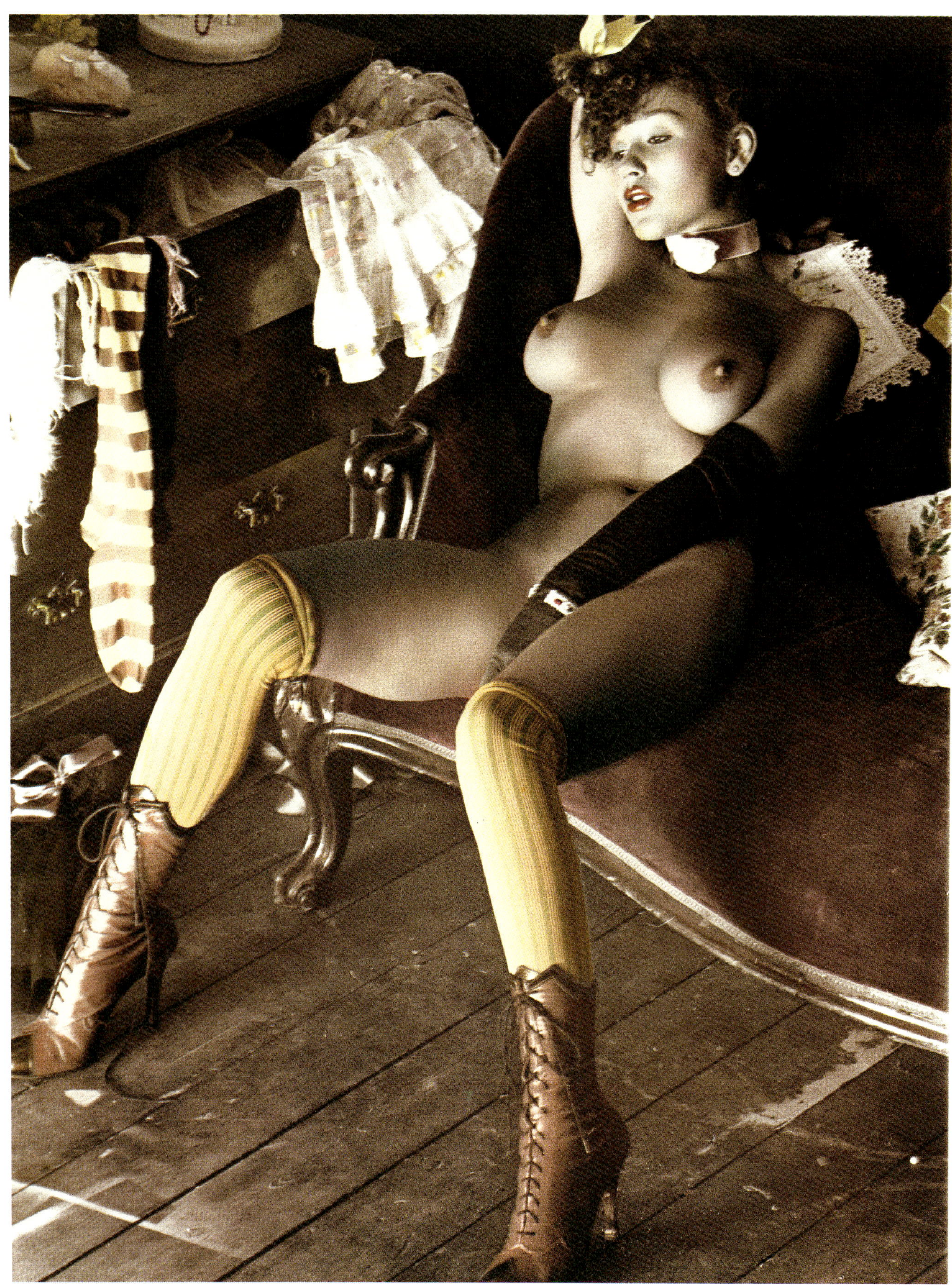

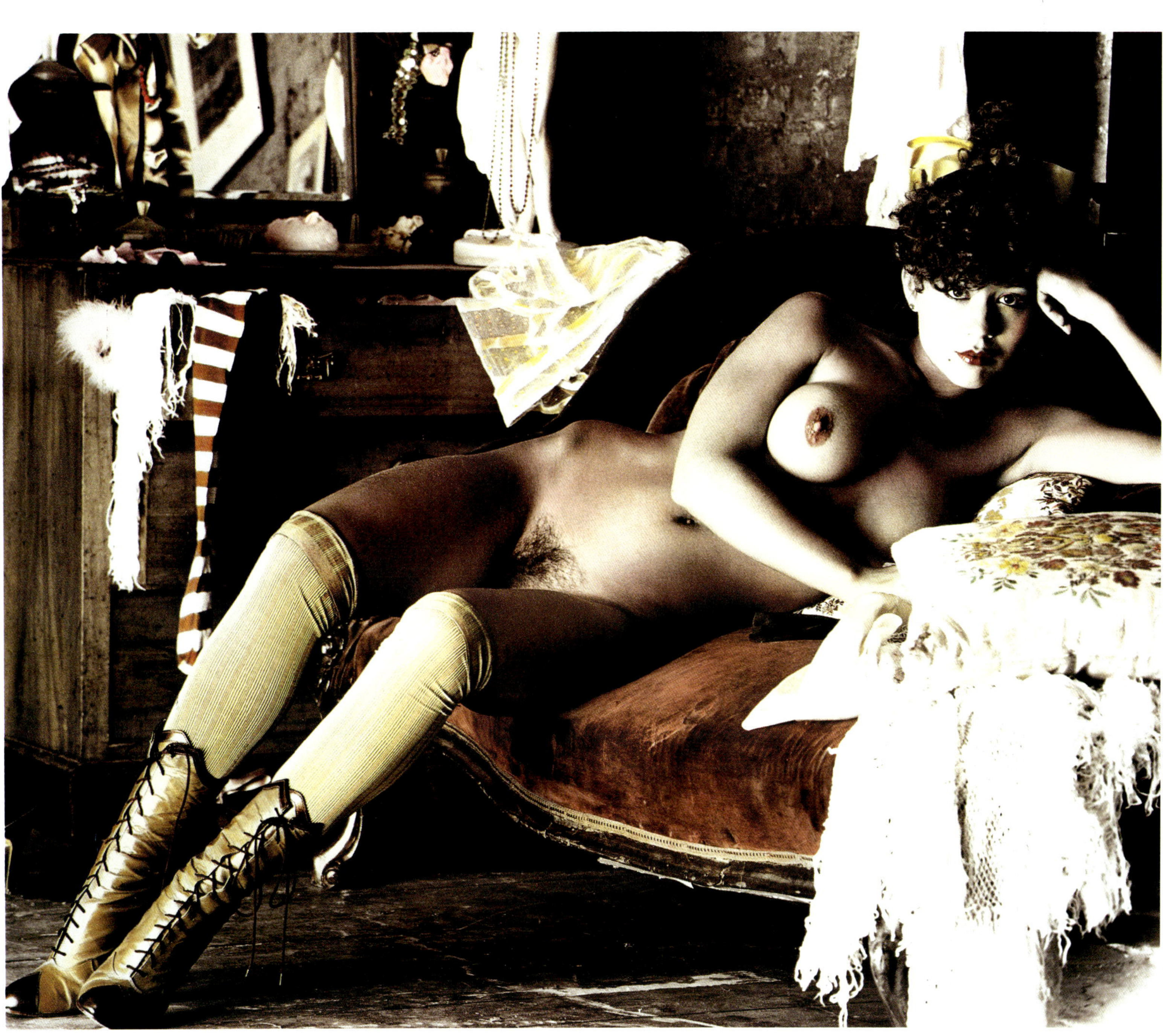

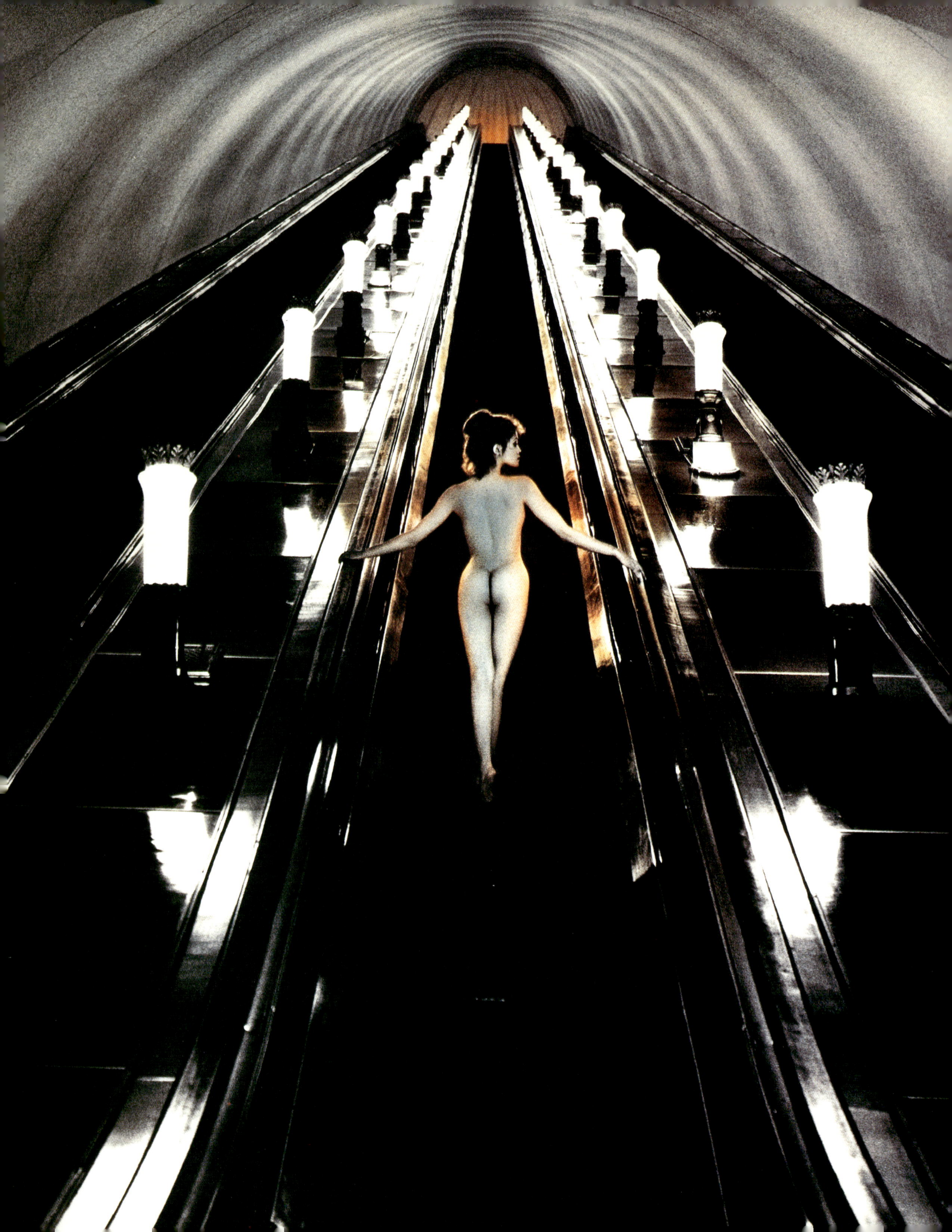

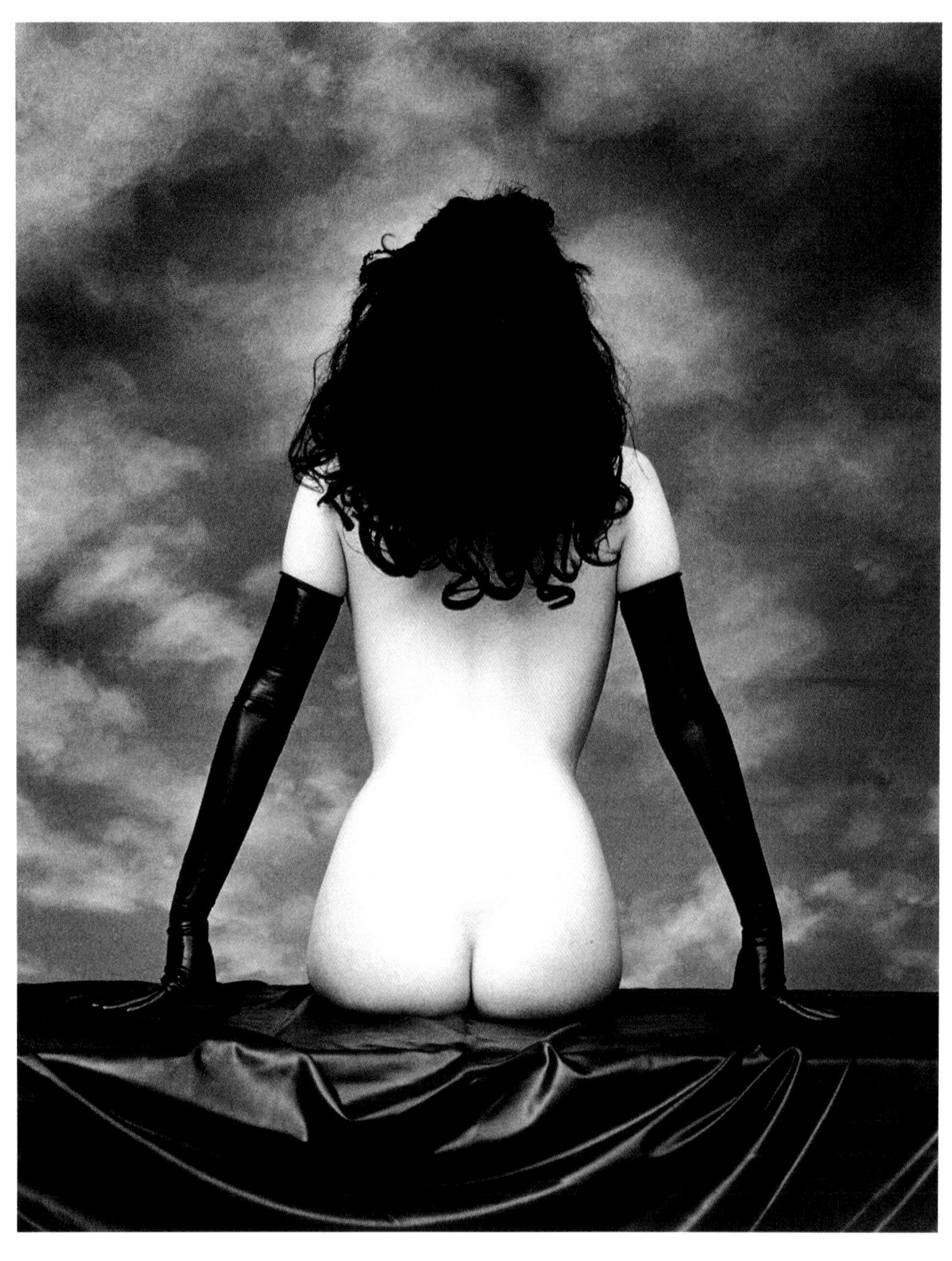

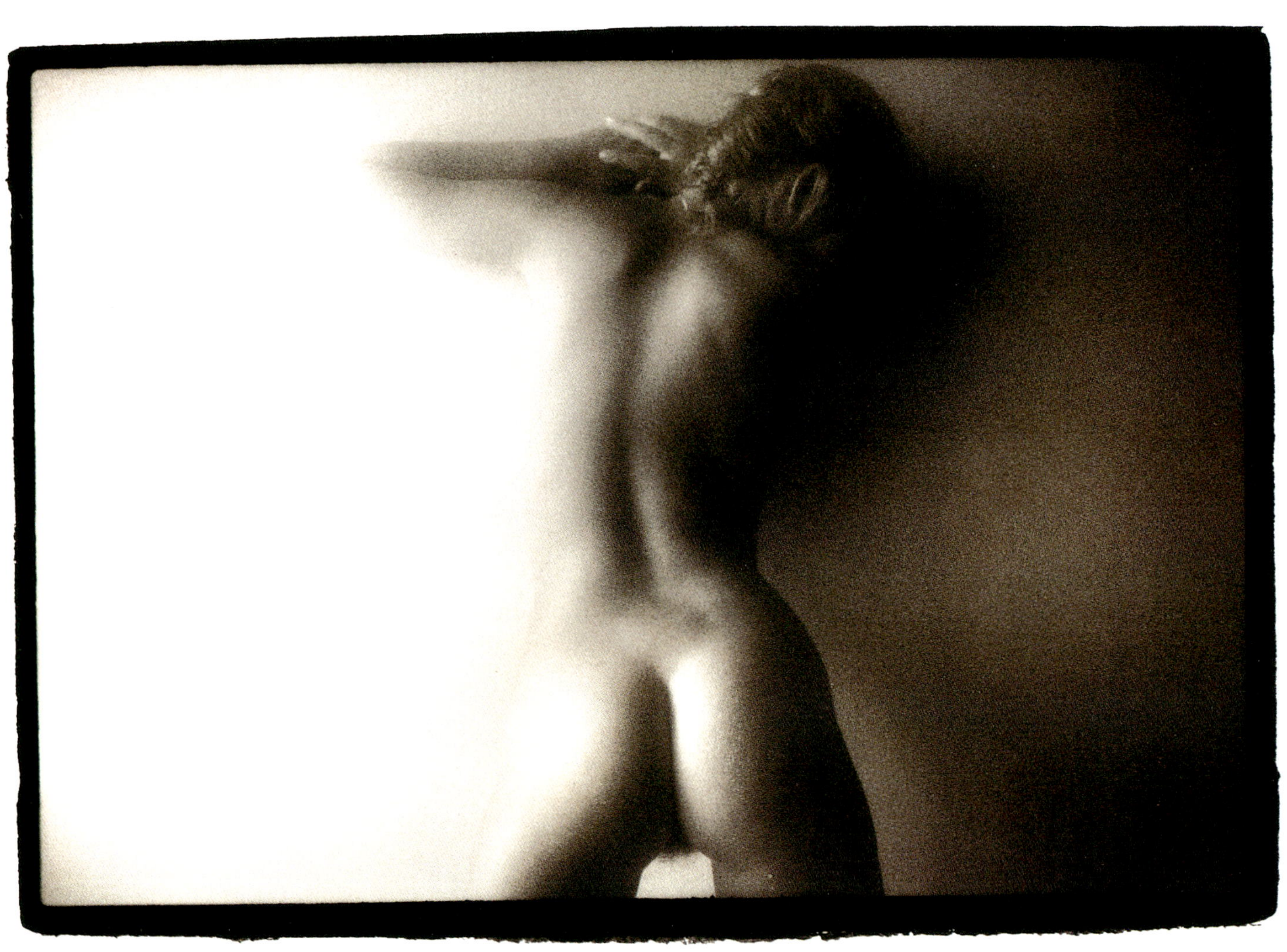

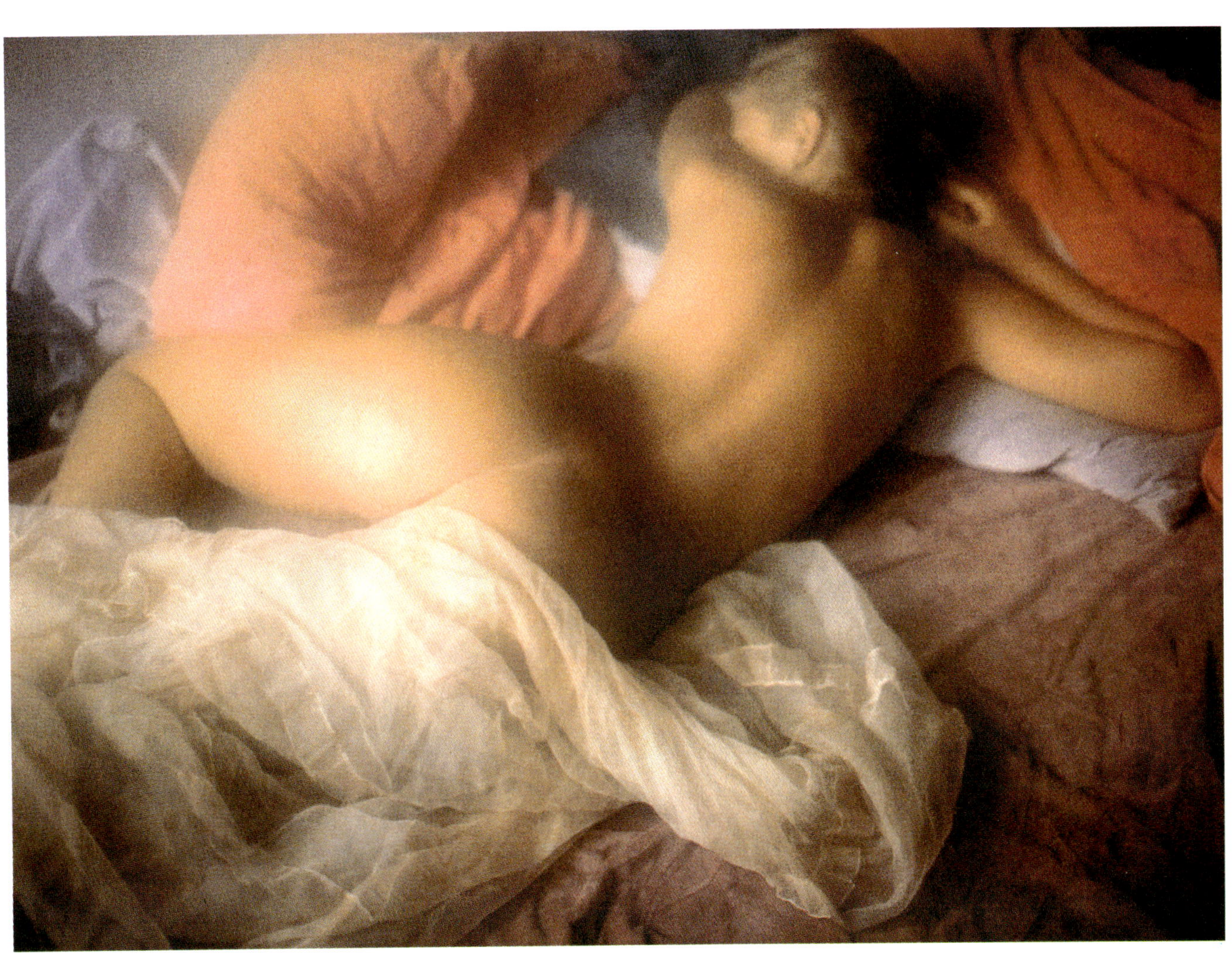

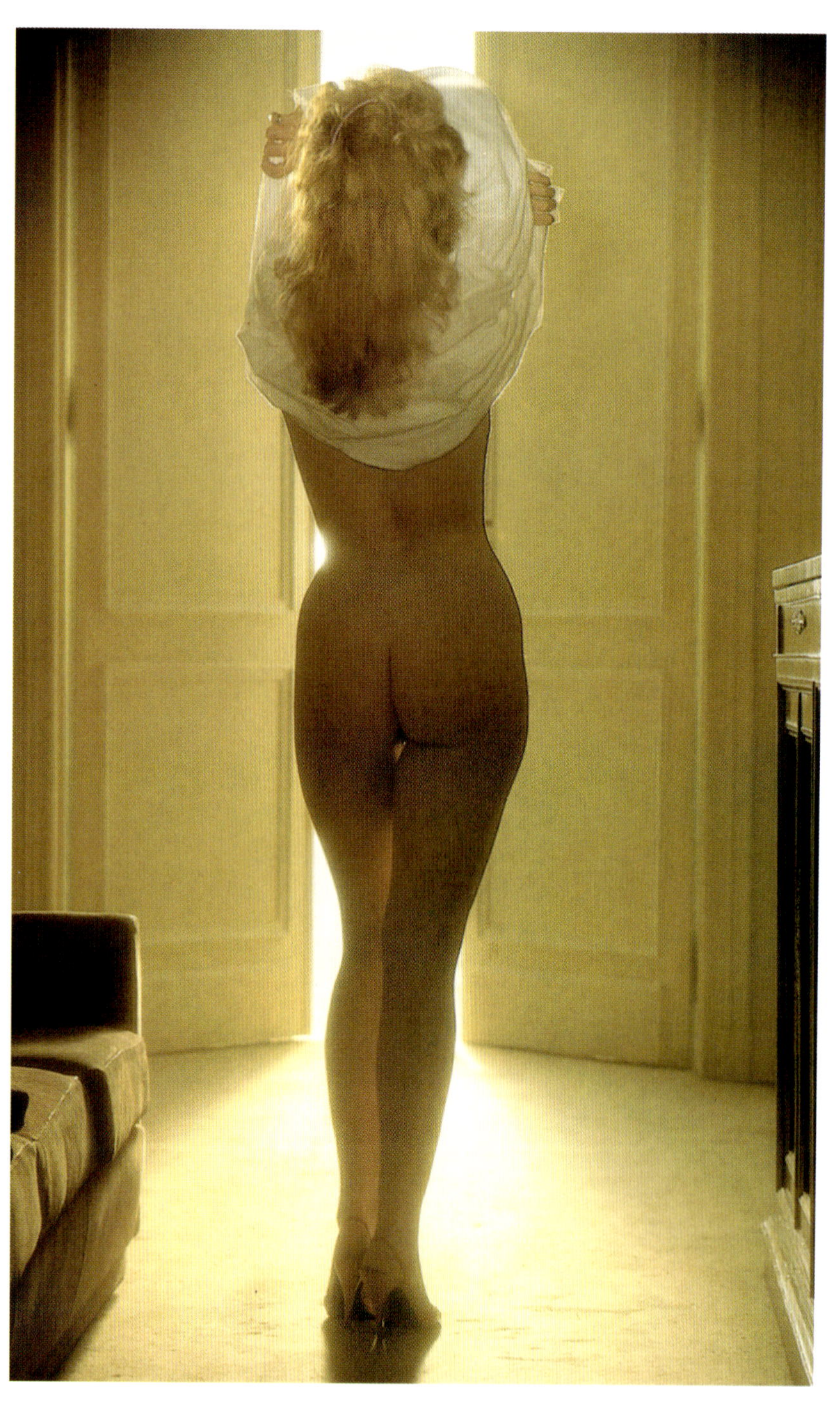

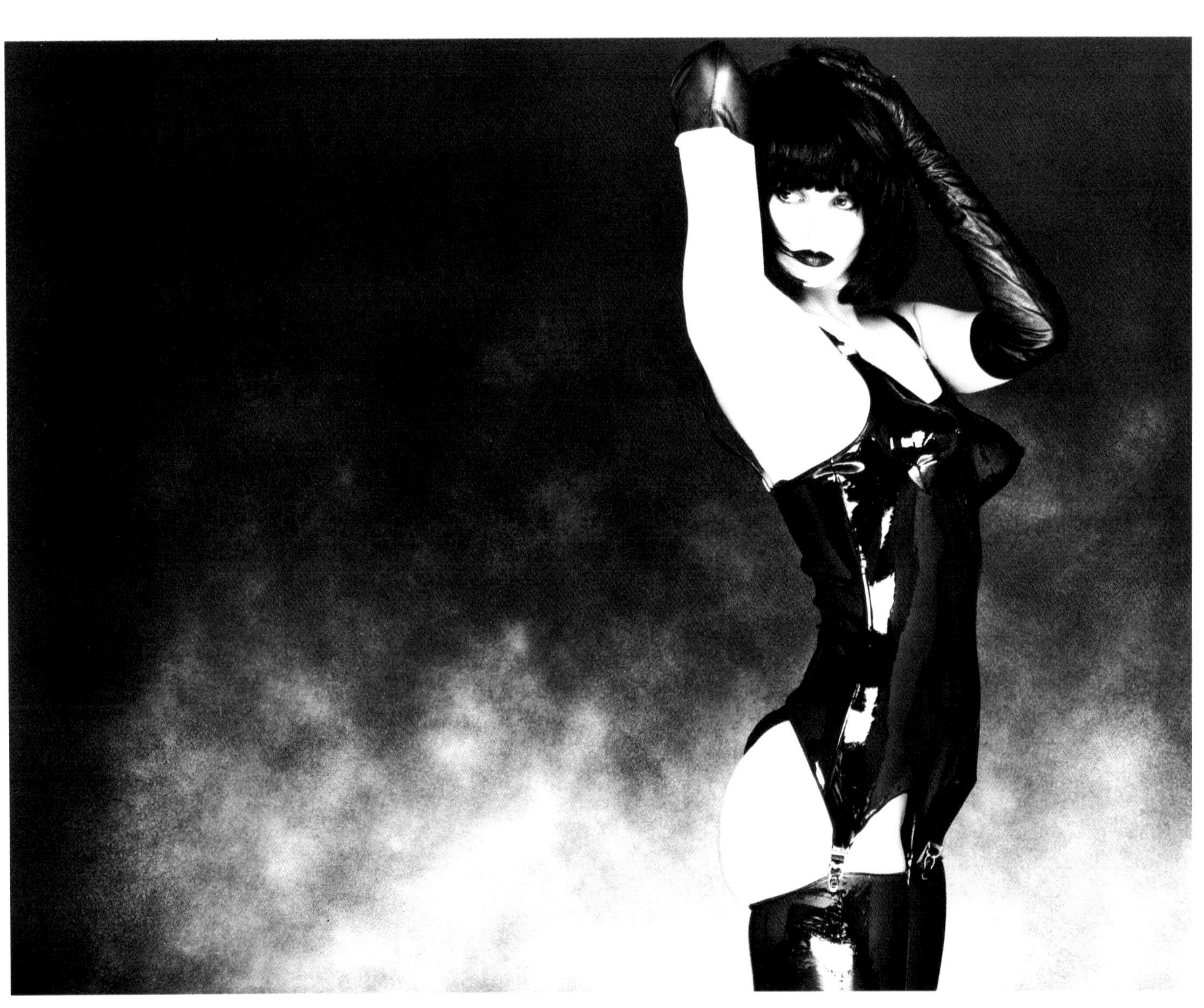

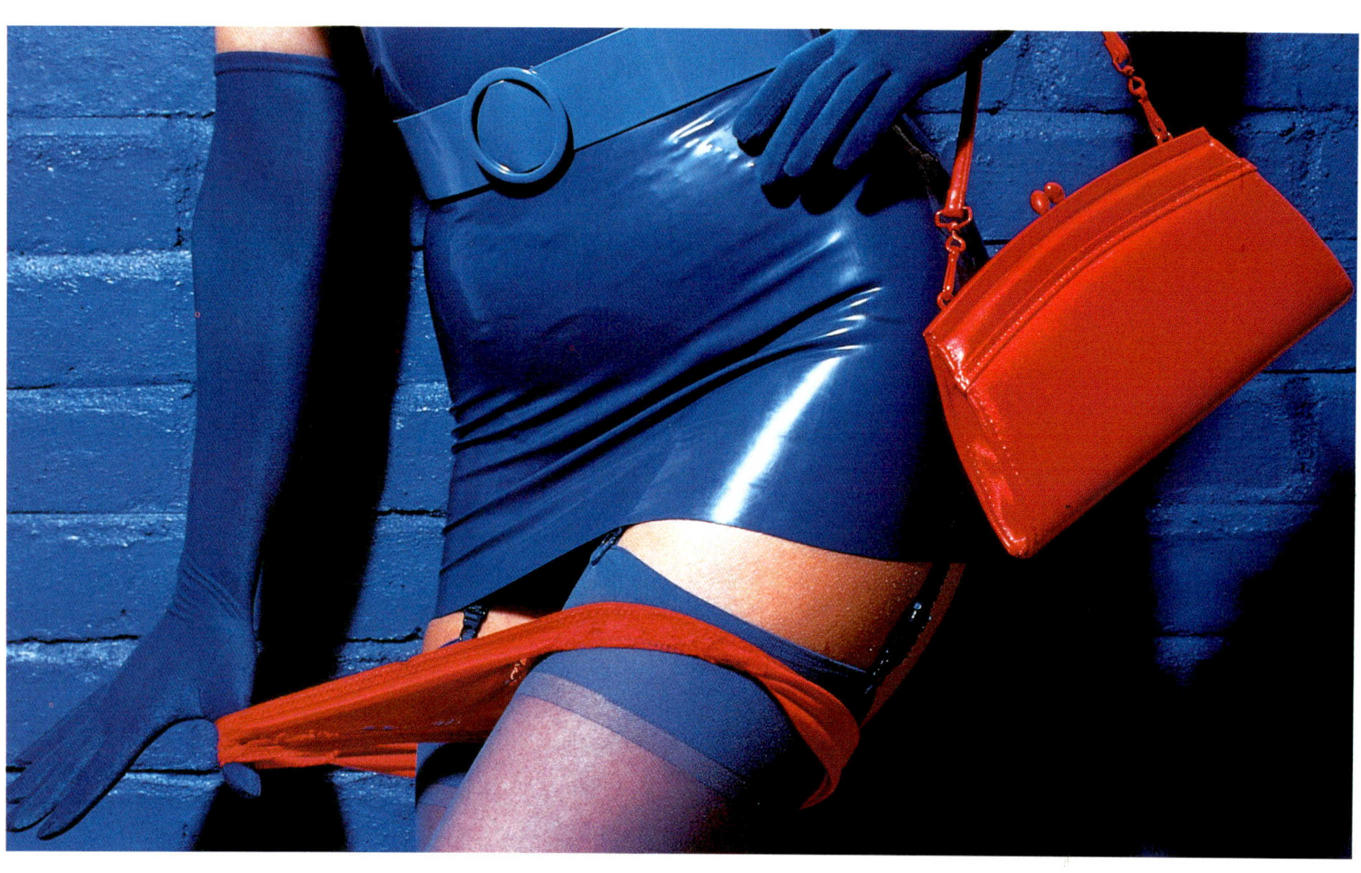

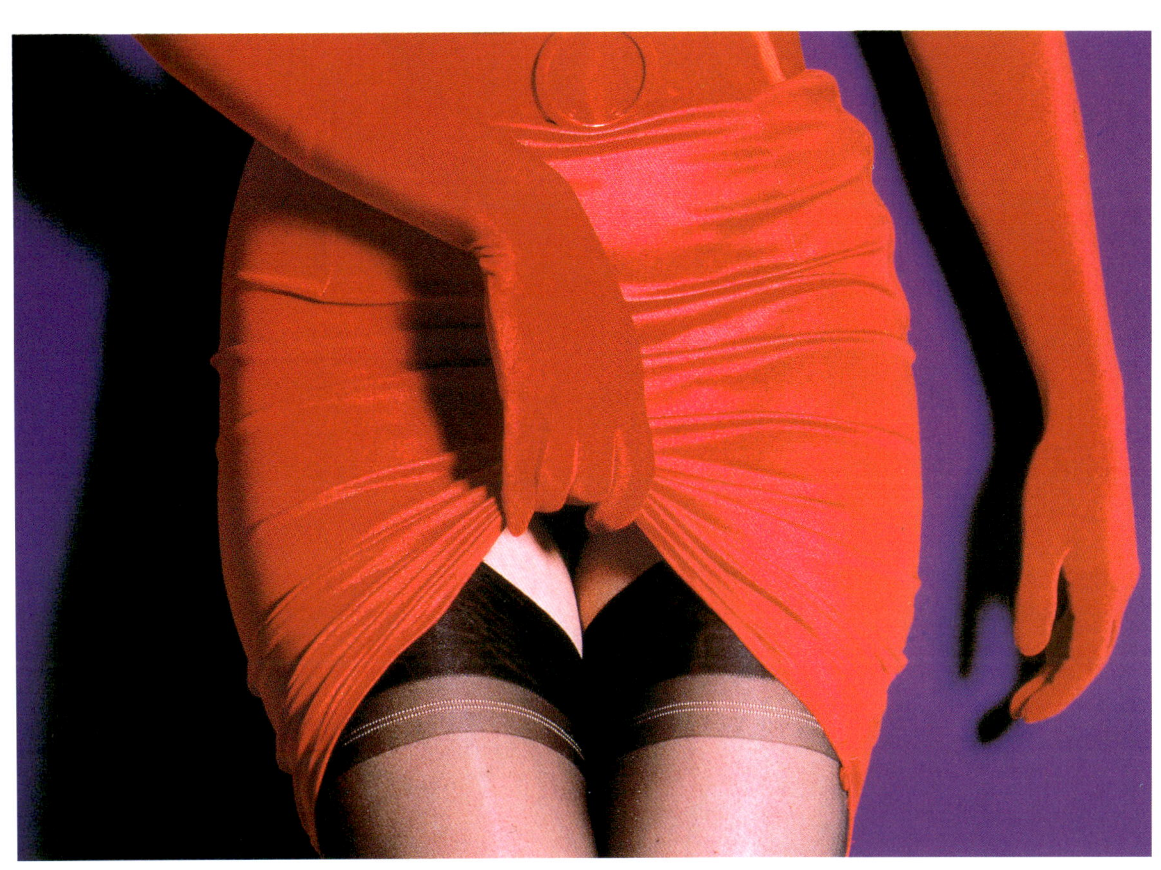

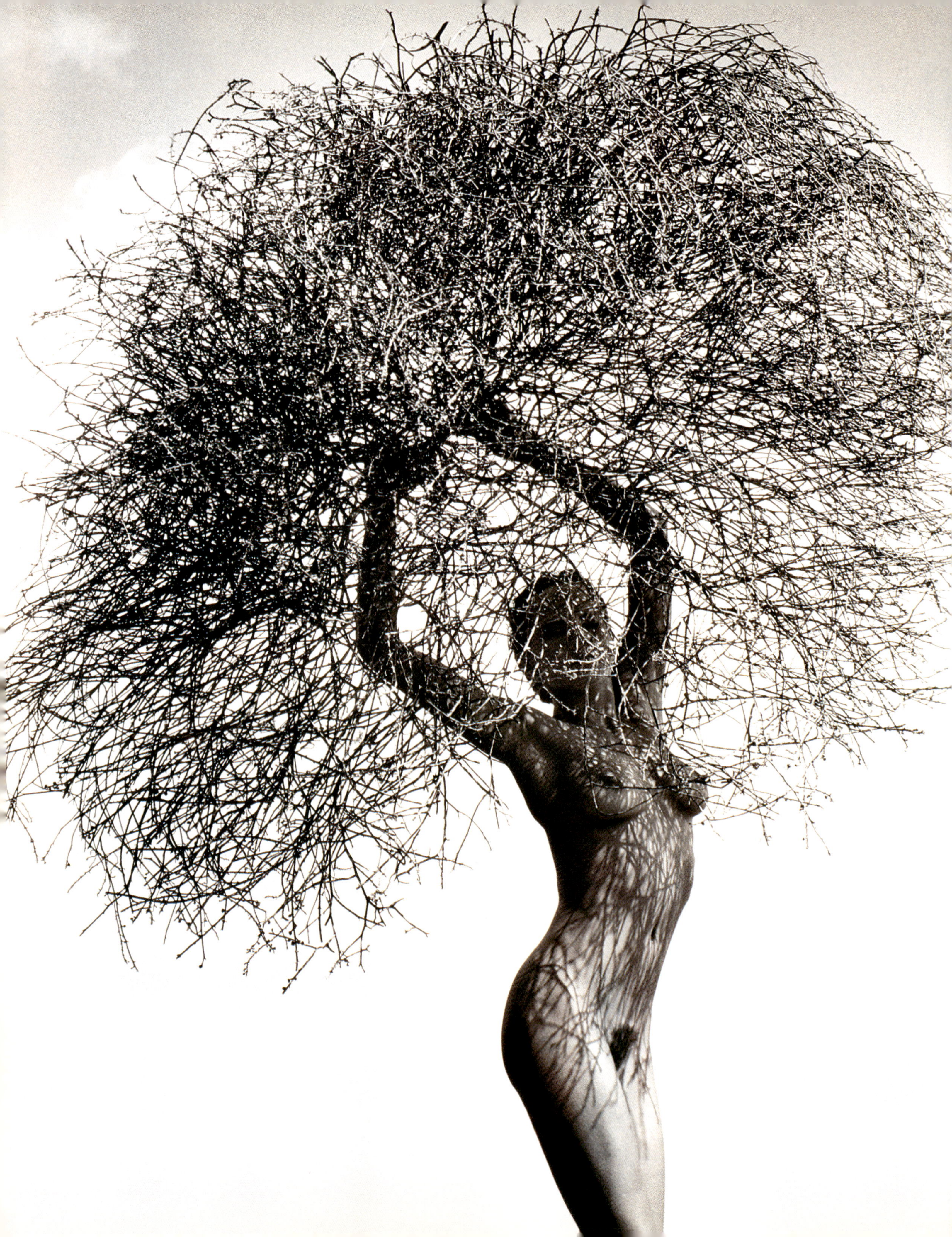

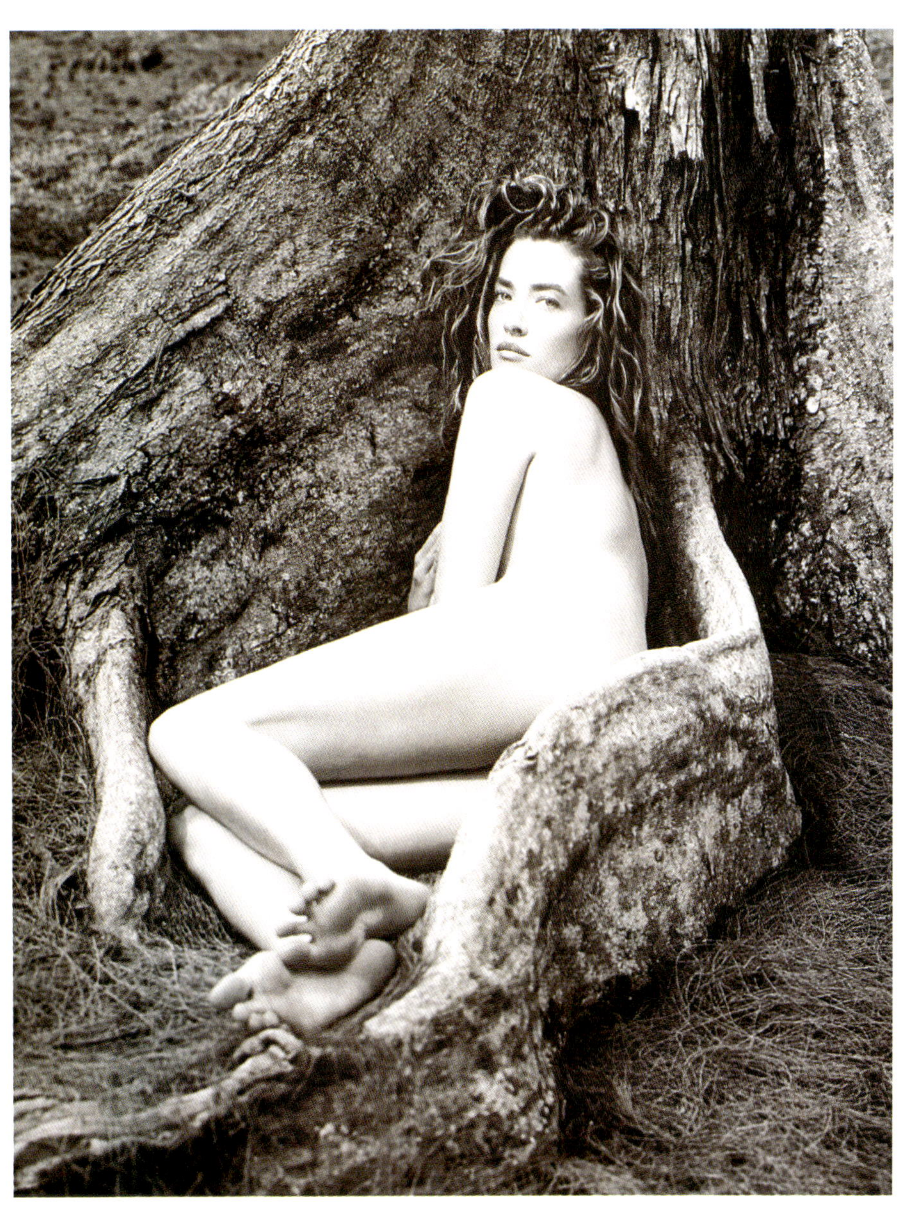

(left) **HERB RITTS** 1986

HERB RITTS 1987

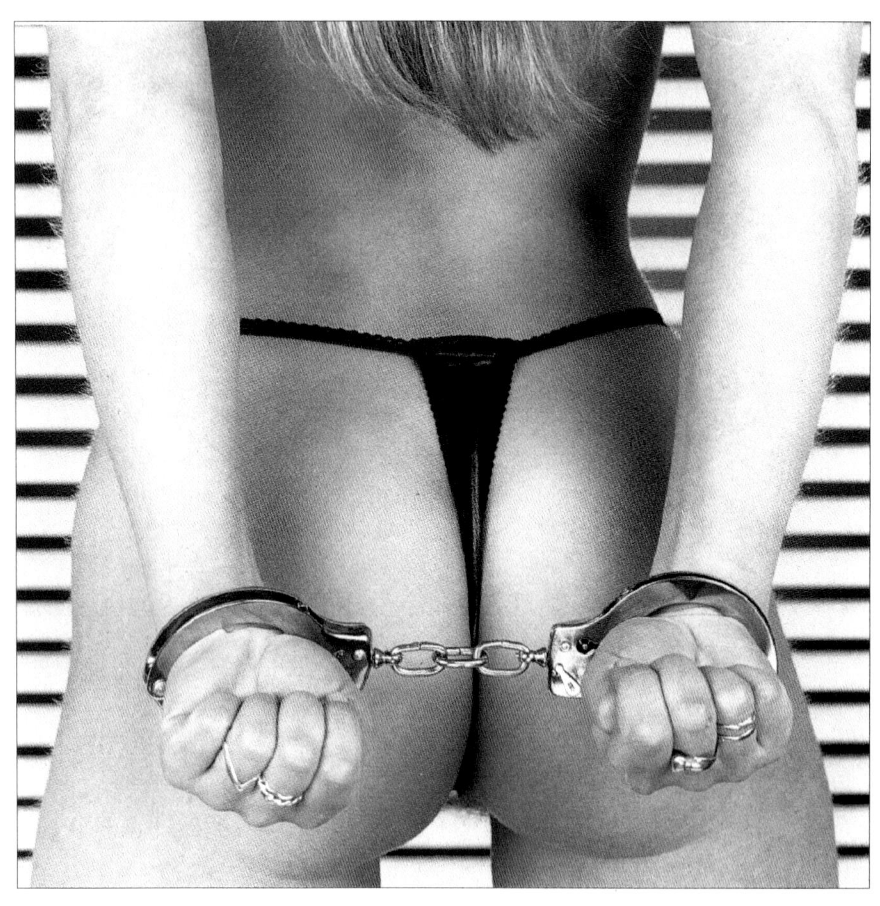

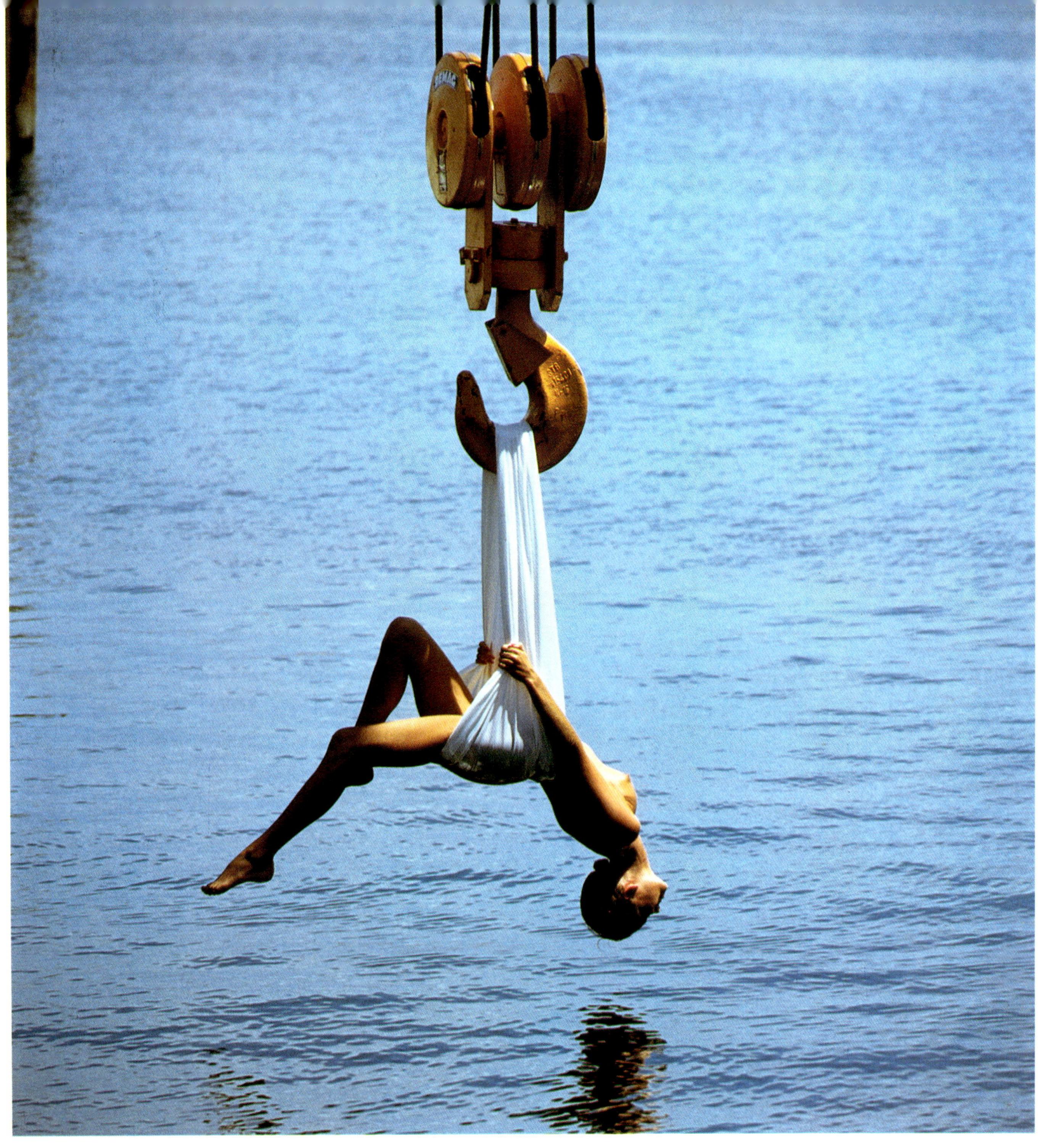

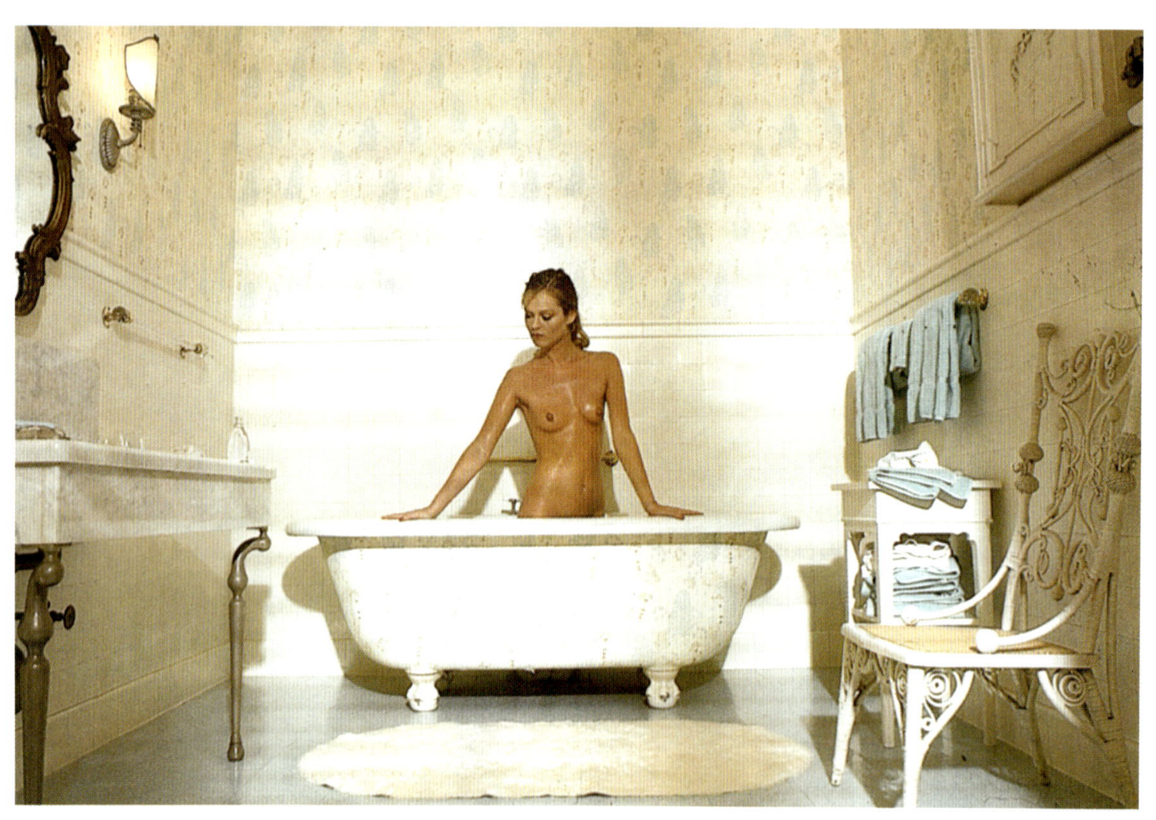

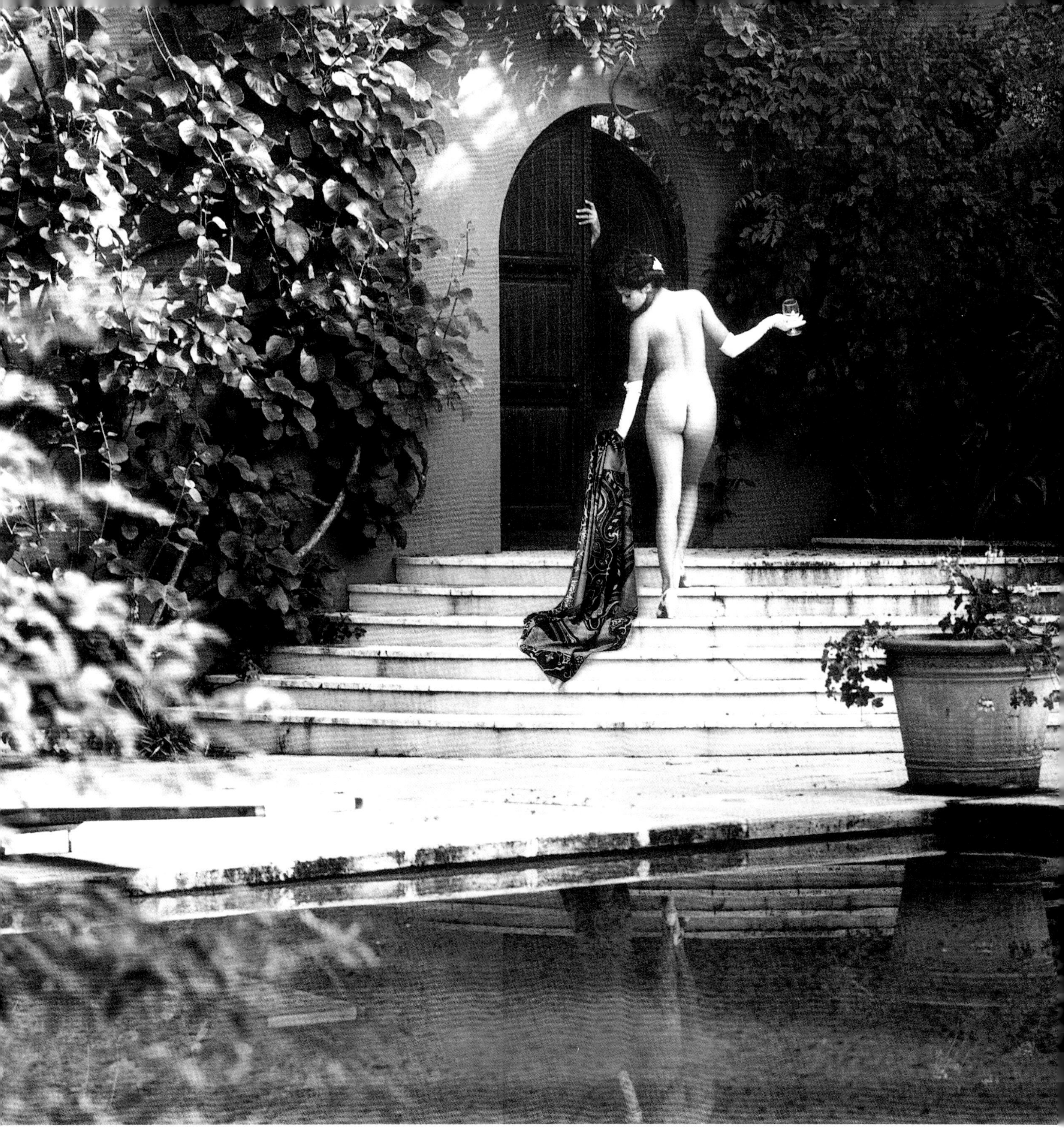

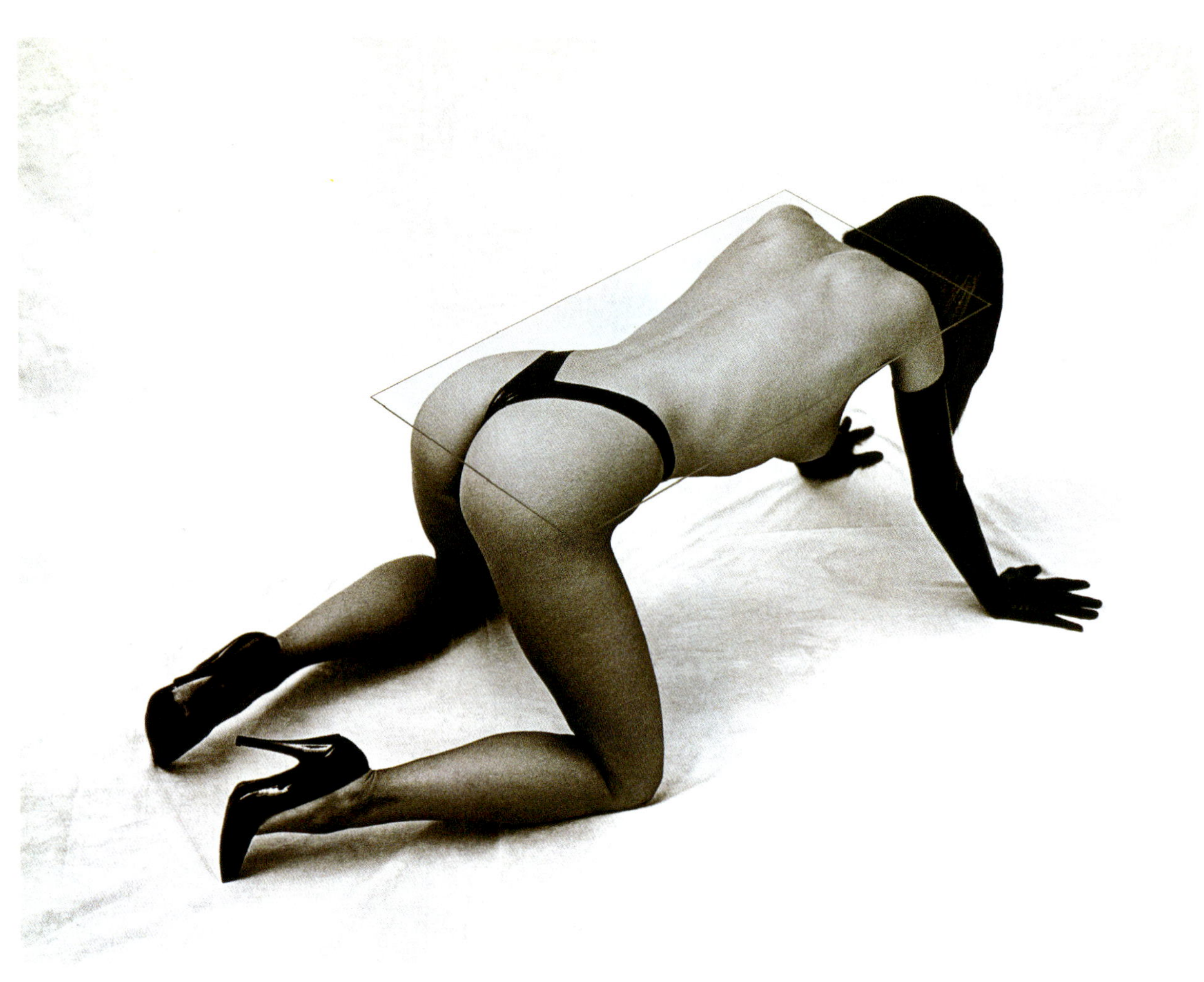

 BOB CARLOS CLARKE c.1987

(right) **BOB CARLOS CLARKE** 1987

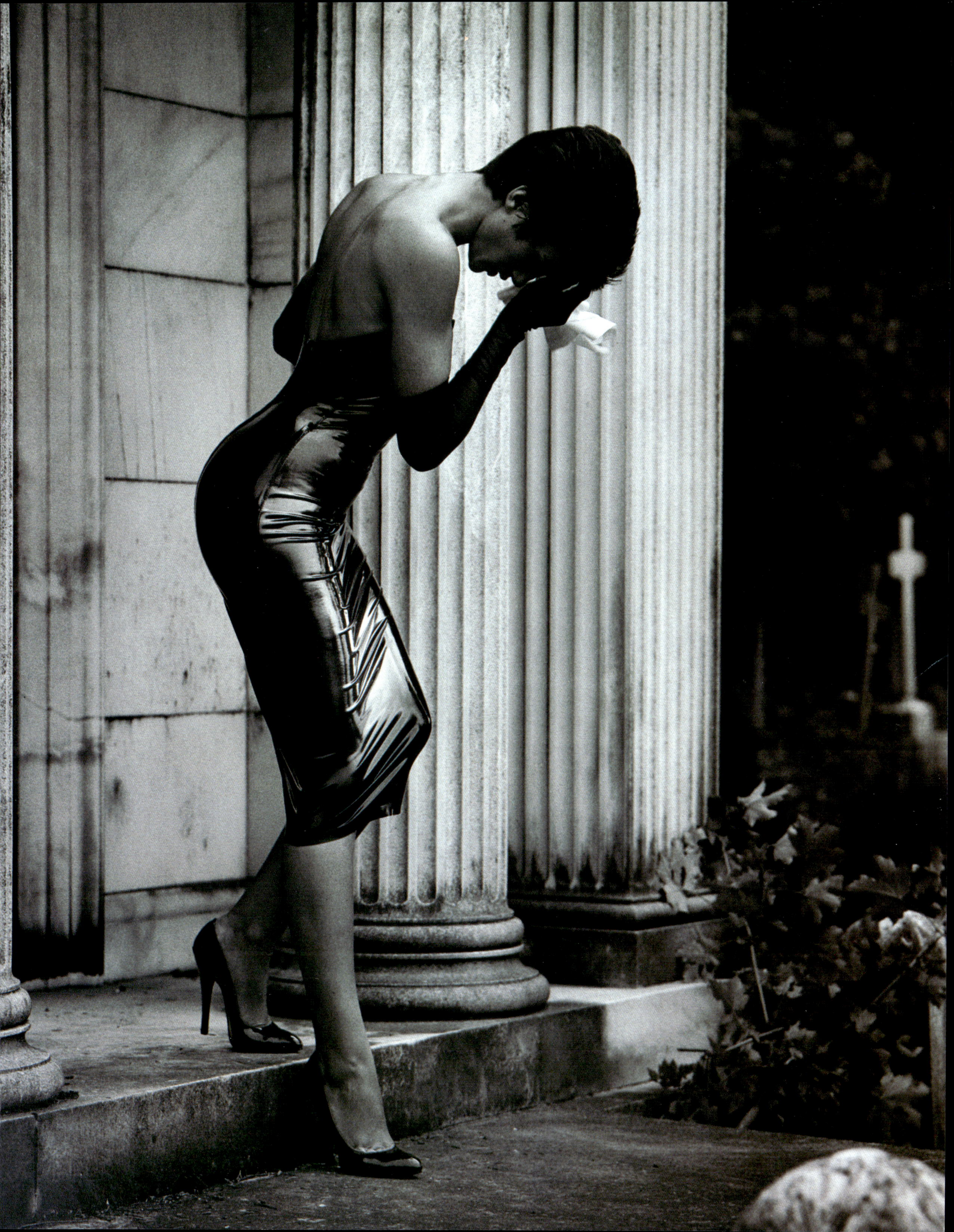

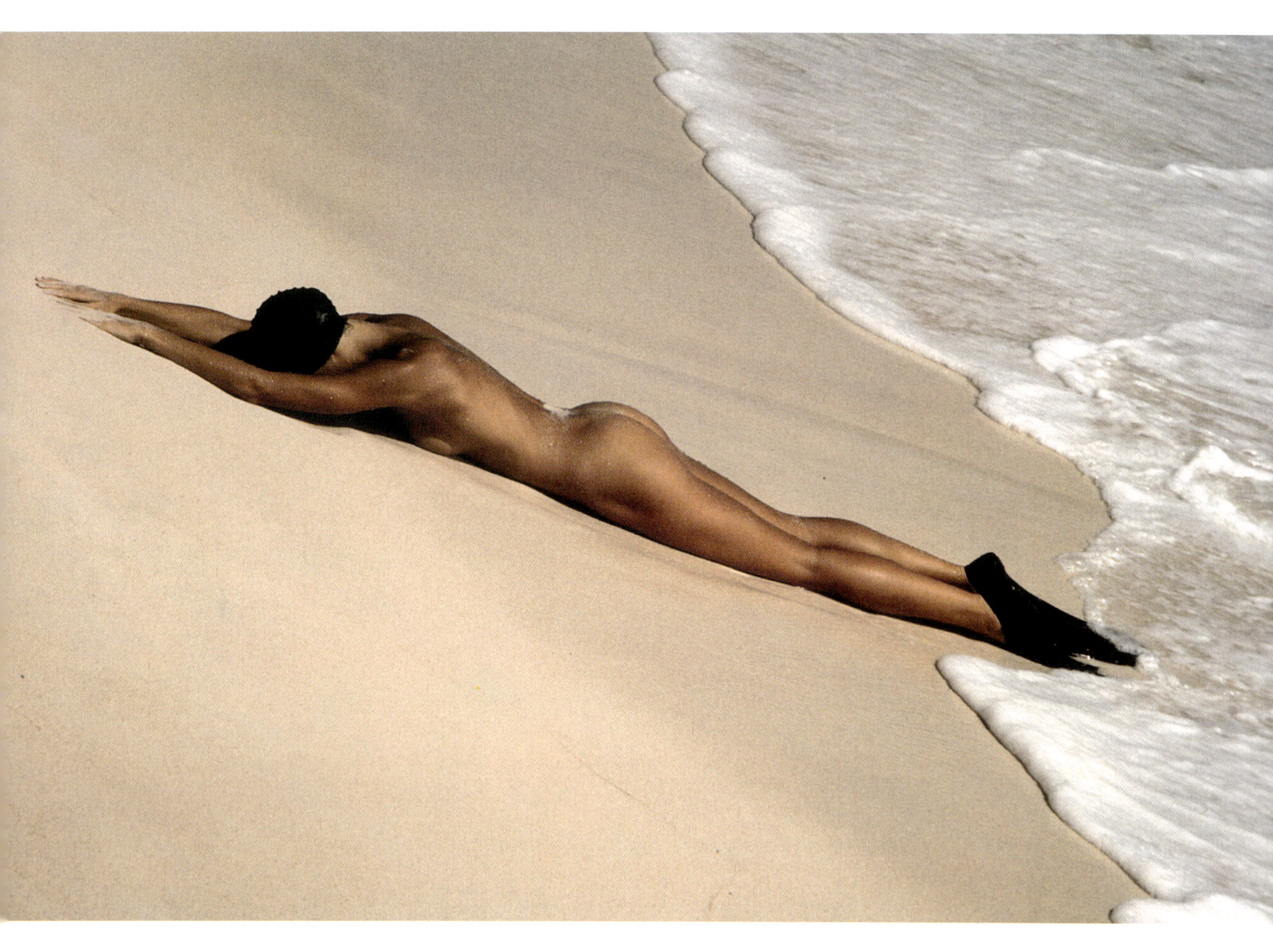

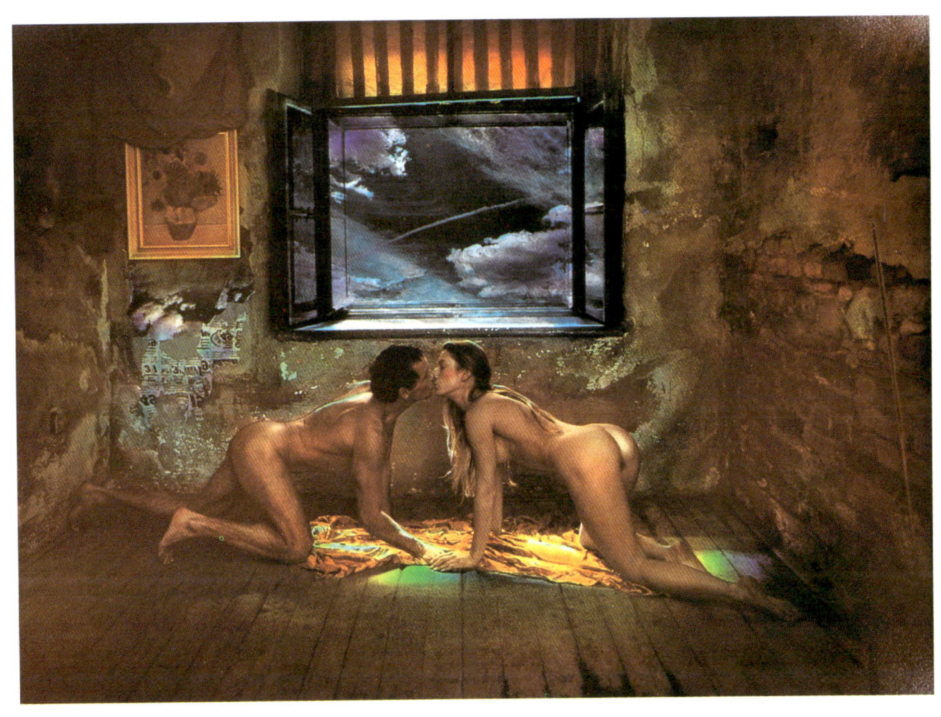

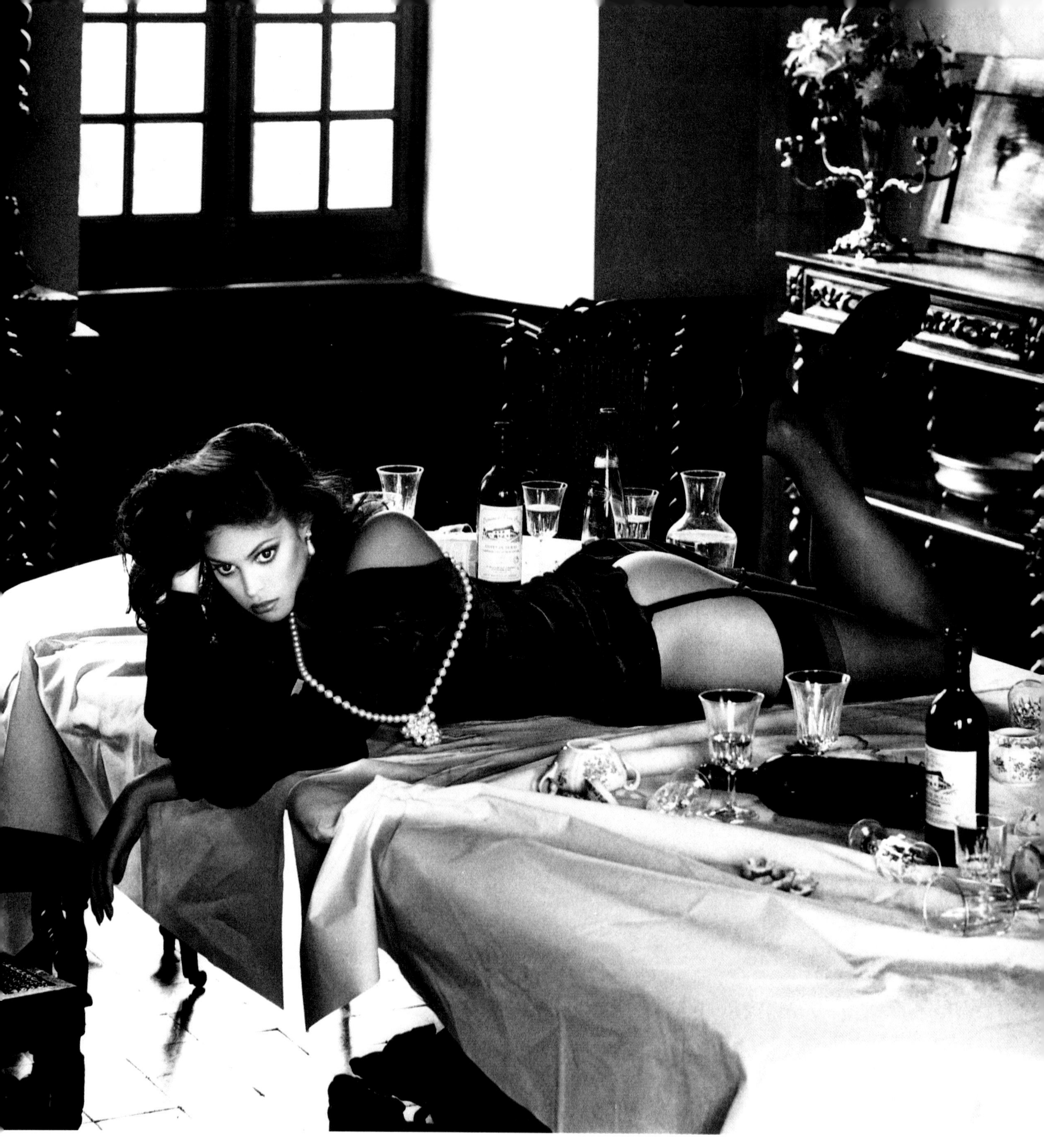

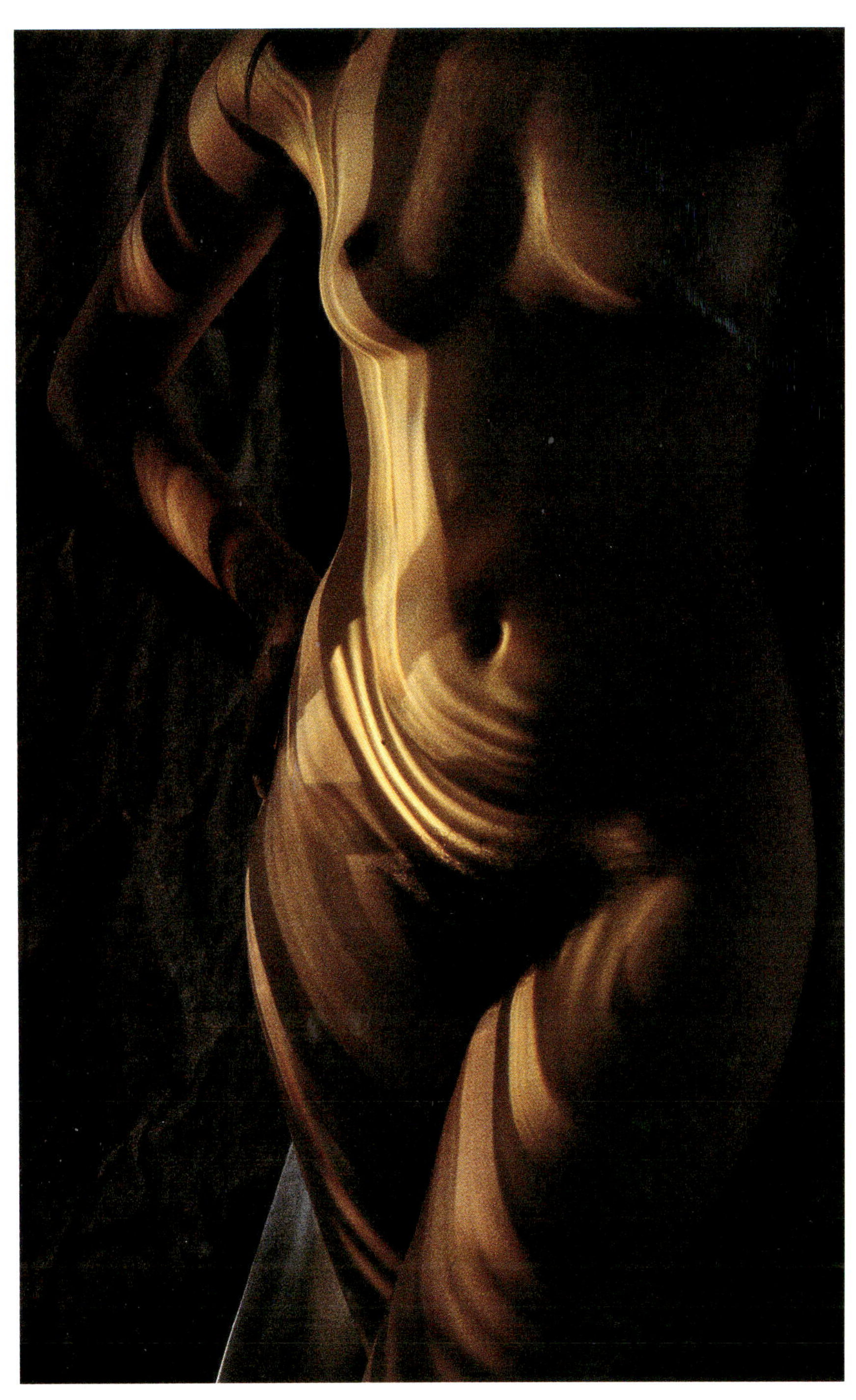

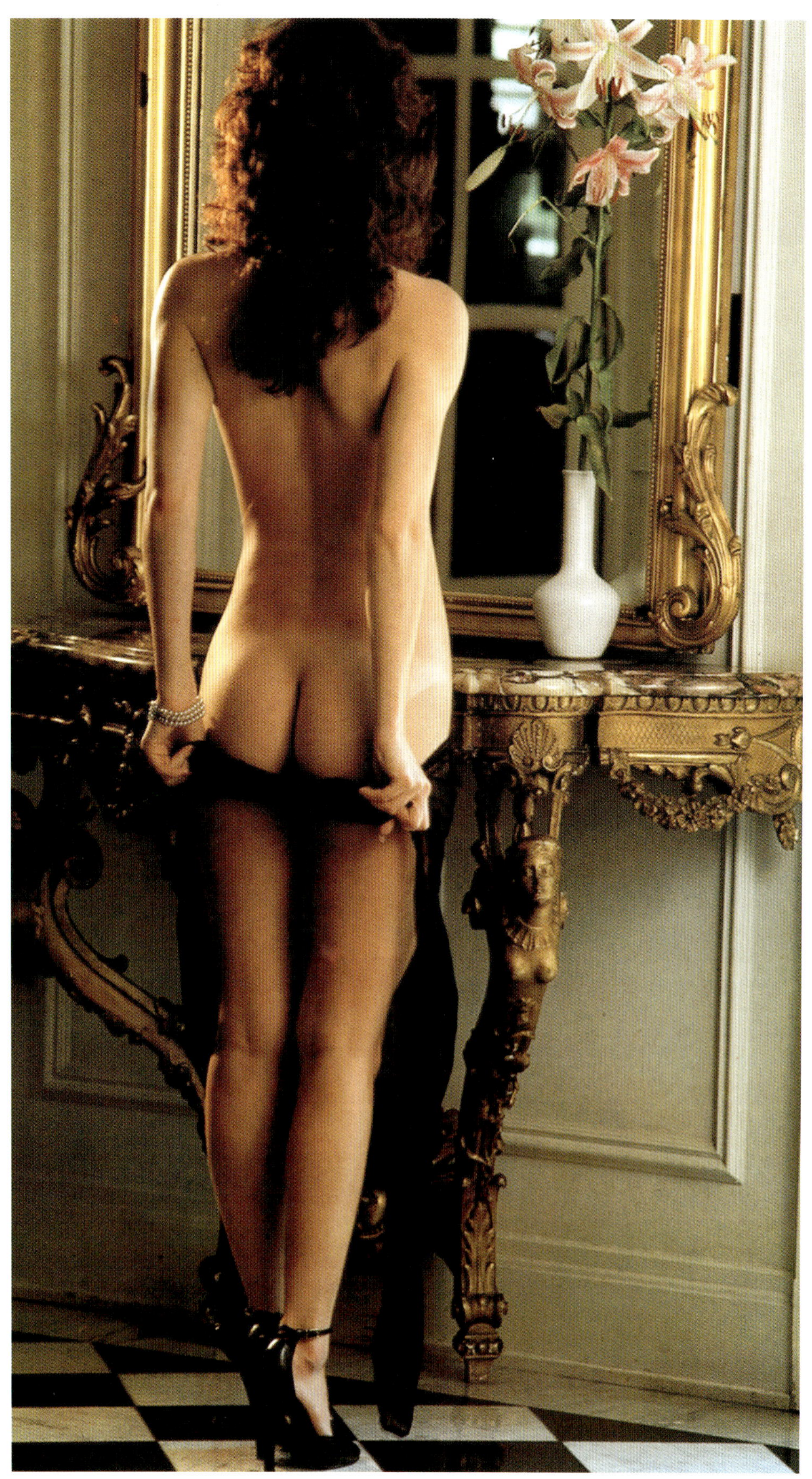

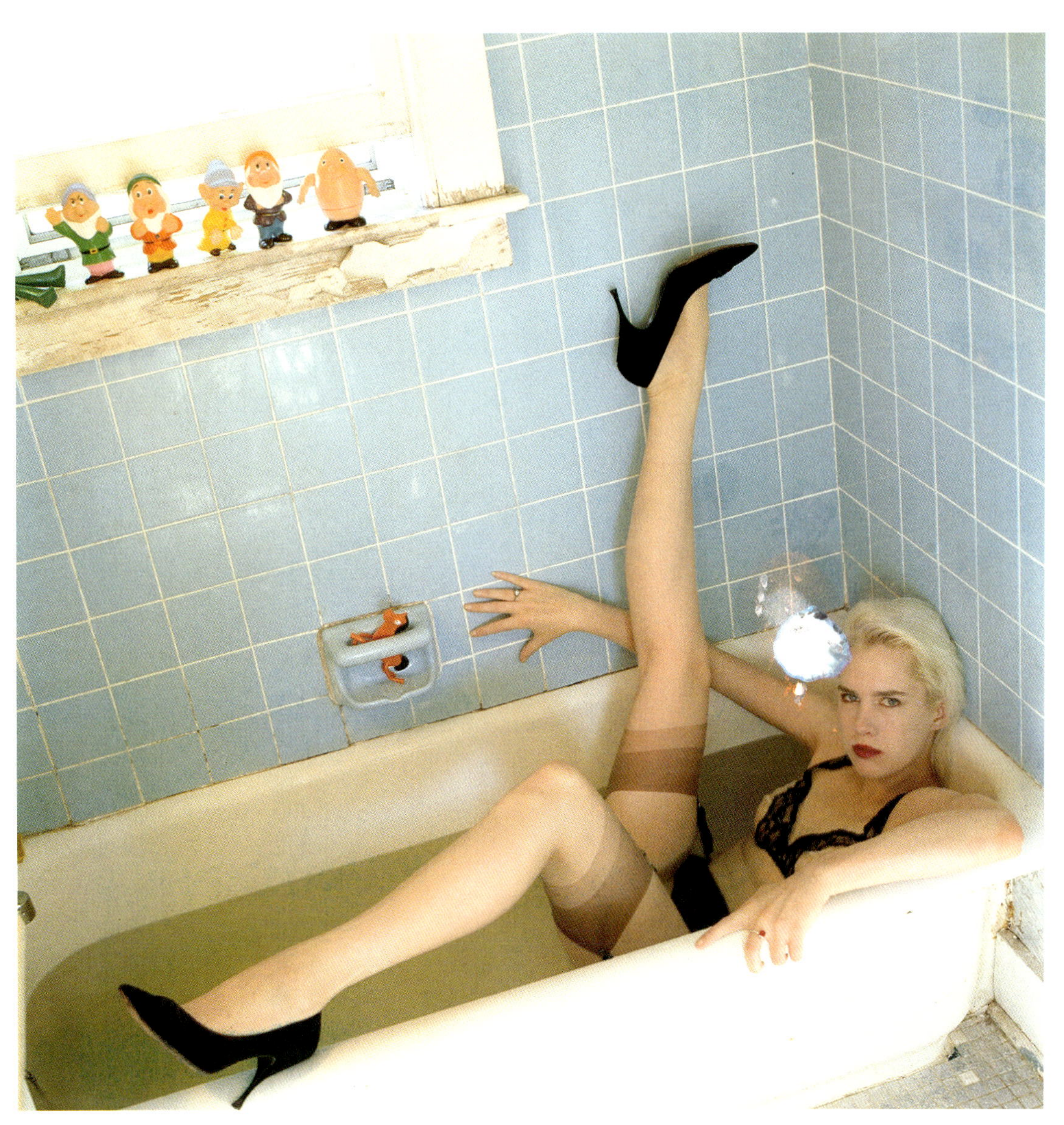

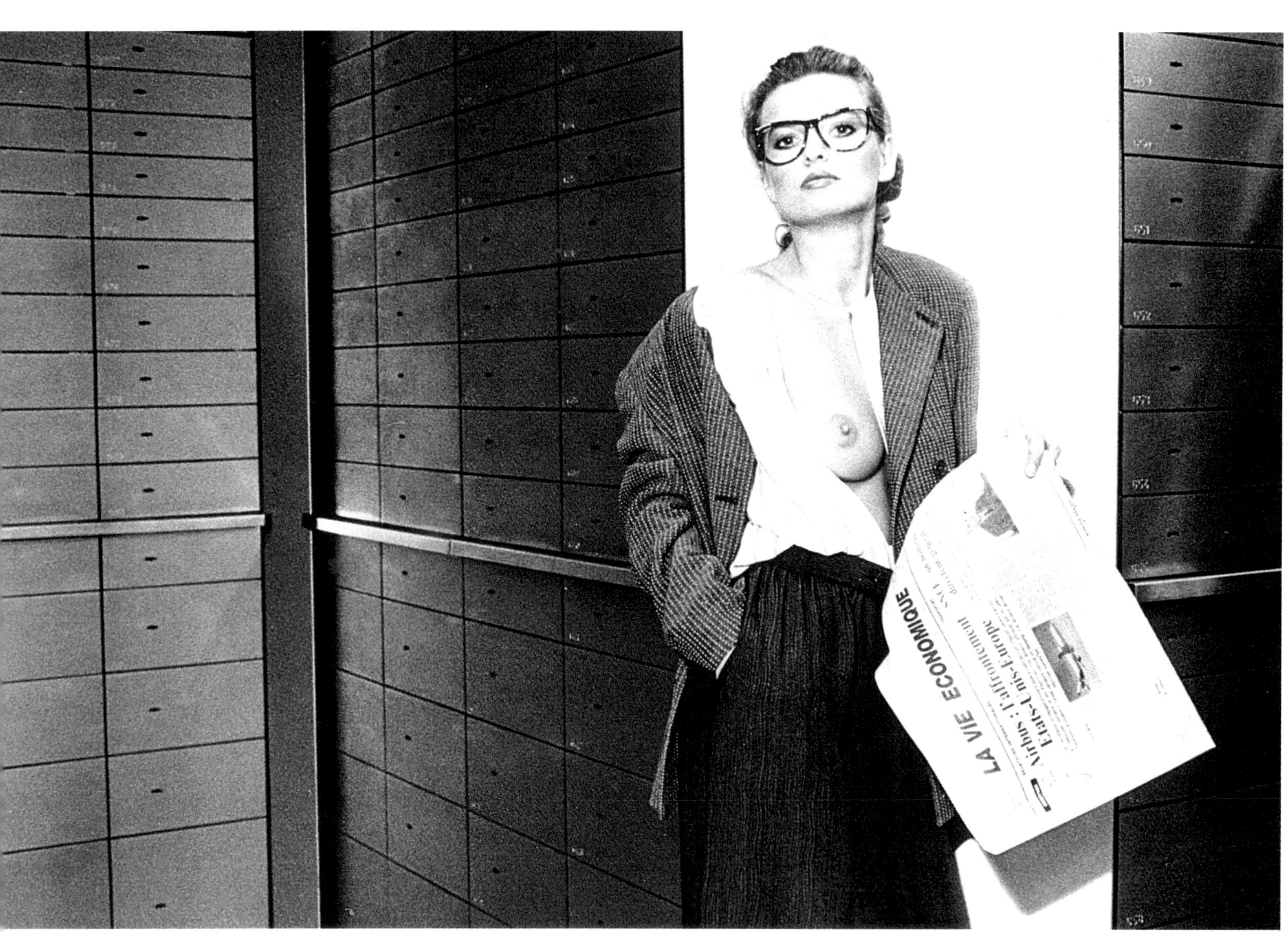
LA VIE ECONOMIQUE
Etats-Unis-Europe

1990s

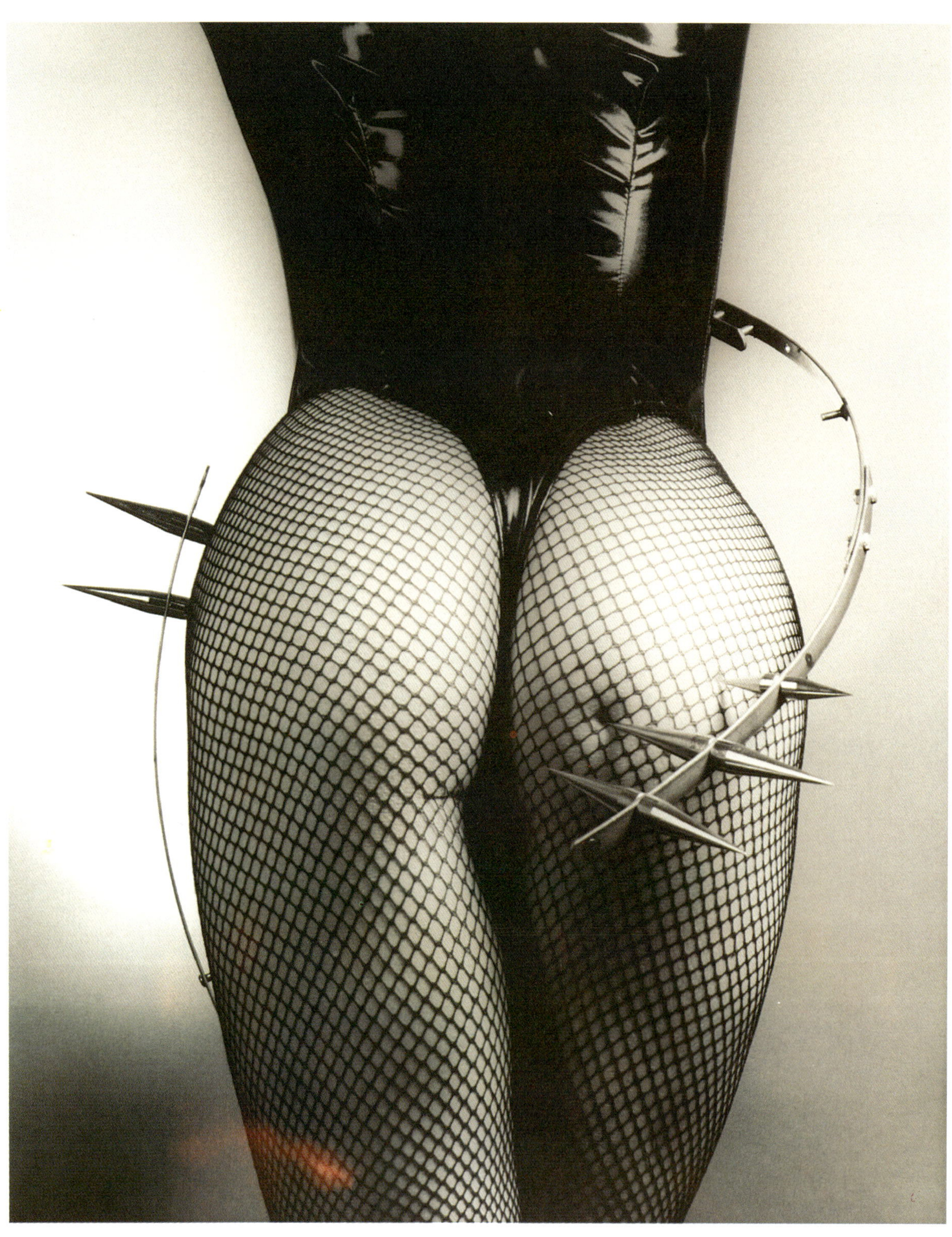

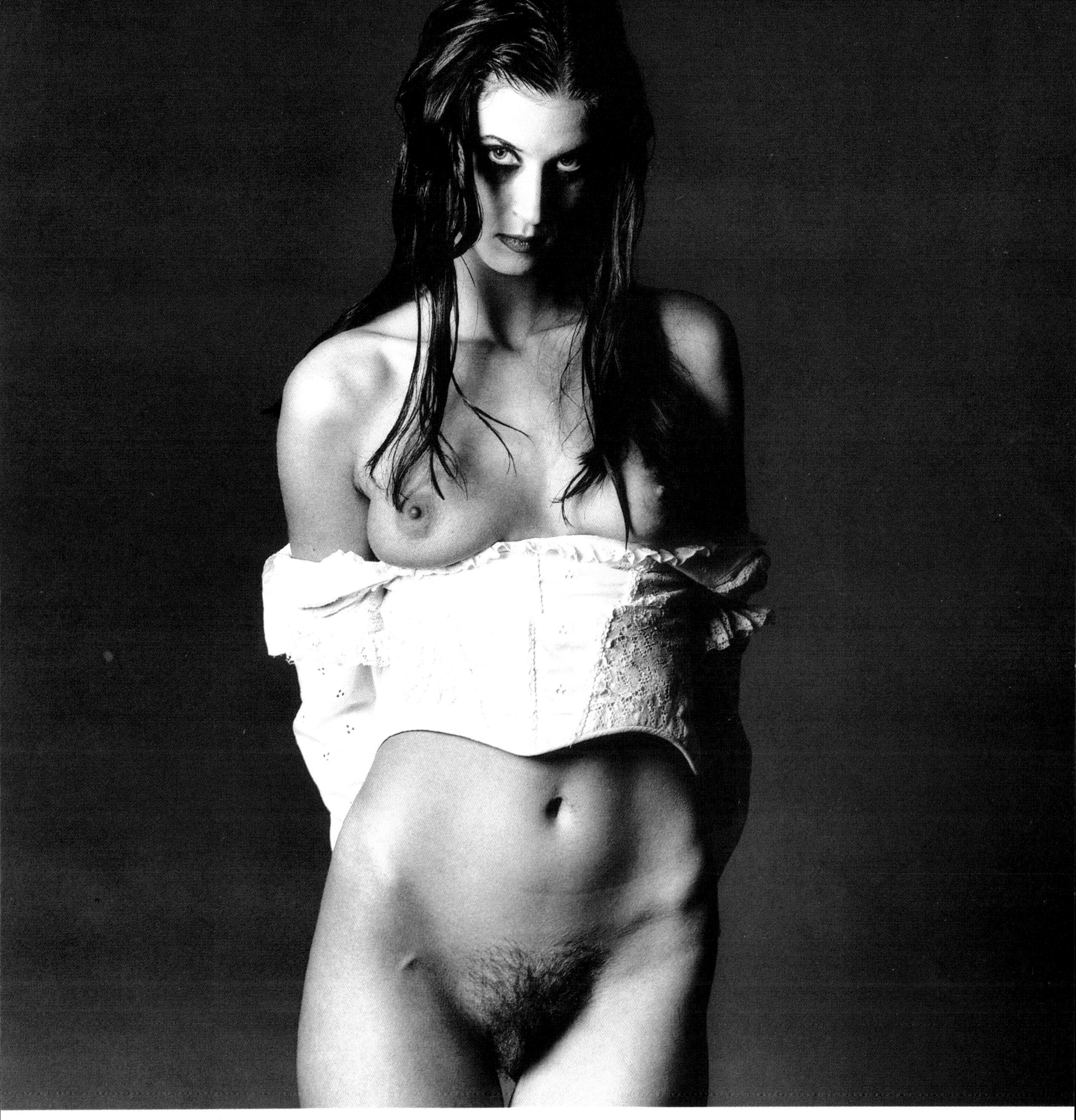

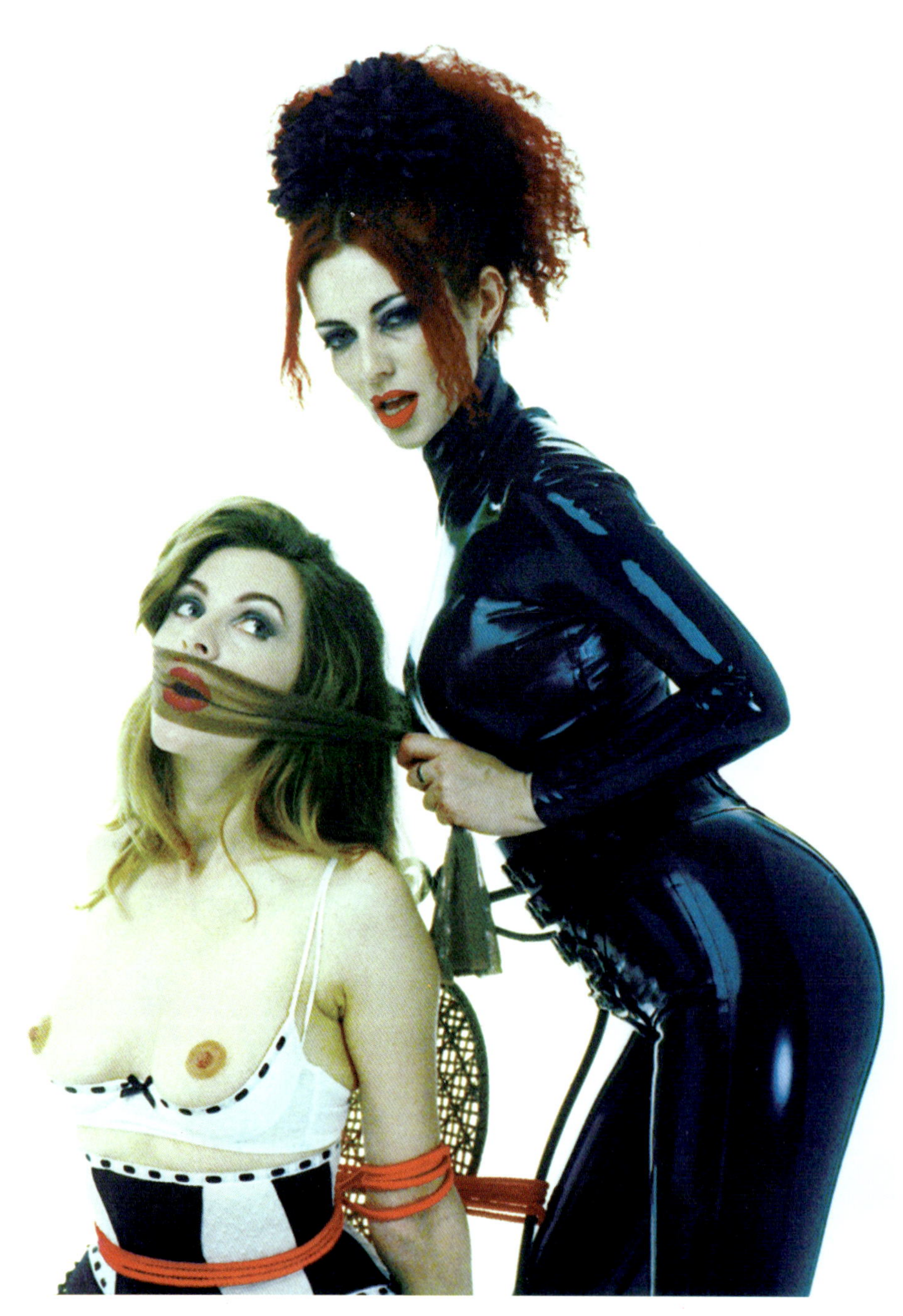

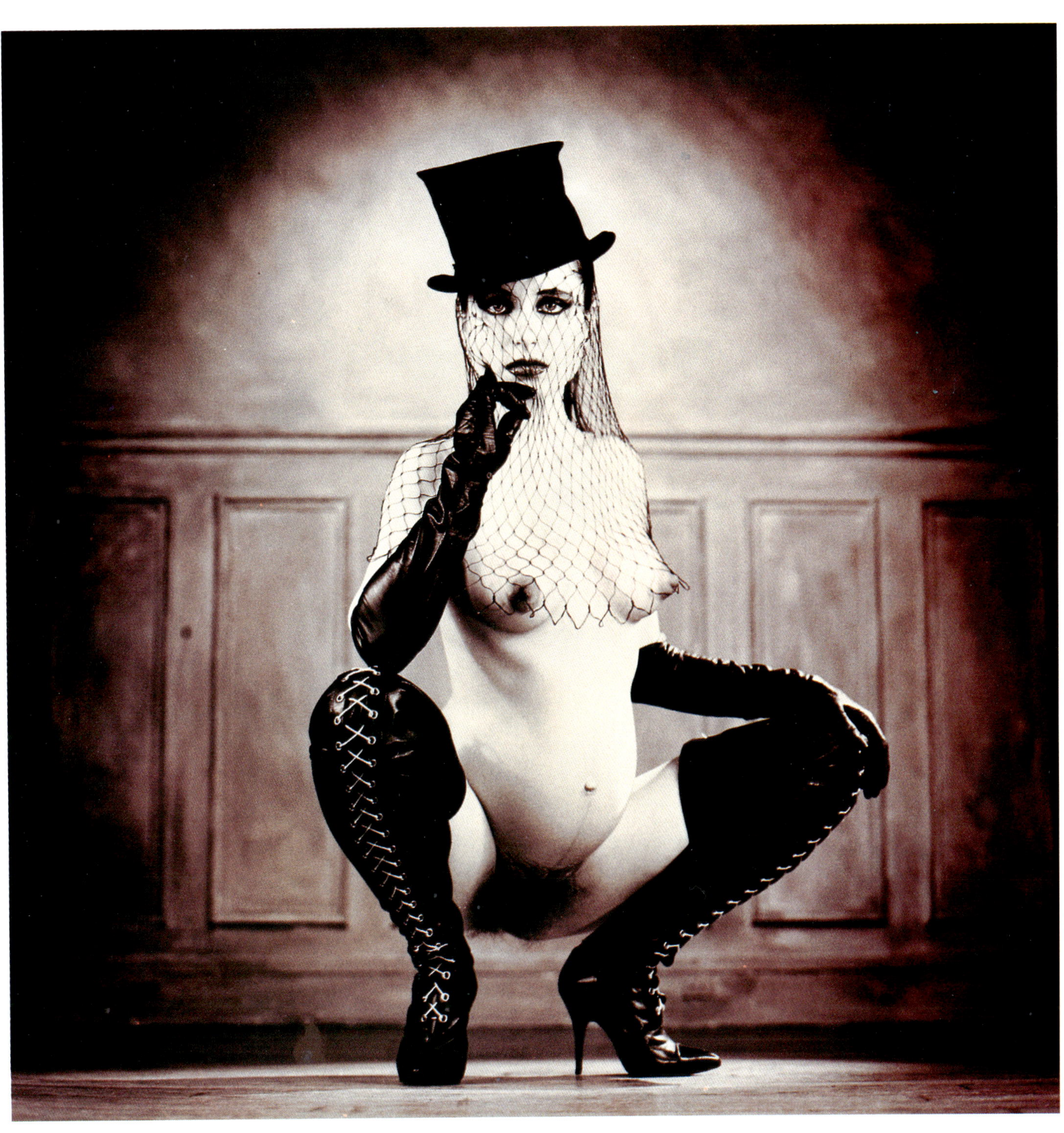

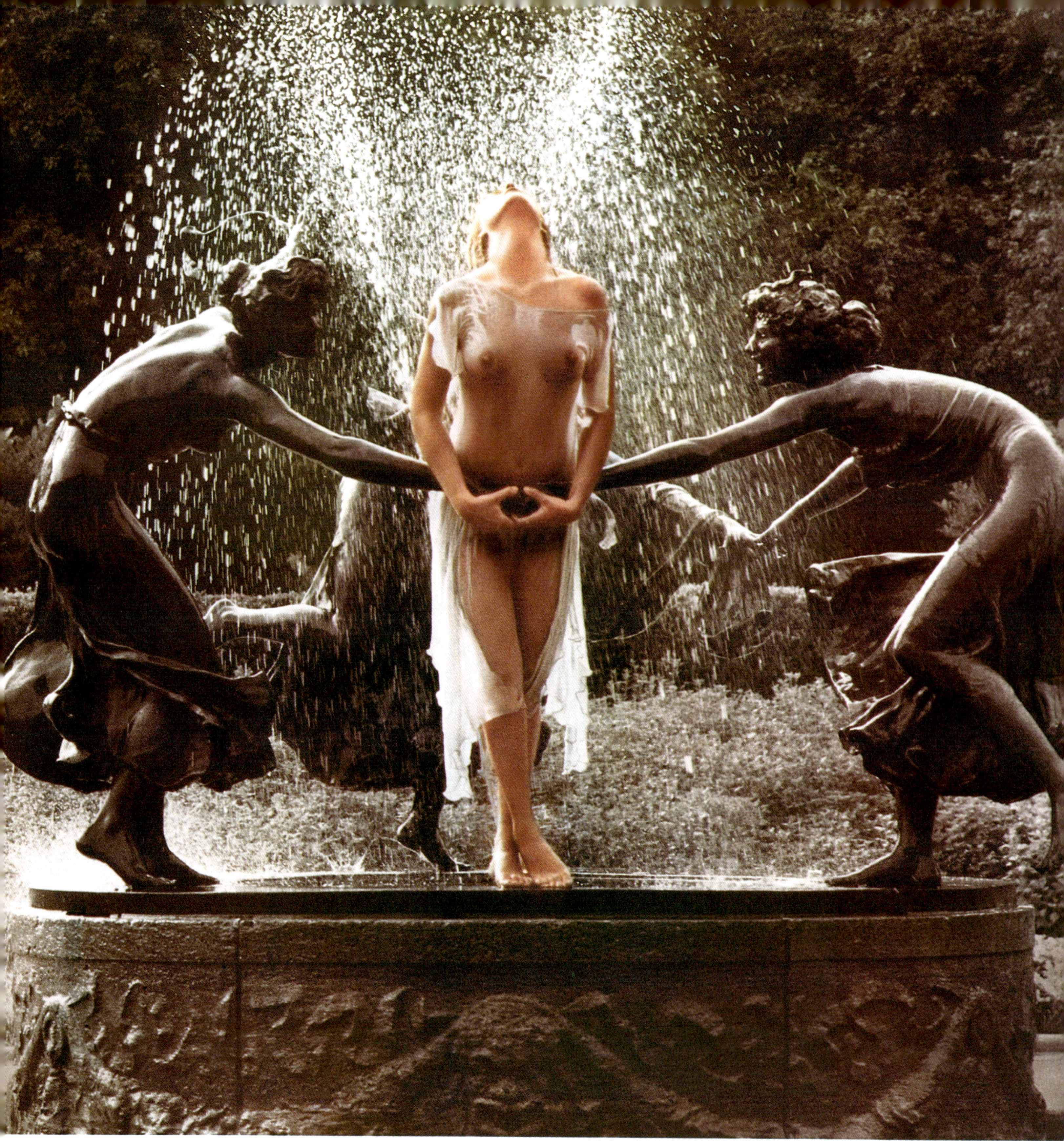

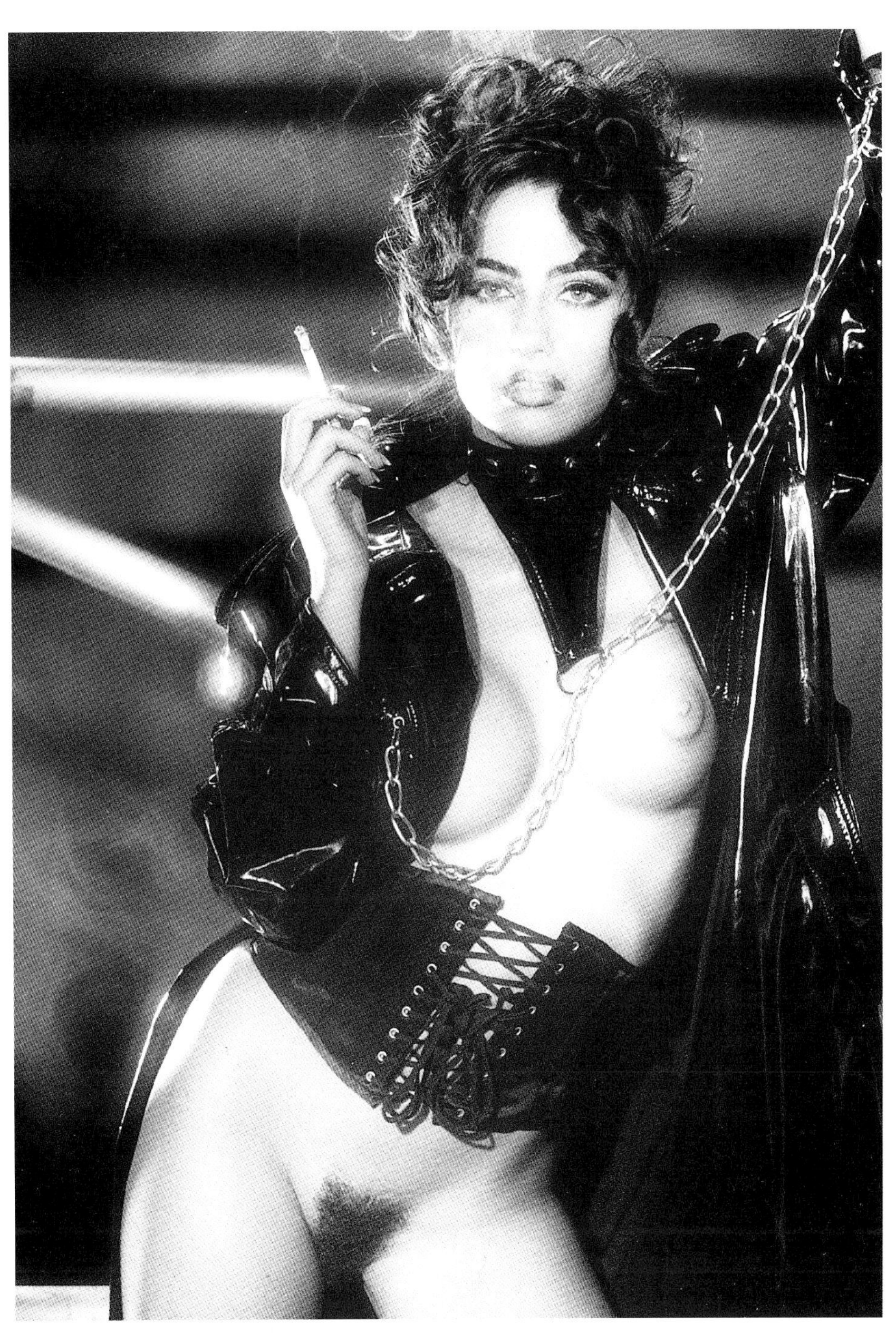

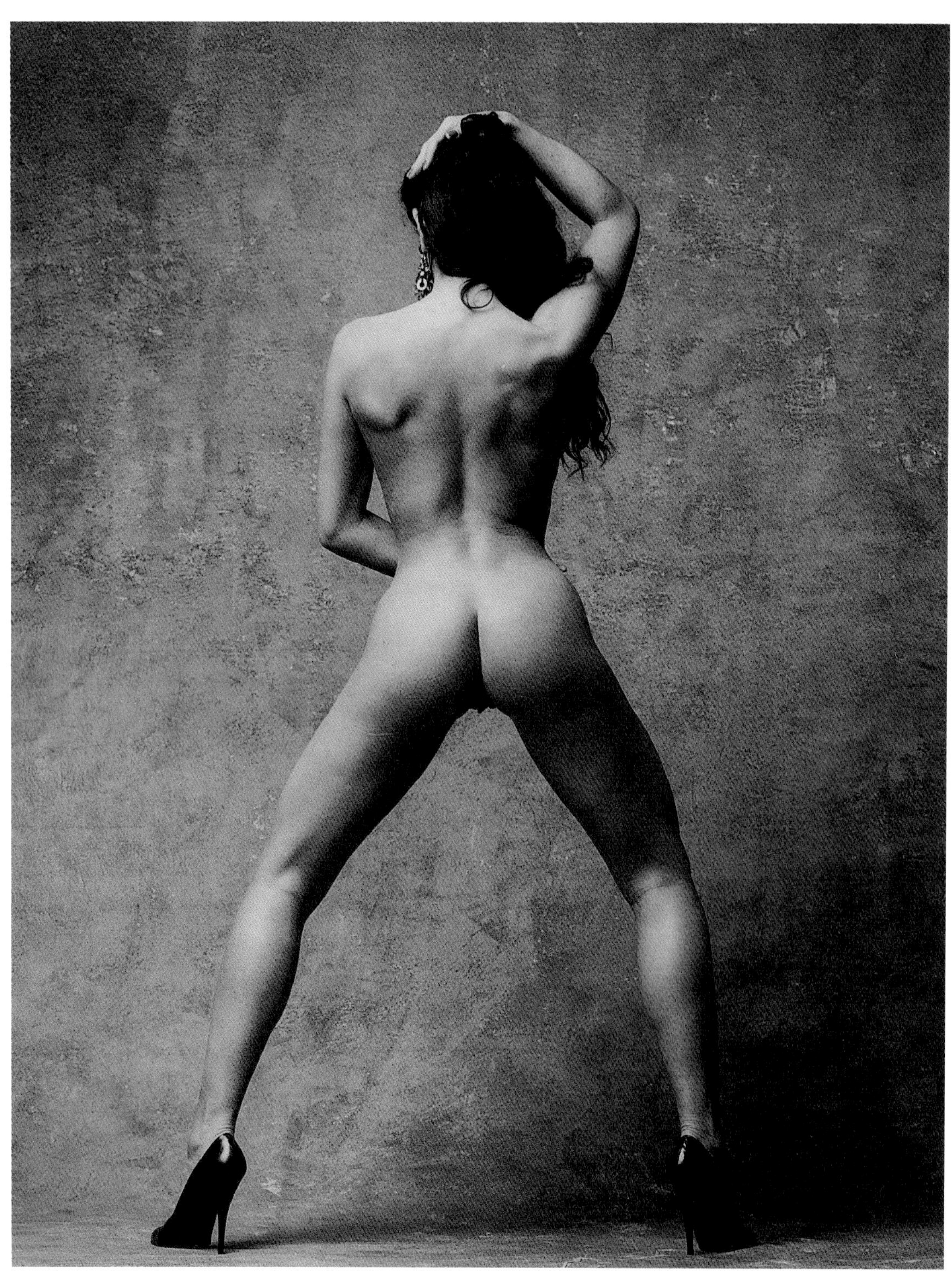

 CRAIG MOREY 1992

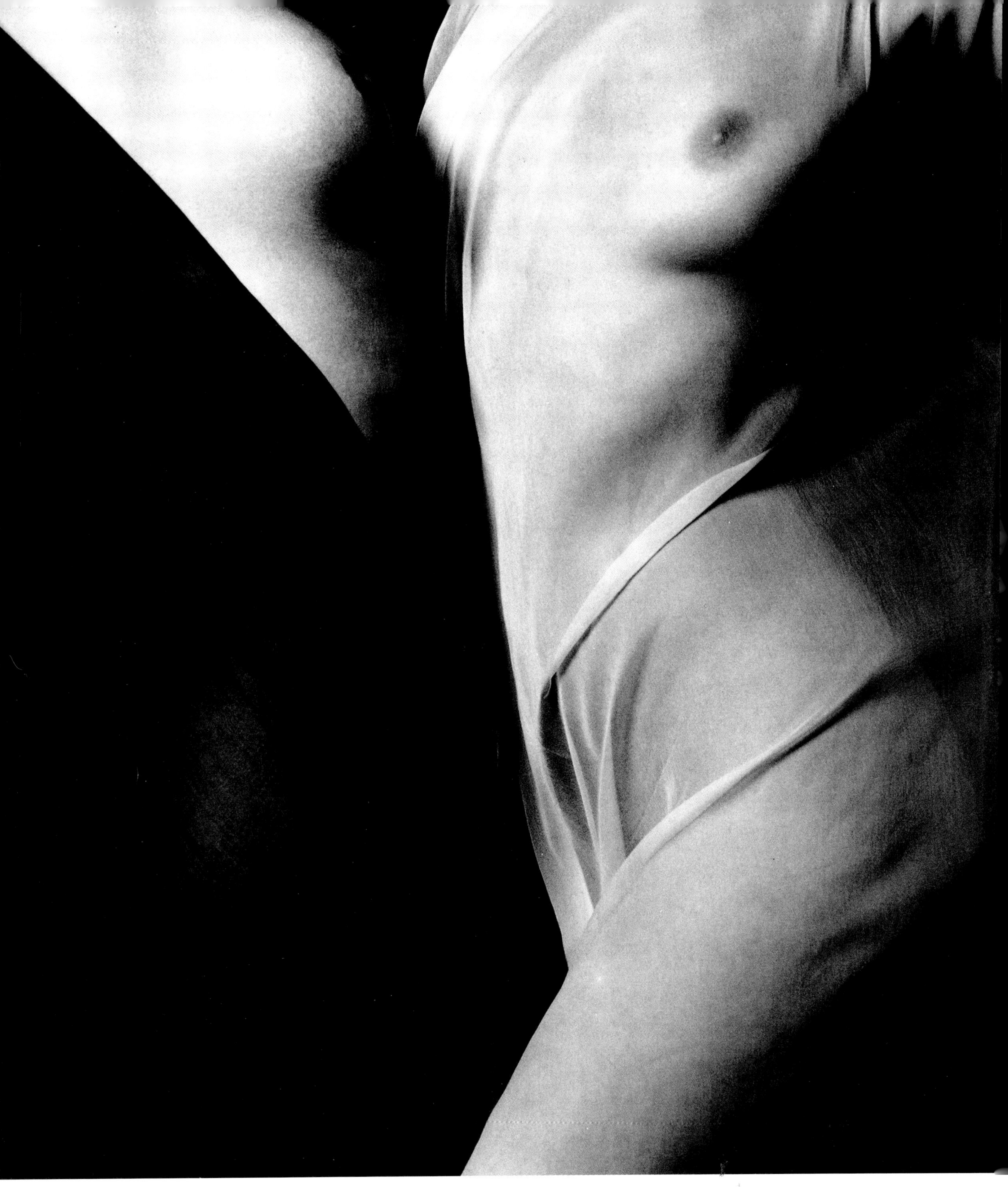

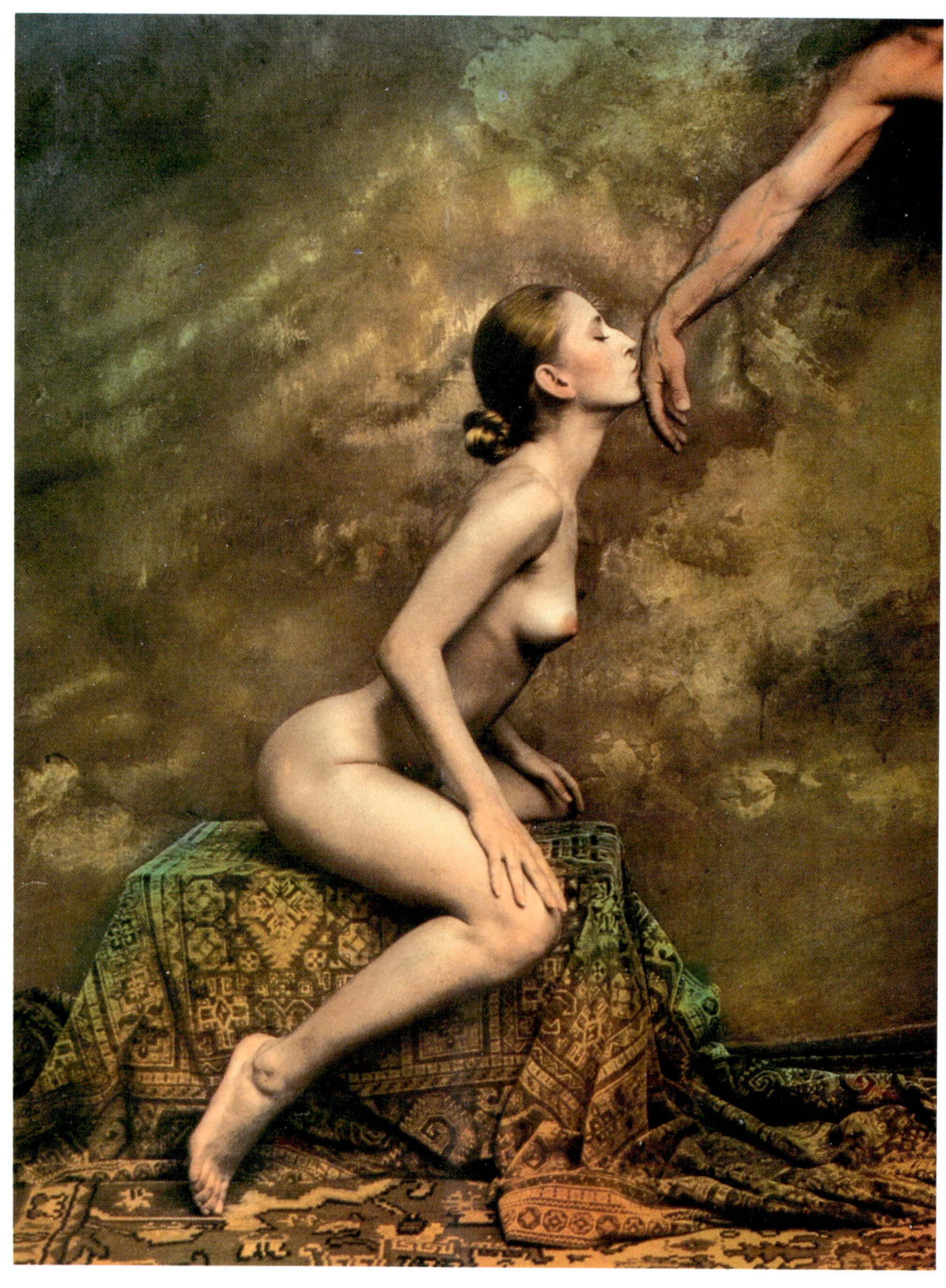

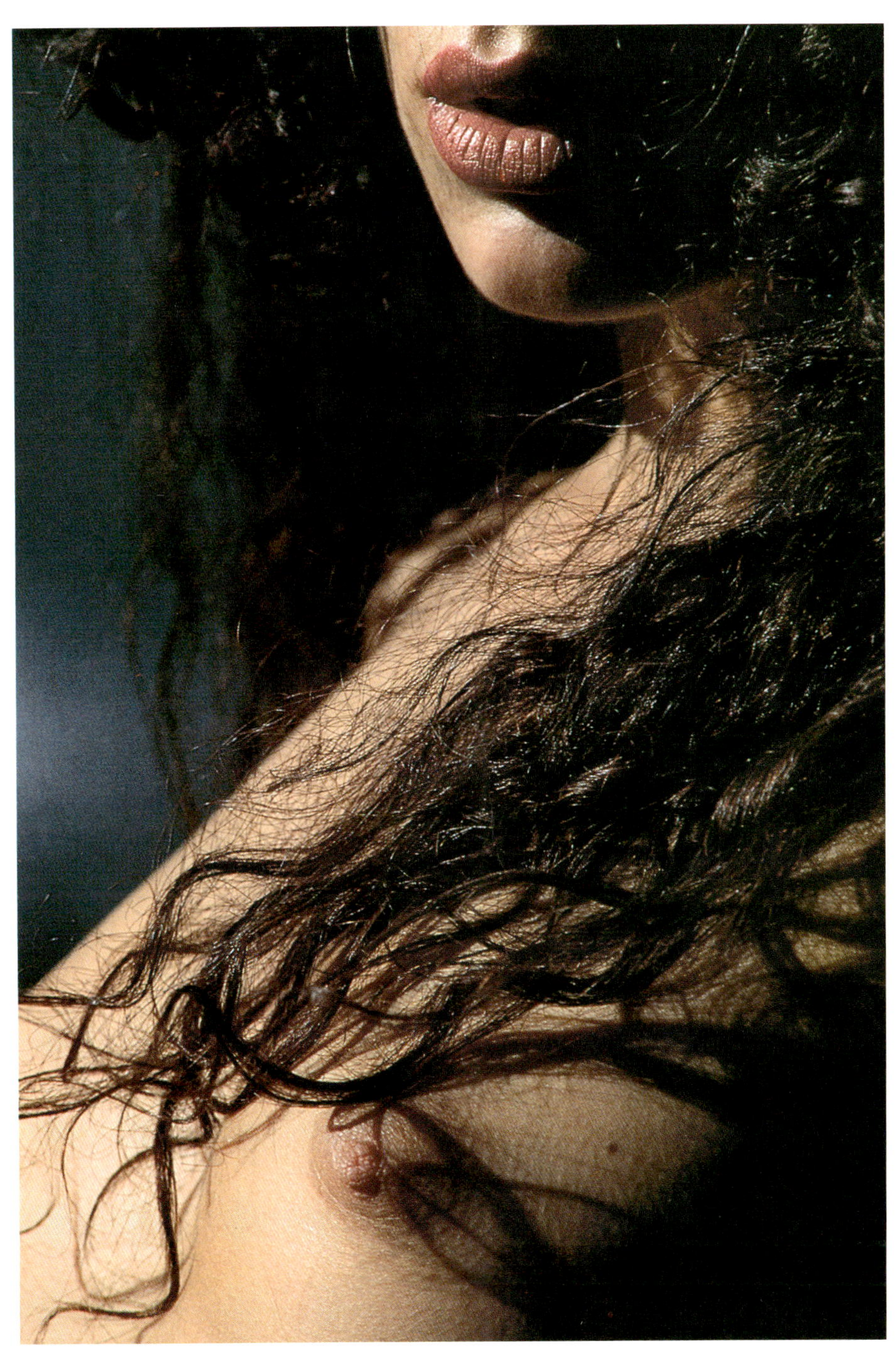

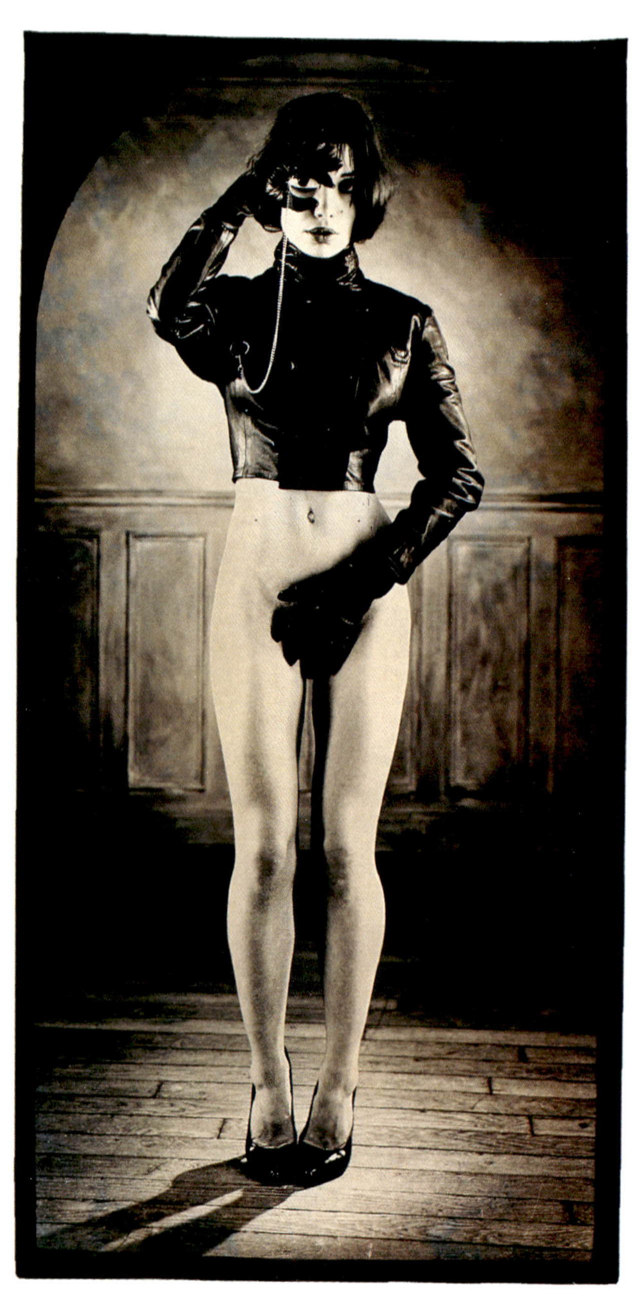

 | **GILLES BERQUET** 1993

(right) **IAIN McKELL** 1998

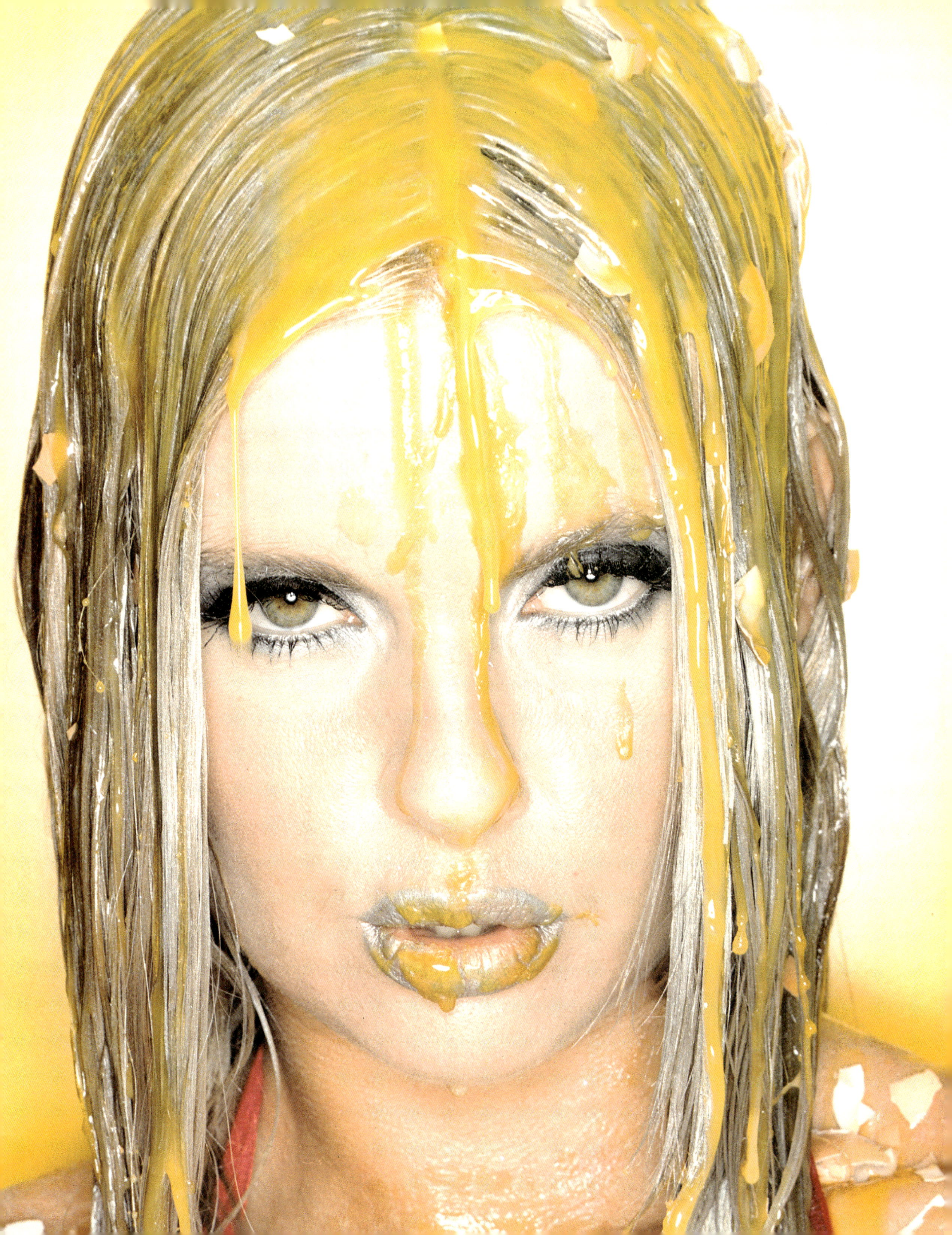

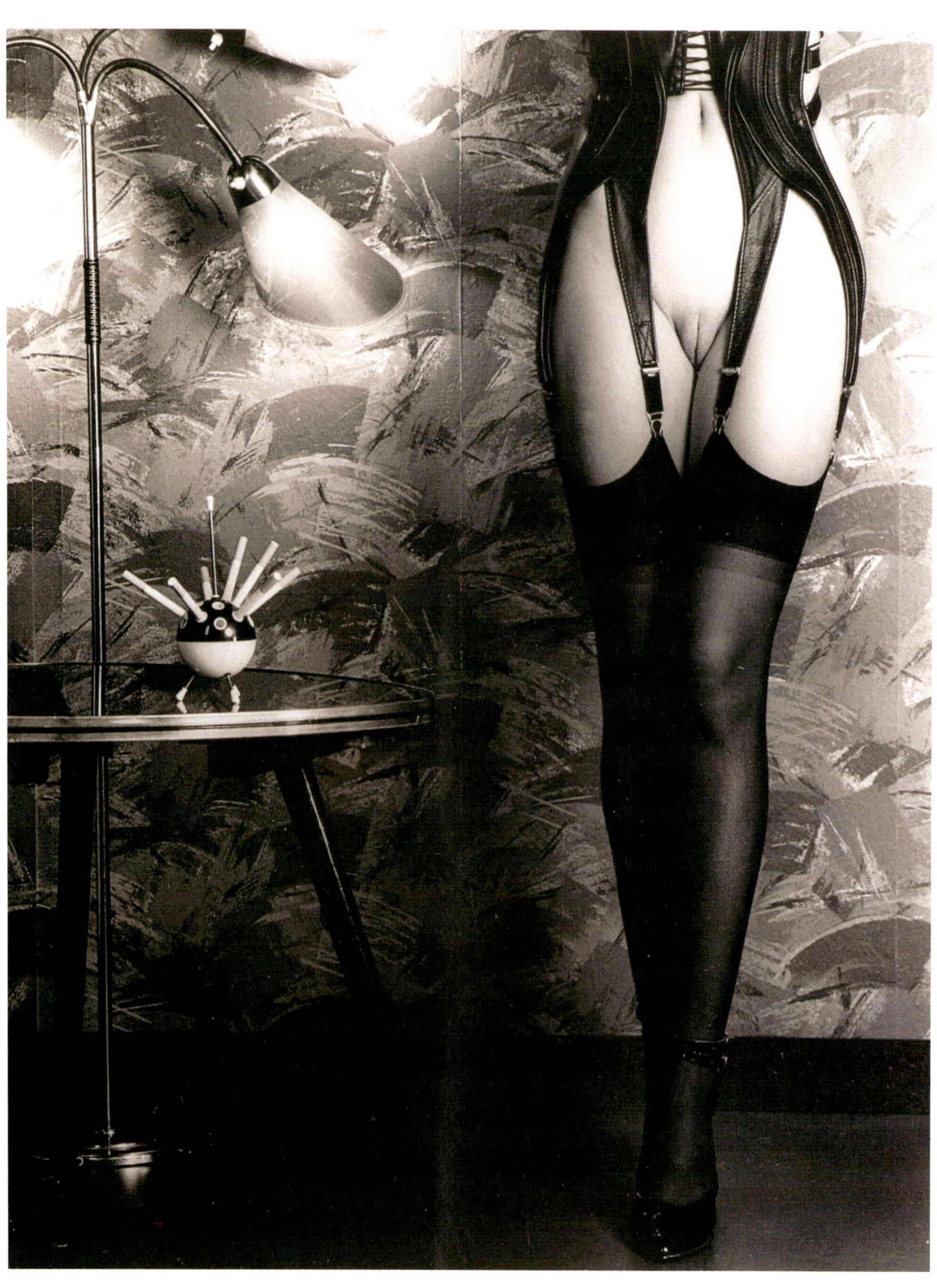

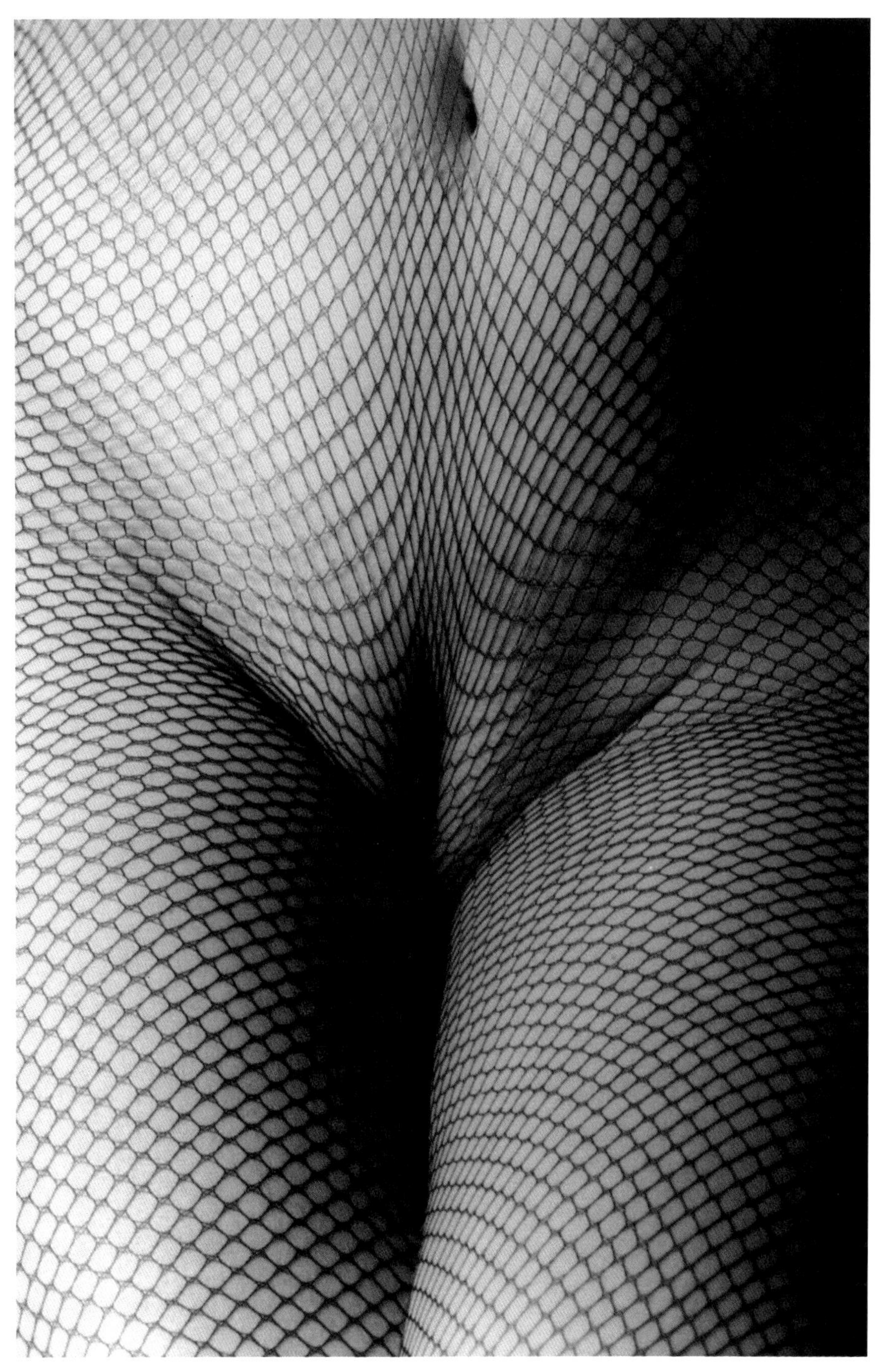

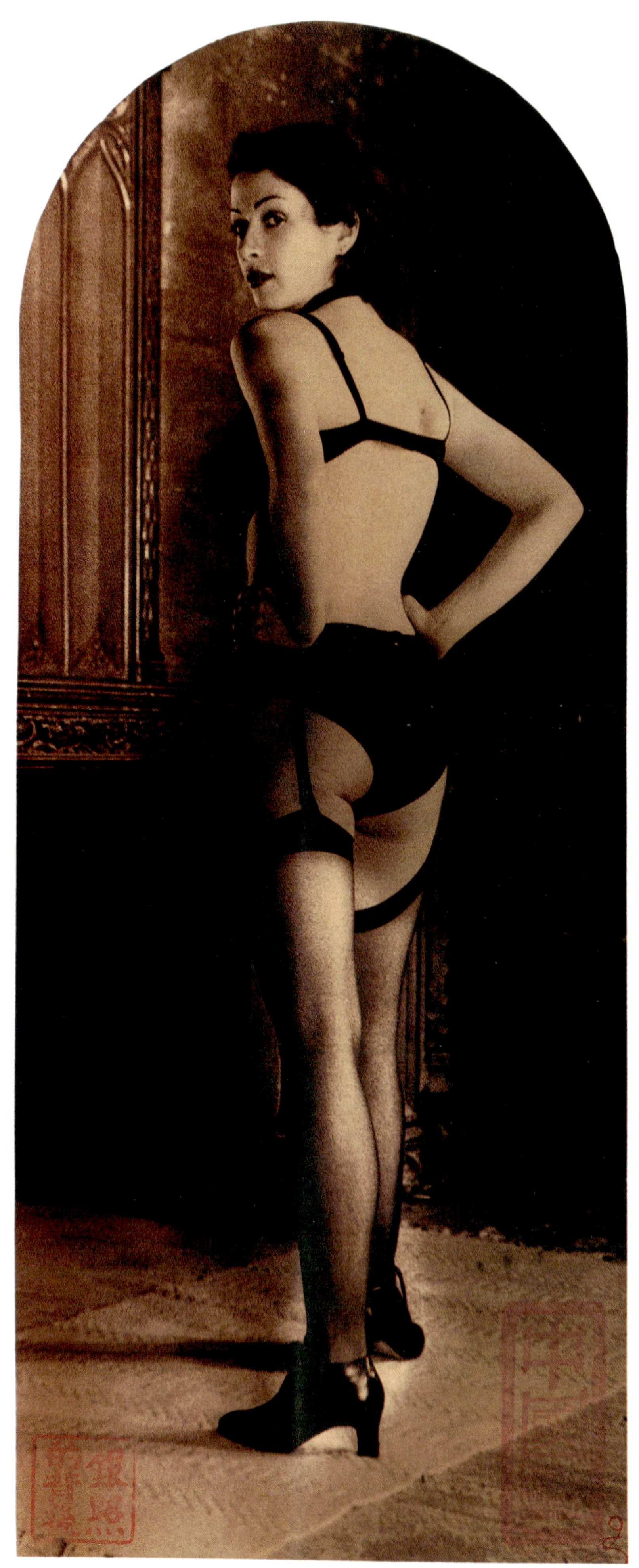

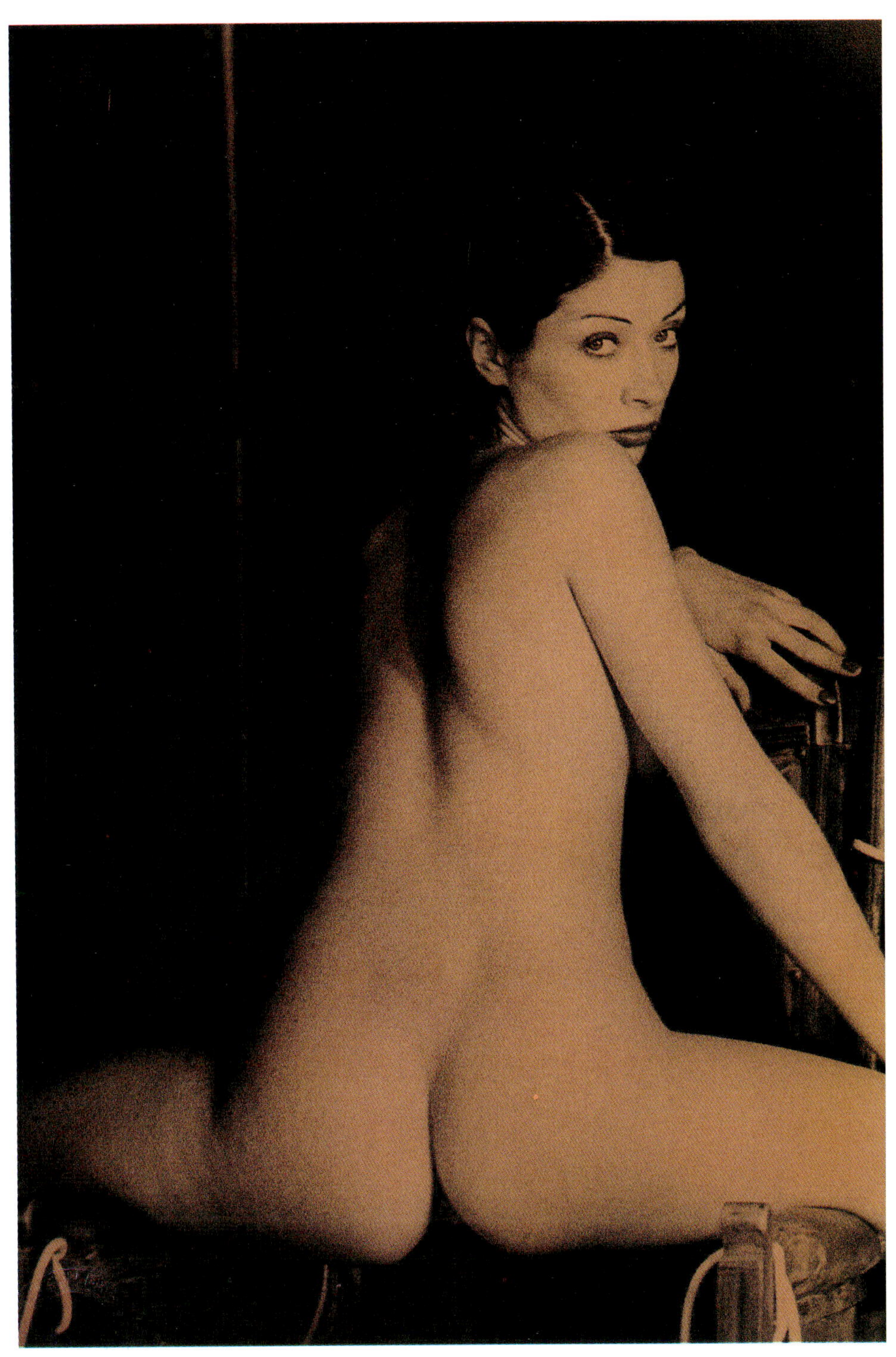

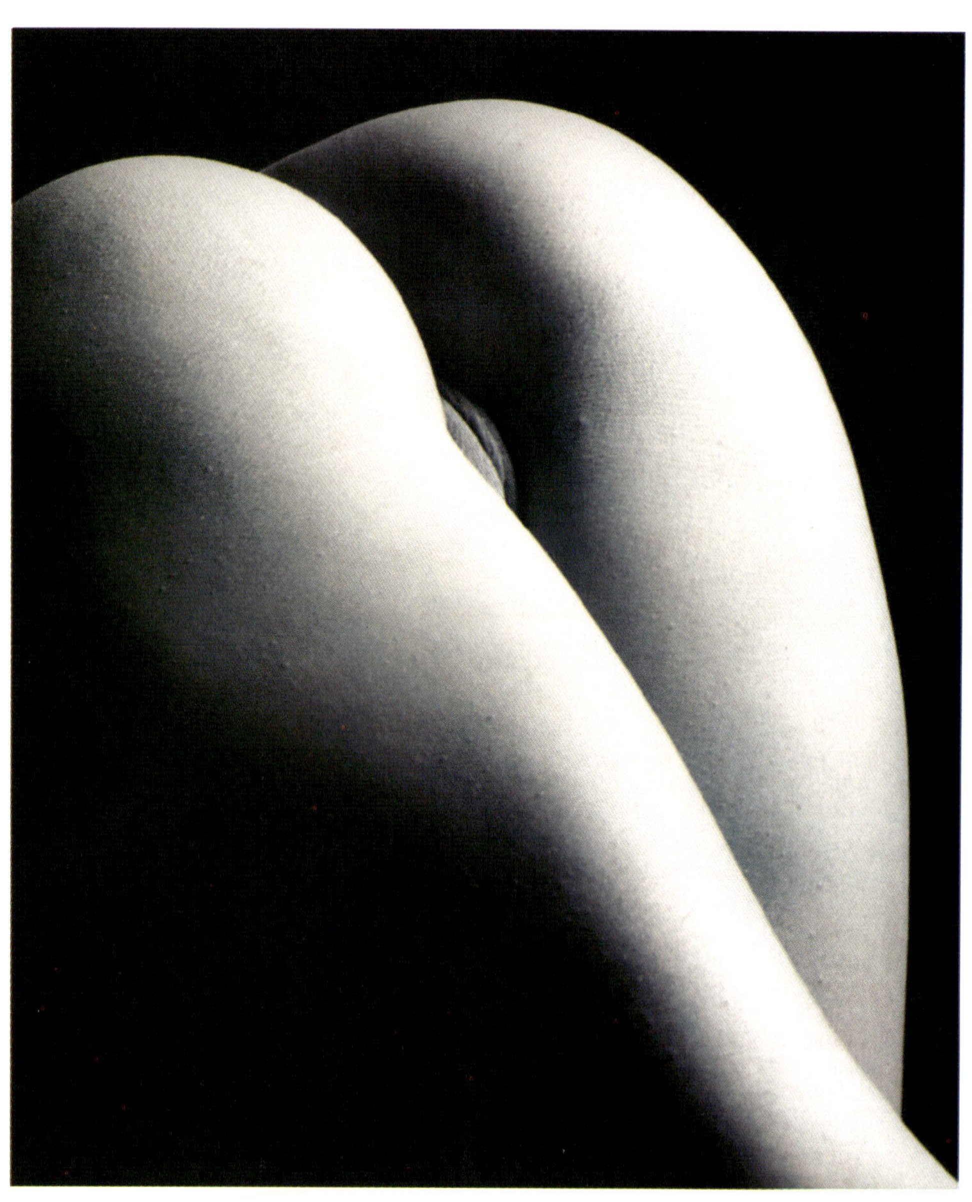

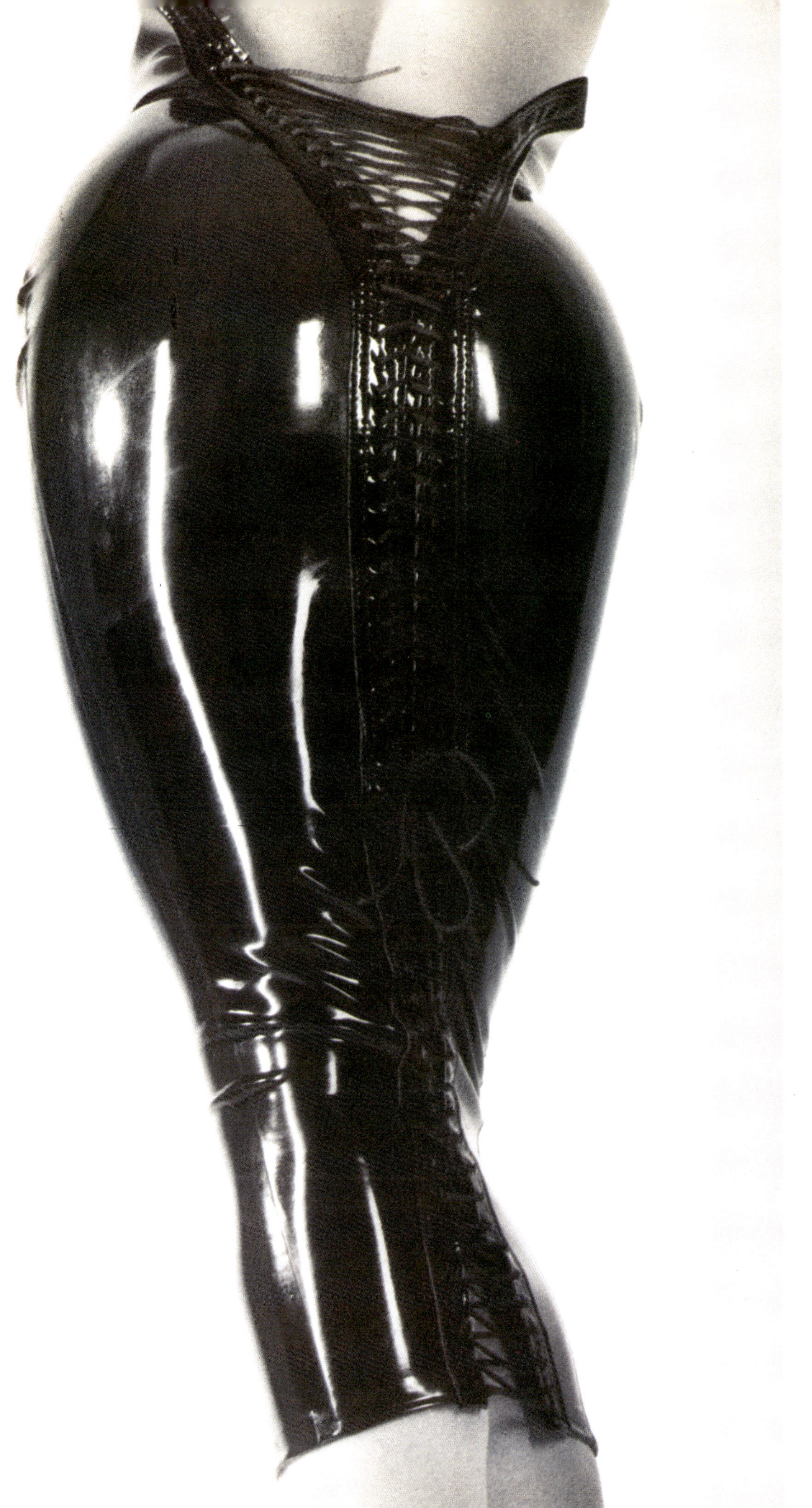

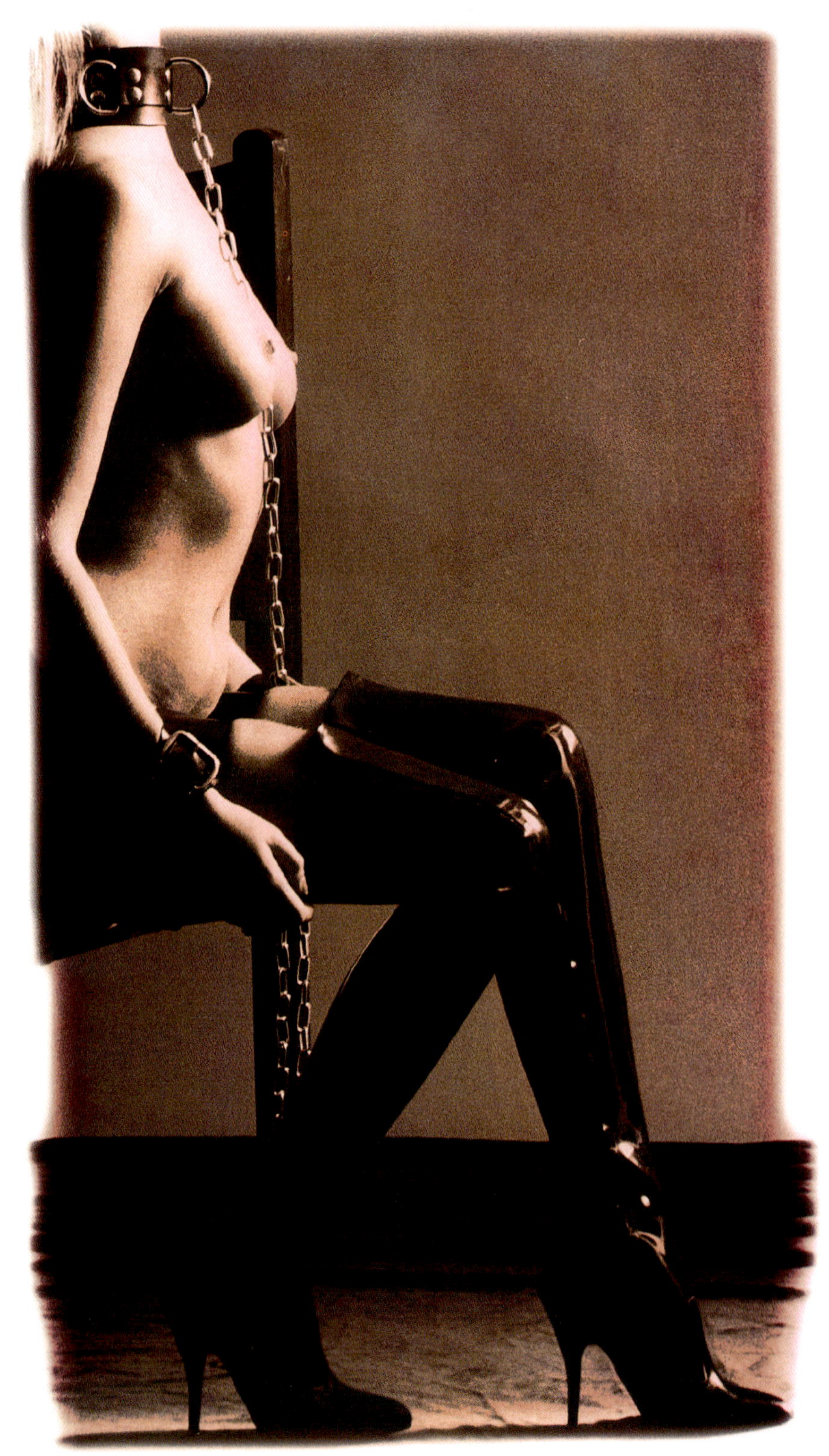

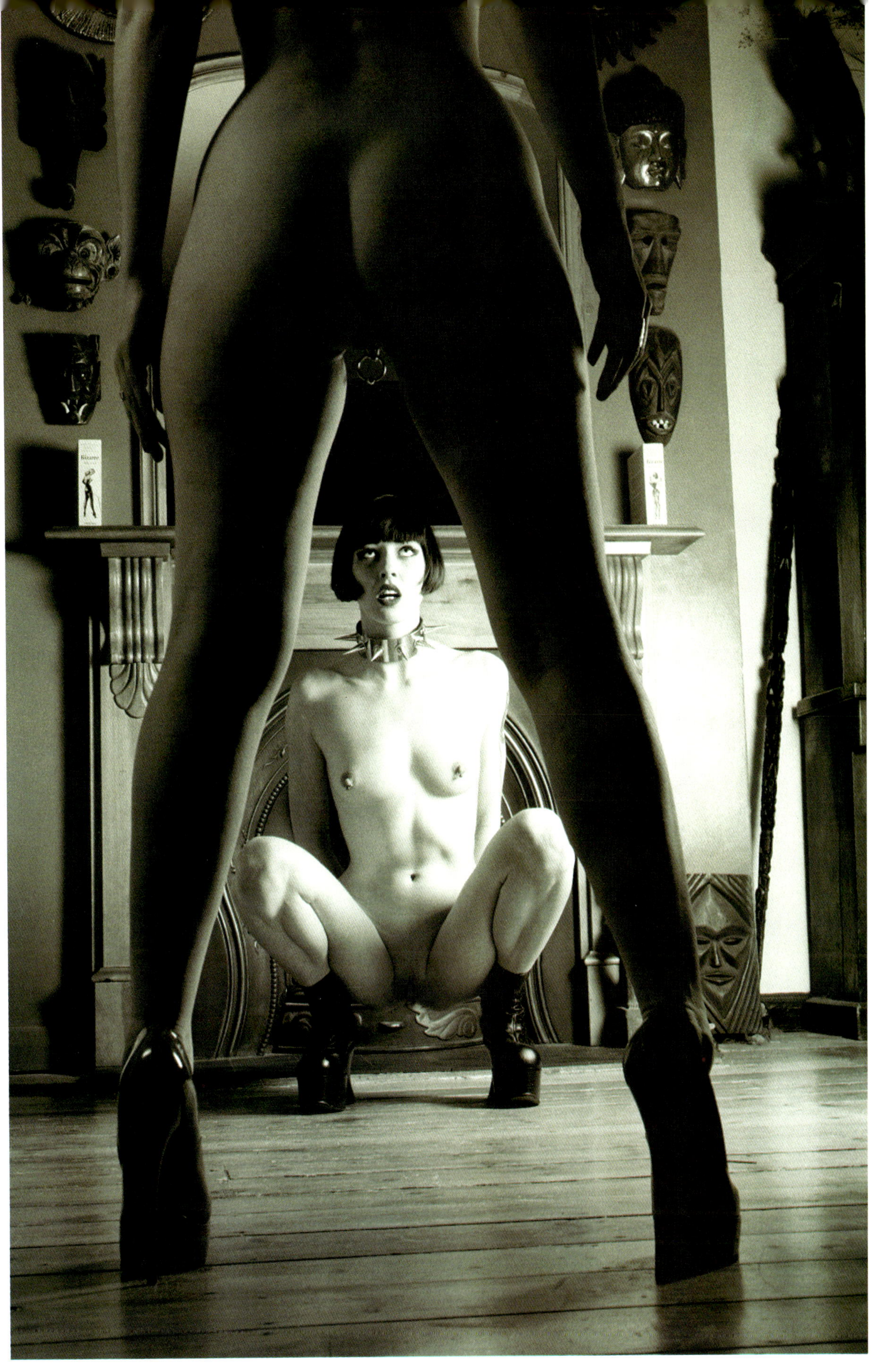

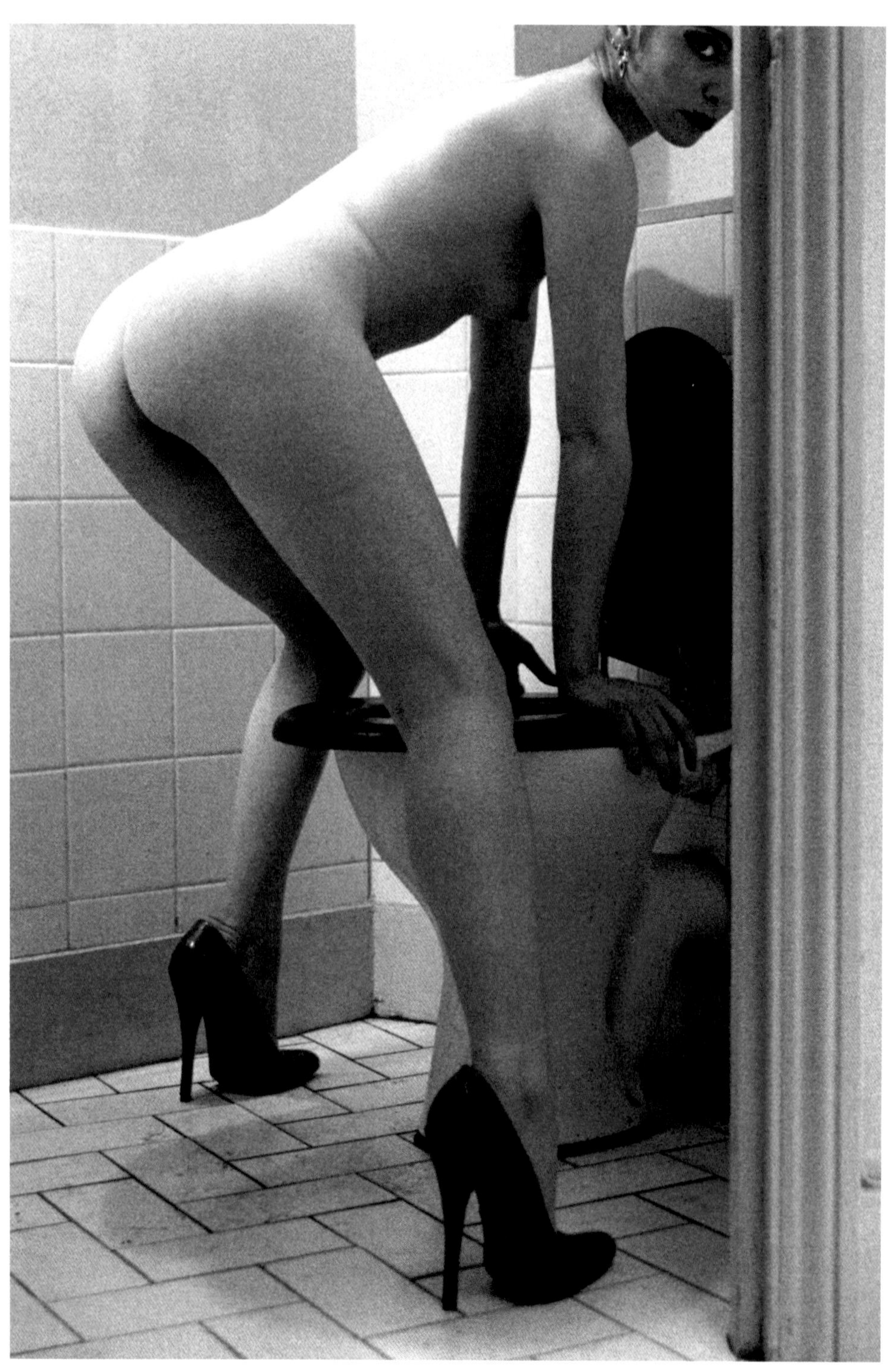

 | TREVOR WATSON 1995

(right) JOHN SWANNELL 1991

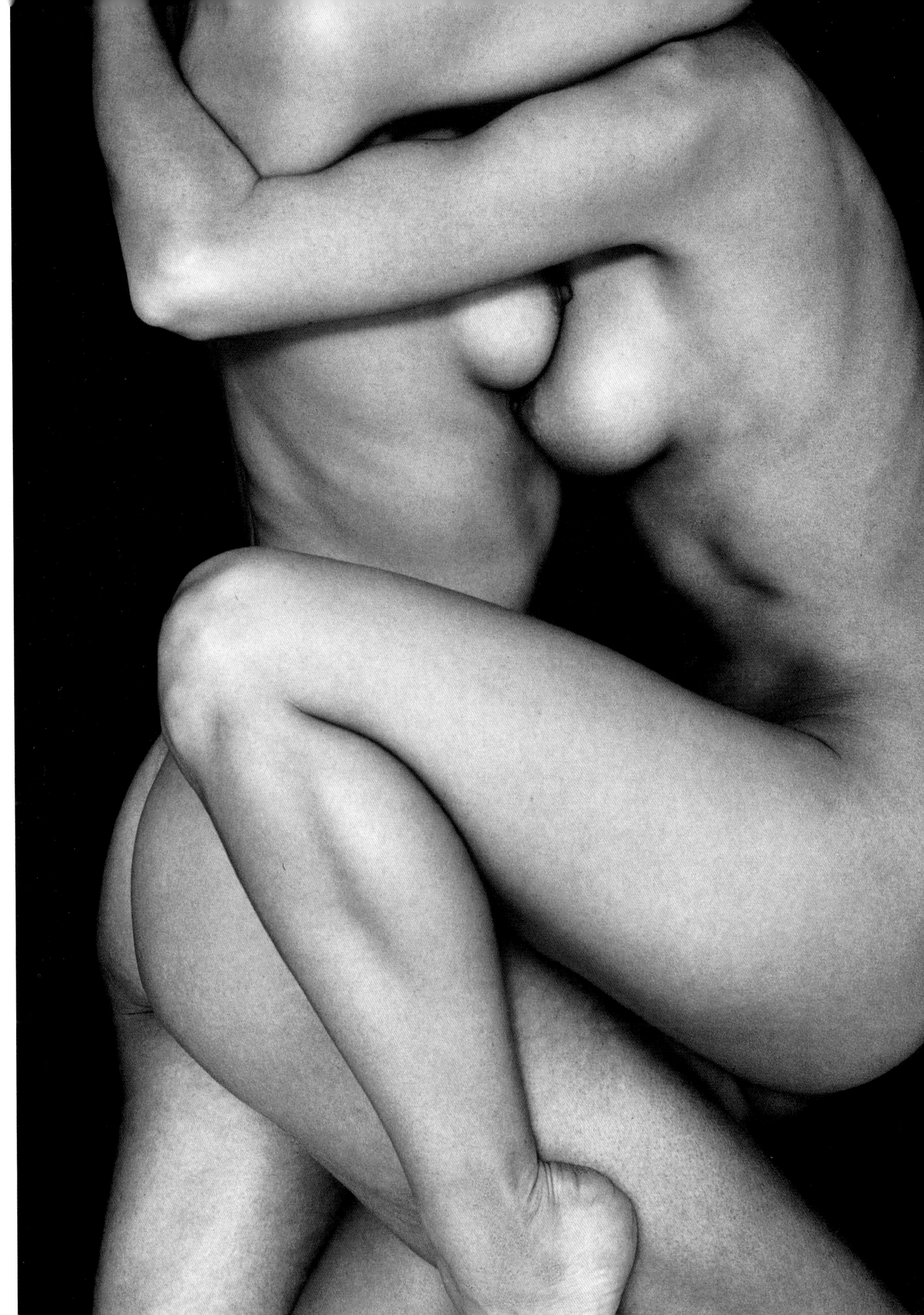

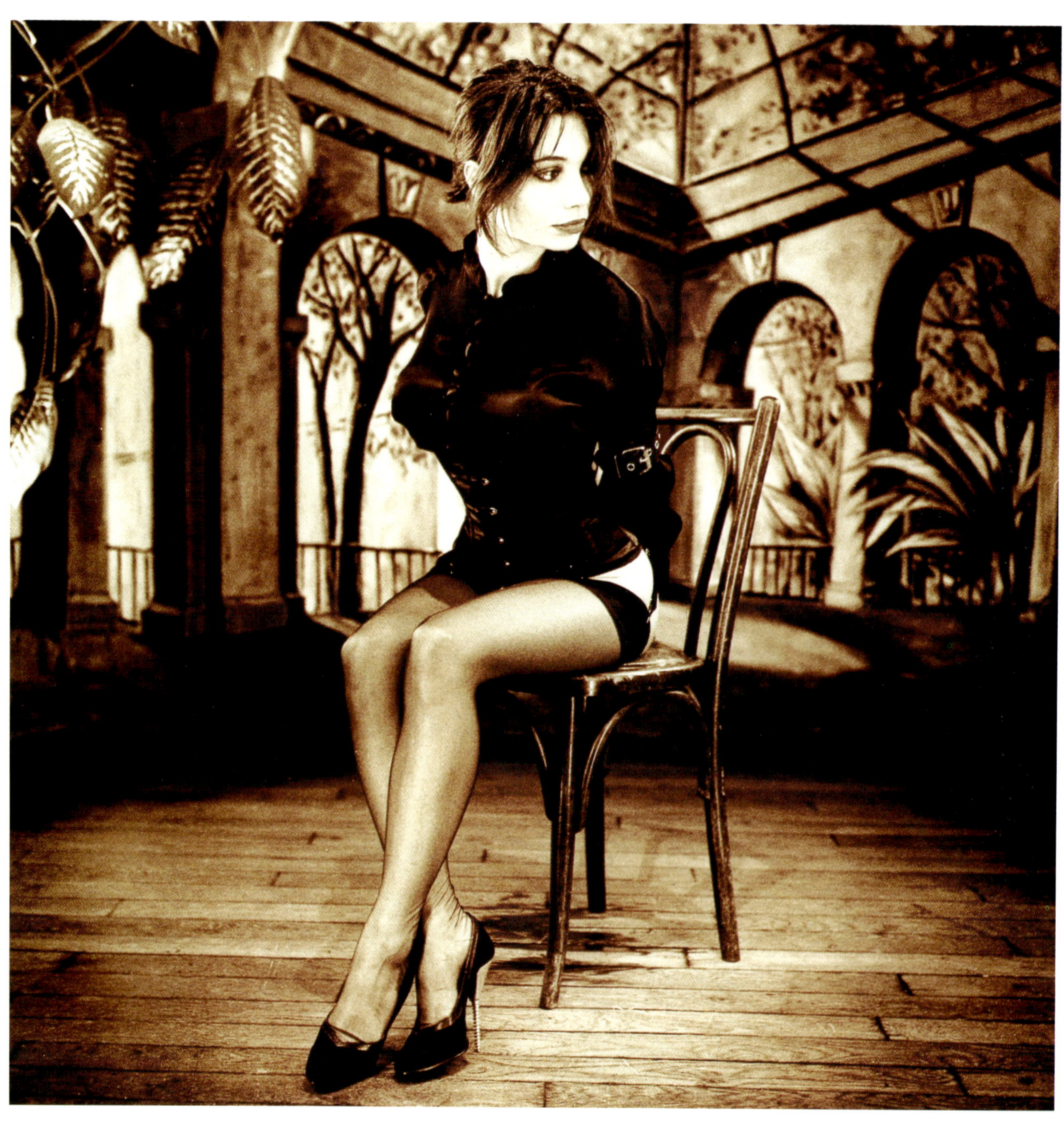

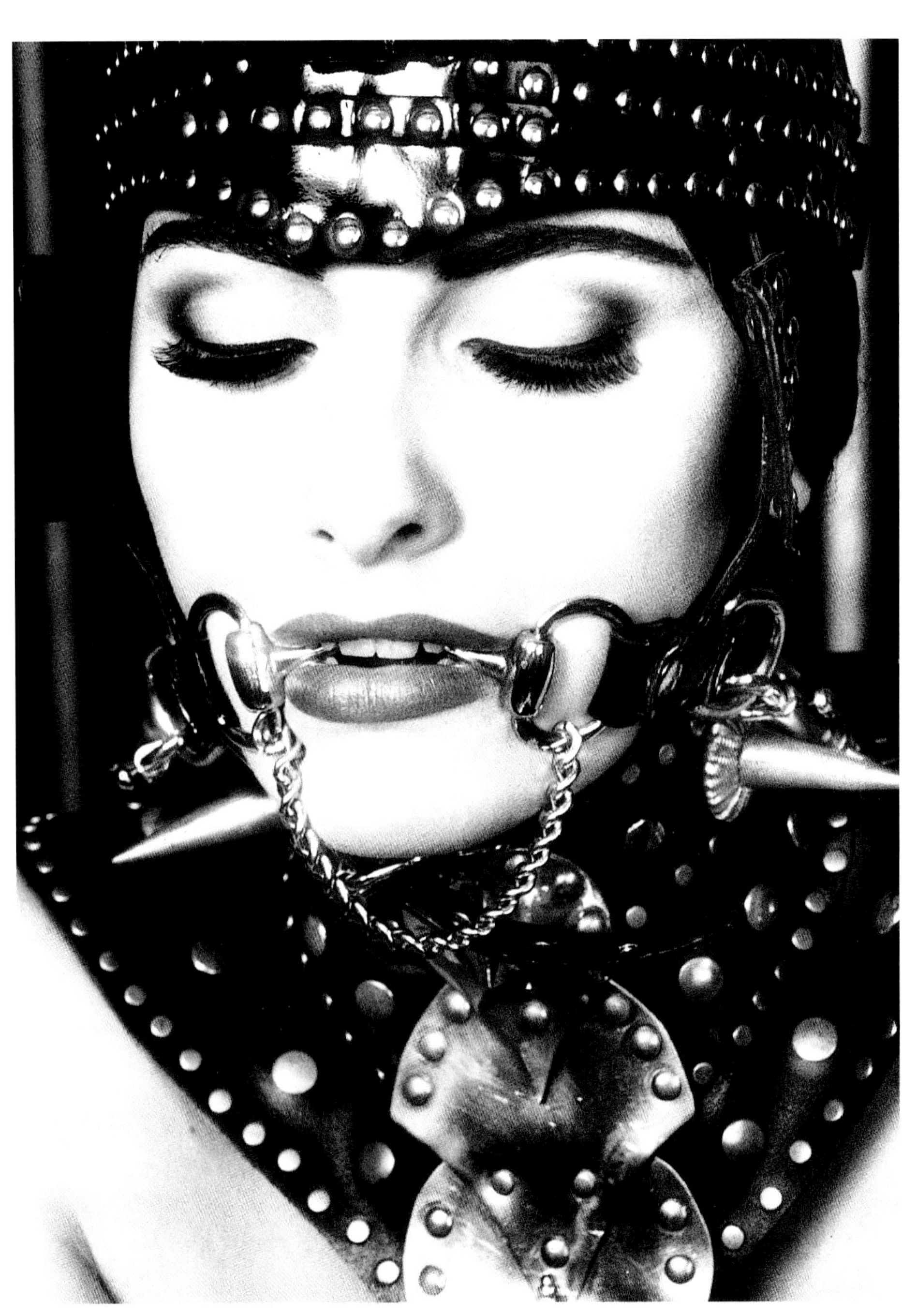

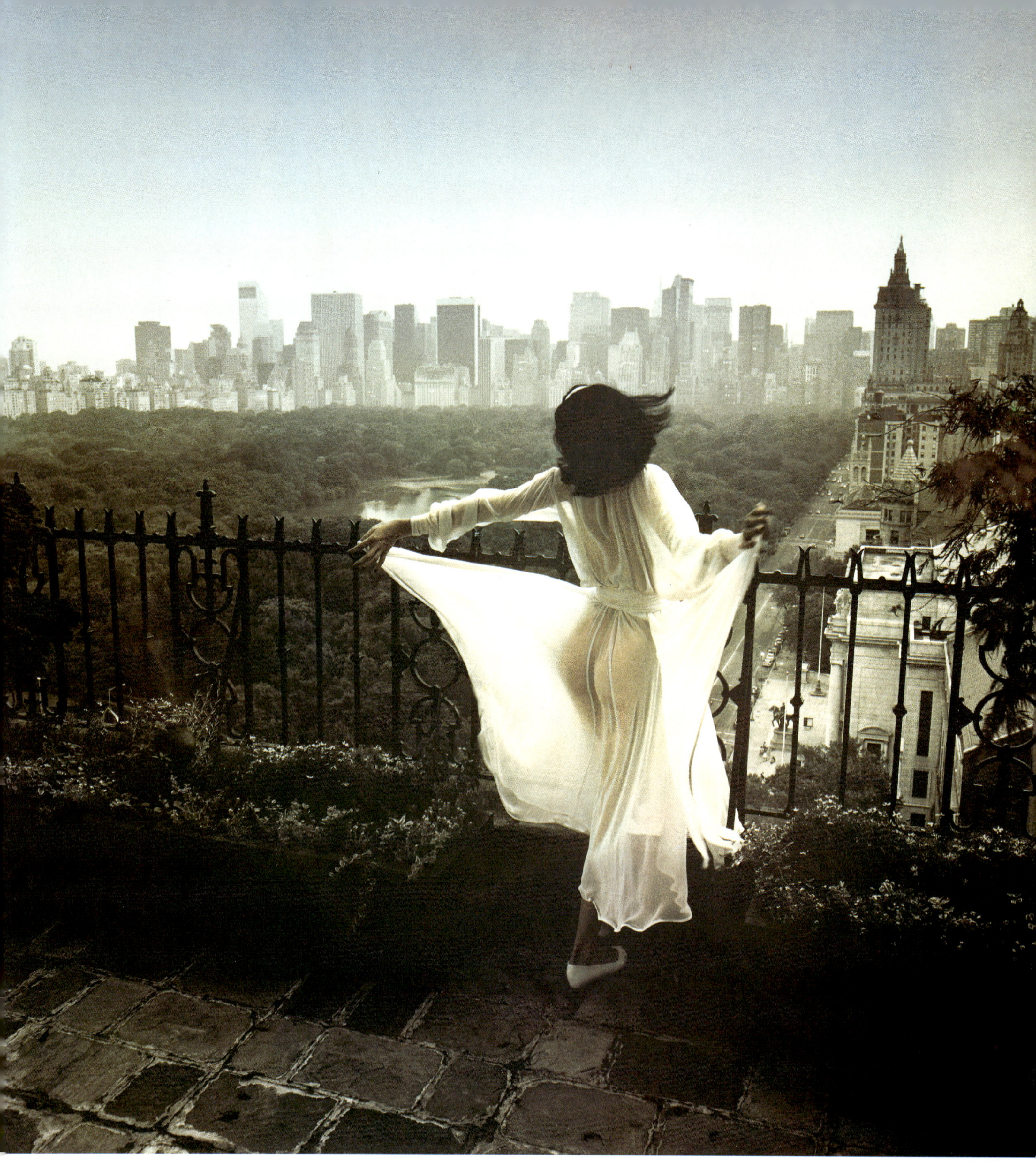

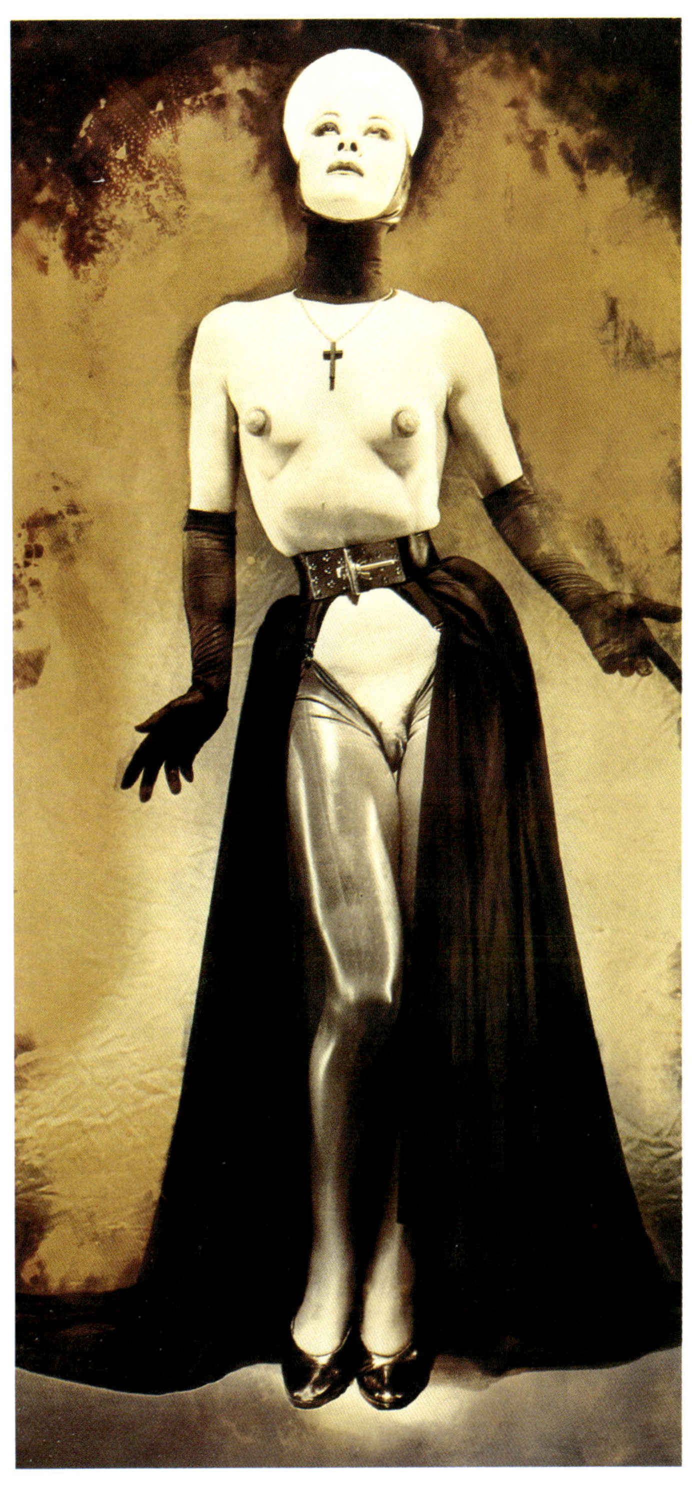

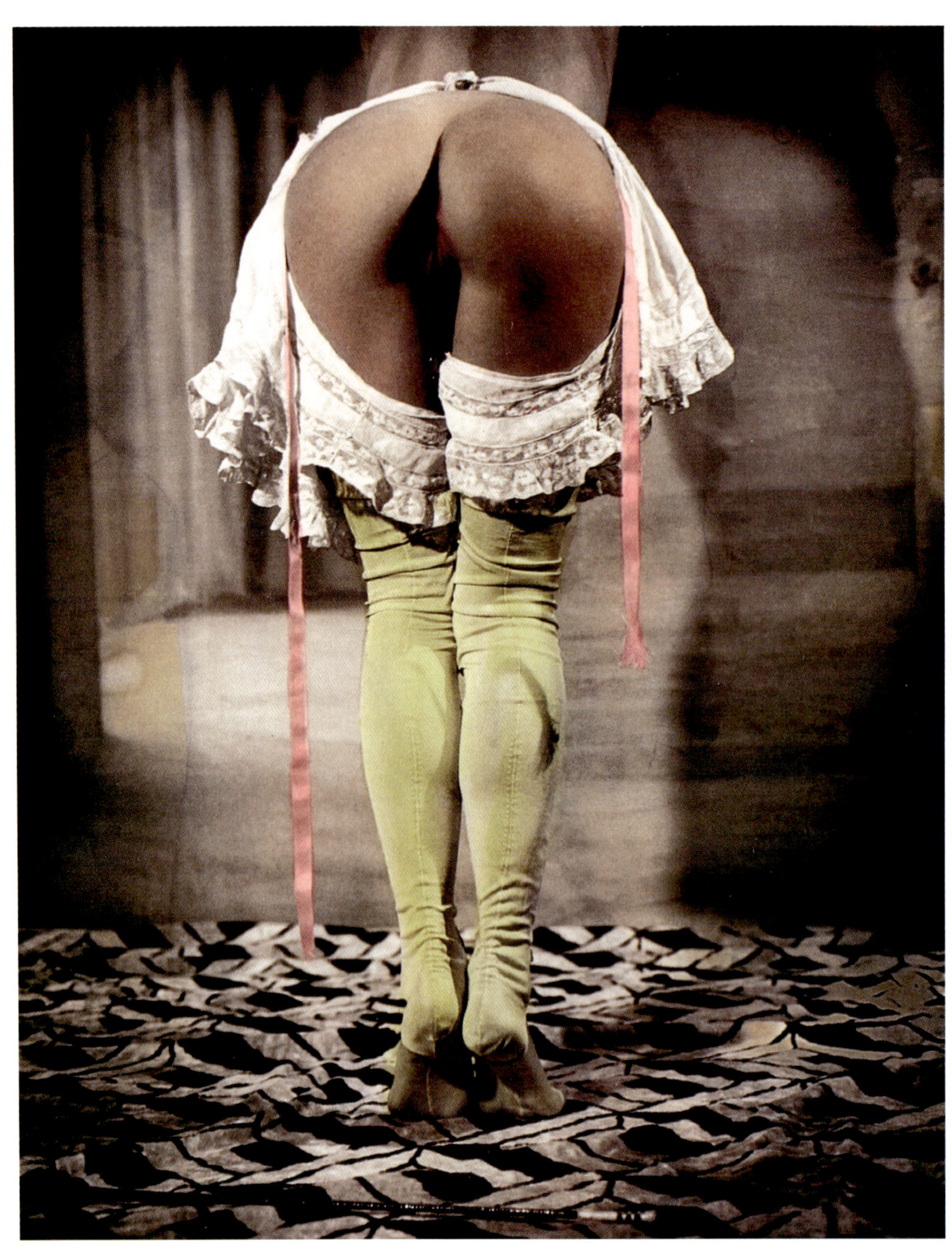

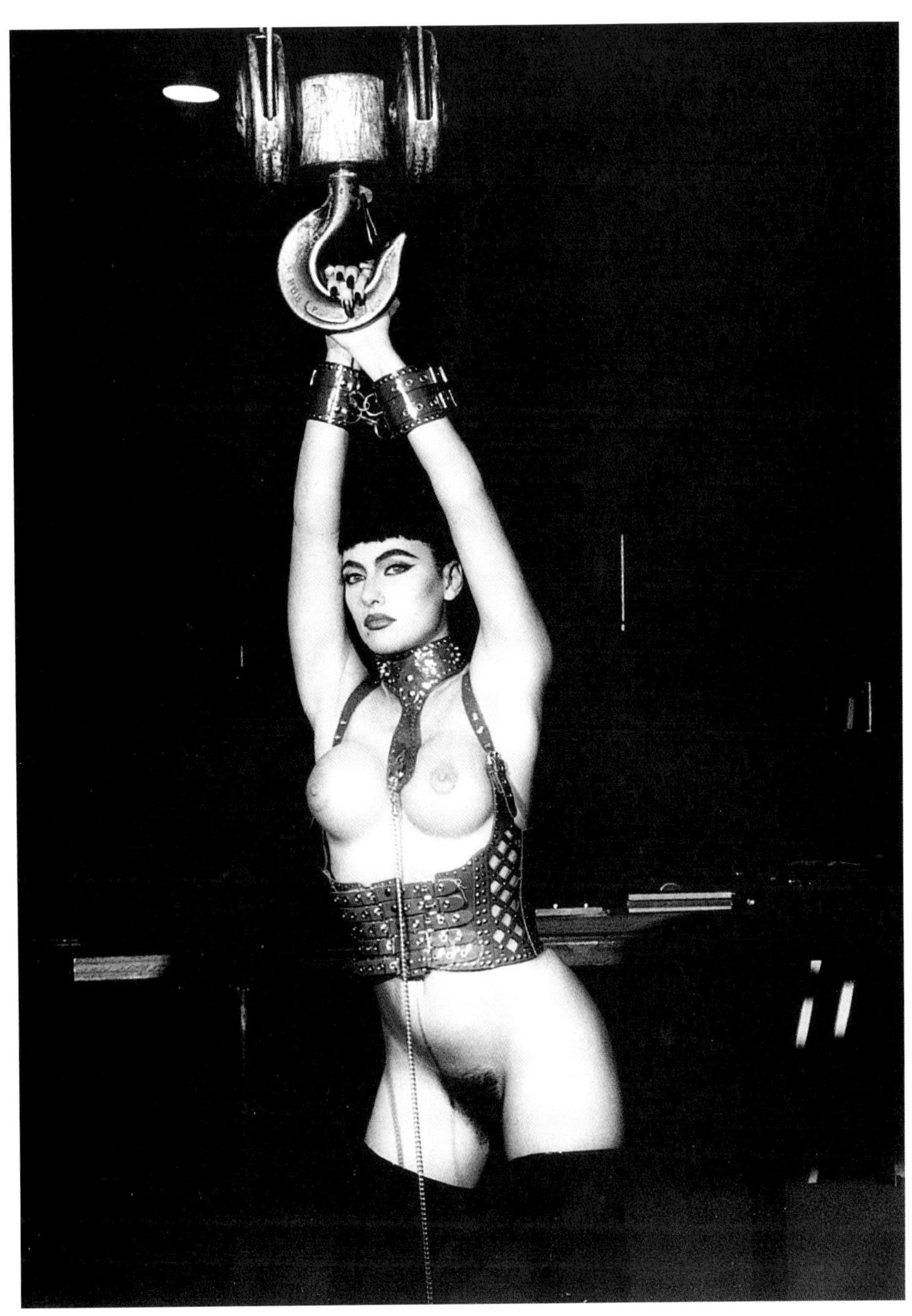

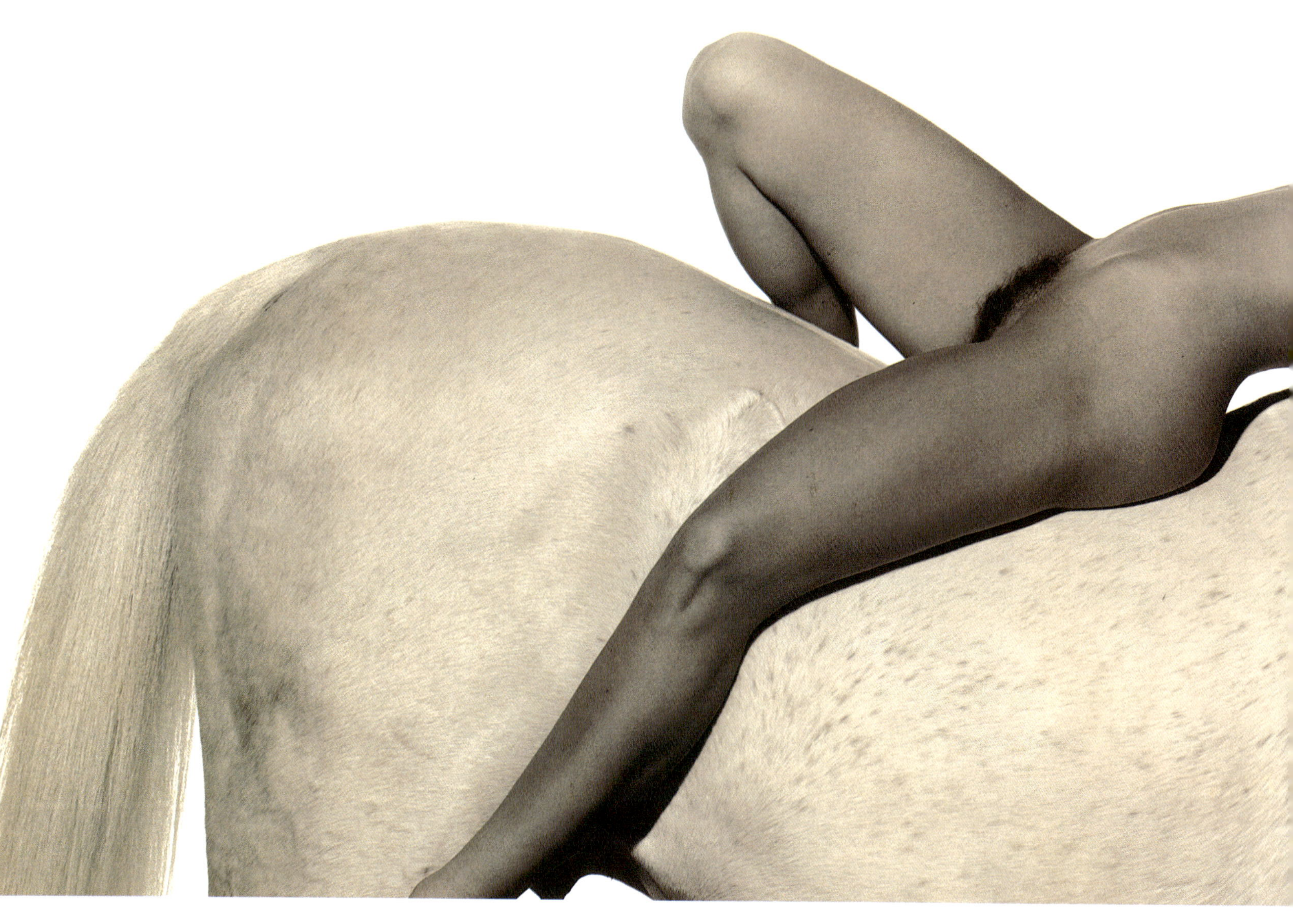

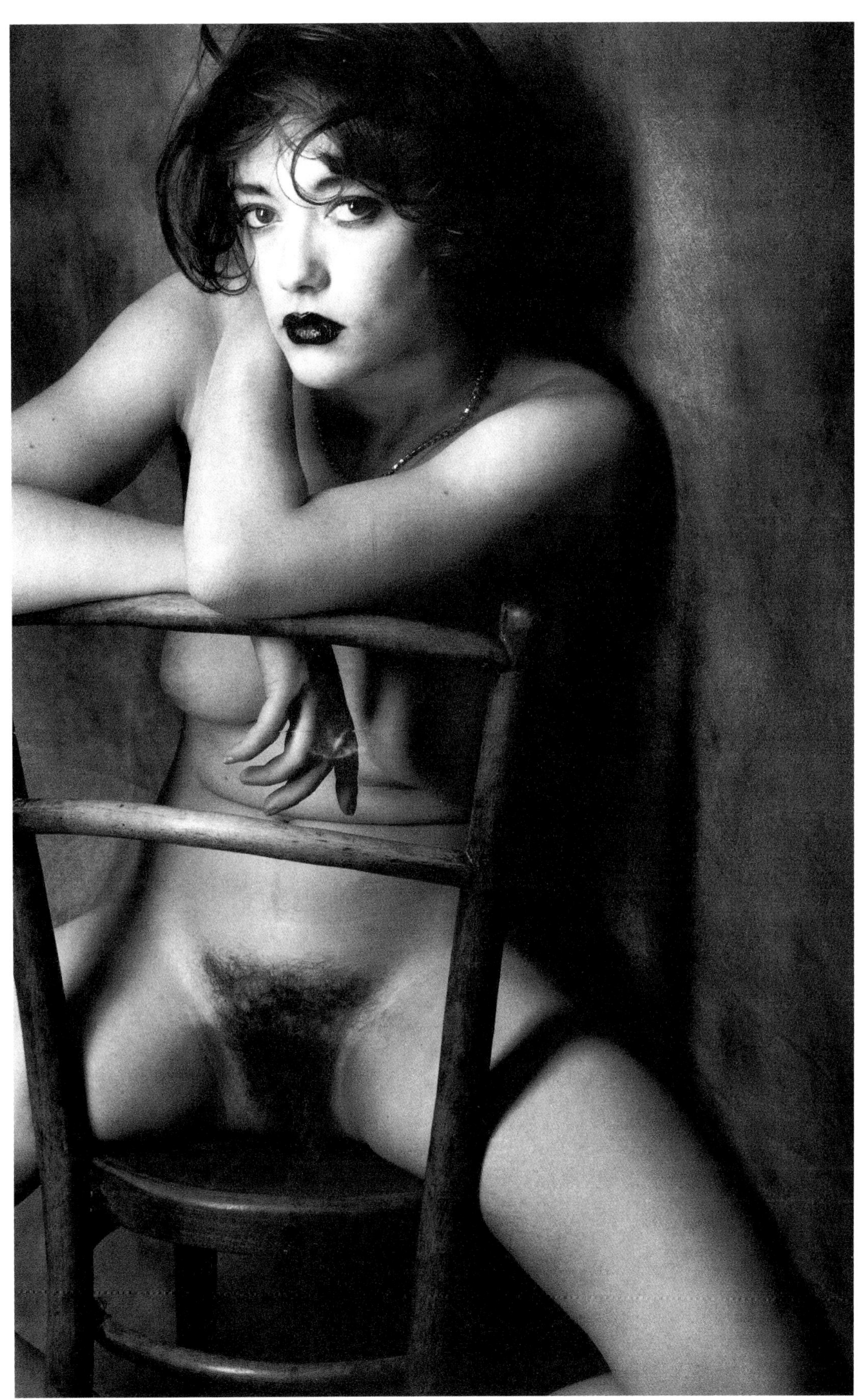

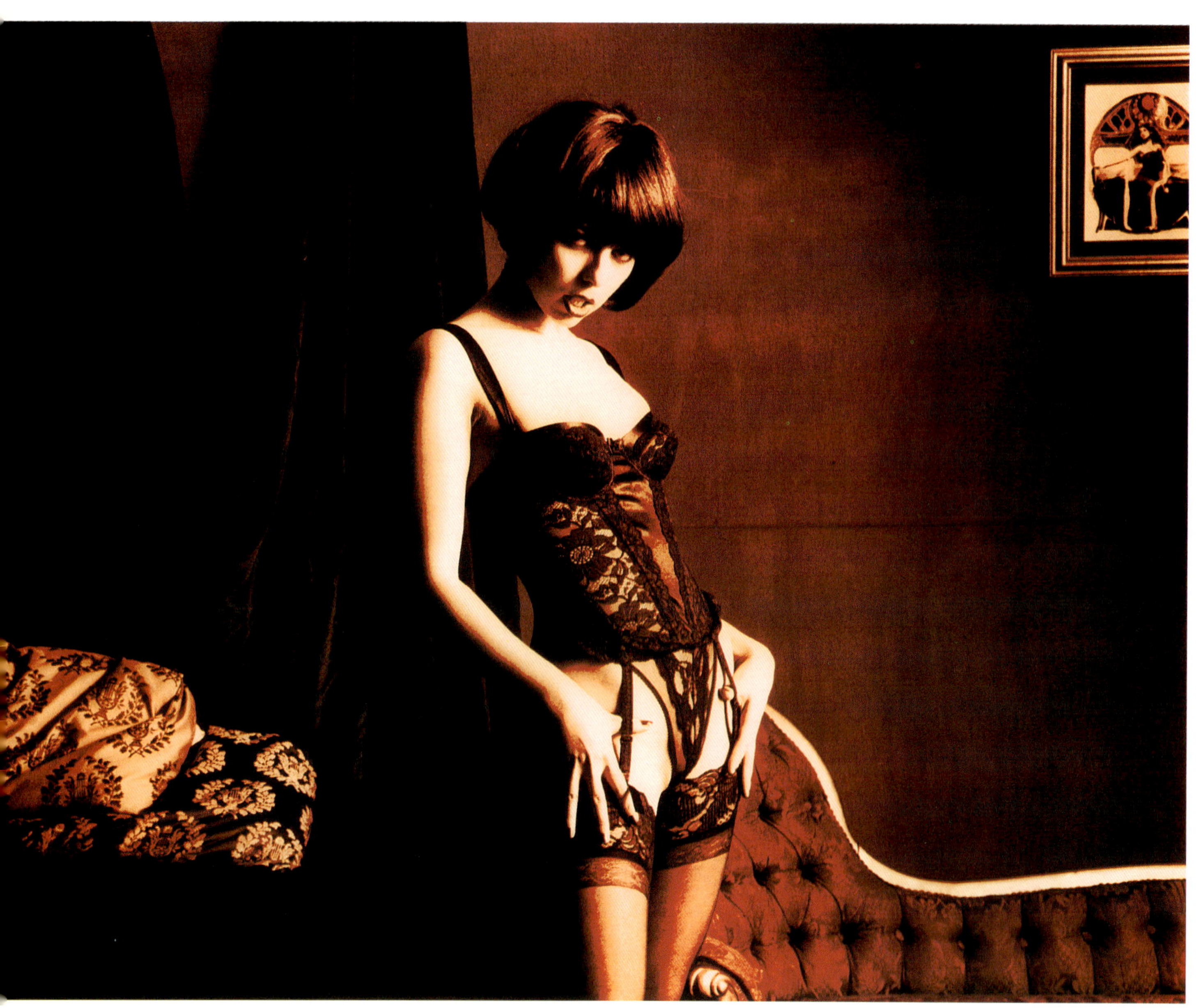

 | **NIC MARCHANT** 1997

(right) **IAIN McKELL** 1997

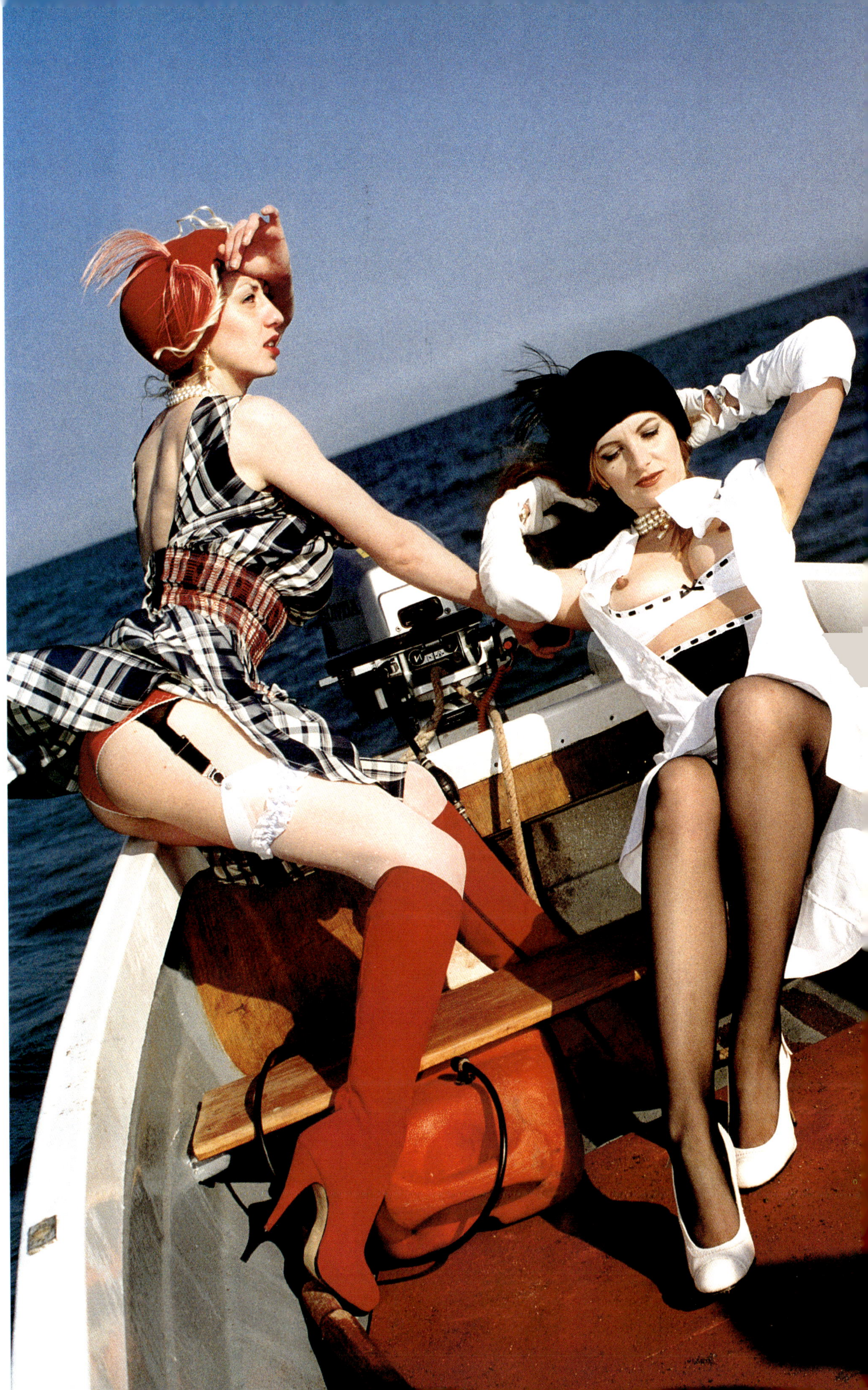

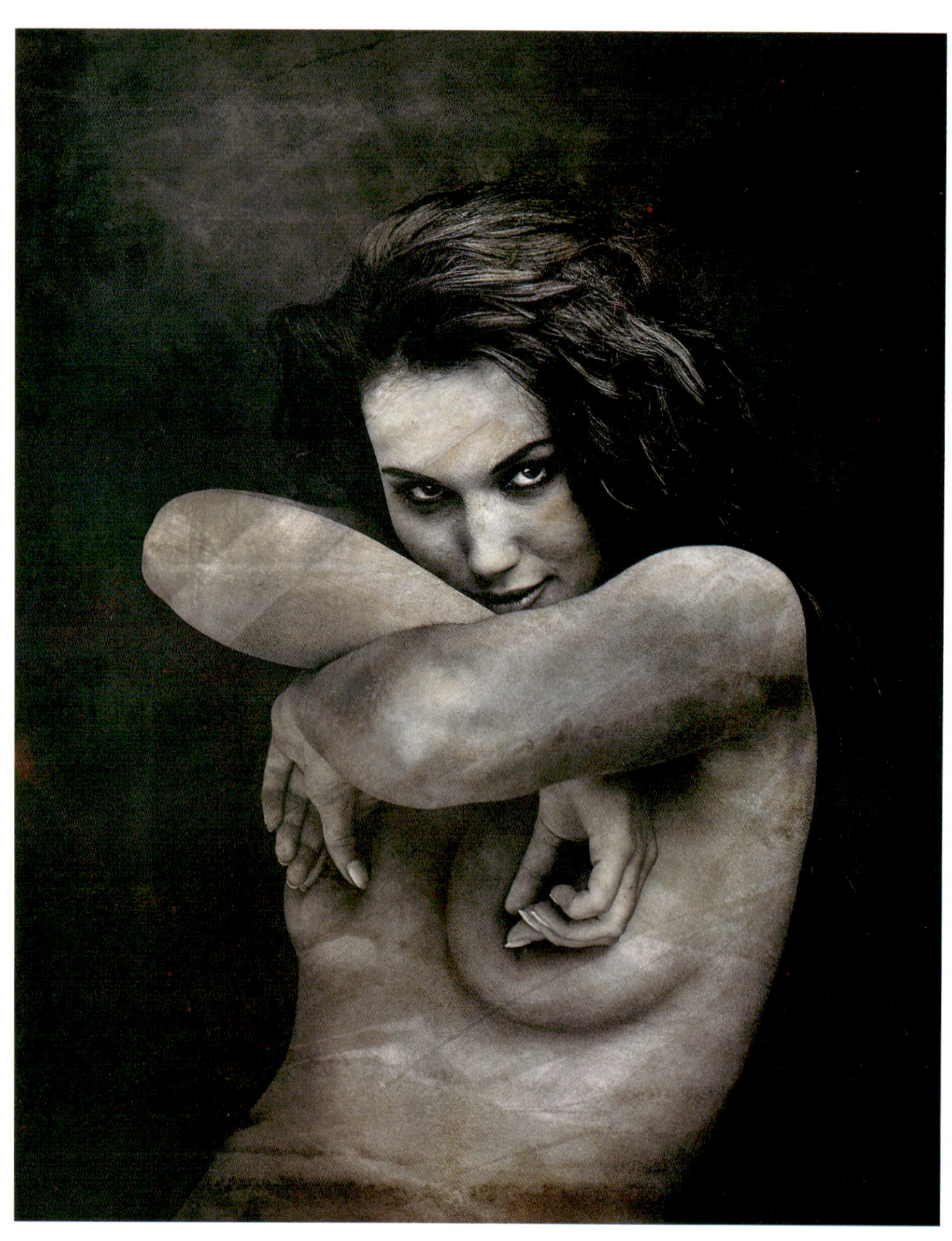

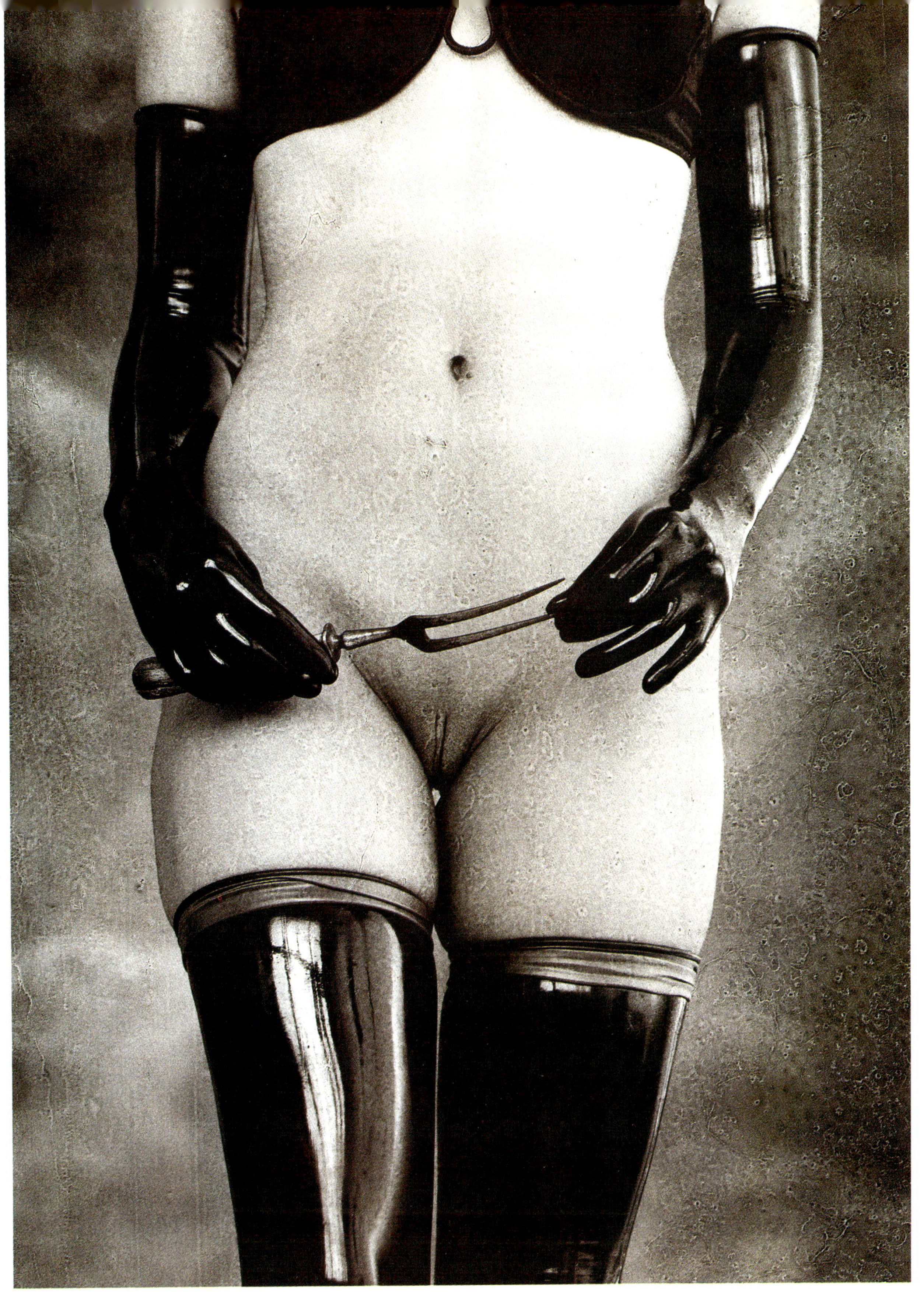

BOB CARLOS CLARKE 1992

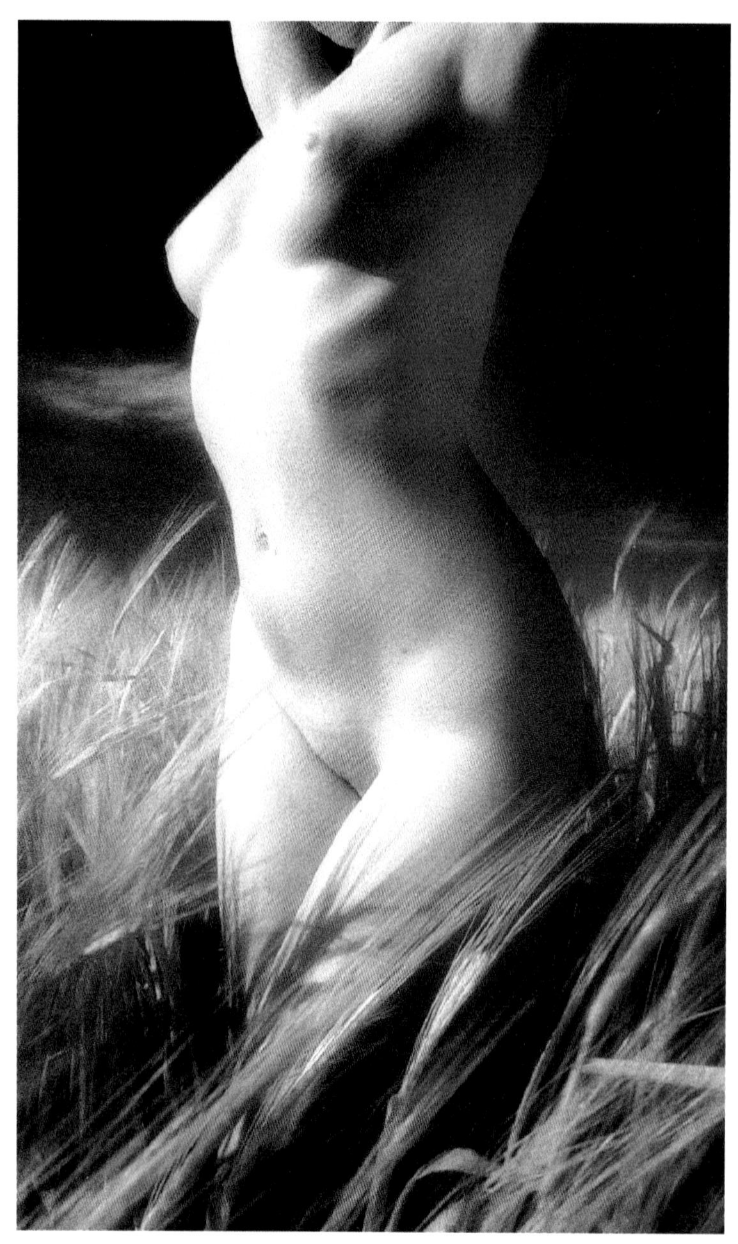

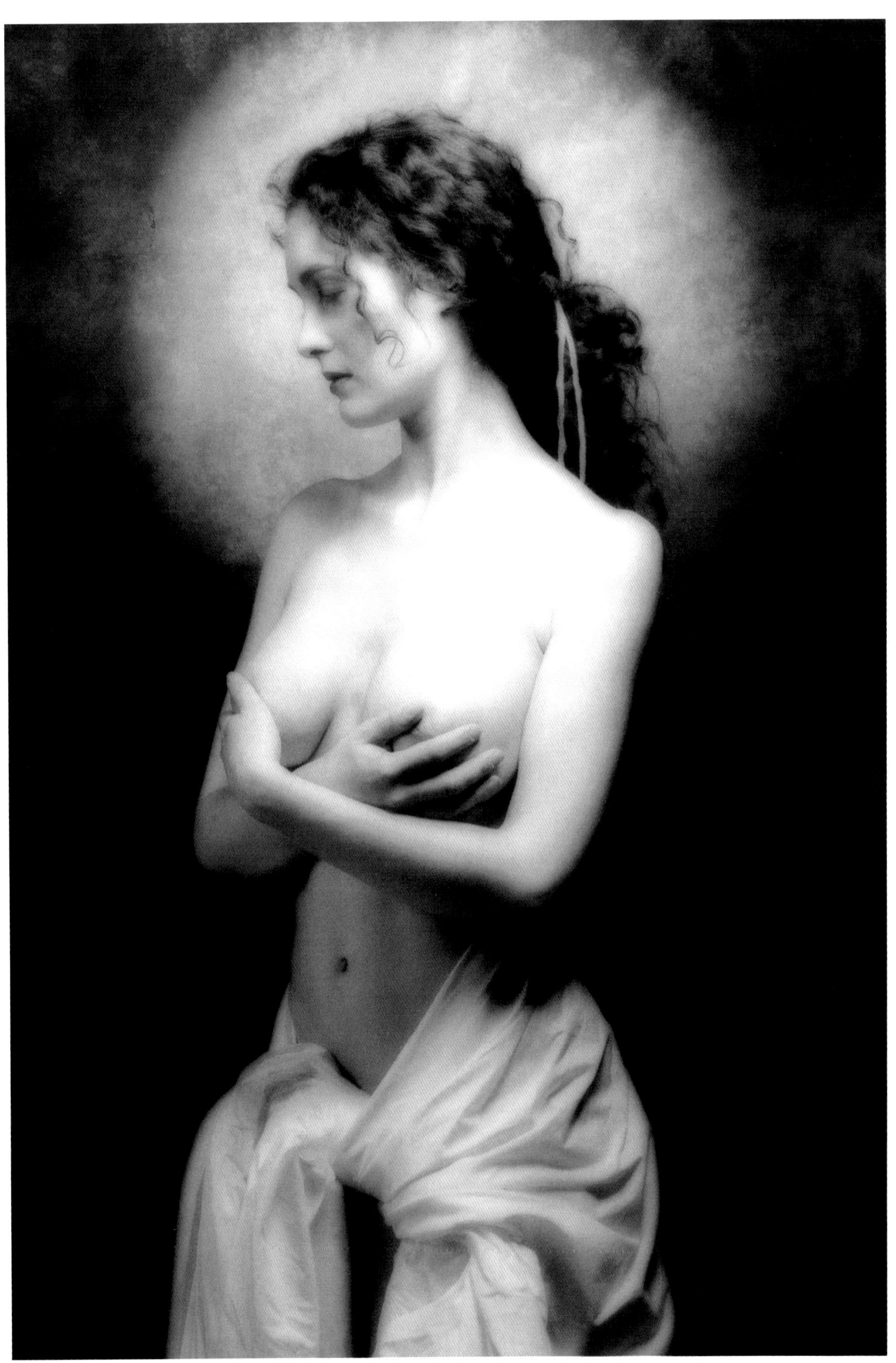

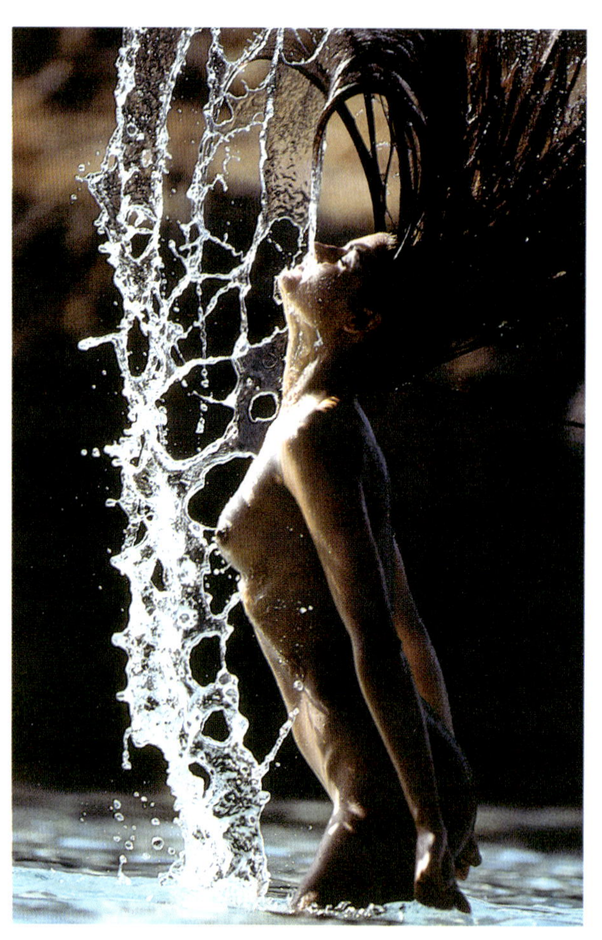

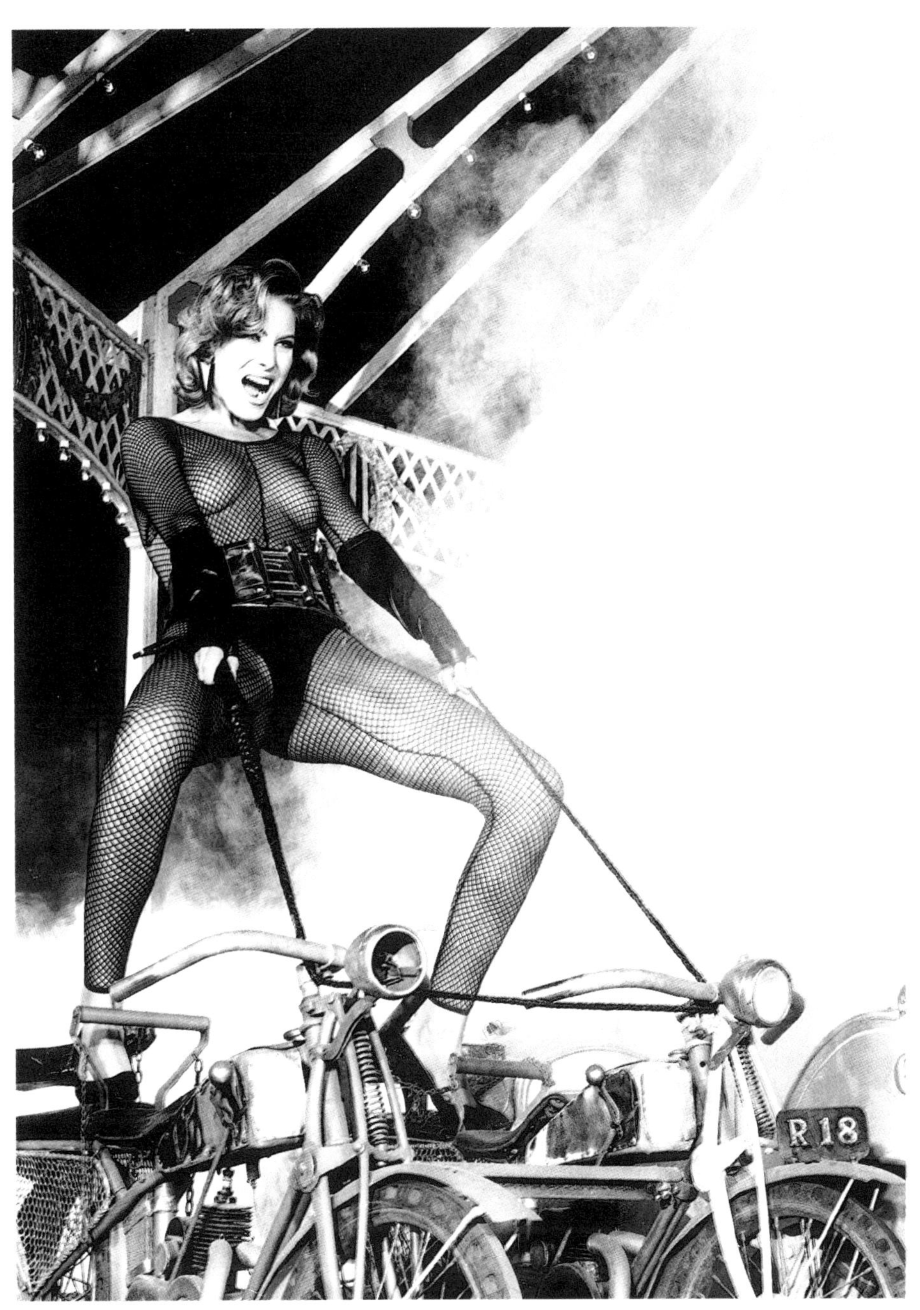
R 18

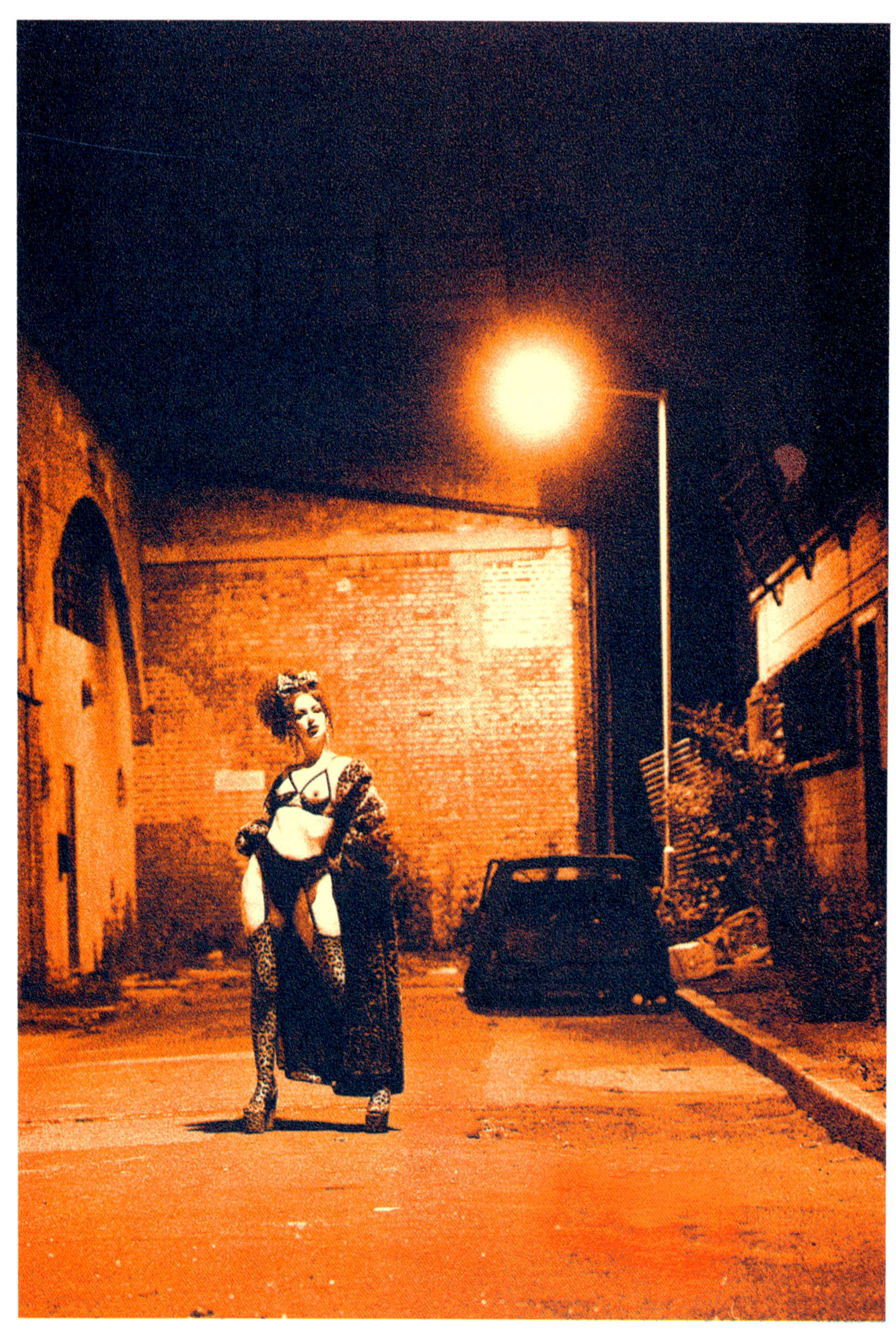

 | **TREVOR WATSON** 1997

(right) **IAIN McKELL** 1996

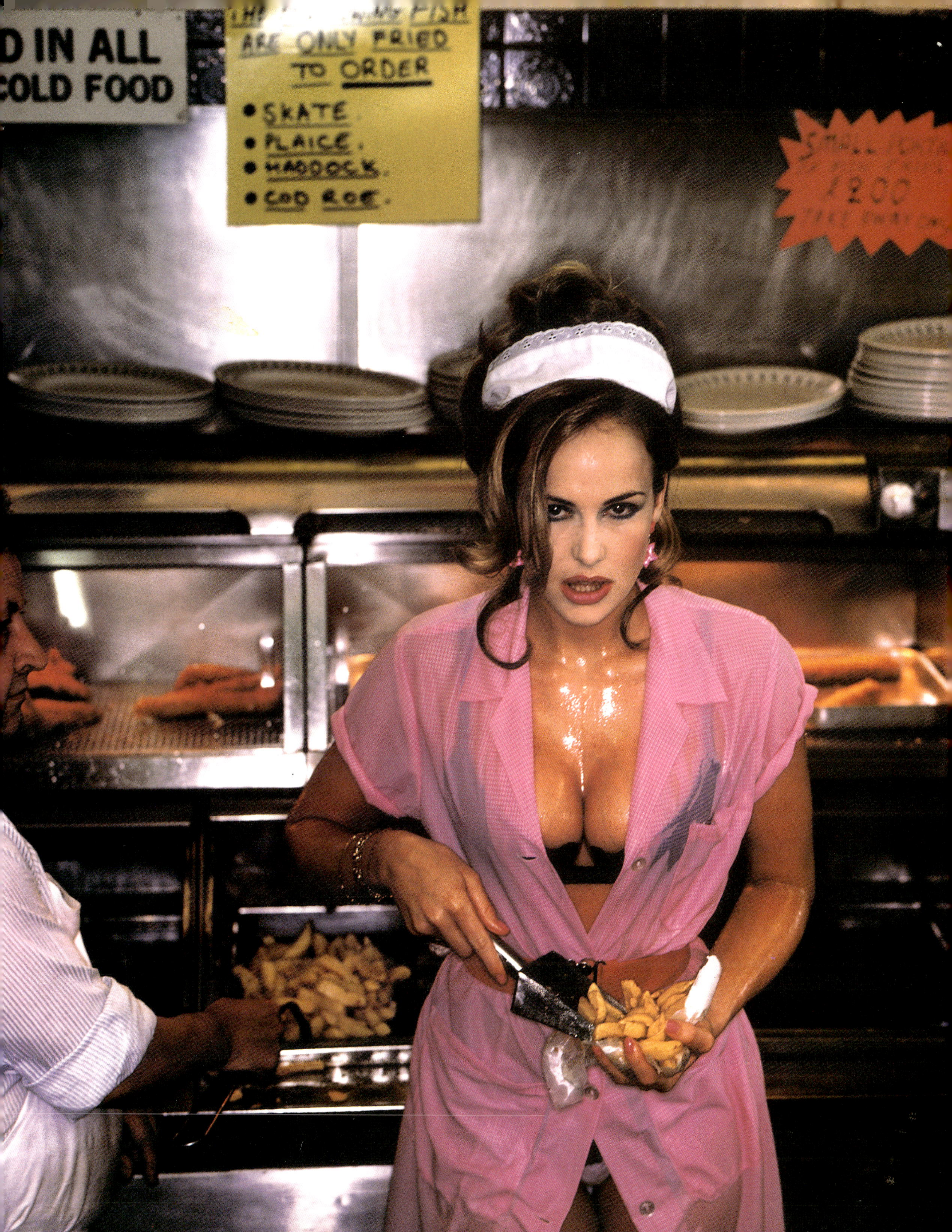
D IN ALL
COLD FOOD
ARE ONLY FRIED
TO ORDER
SKATE
PLAICE
HADDOCK
COD ROE

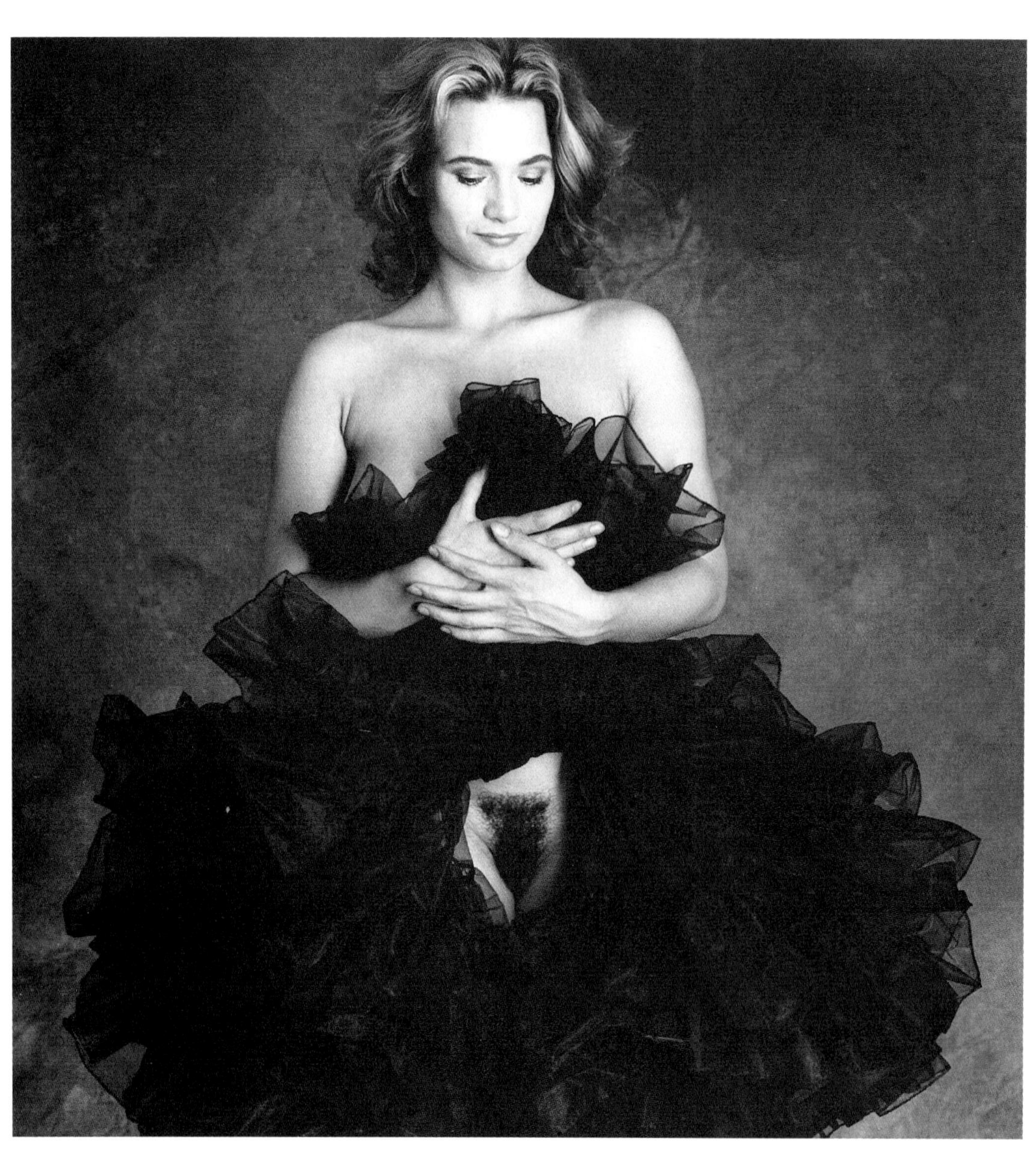

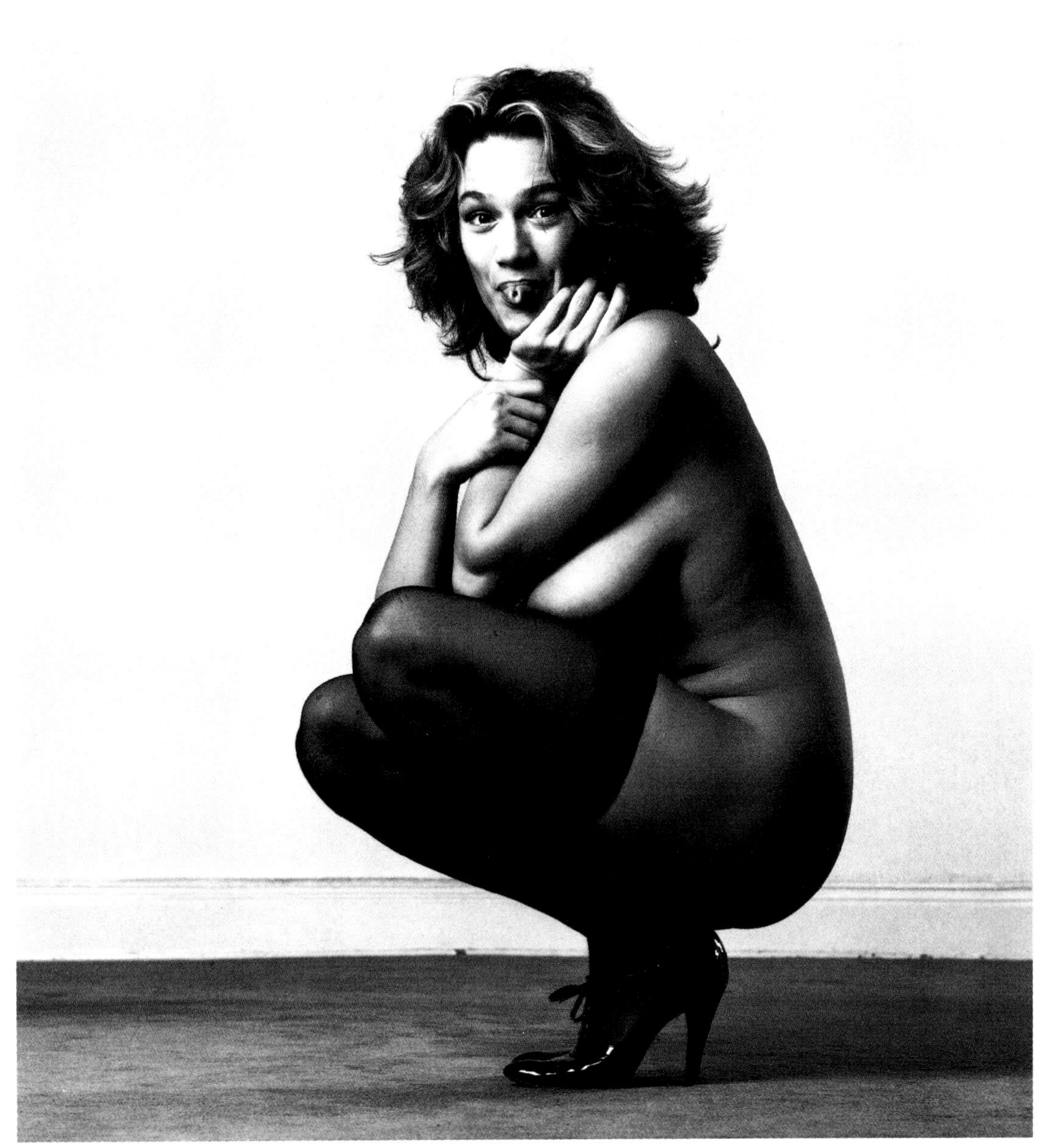

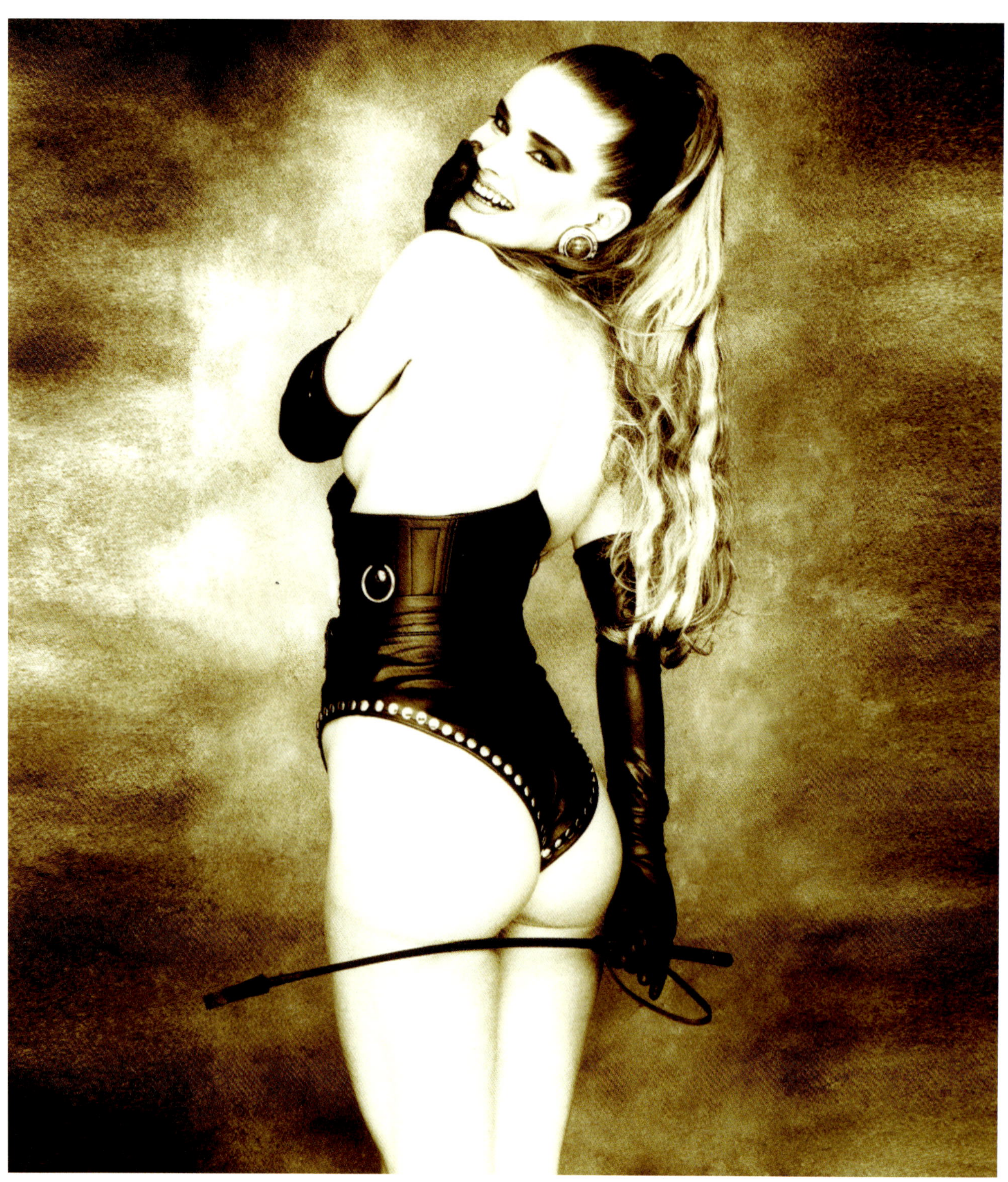

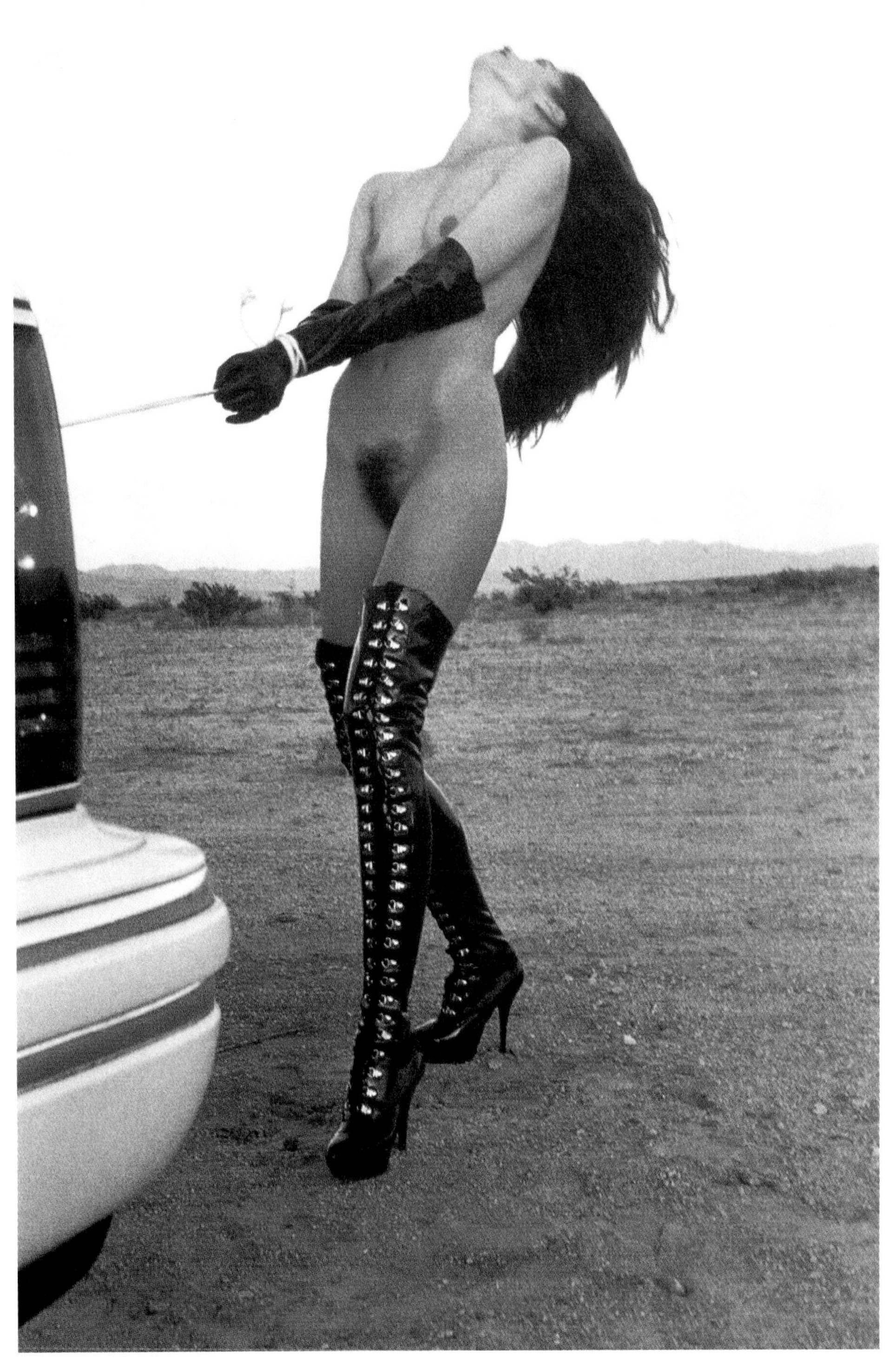

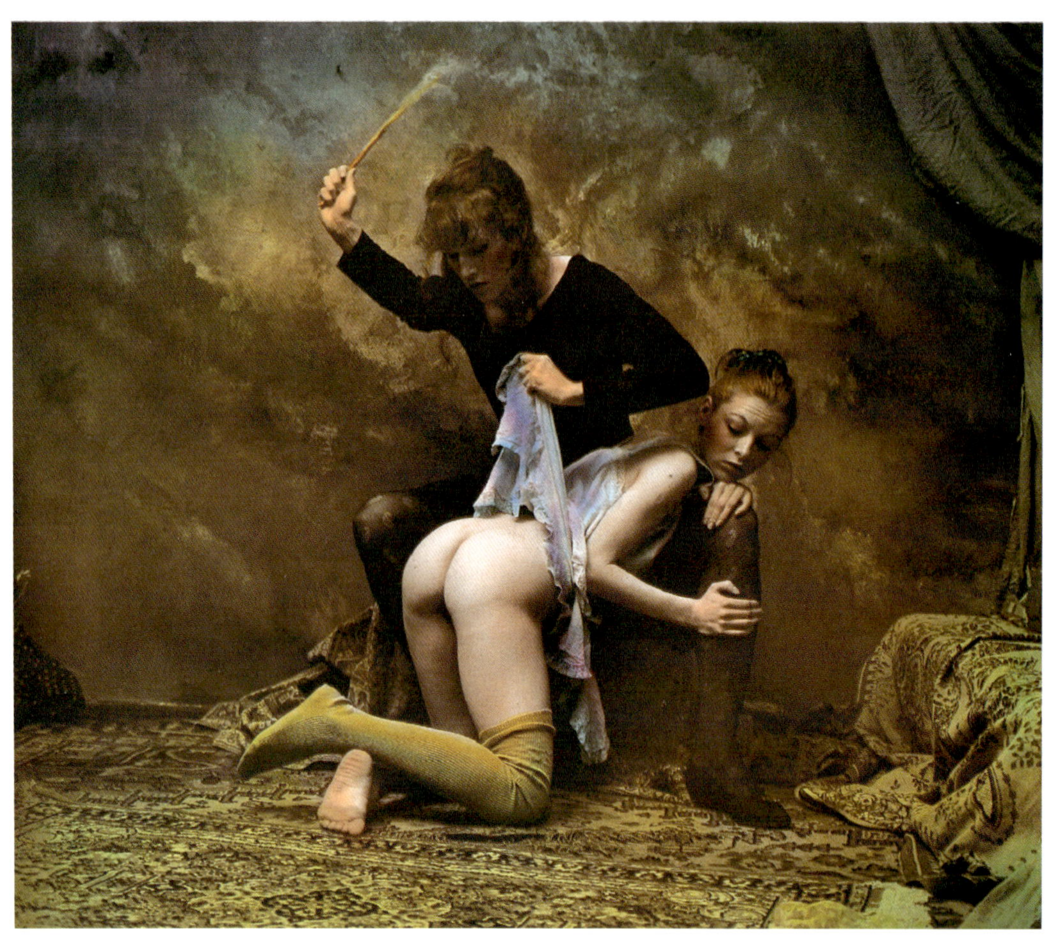

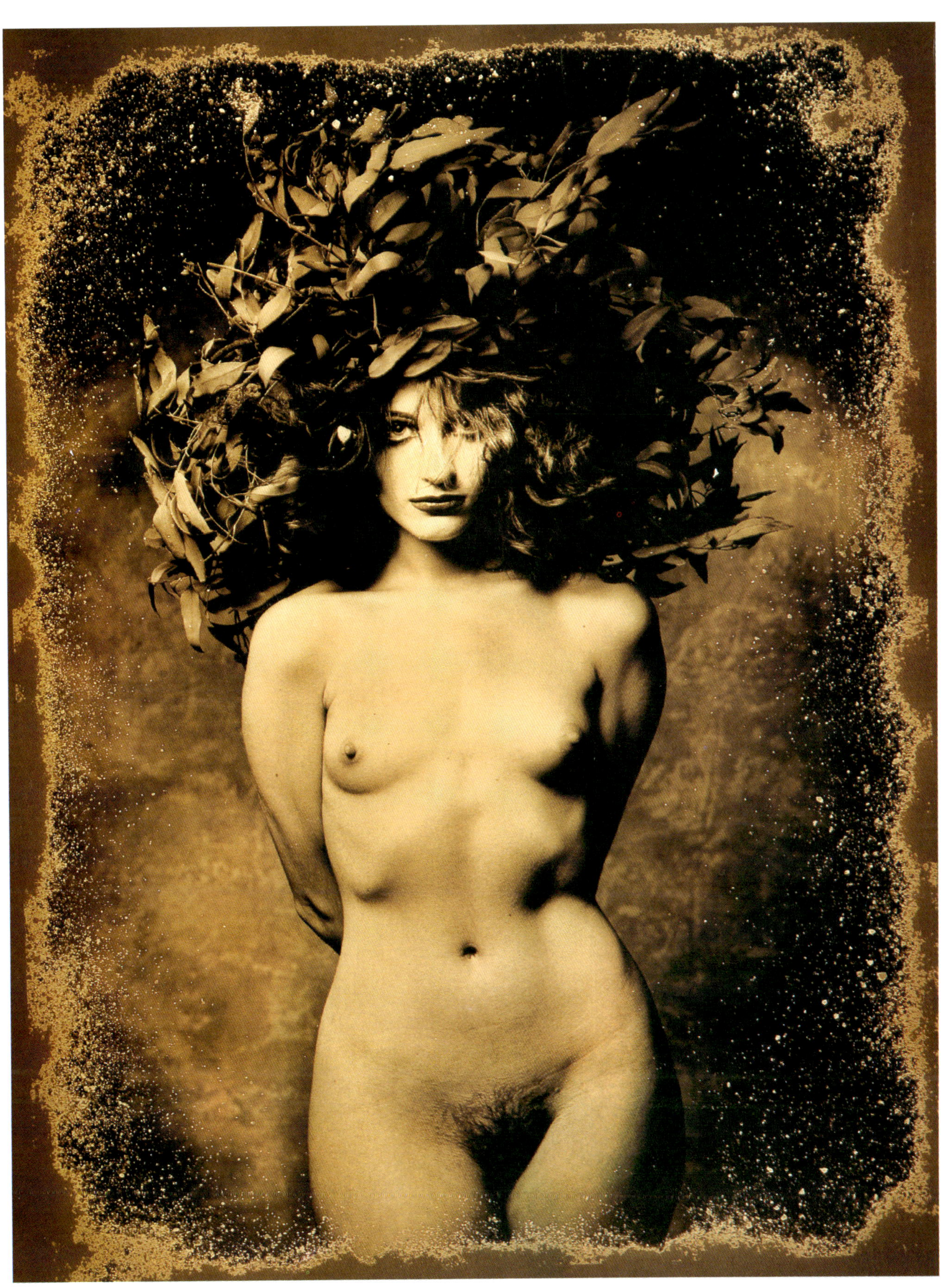

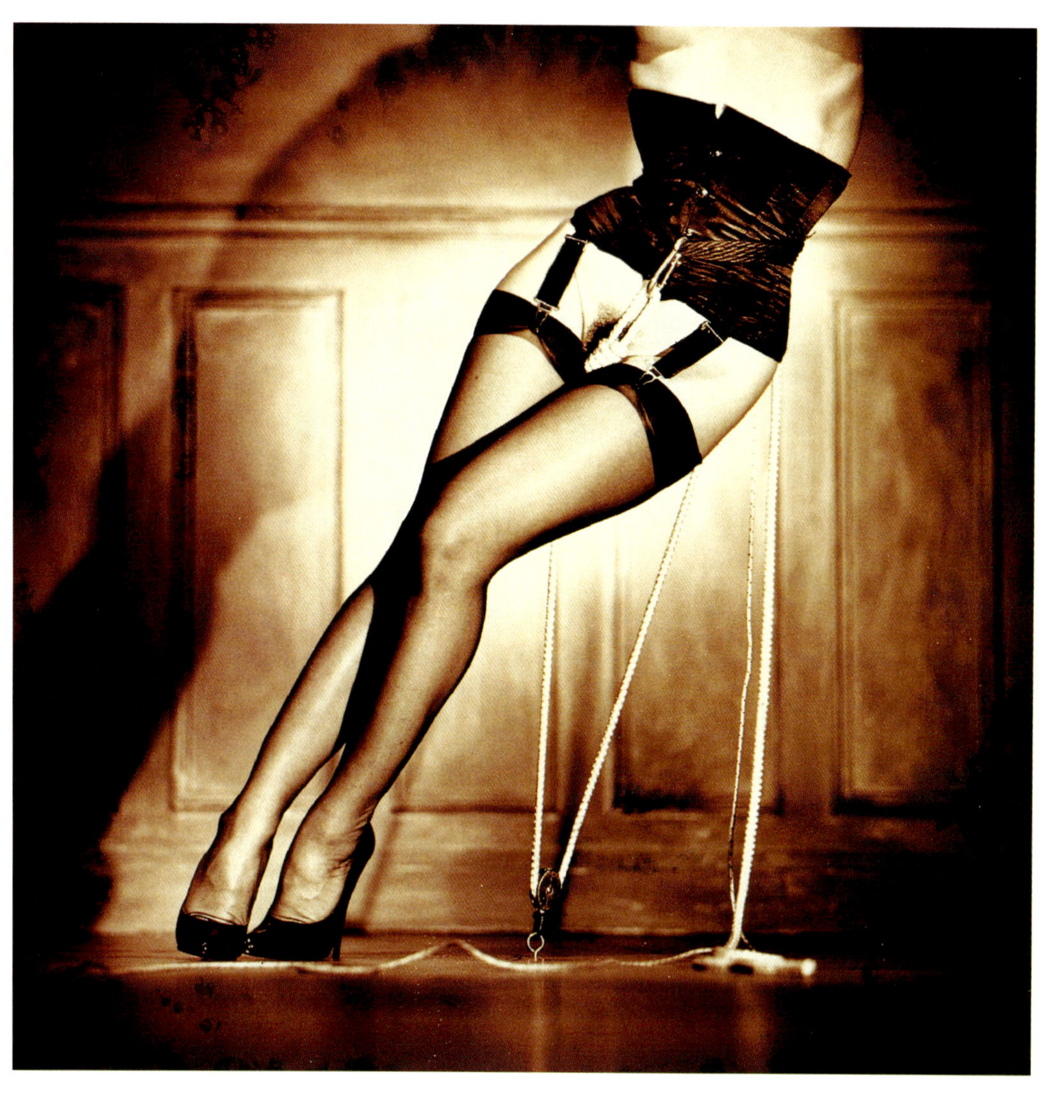

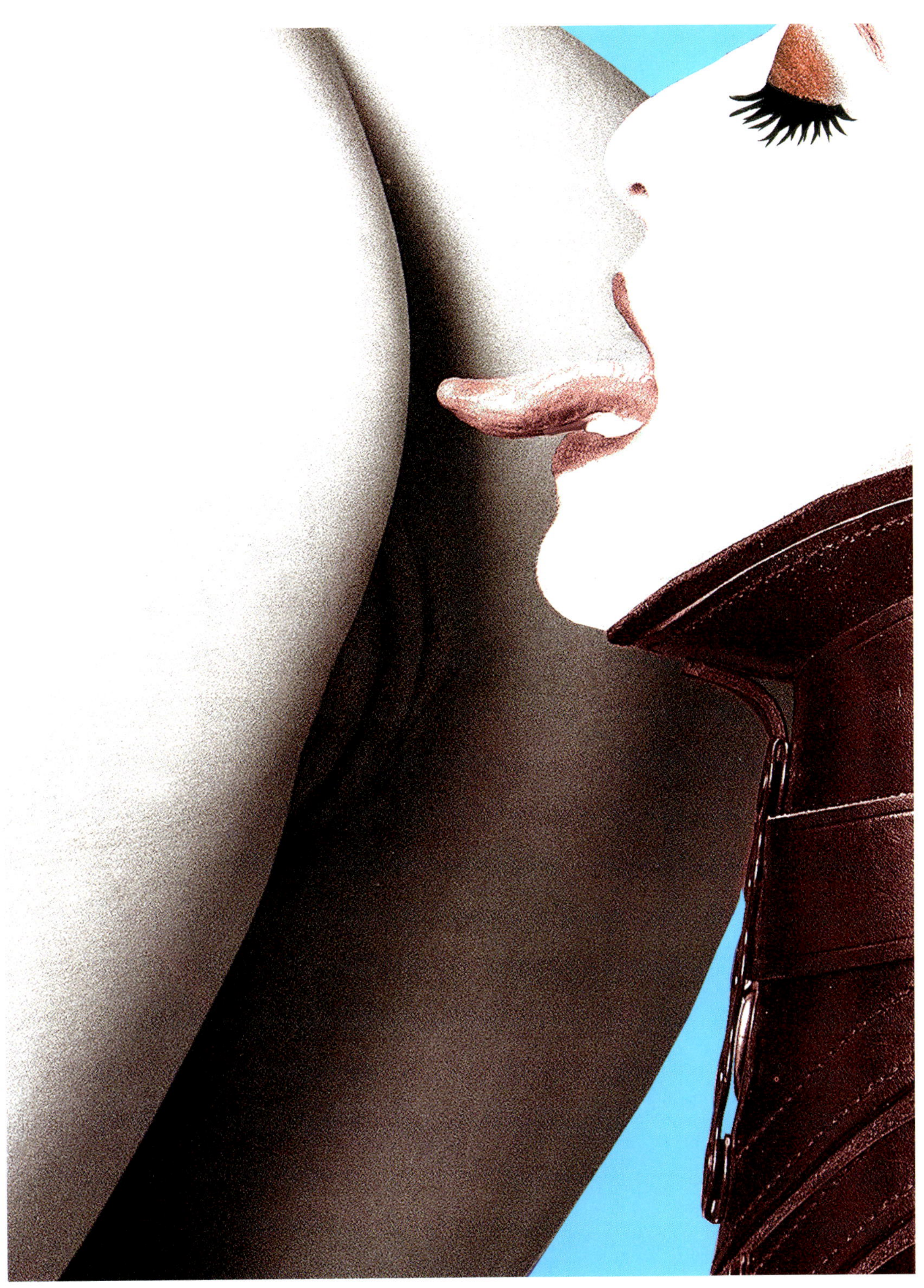

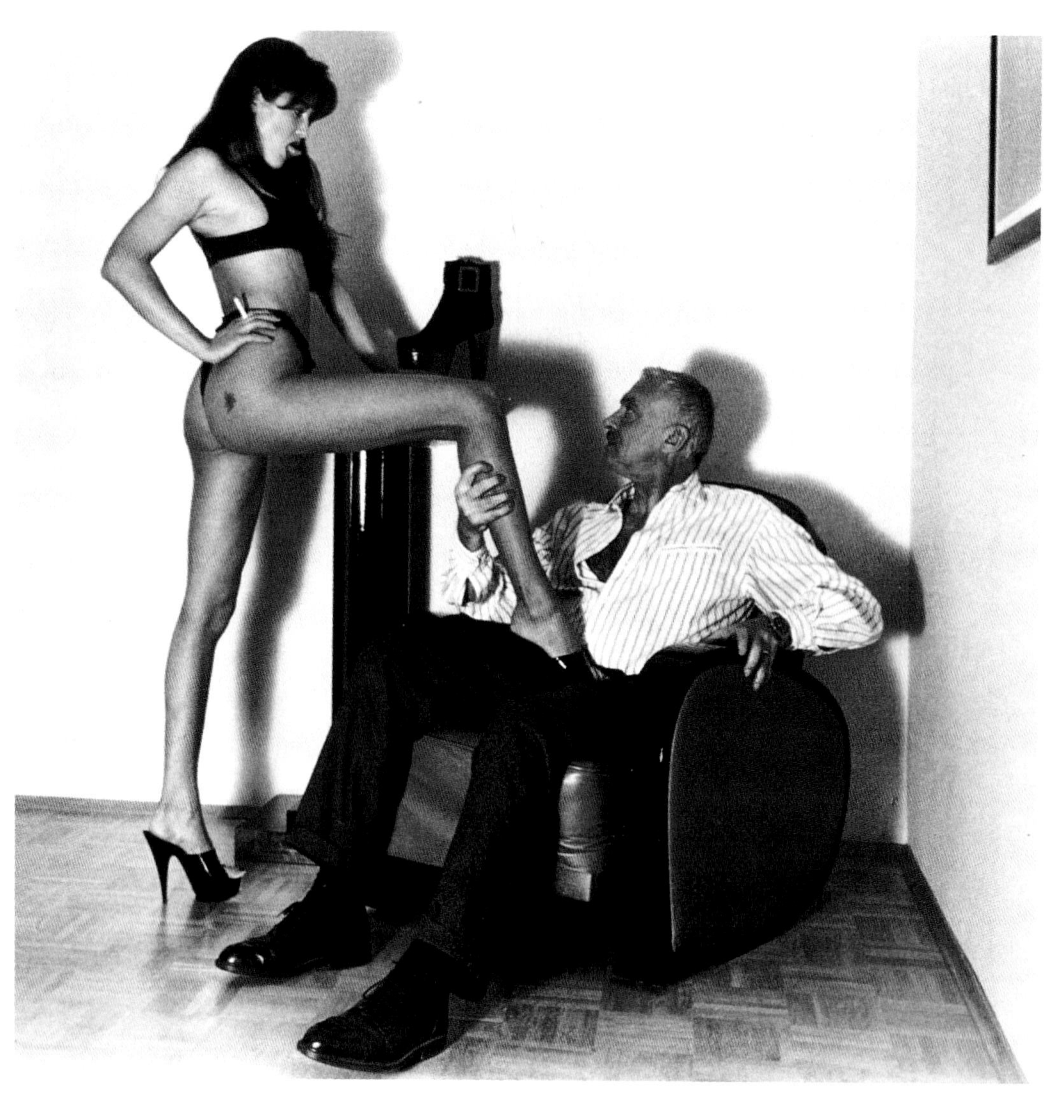

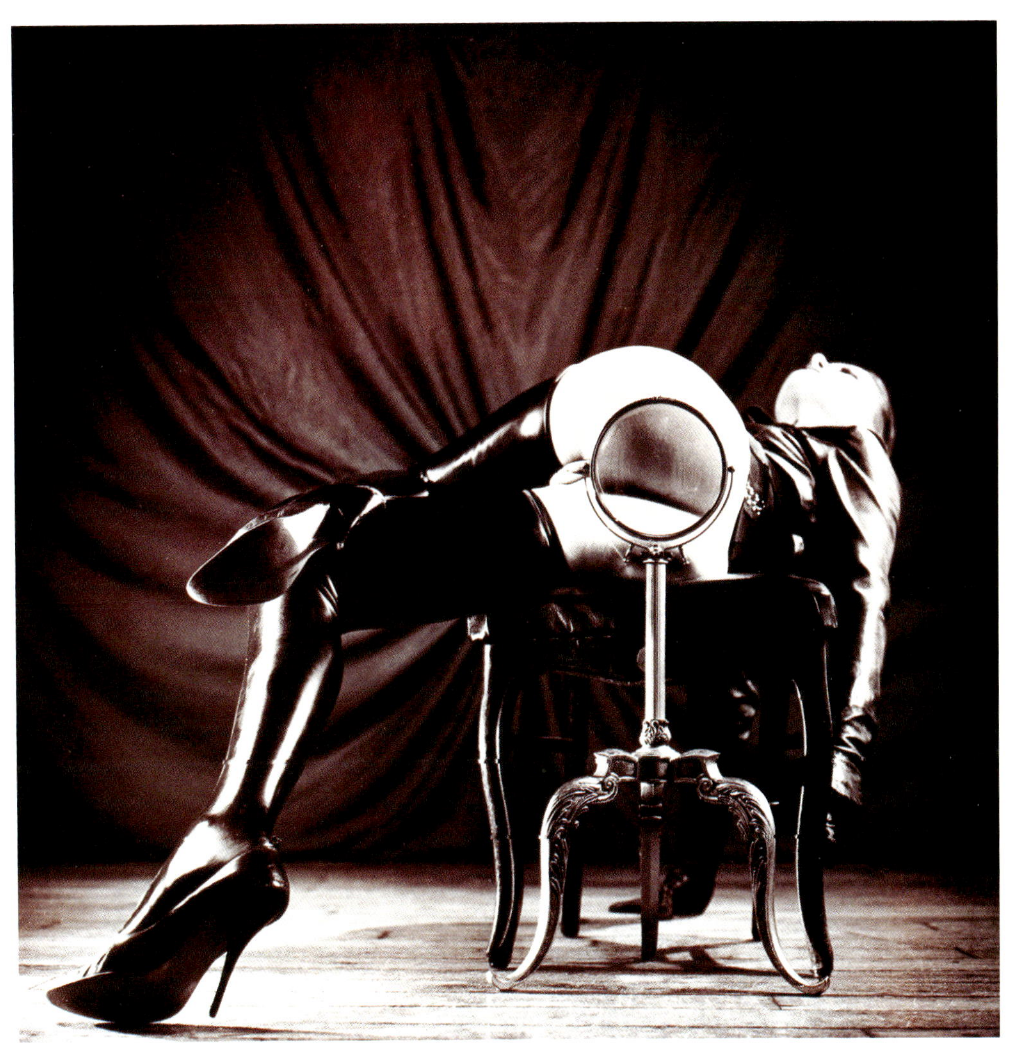

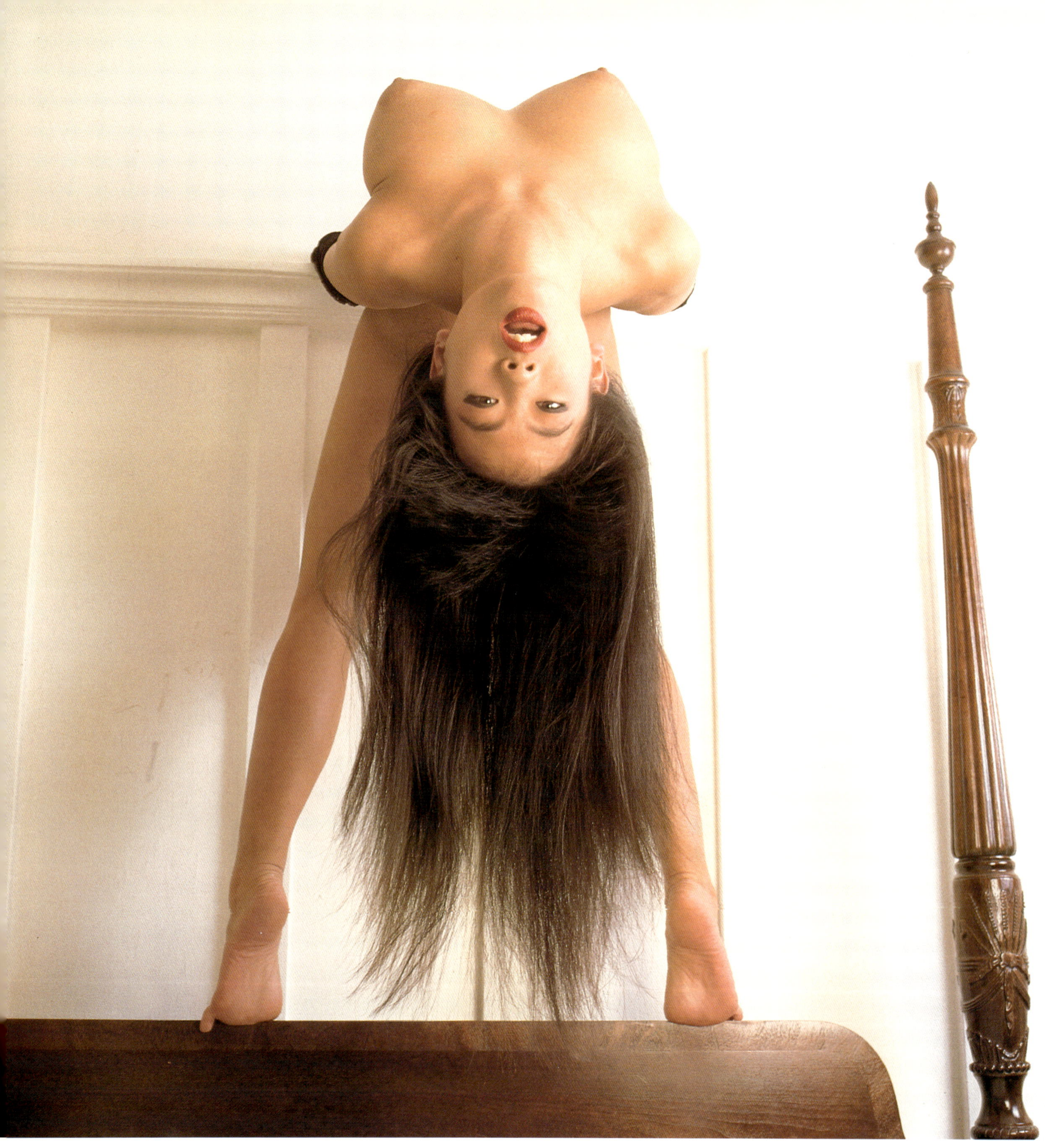

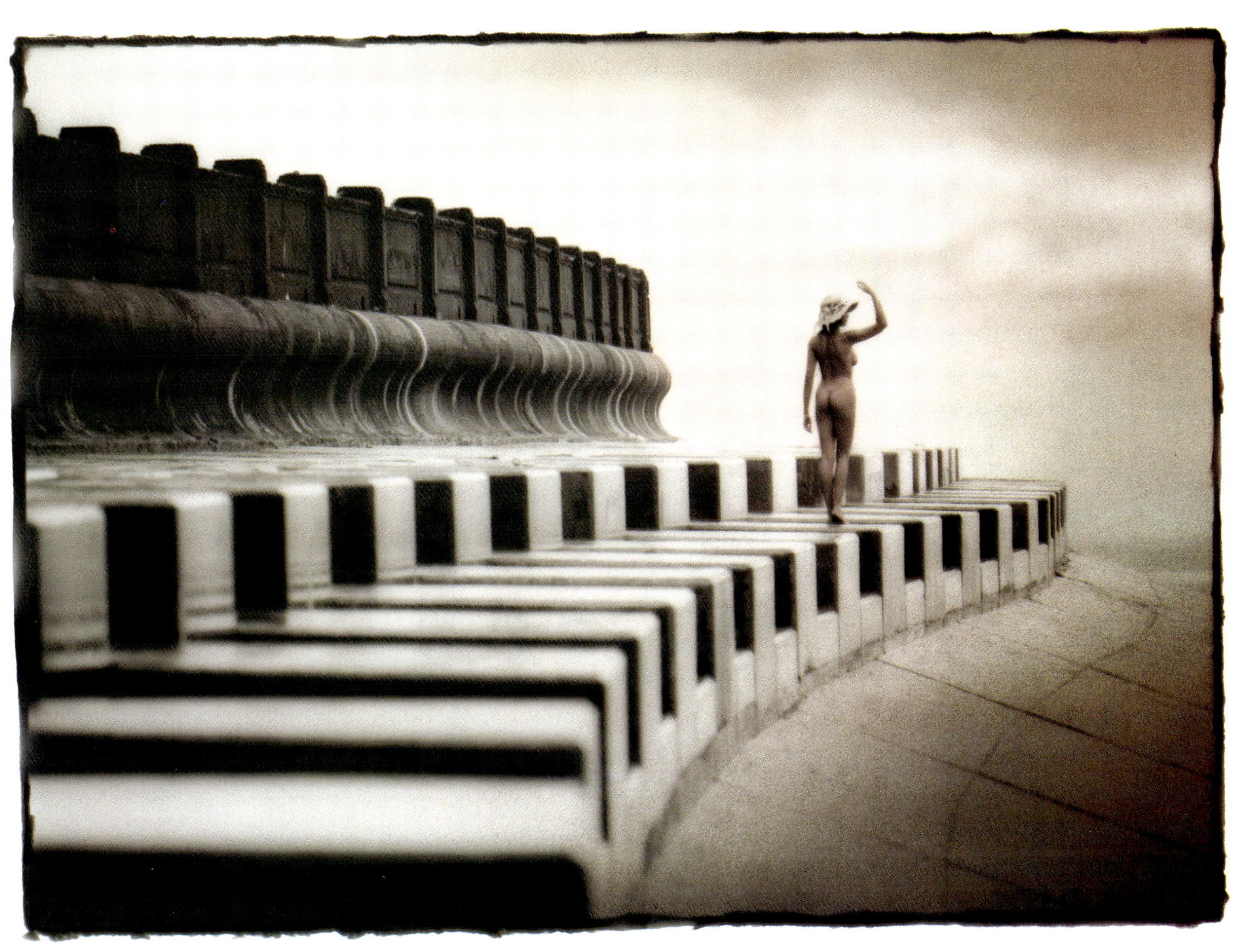

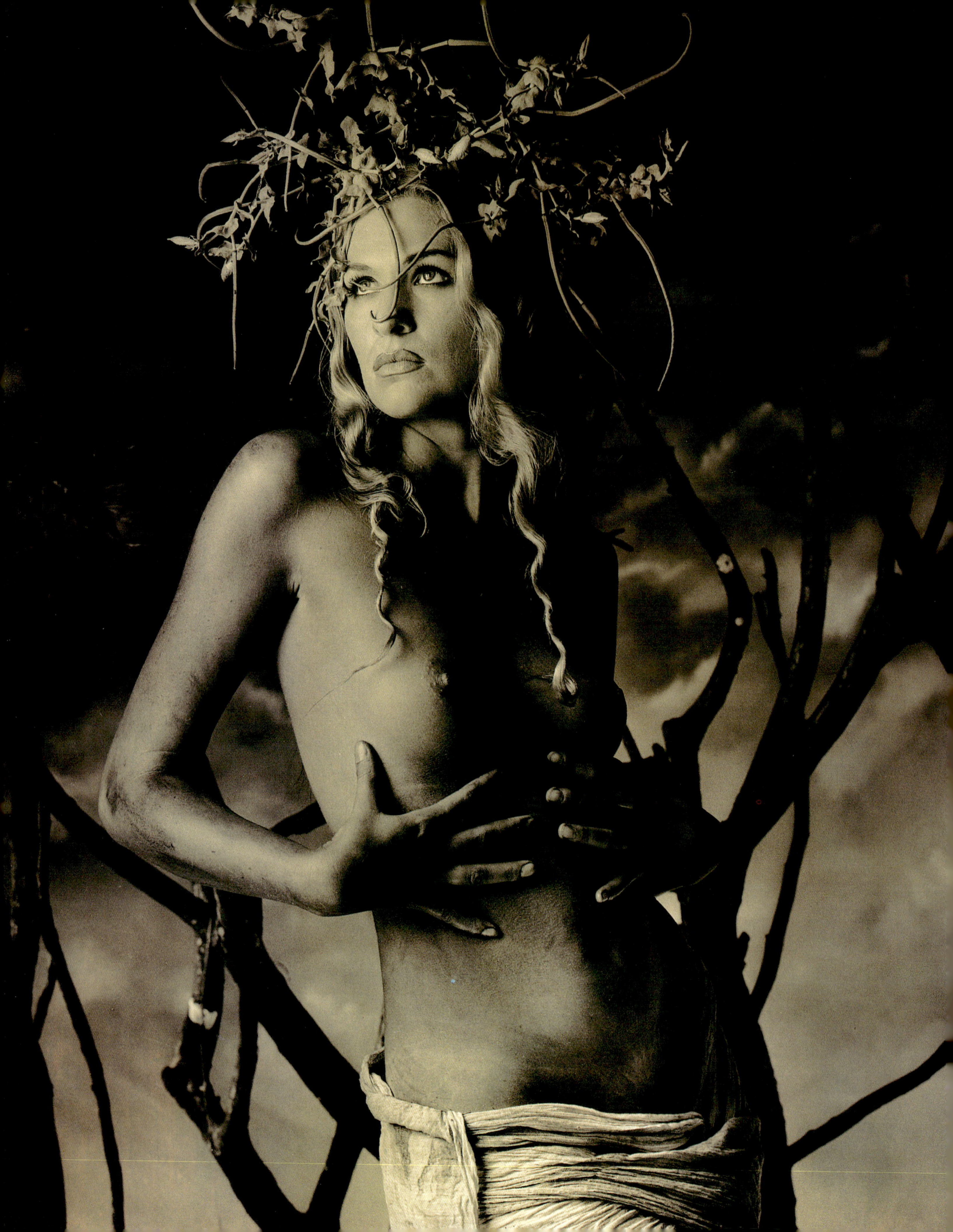

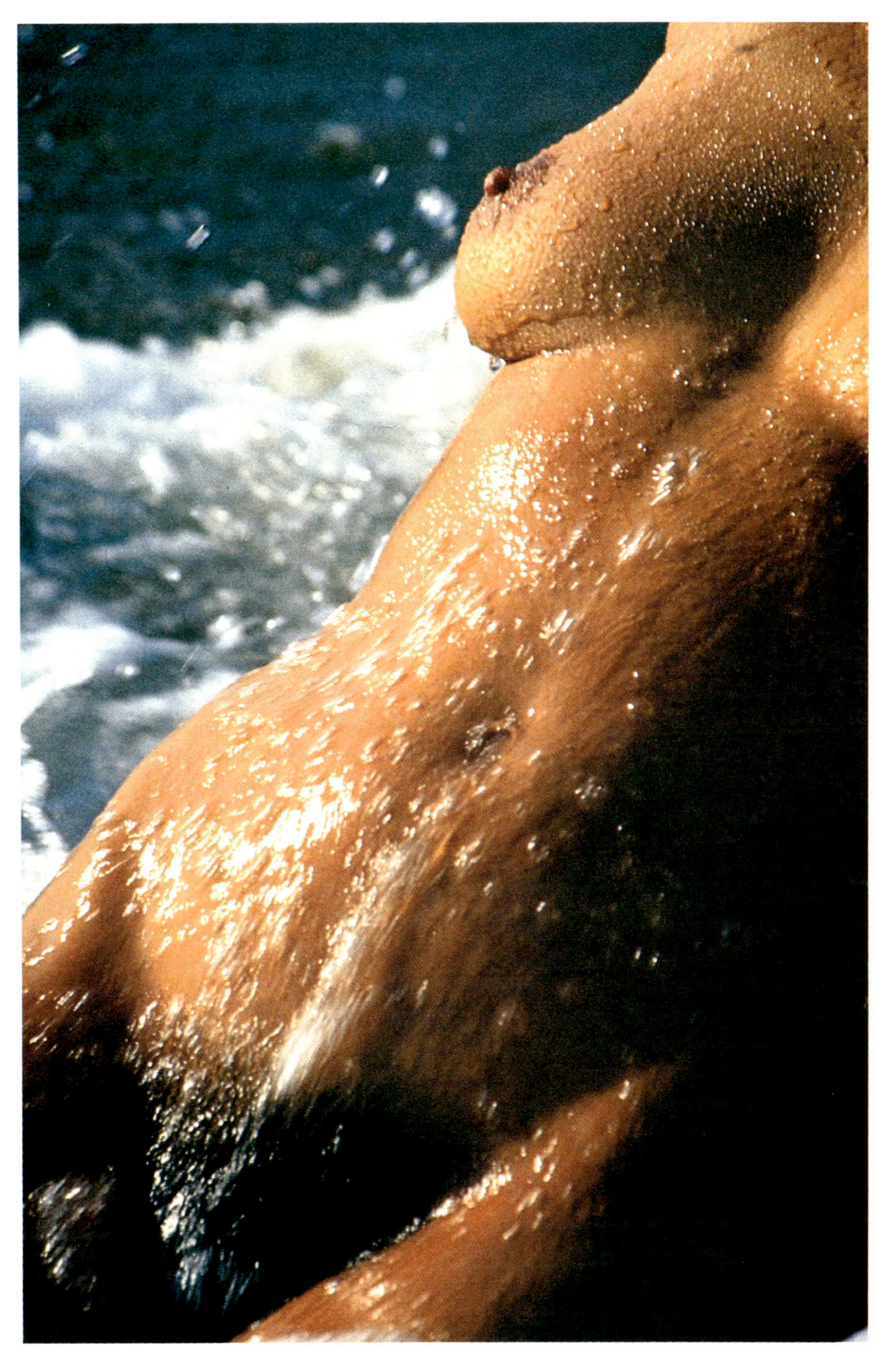

(left) **DAVID PENPRASE** 1997

LUCIEN CLERGUE 1990

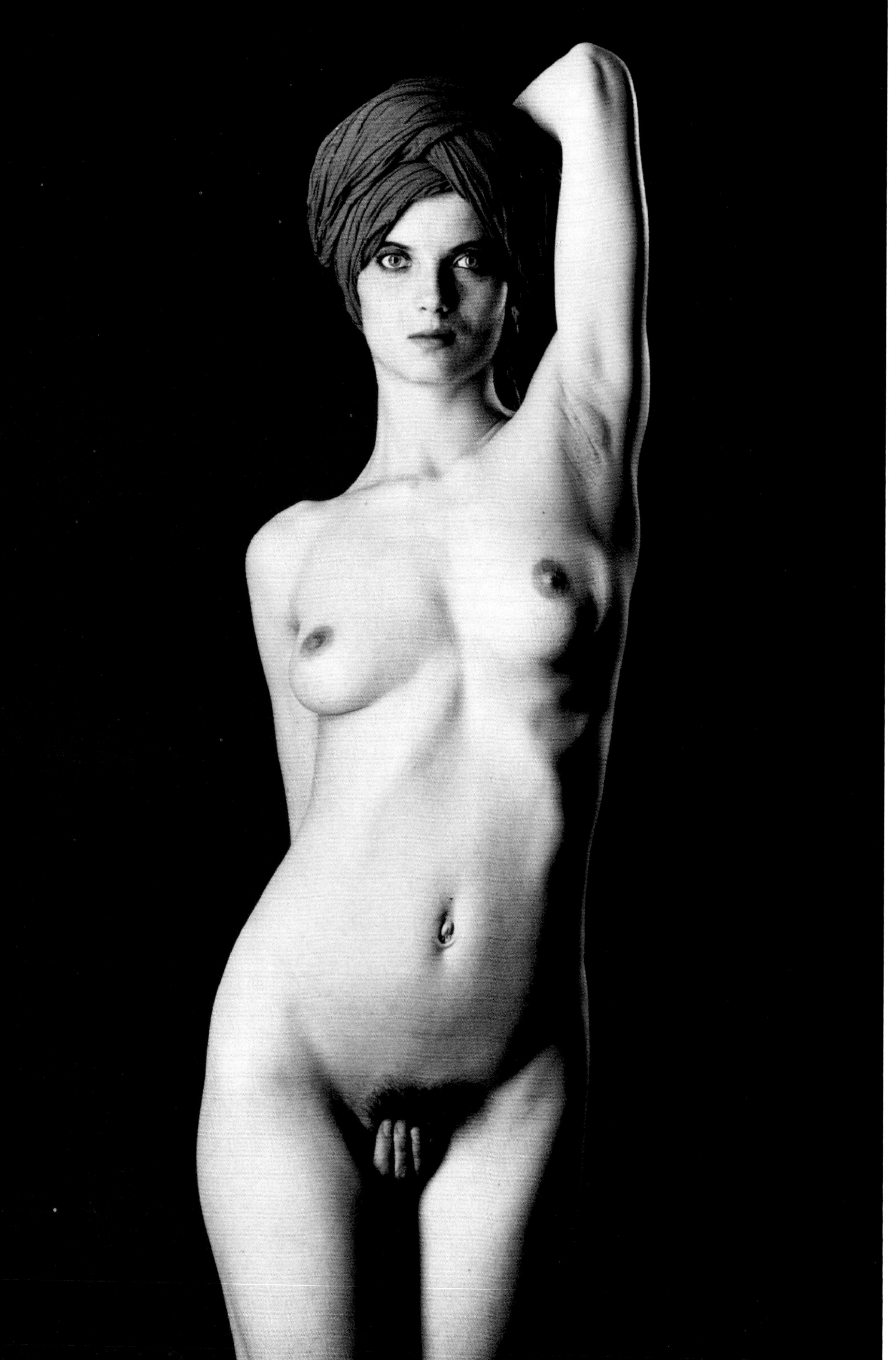

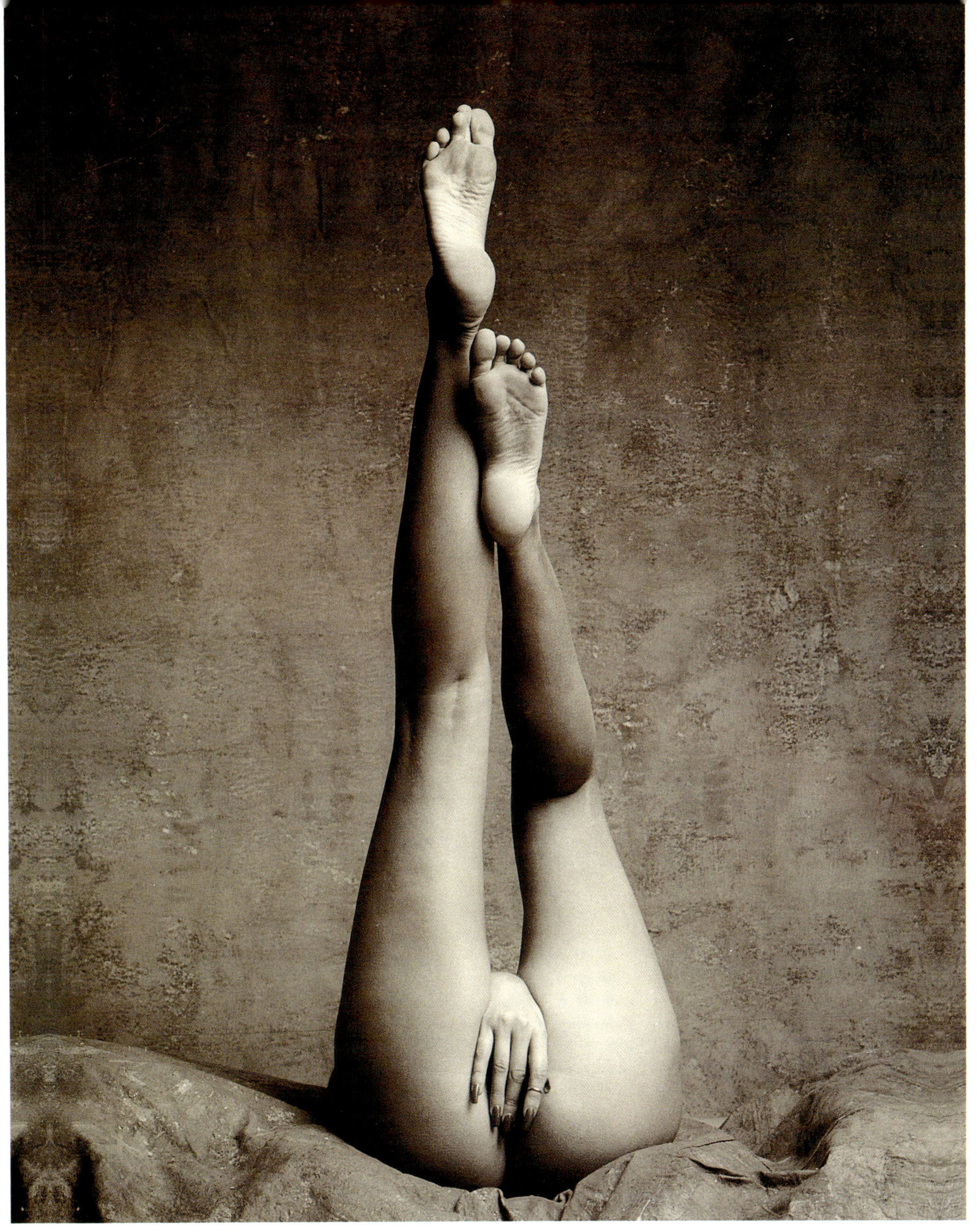

(left) **THOMAS KARSTEN** 1991

CRAIG MOREY 1990

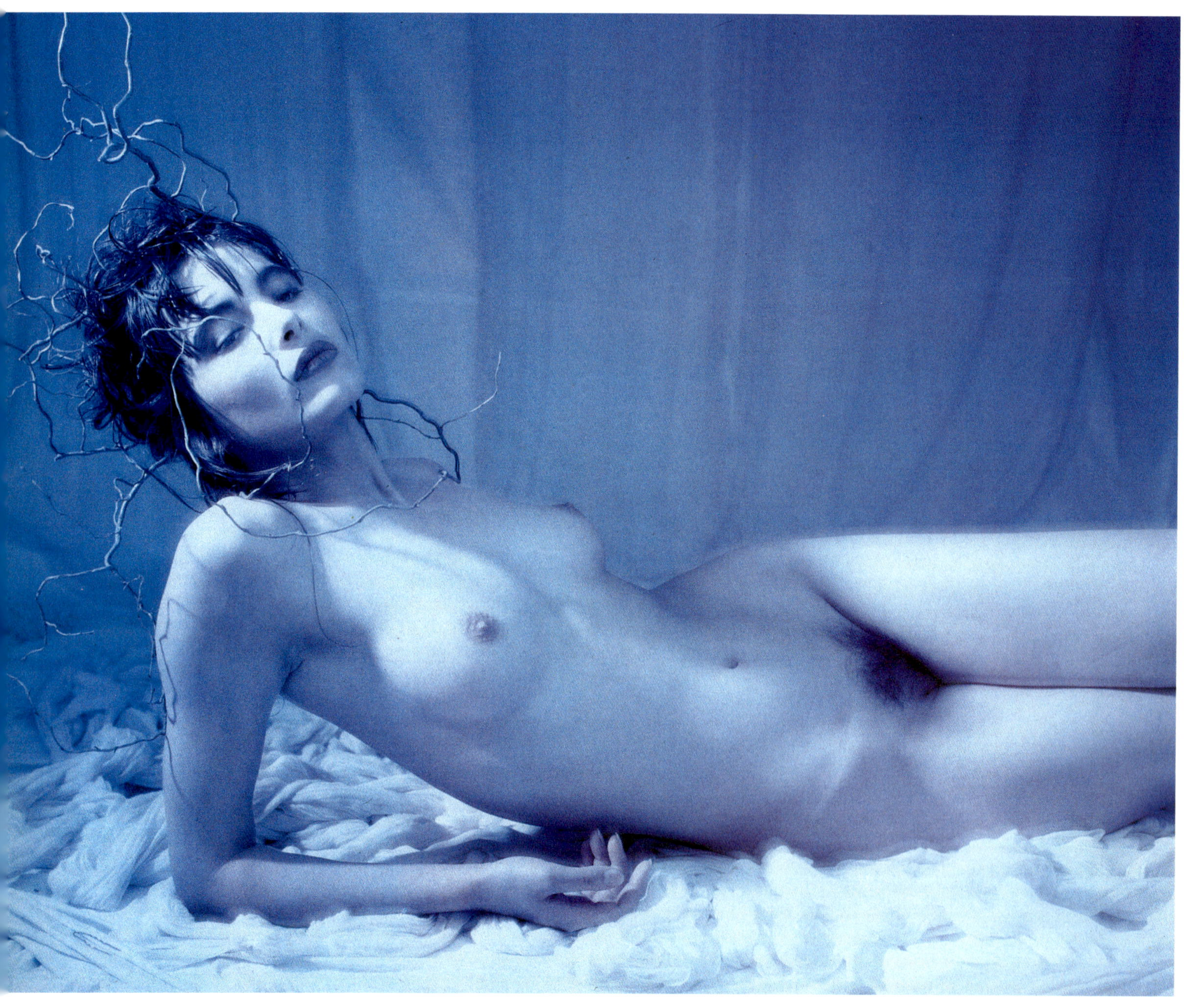

 MONIKA ROBL 1990

(right) IAIN McKELL 1996

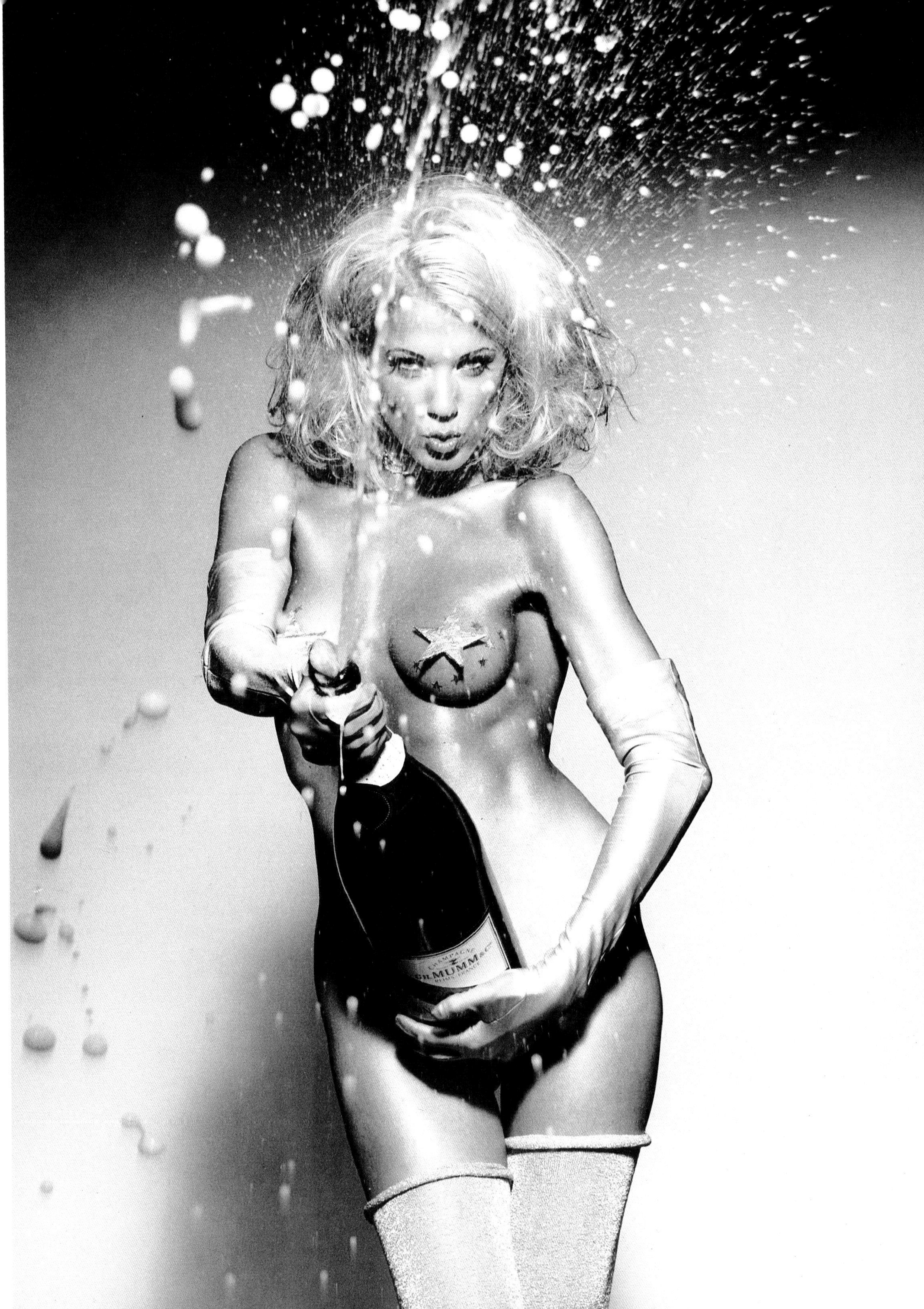
MUMM

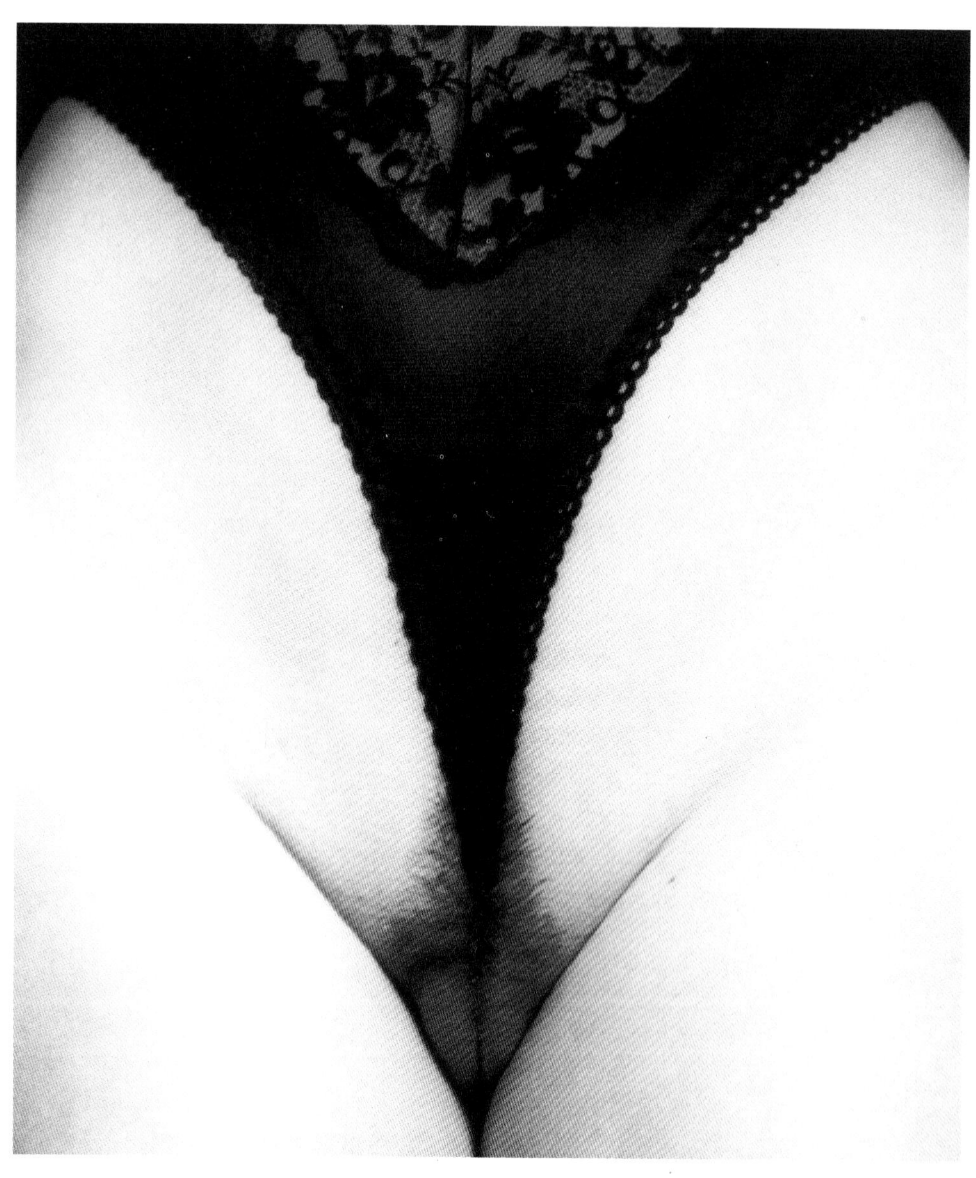

(right) **JOHN DIETRICH** 1990

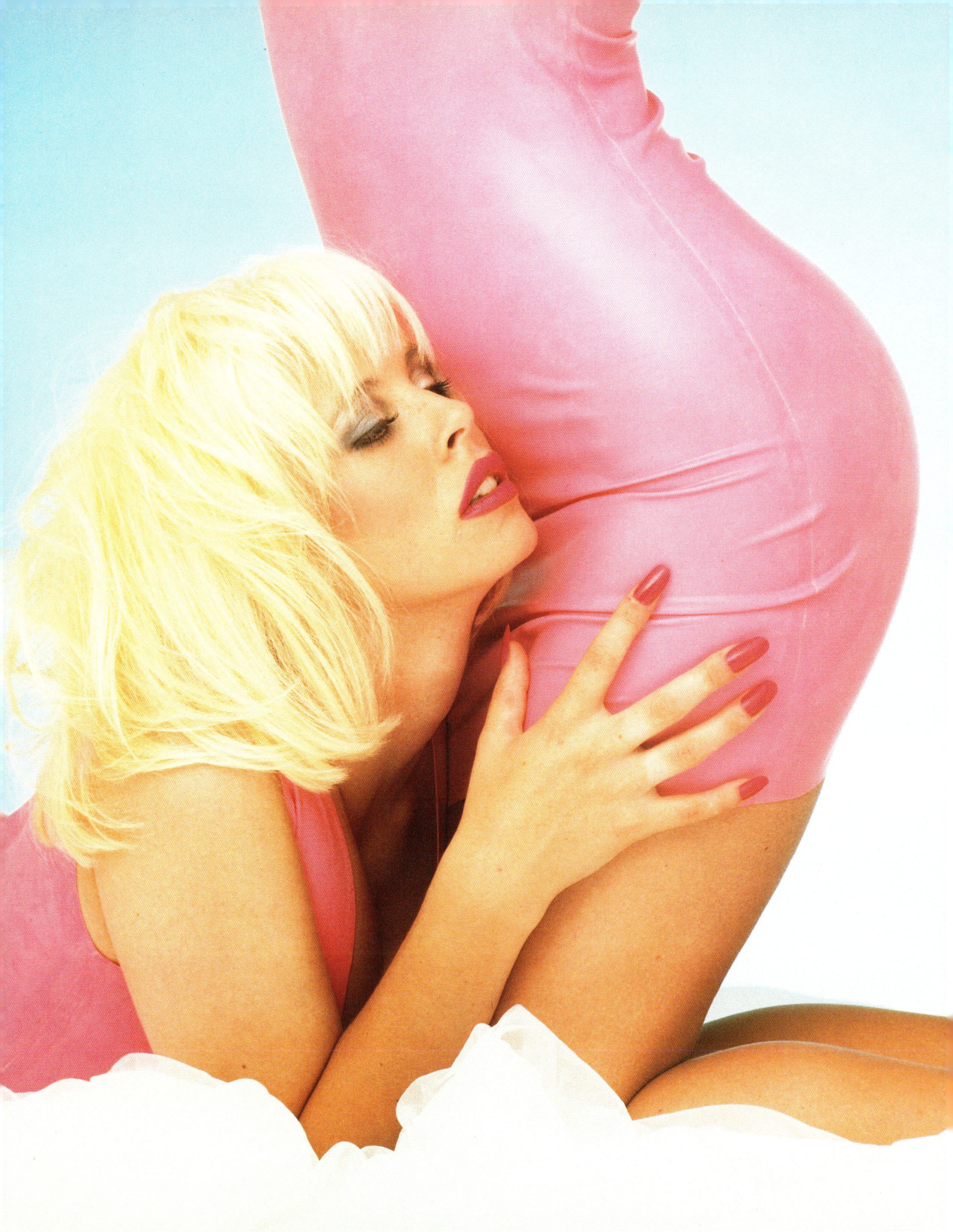

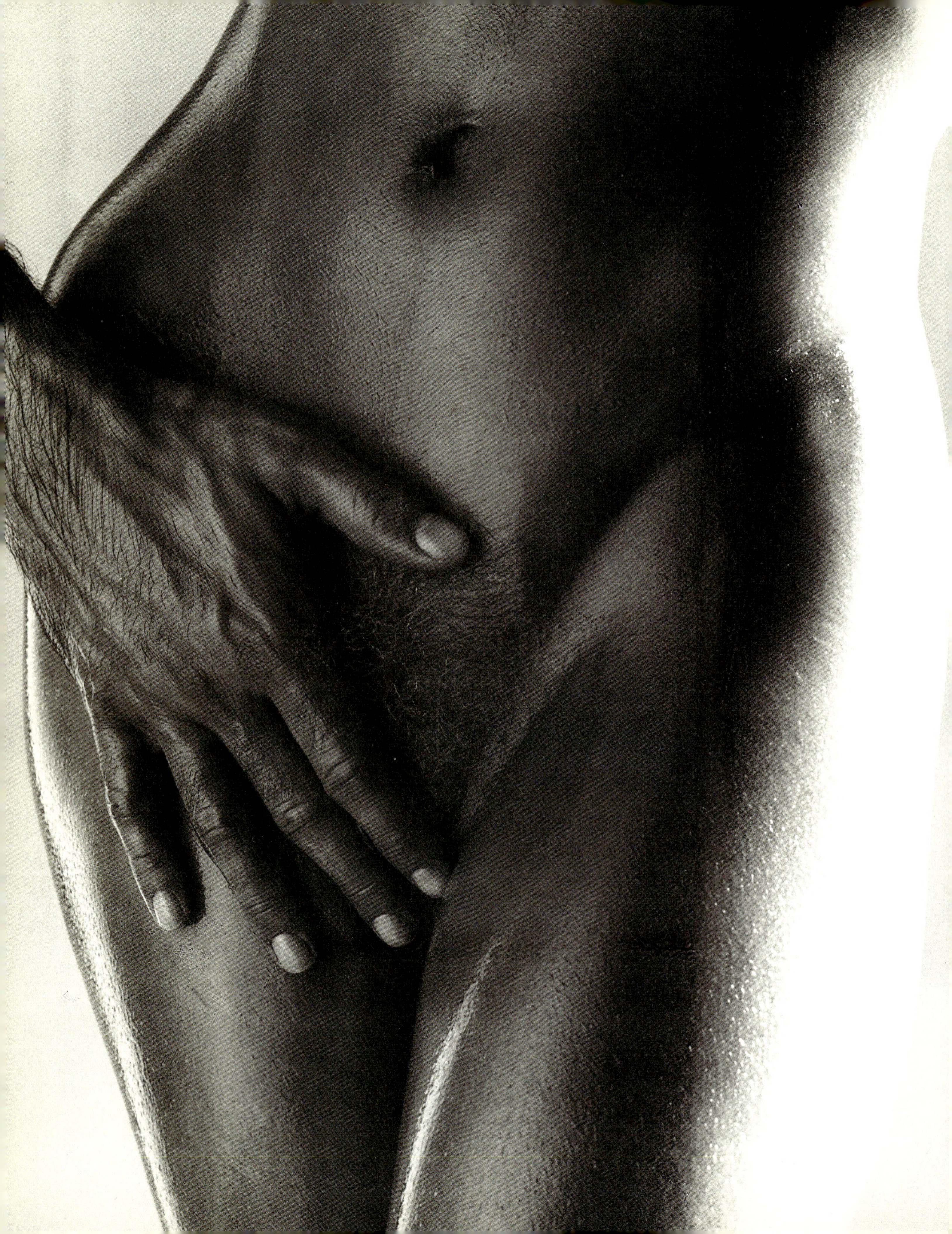

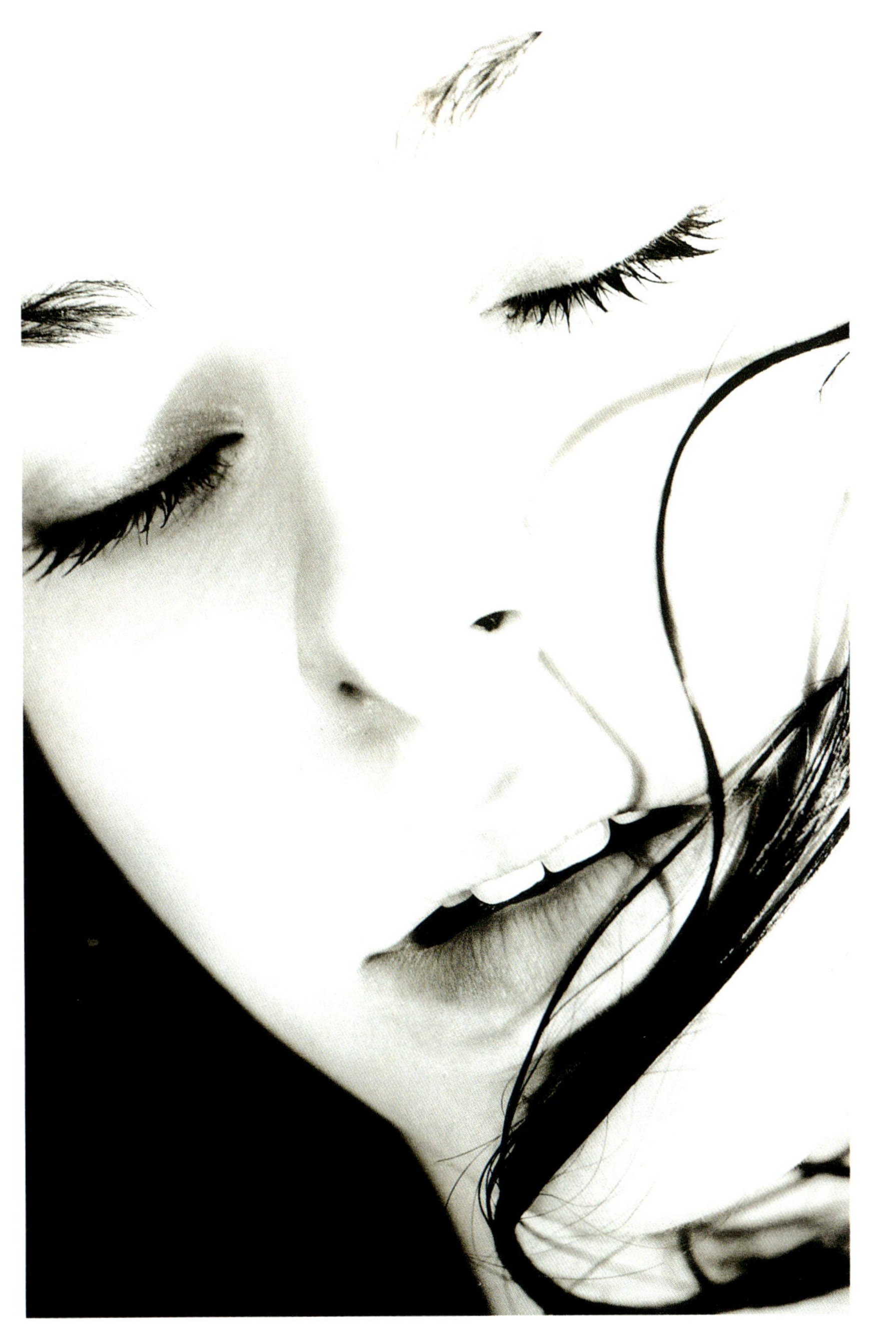

(left) **MONIKA ROBL** 1993

CHARLES ROFF 1998

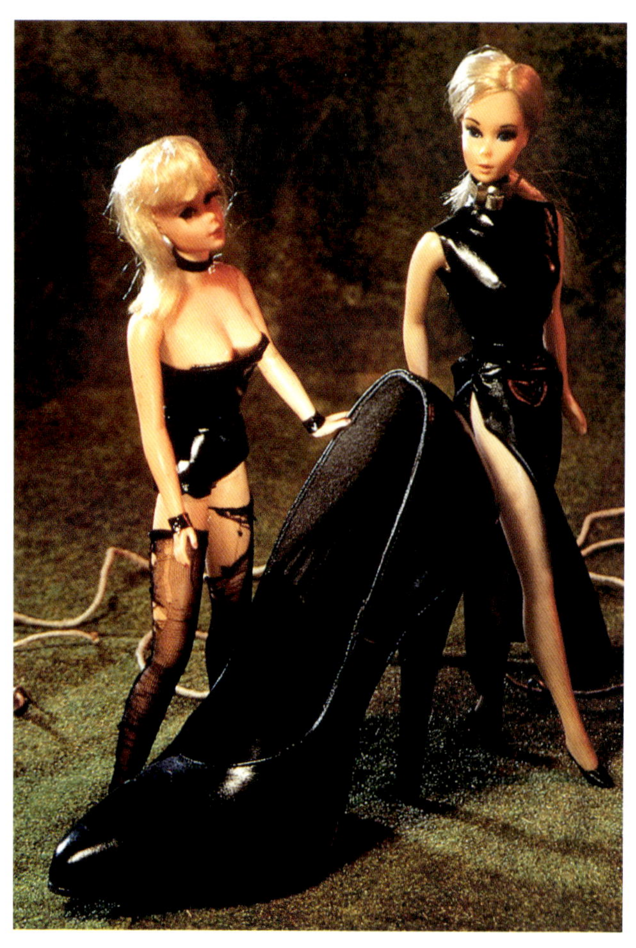

(right) **TREVOR WATSON** 1996

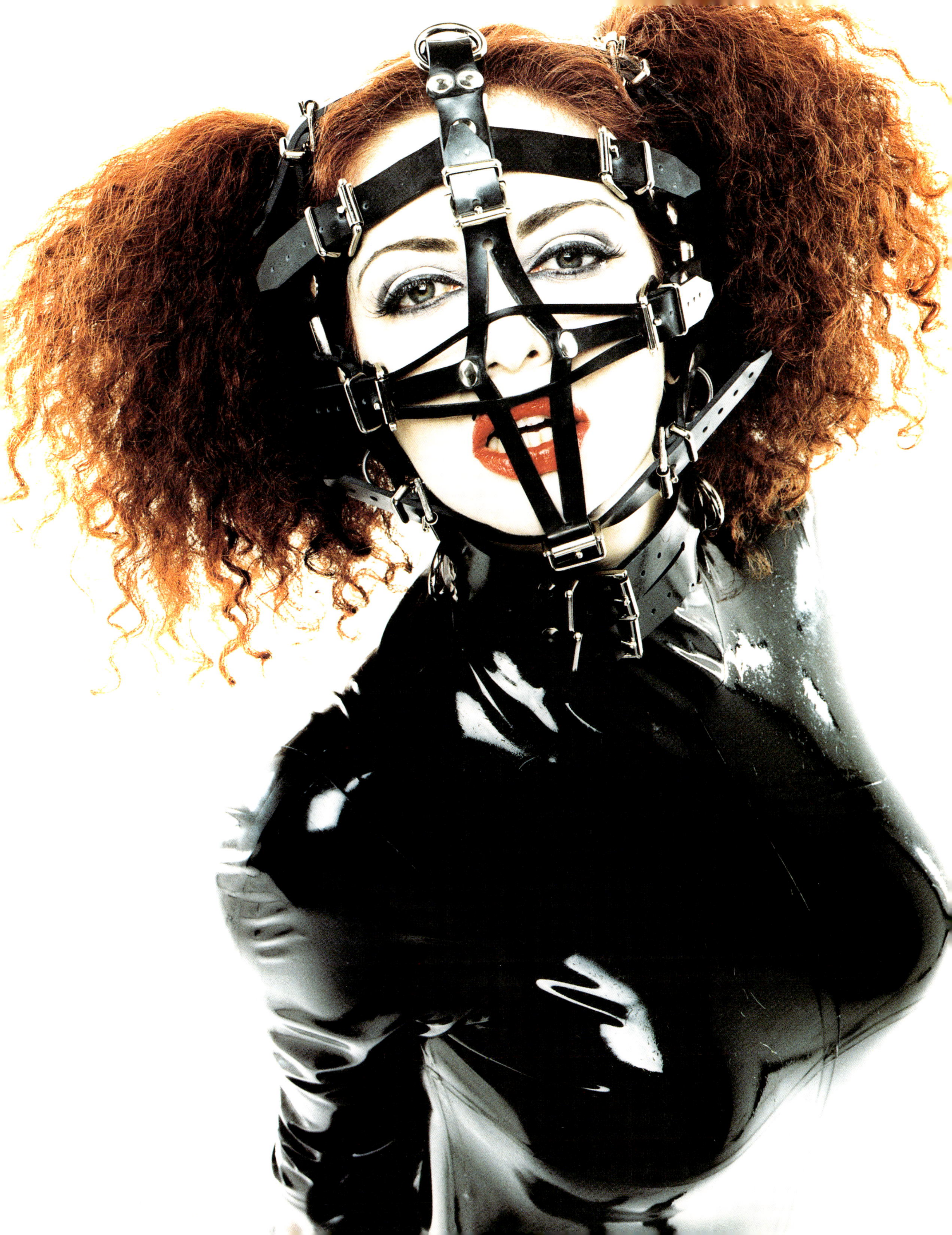

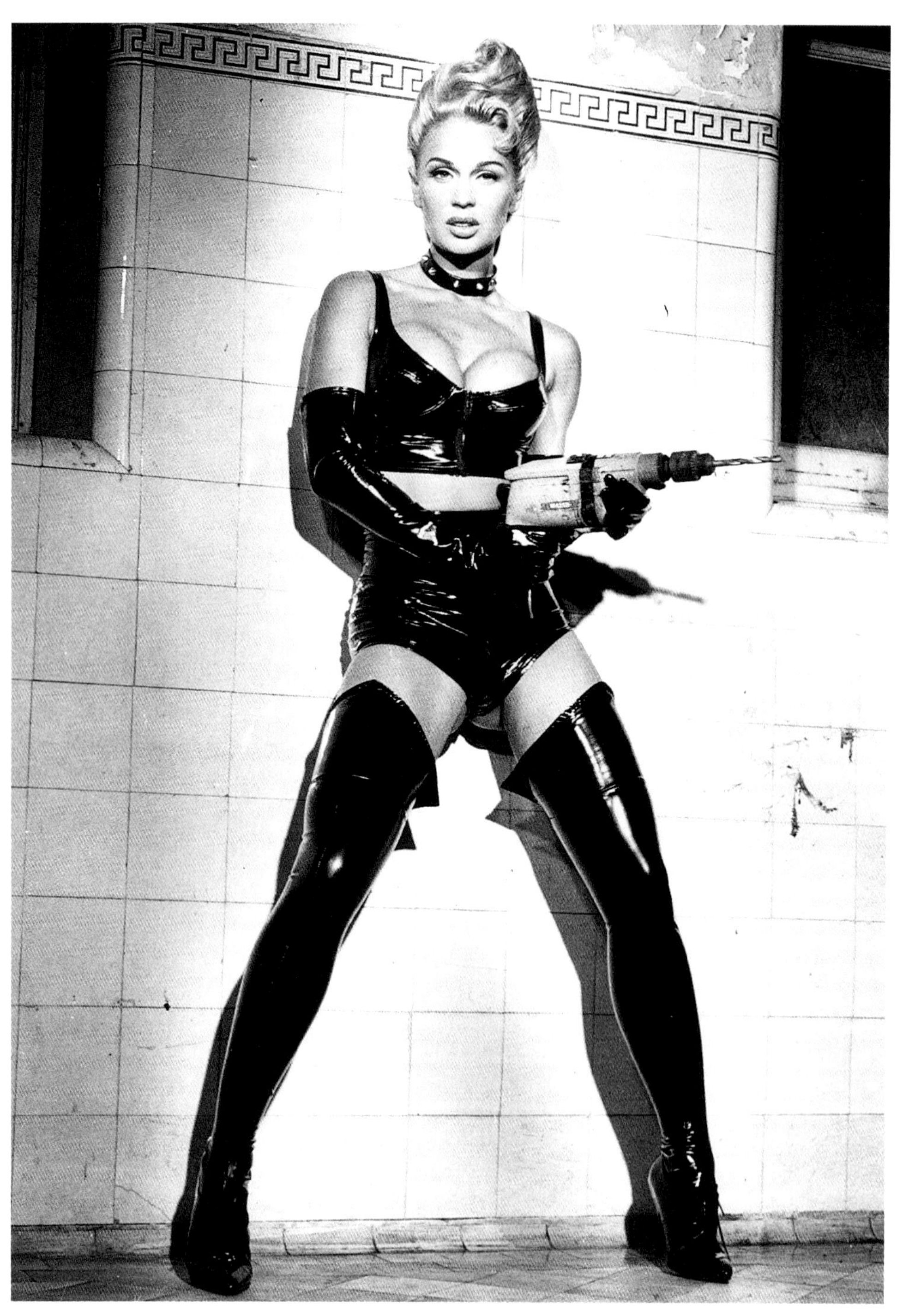

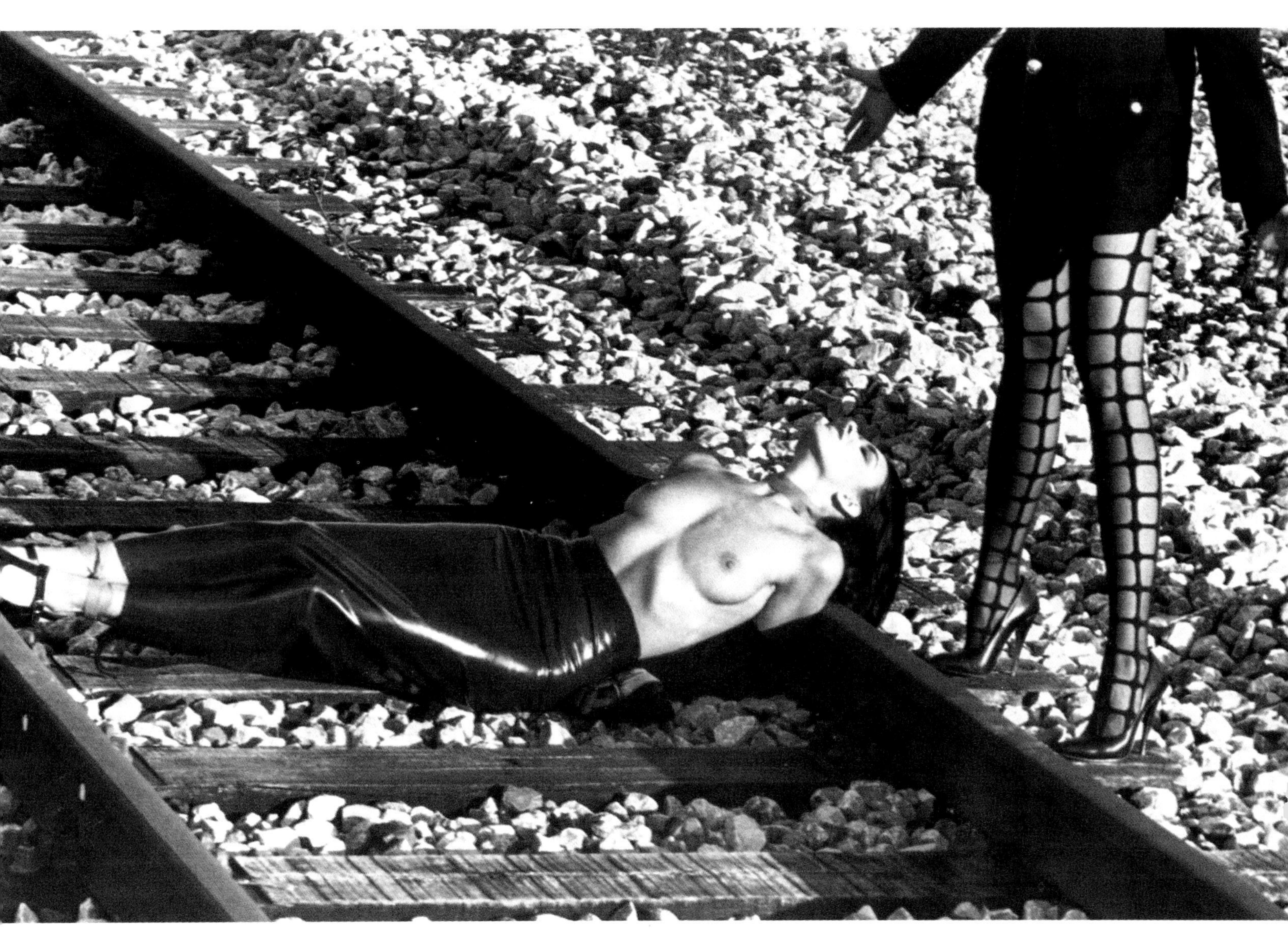

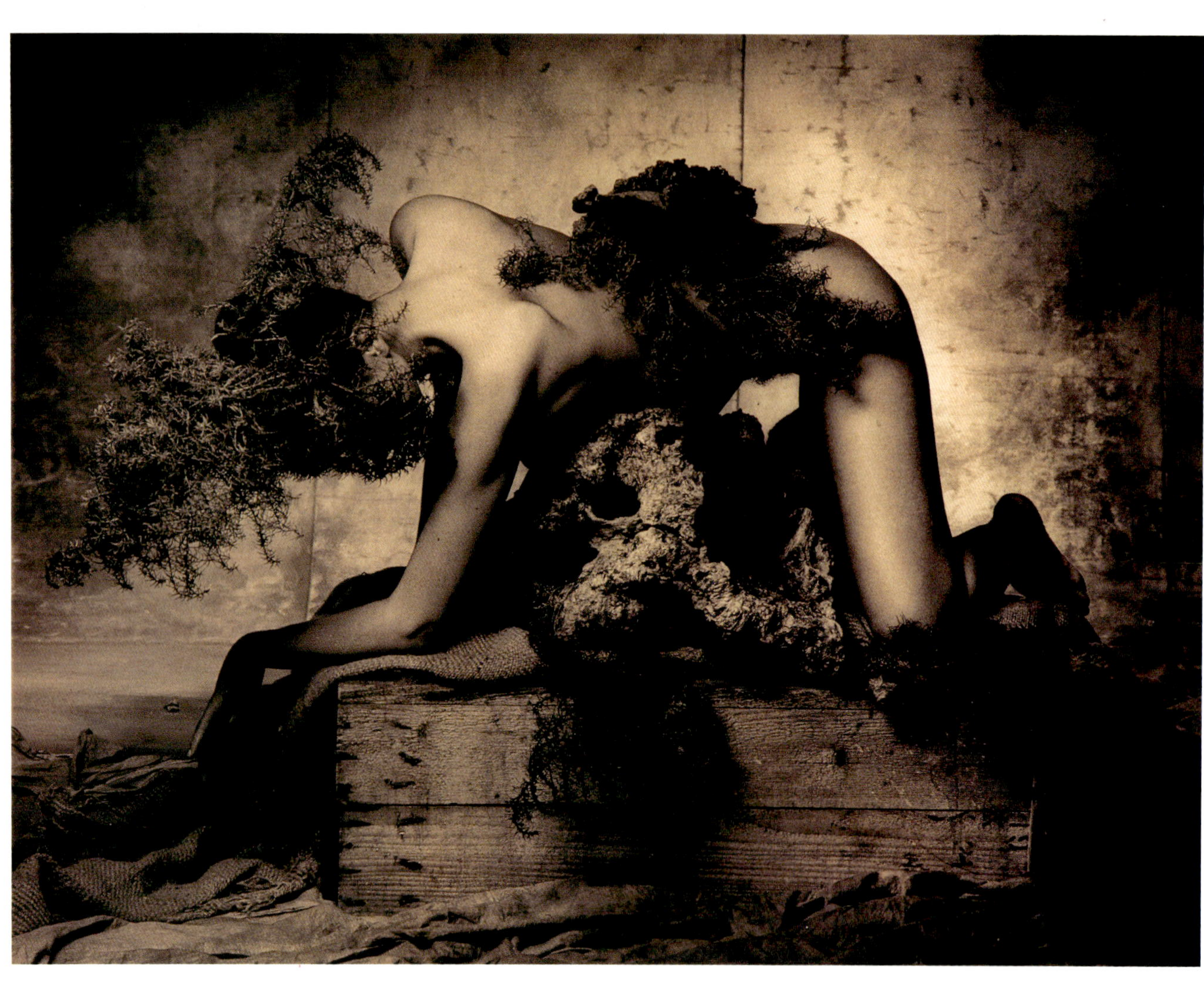

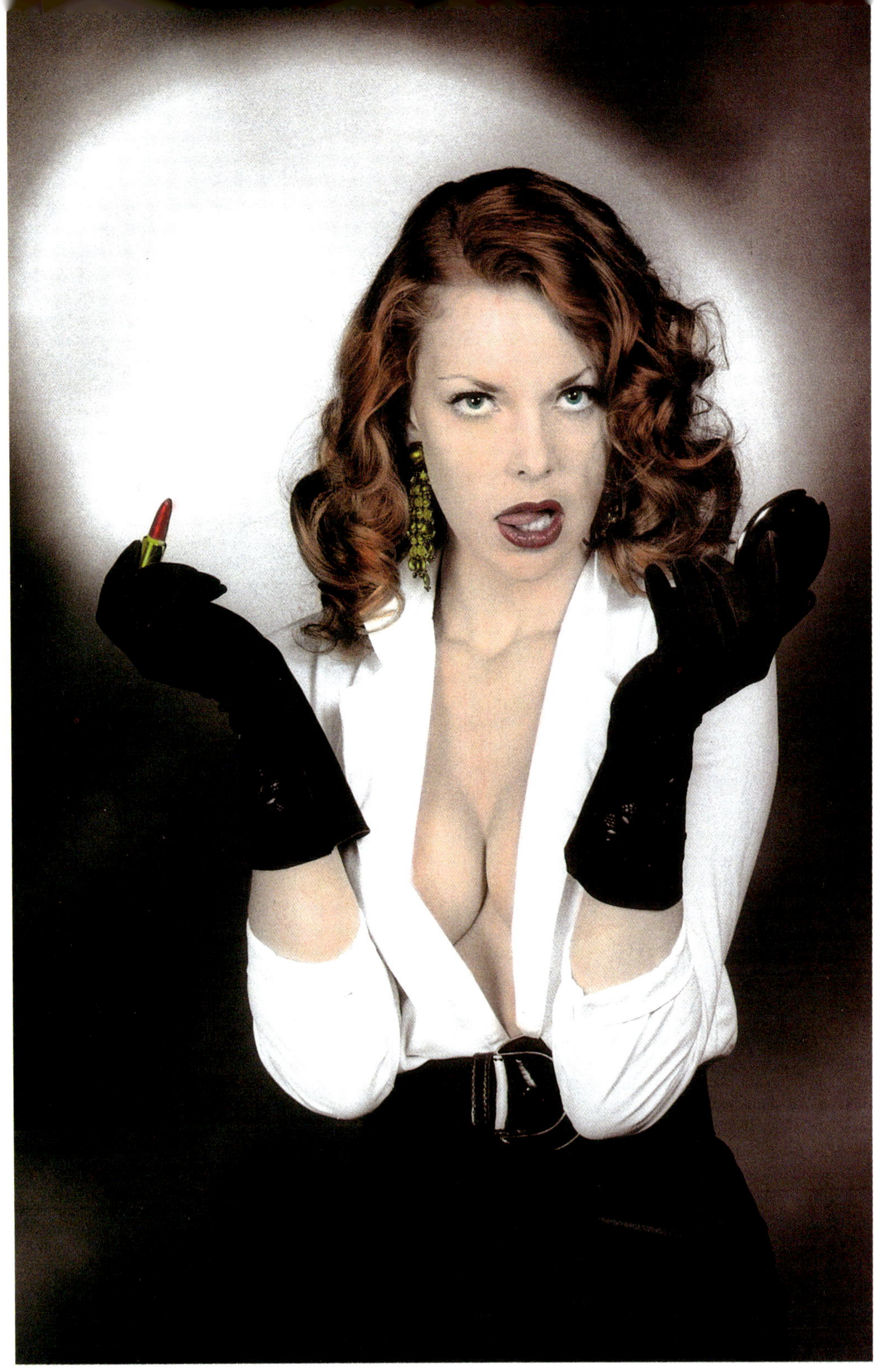

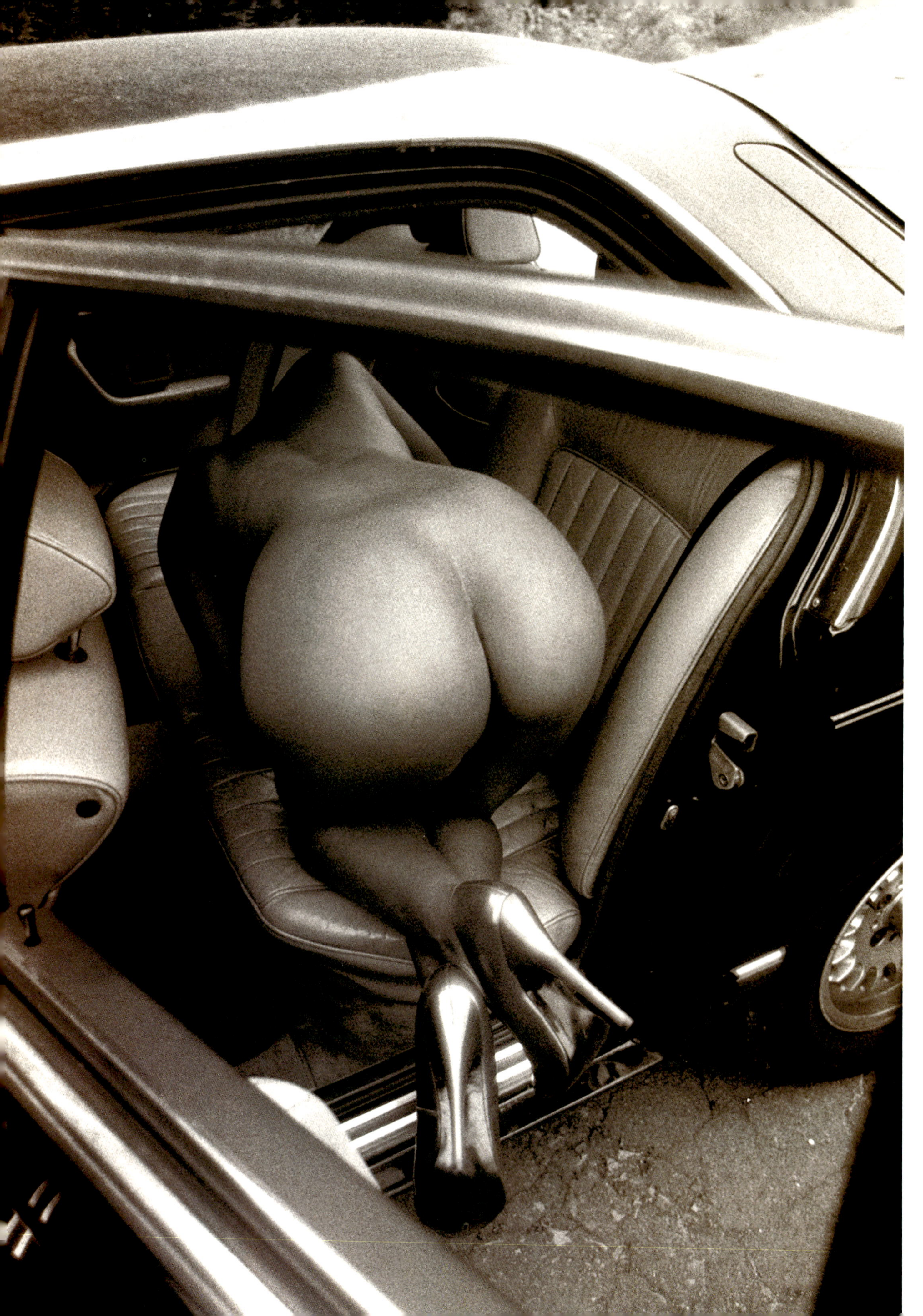

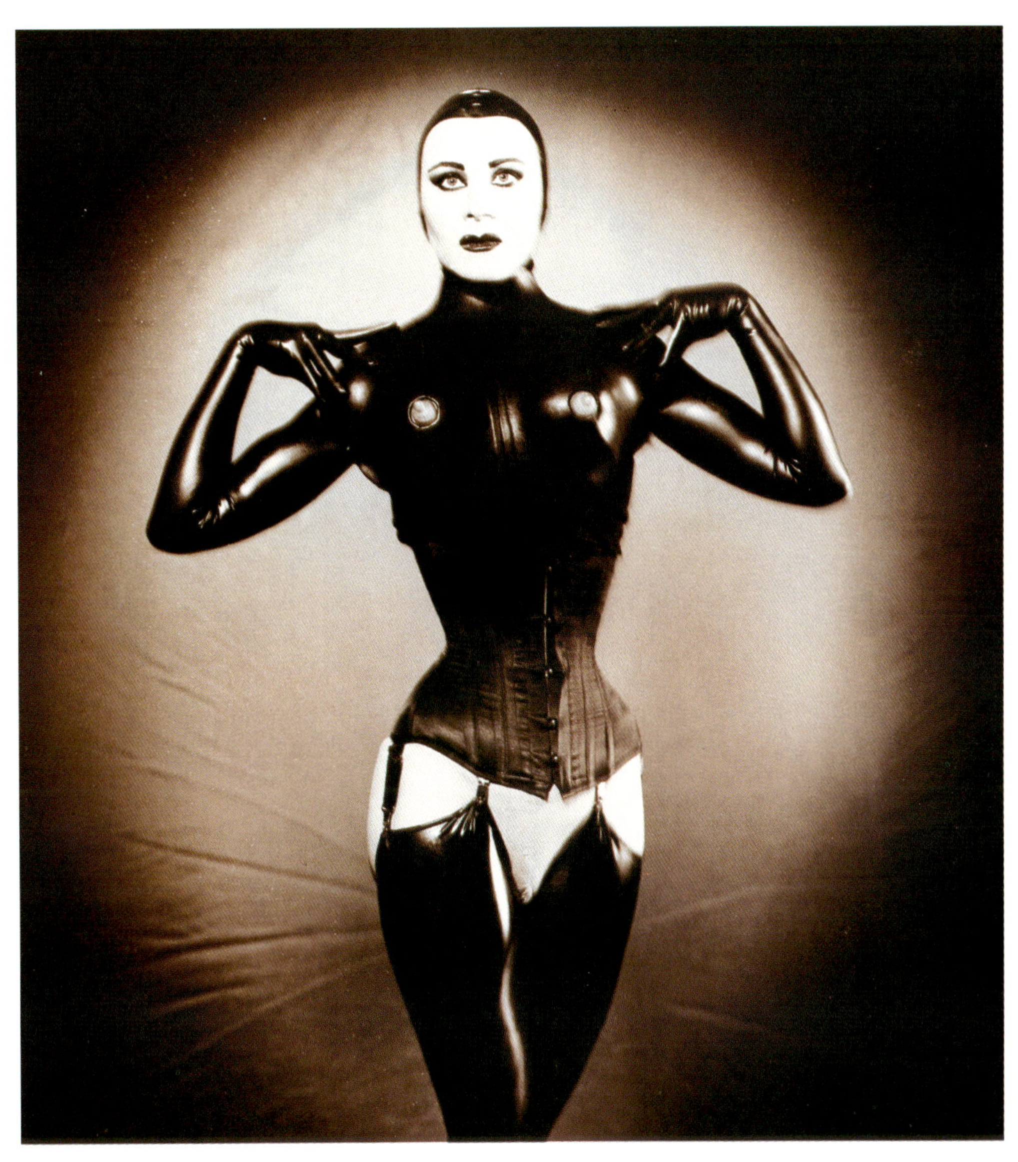

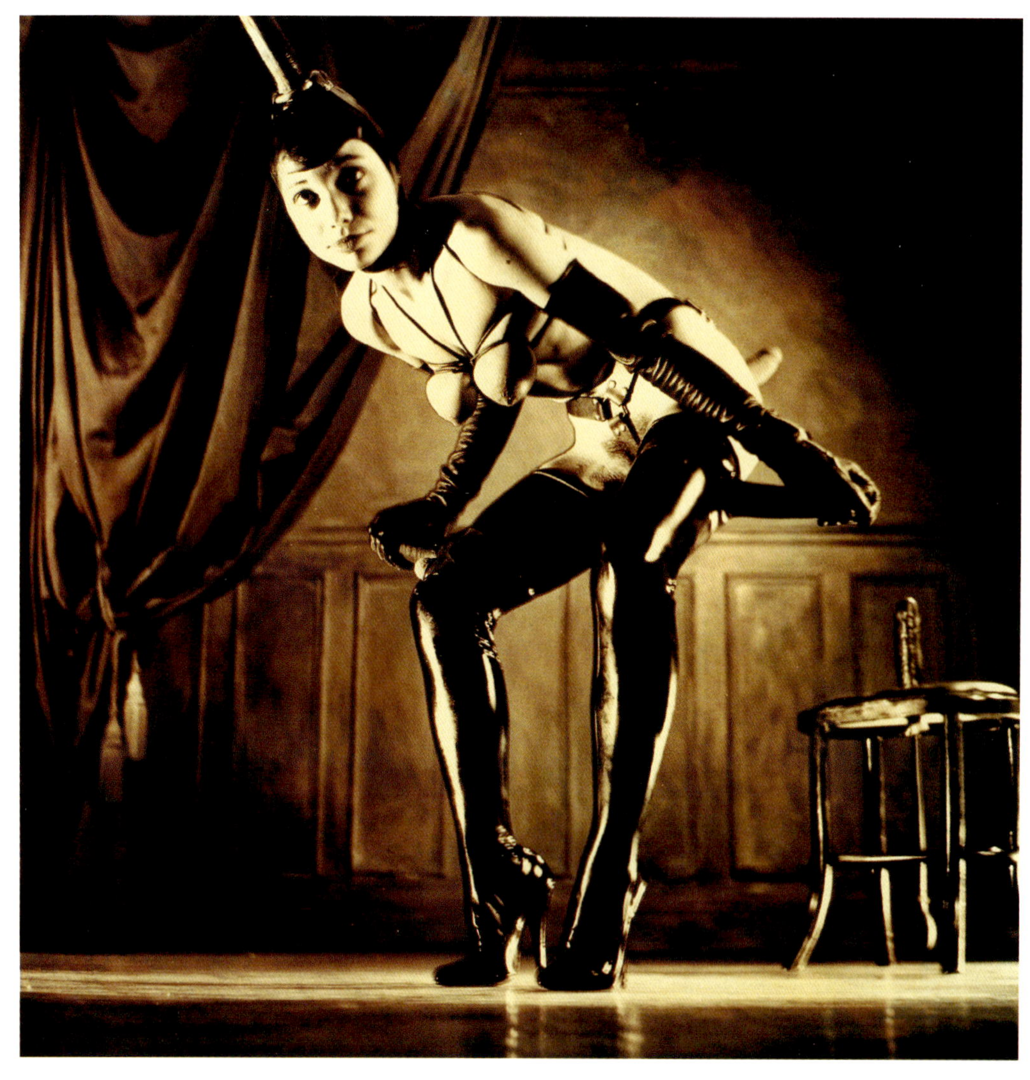

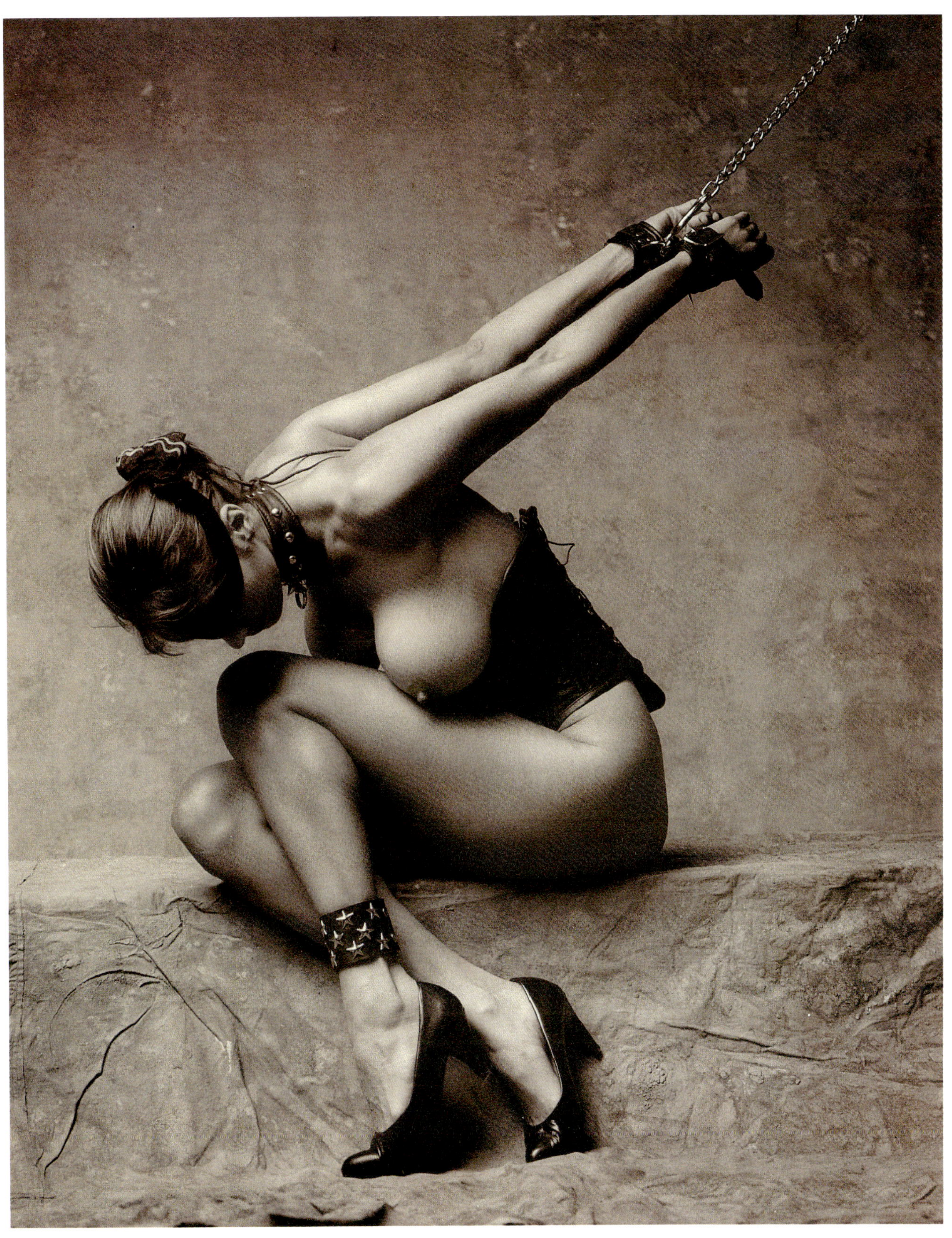

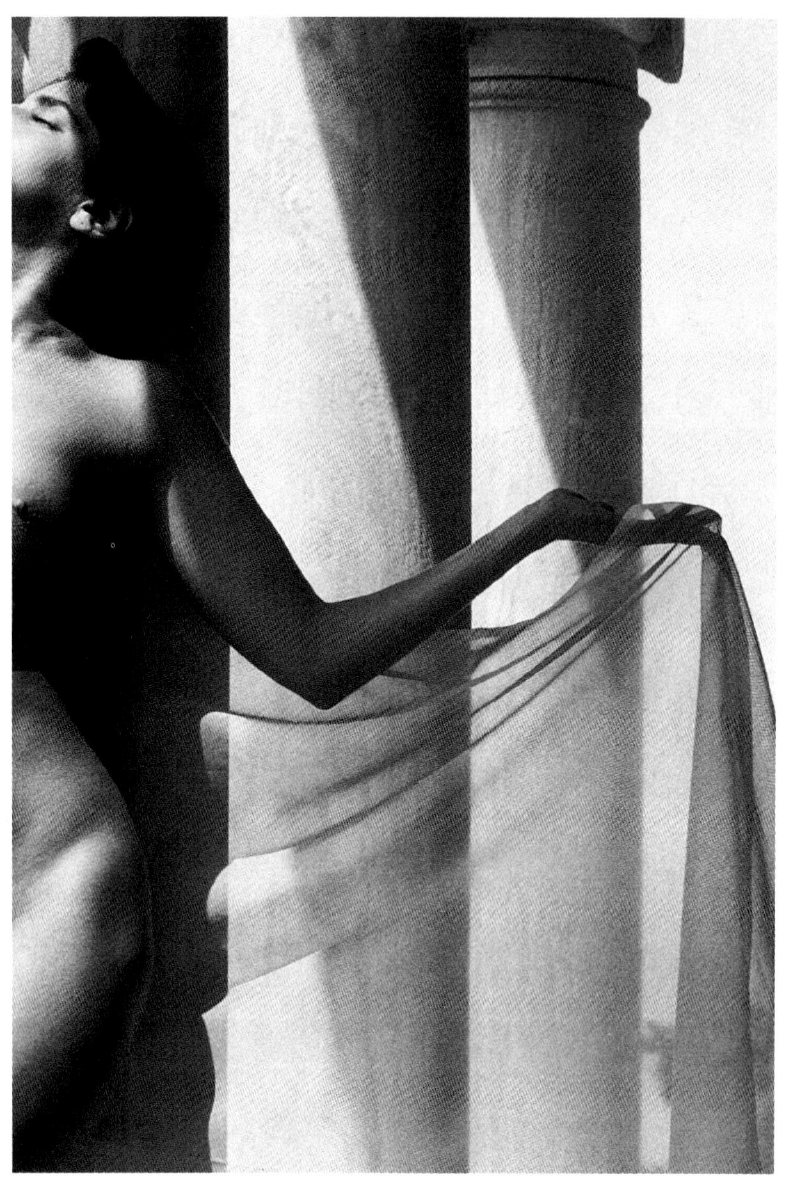

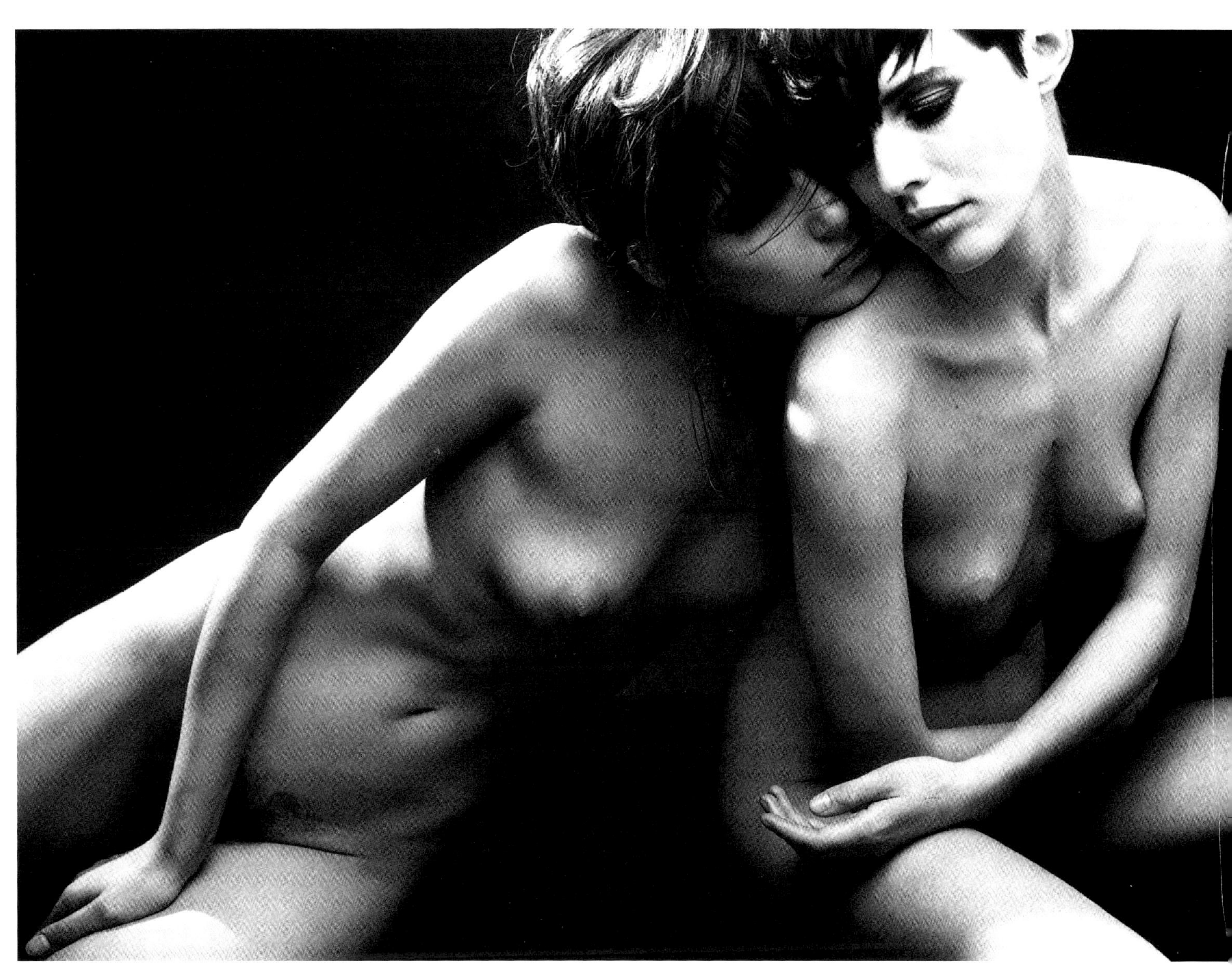

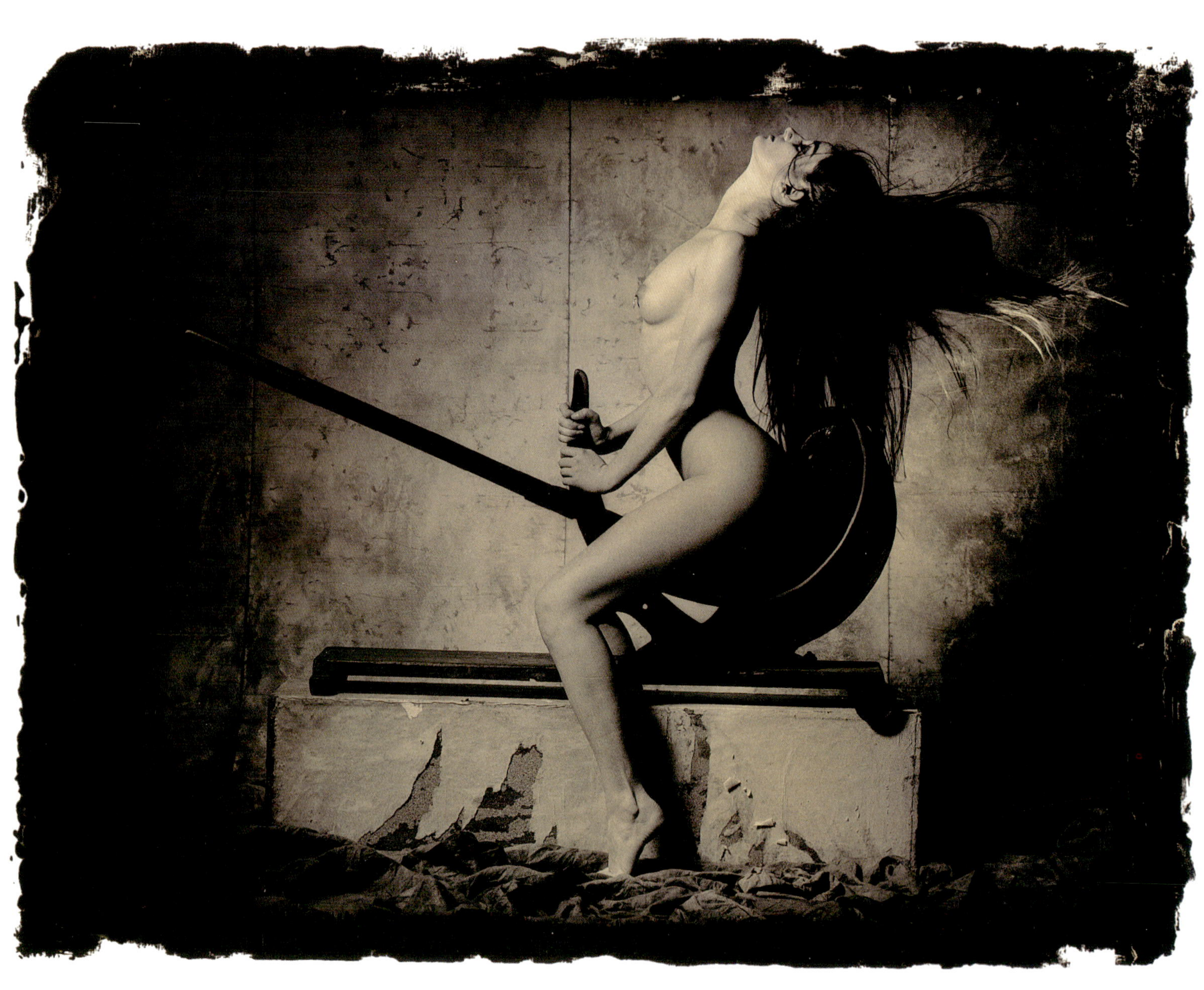

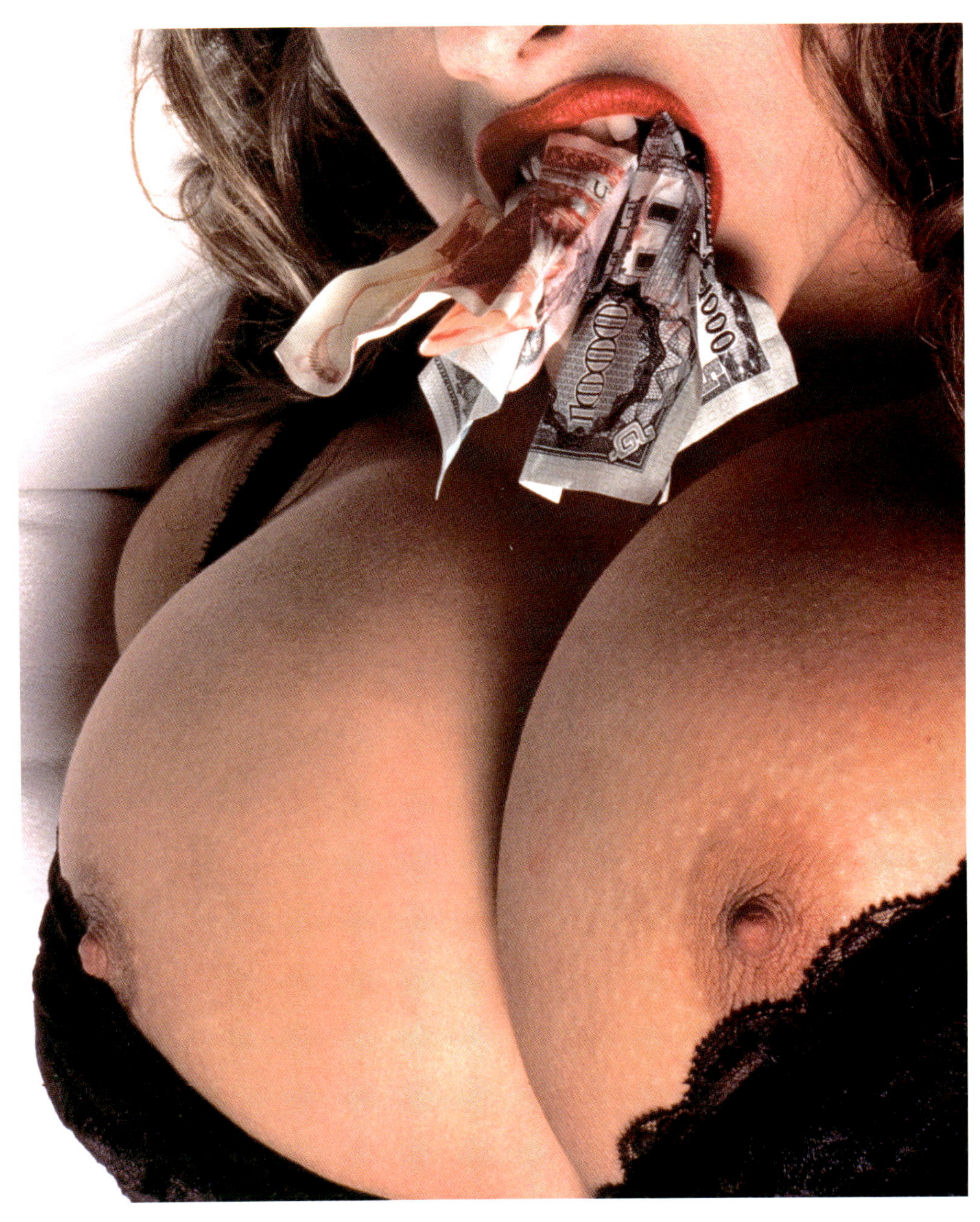

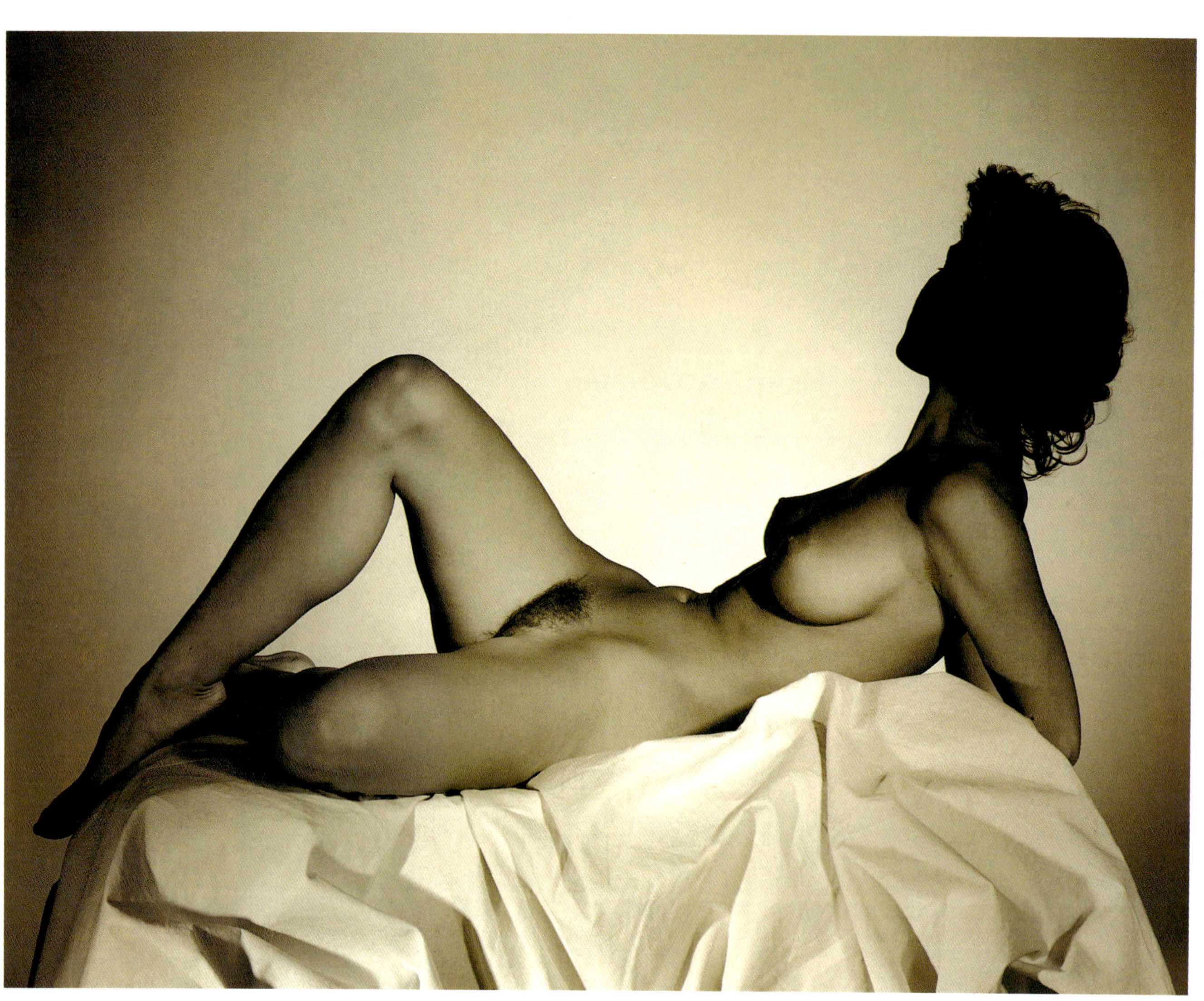

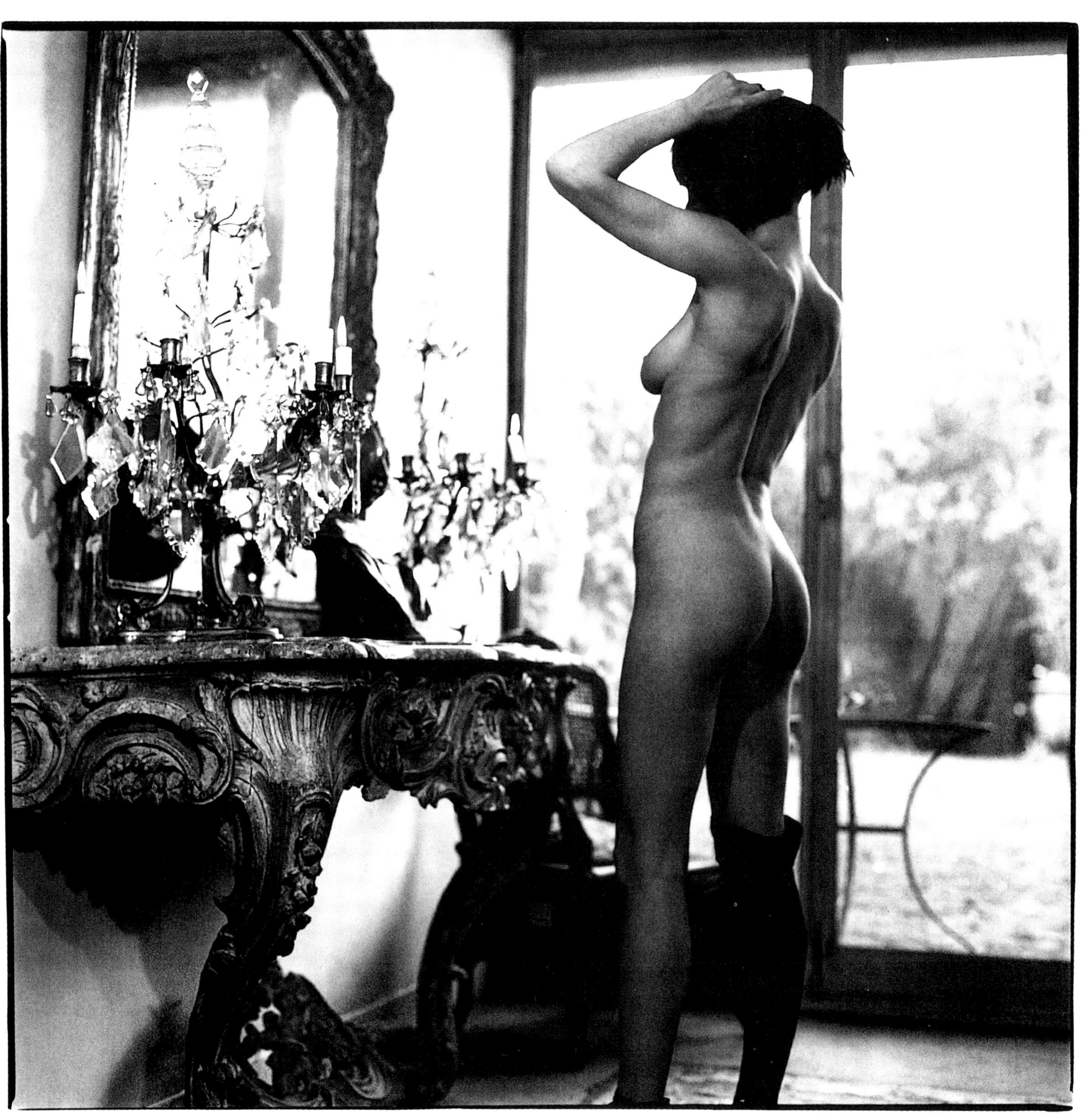

CHARLES ROFF 1996

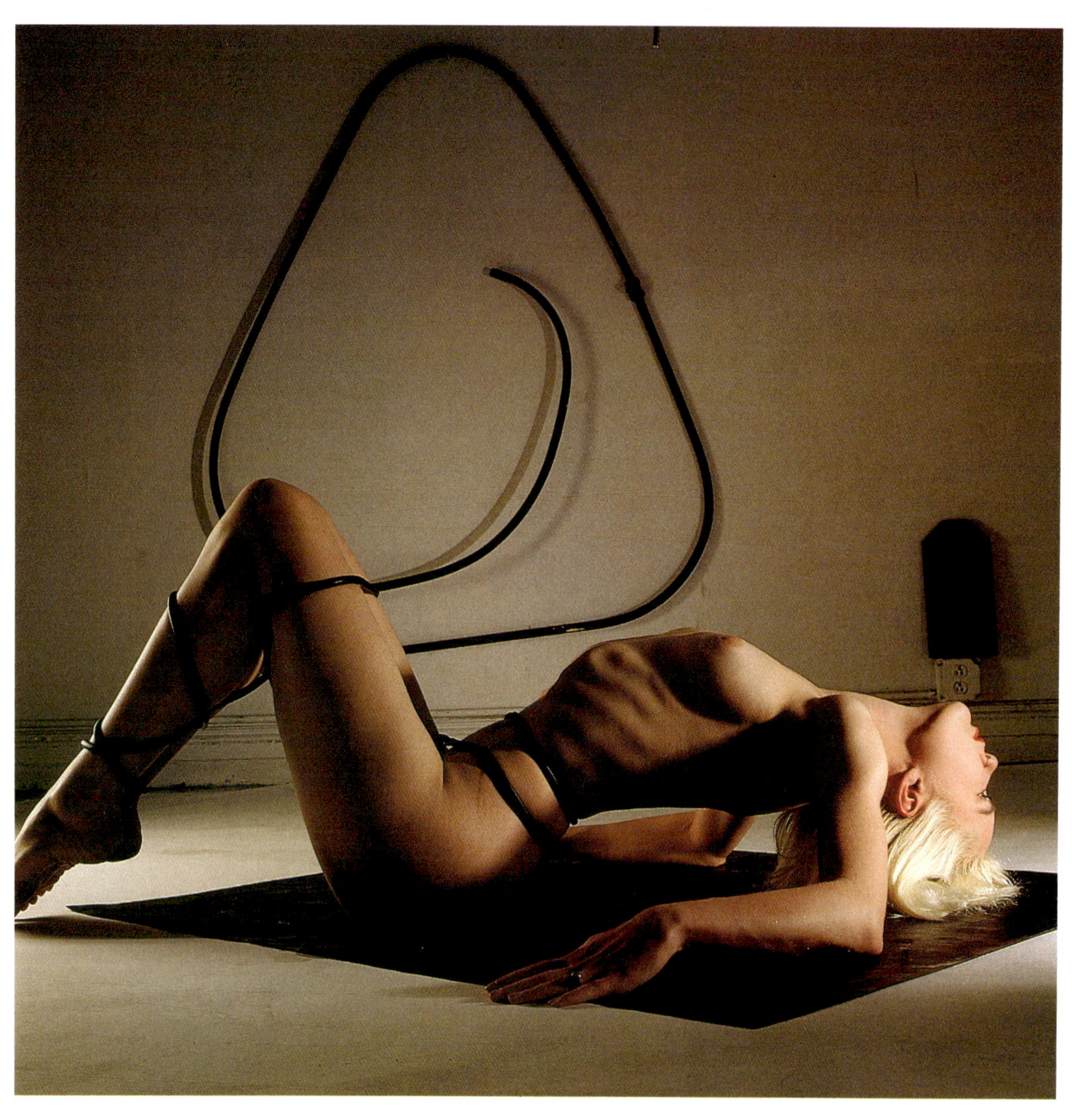

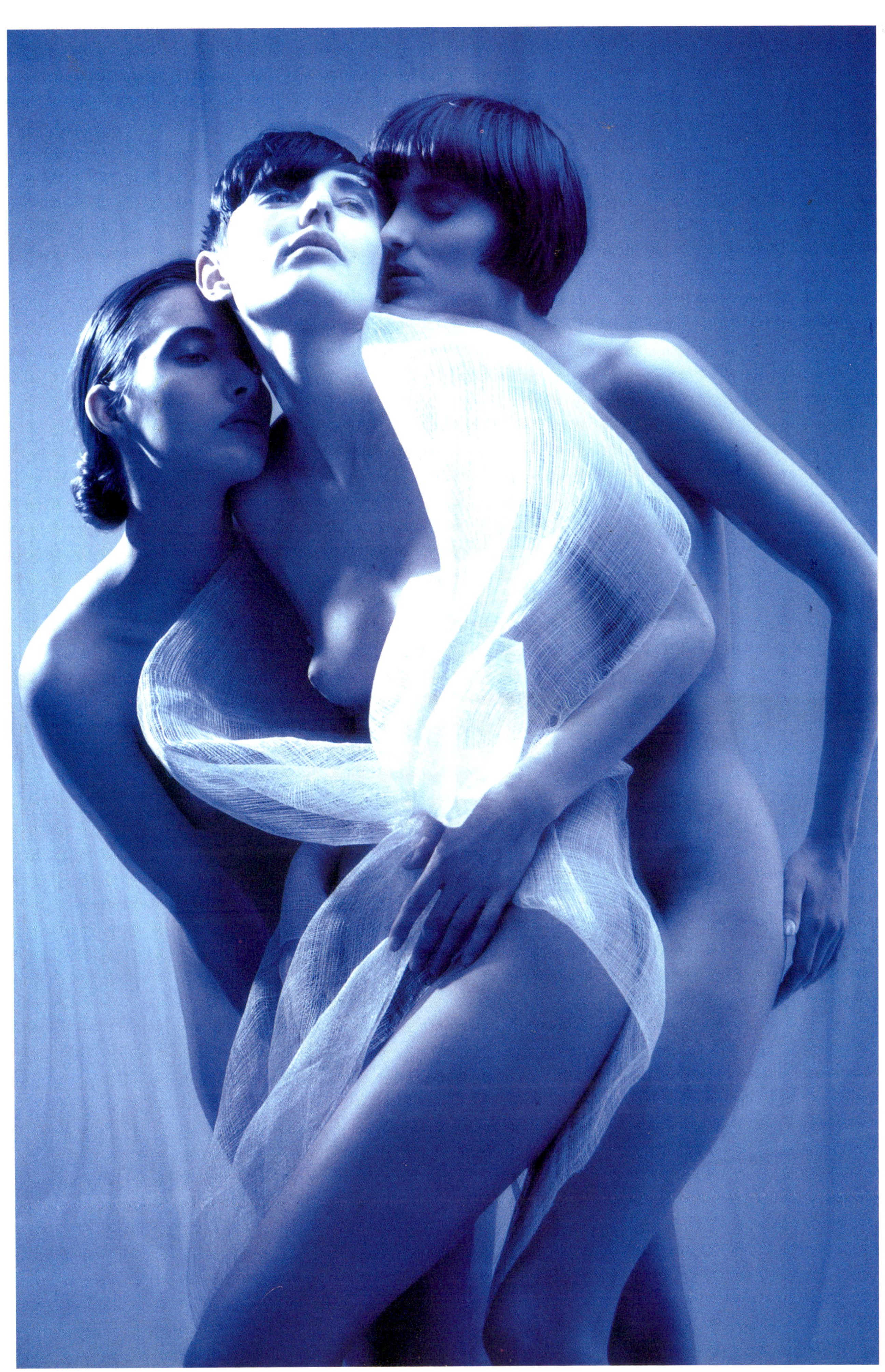

MONIKA ROBL 1990

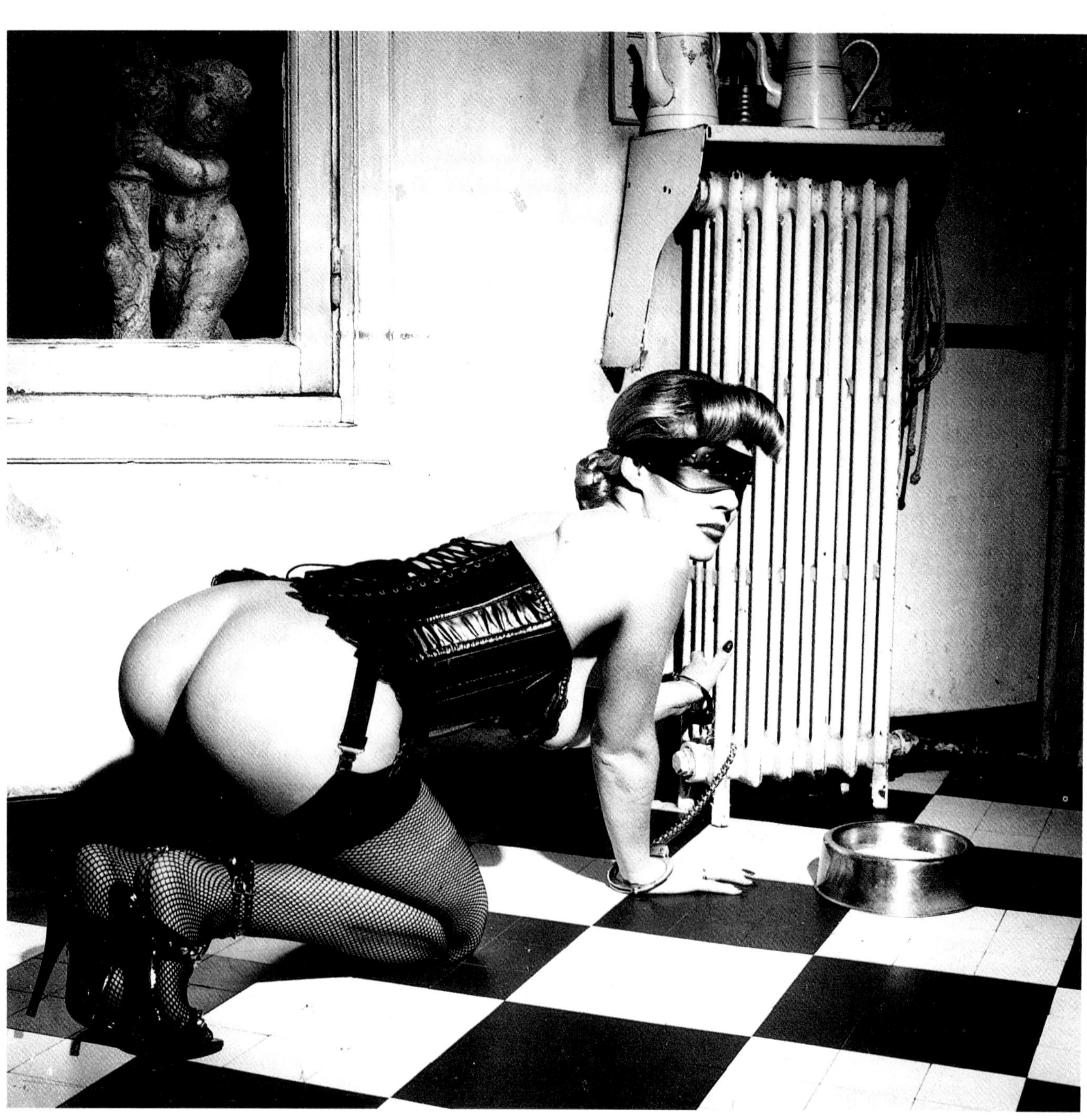

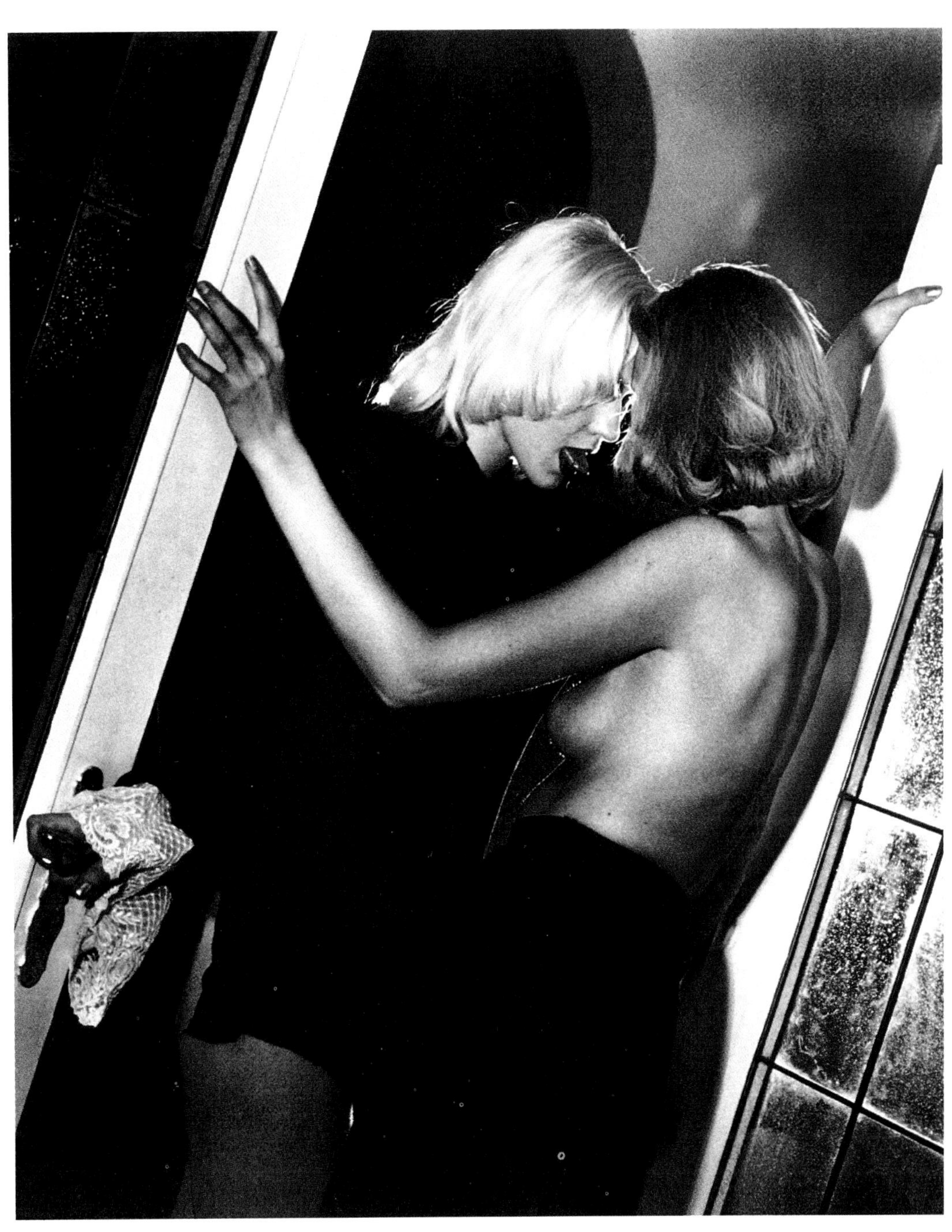

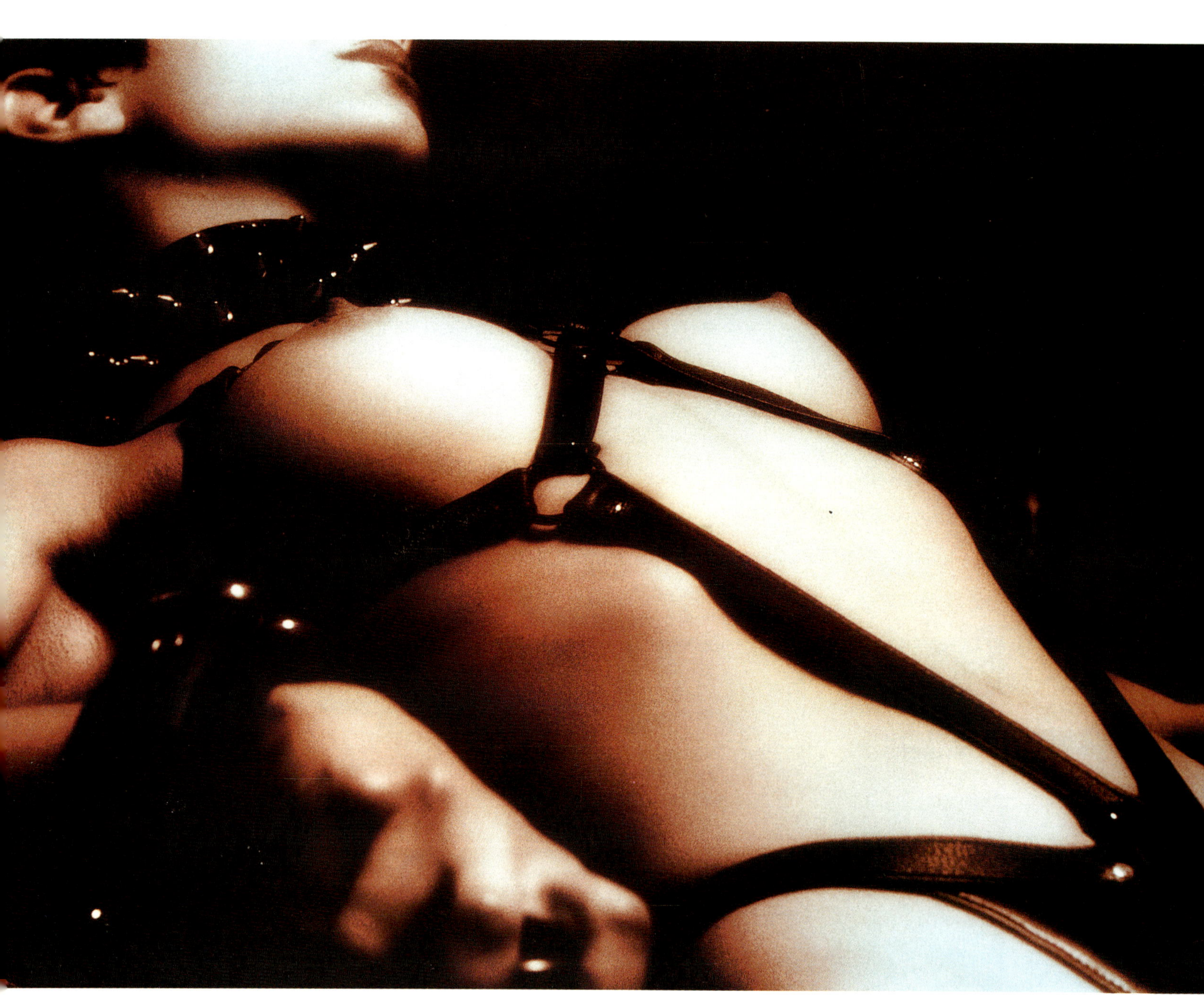

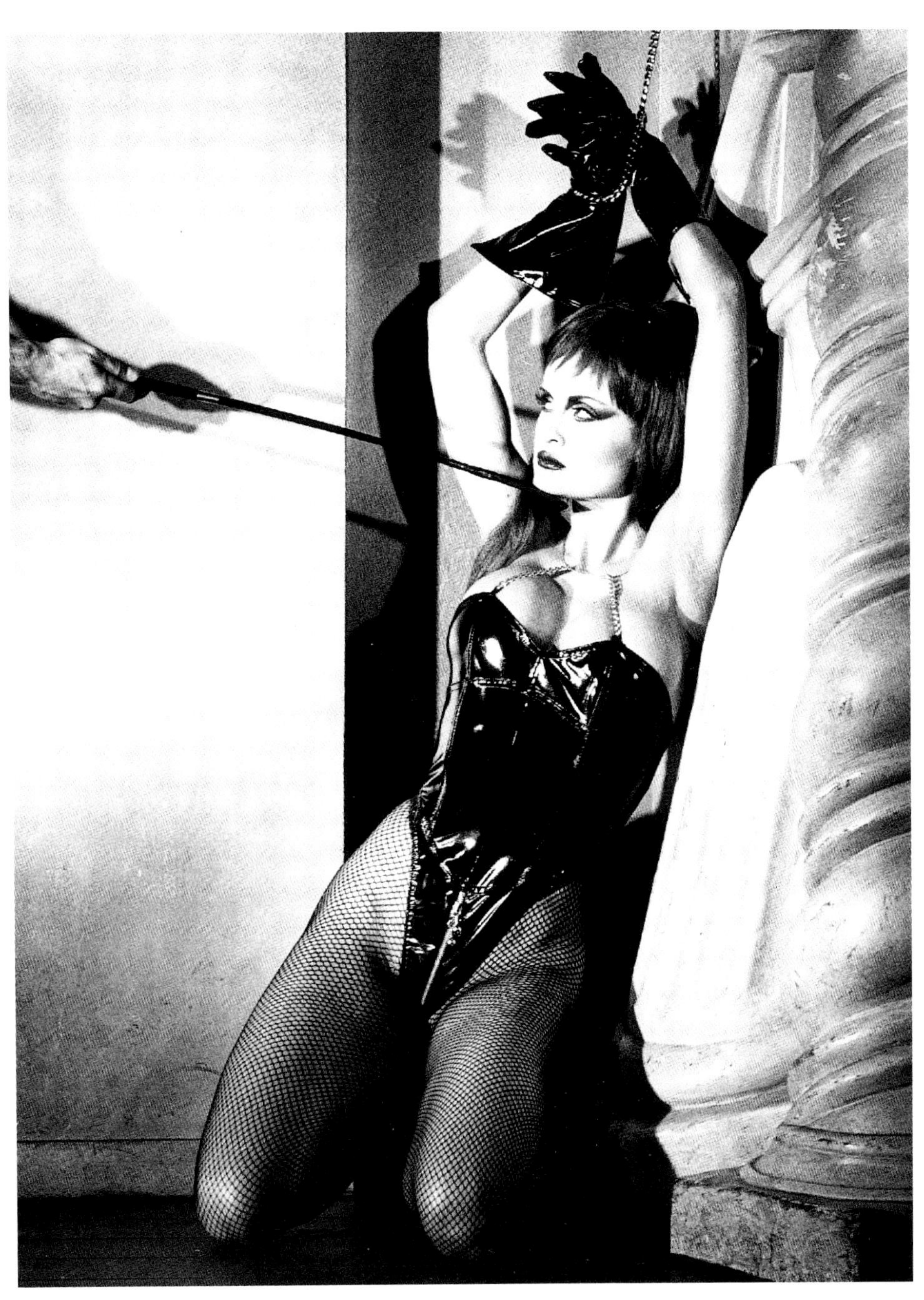

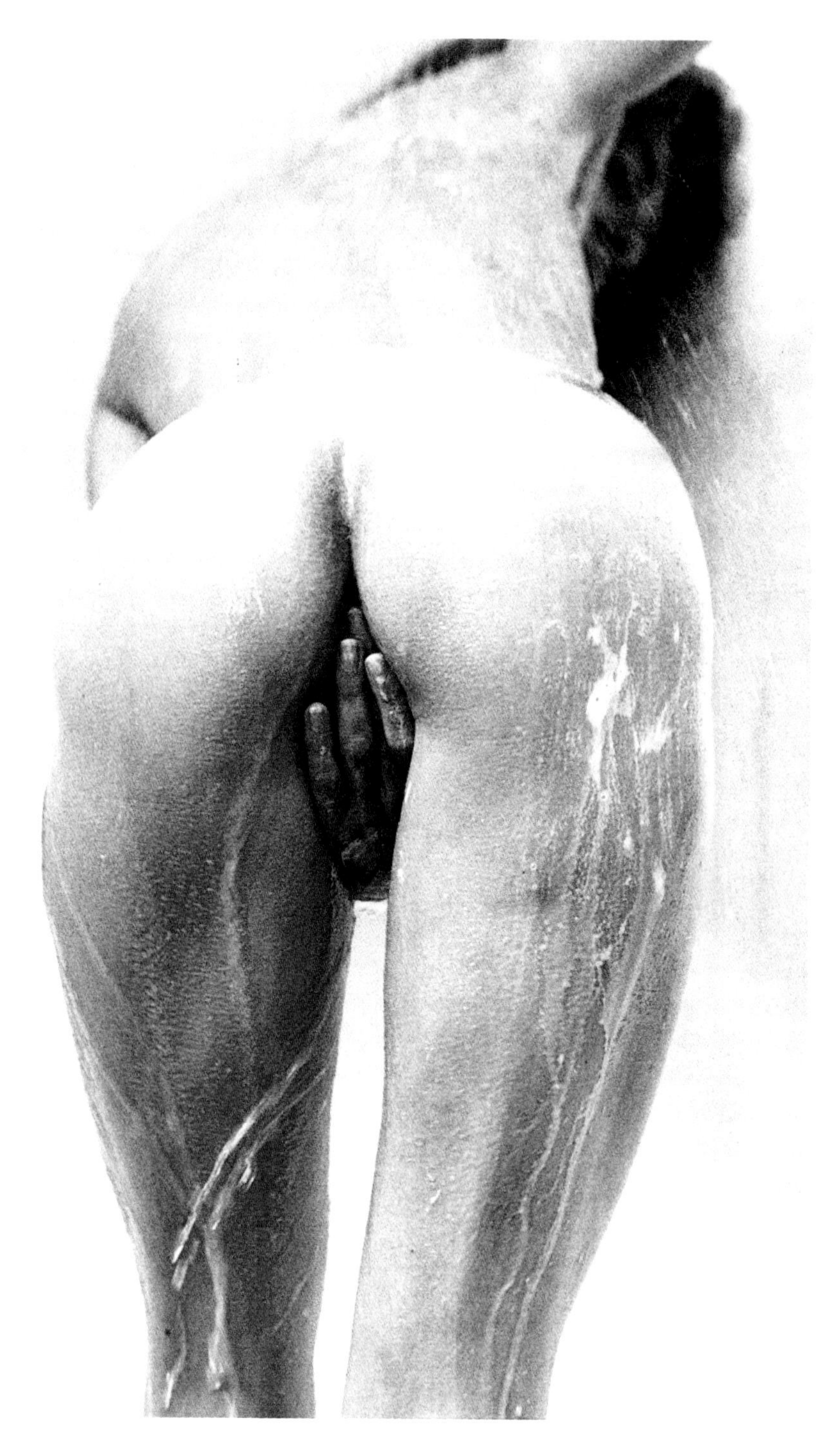

 CHARLES ROFF 1994

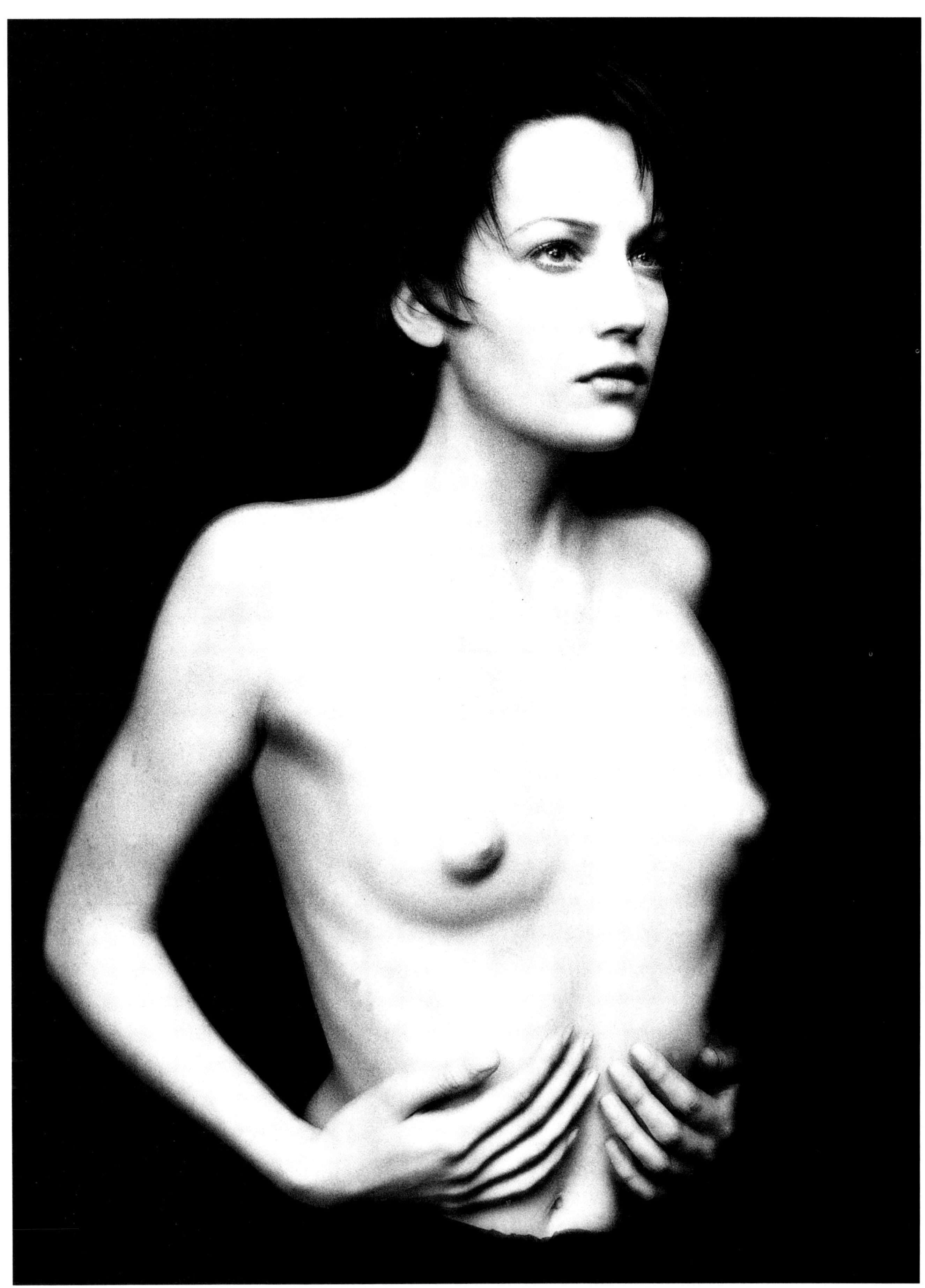

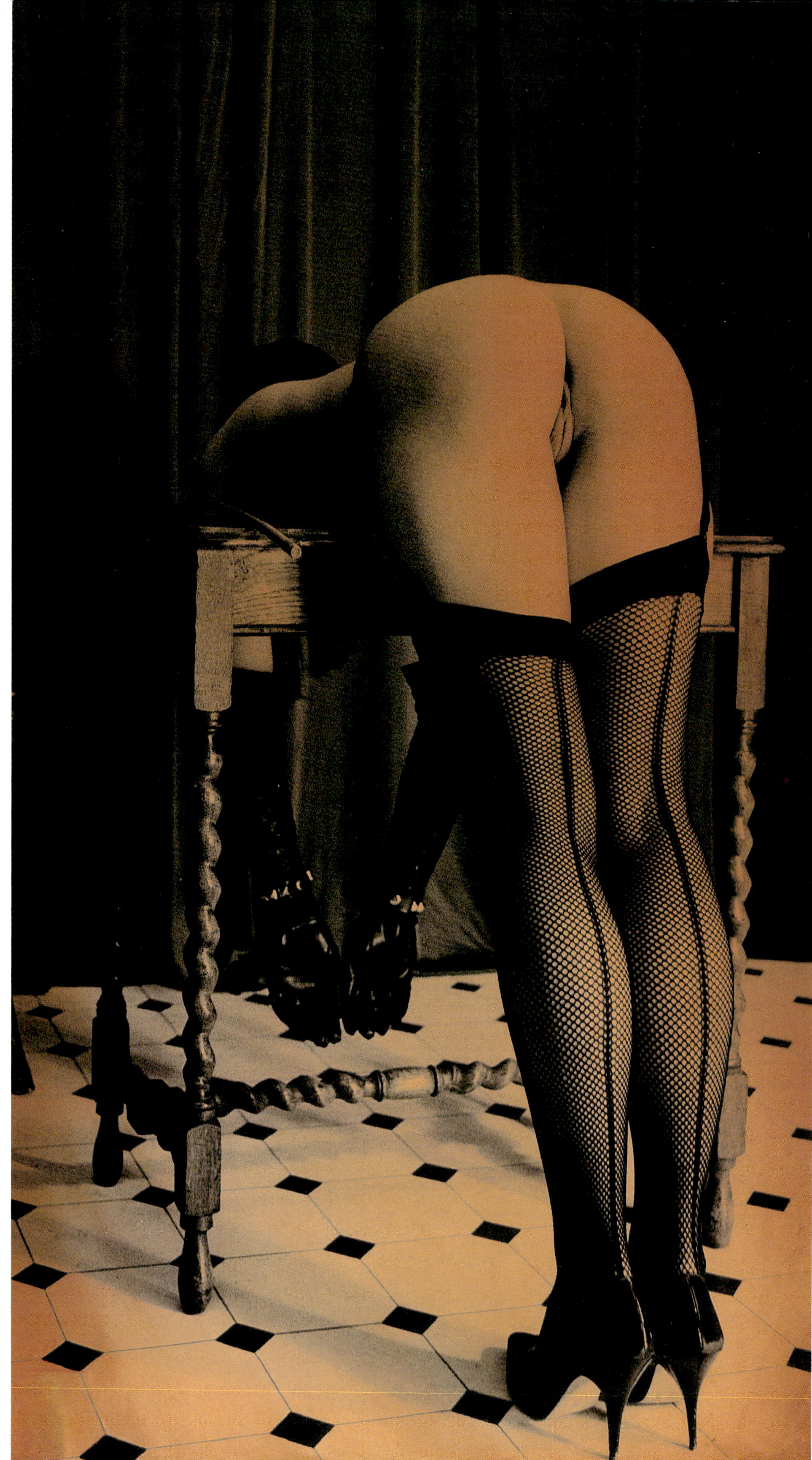

192 | **CHINA HAMILTON** 1994

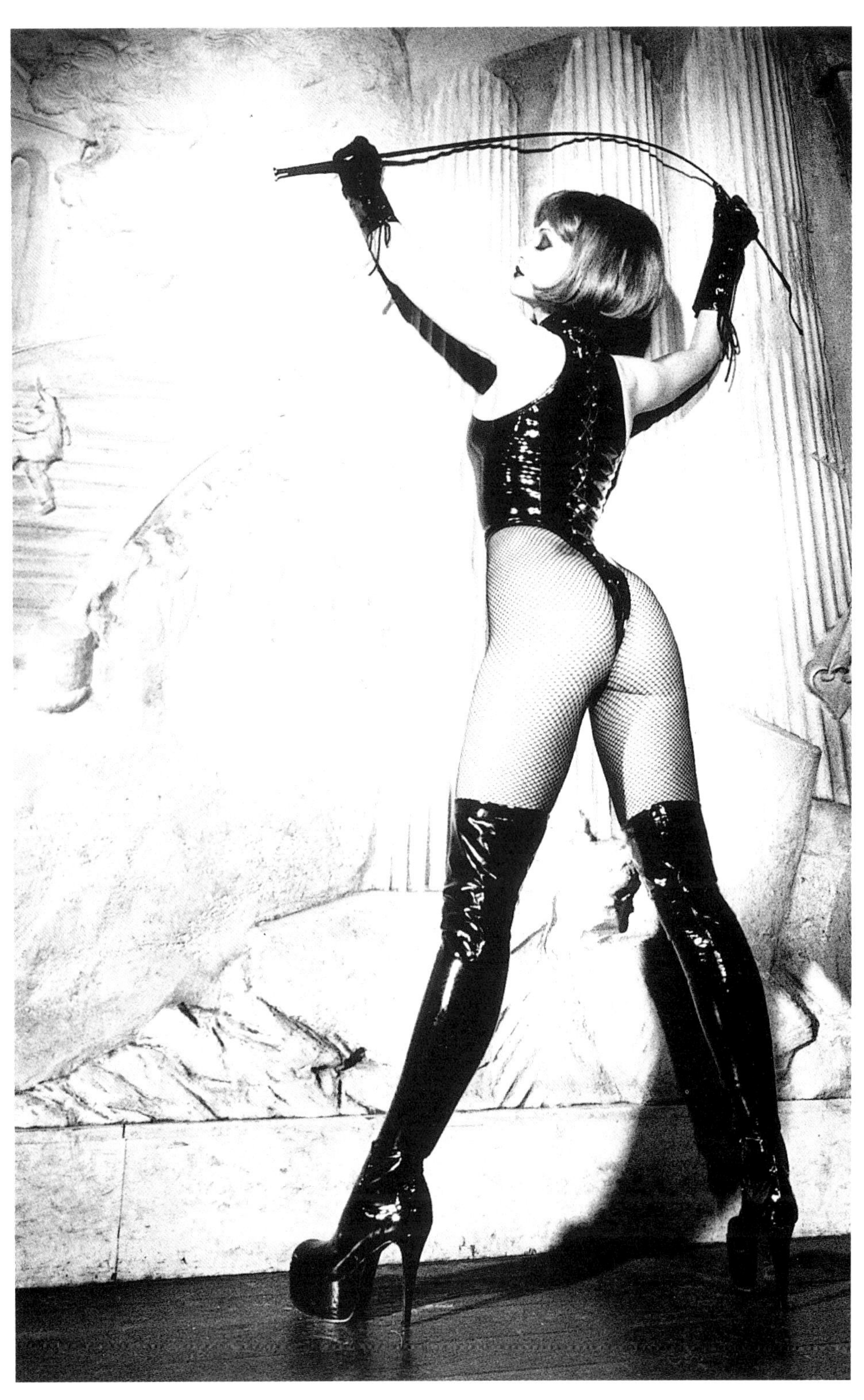

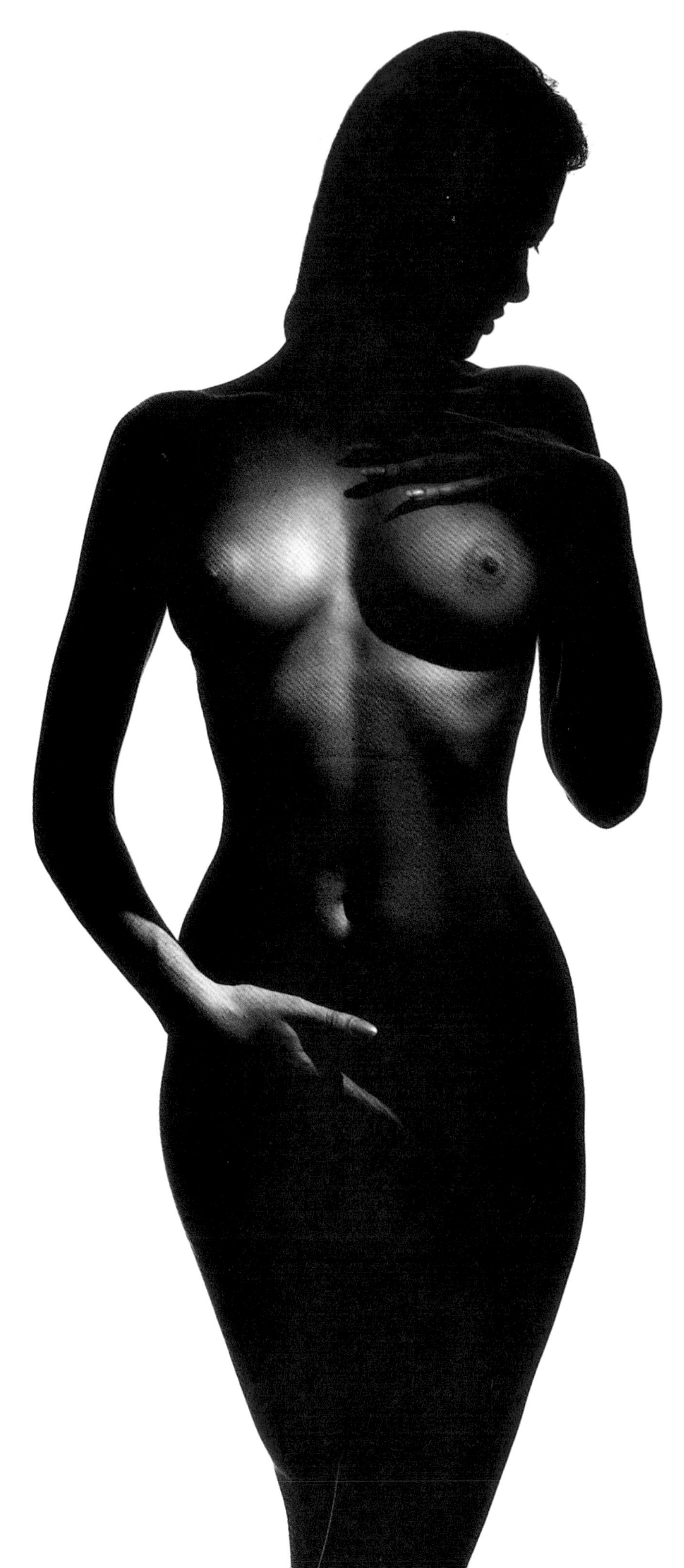

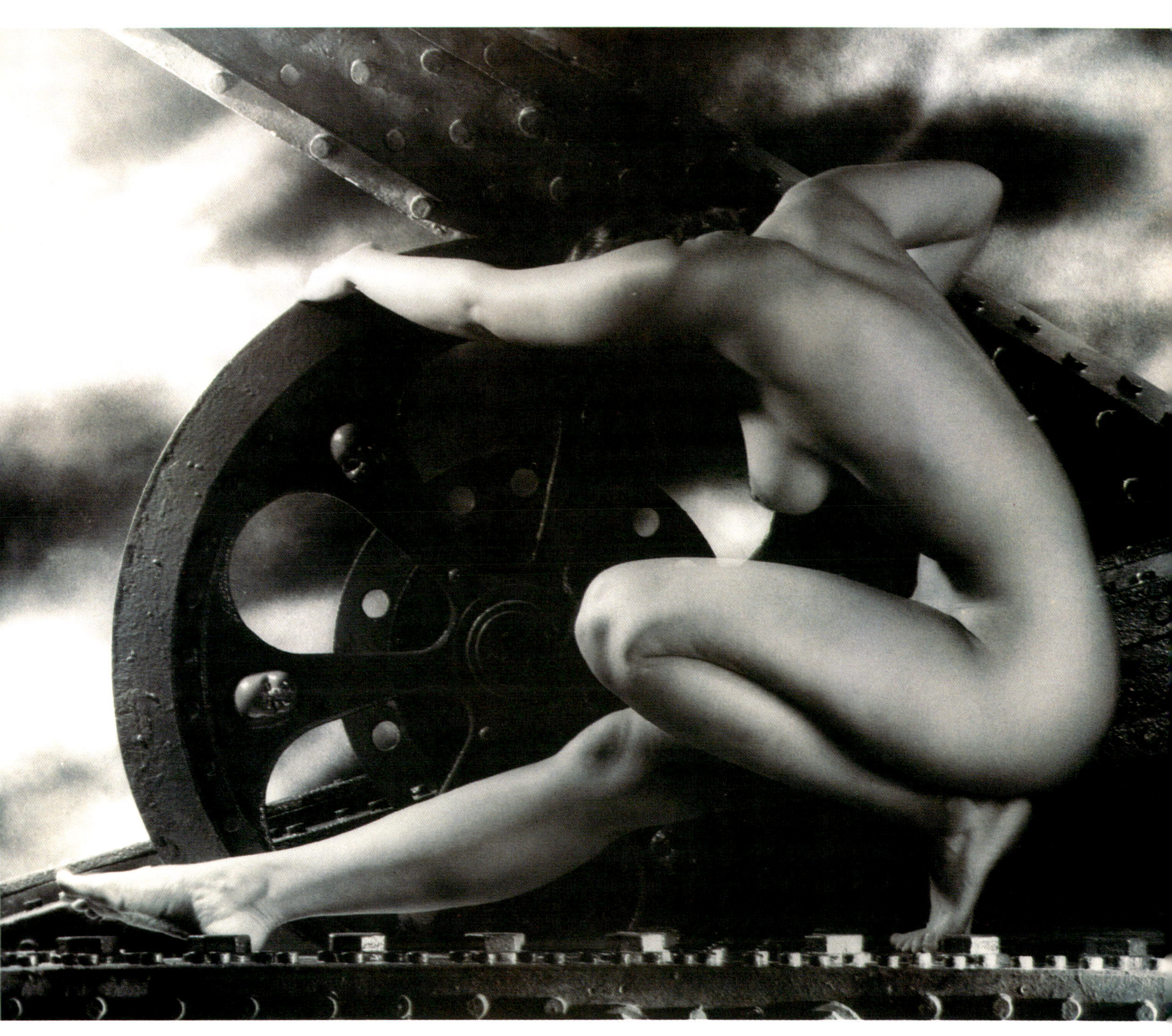

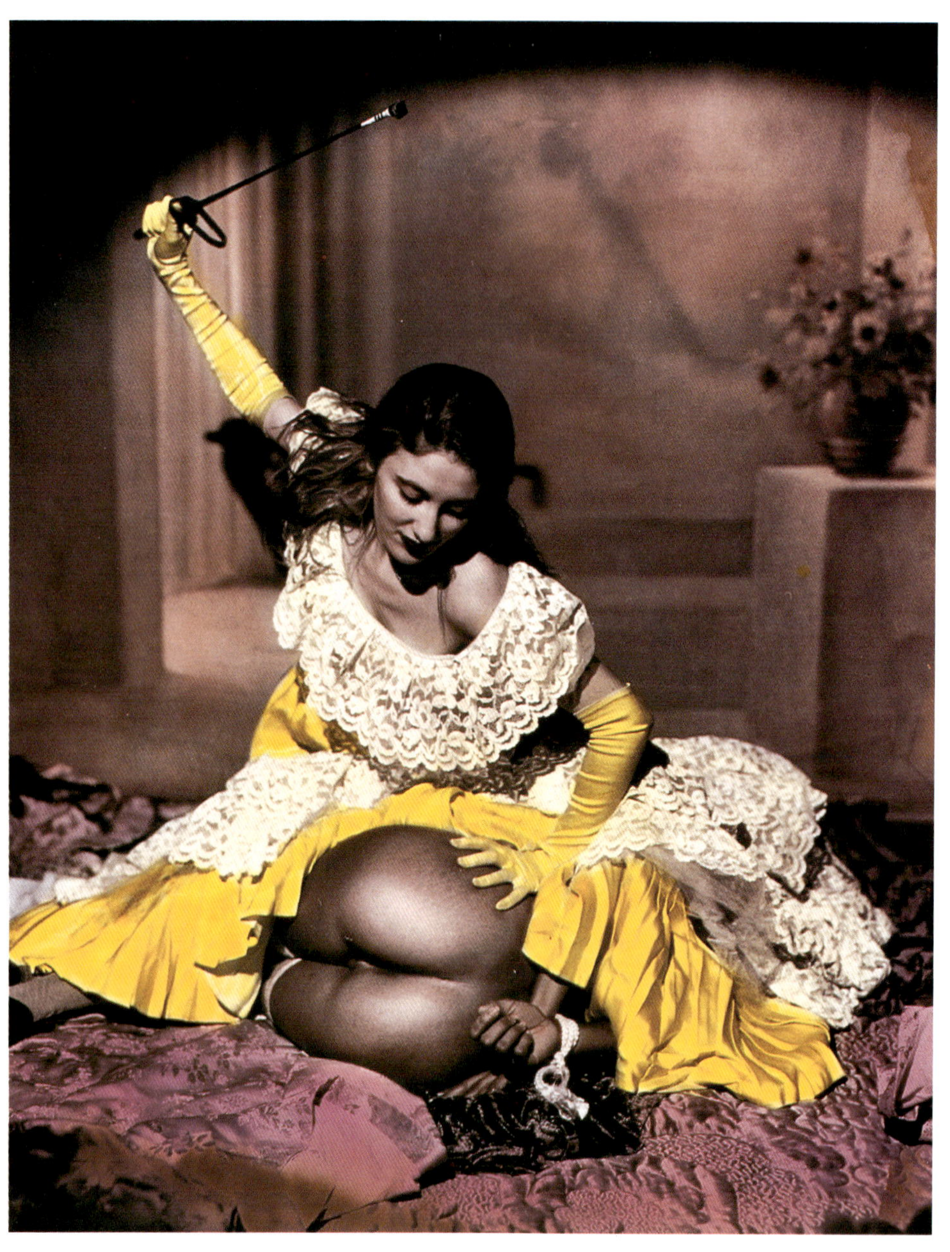

 ALEXANDRE DUPOUY 1995

(right) **IAIN McKELL** 1997

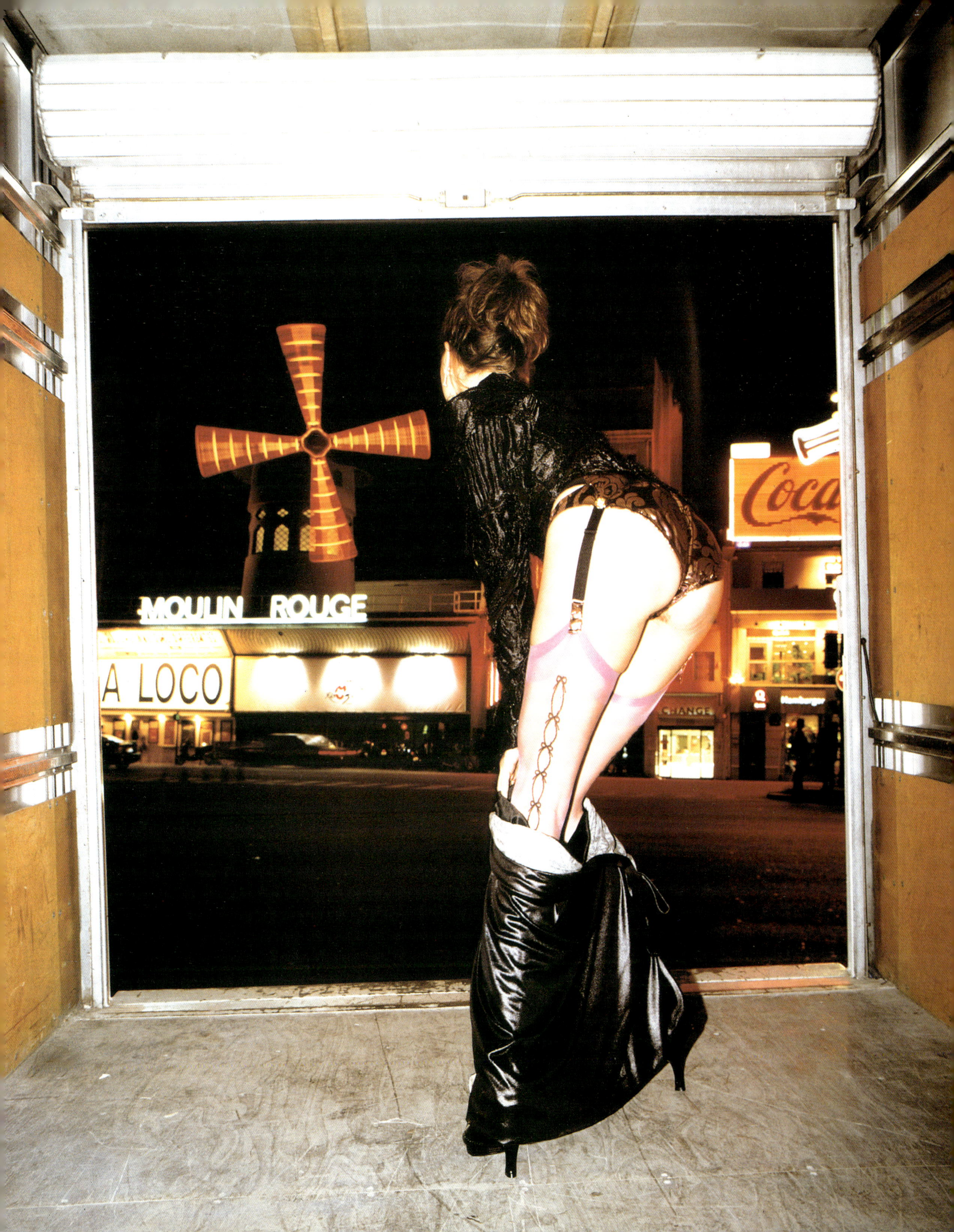
MOULIN ROUGE
A LOCO
Coca
CHANGE

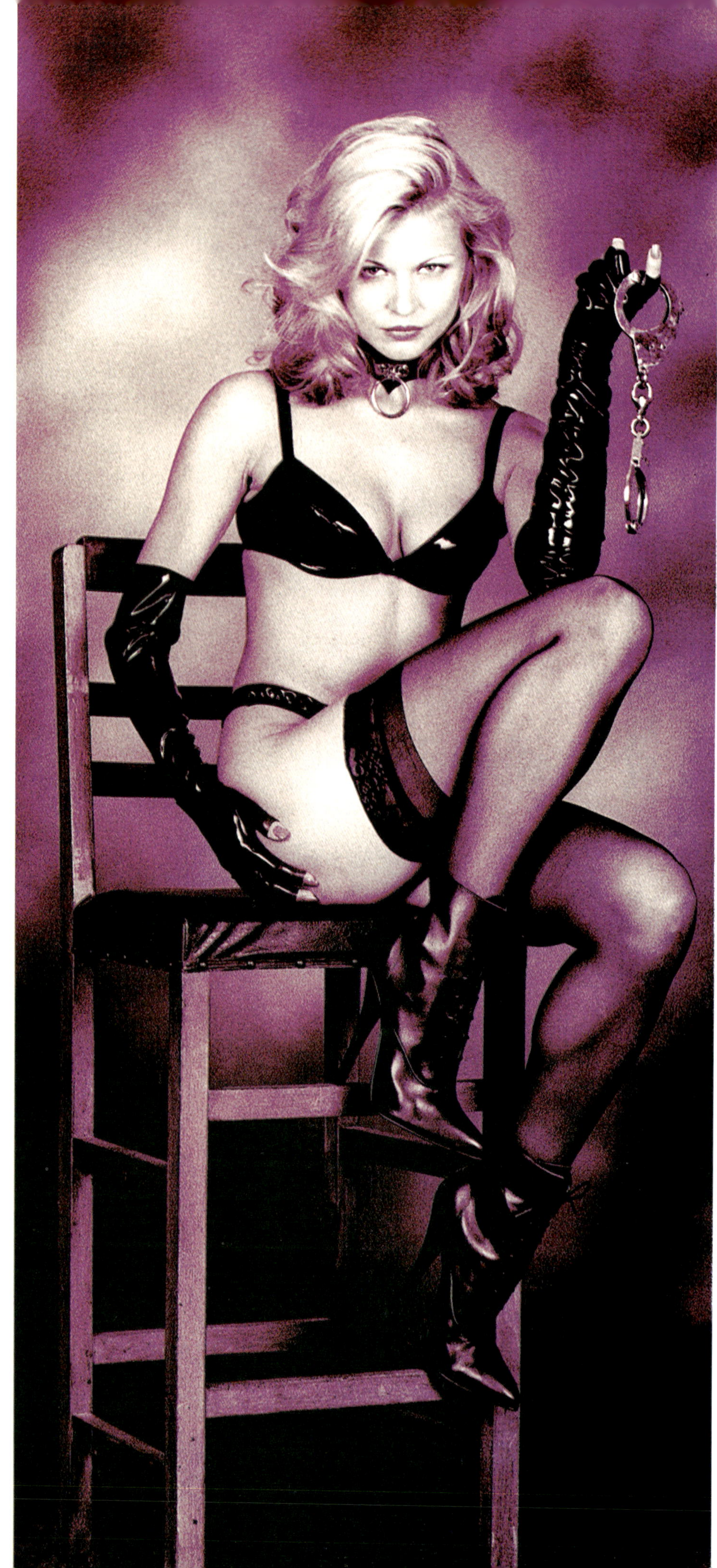

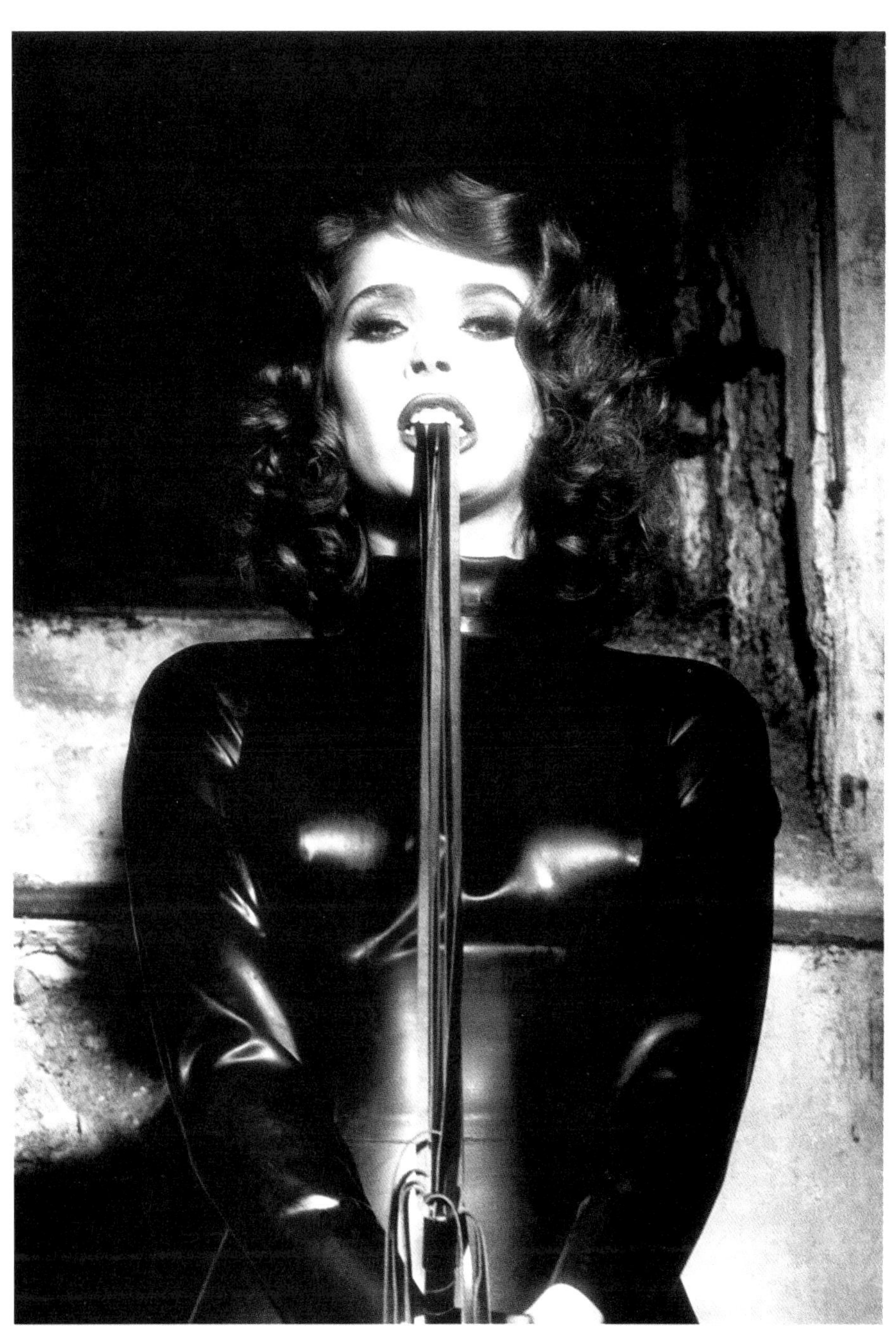

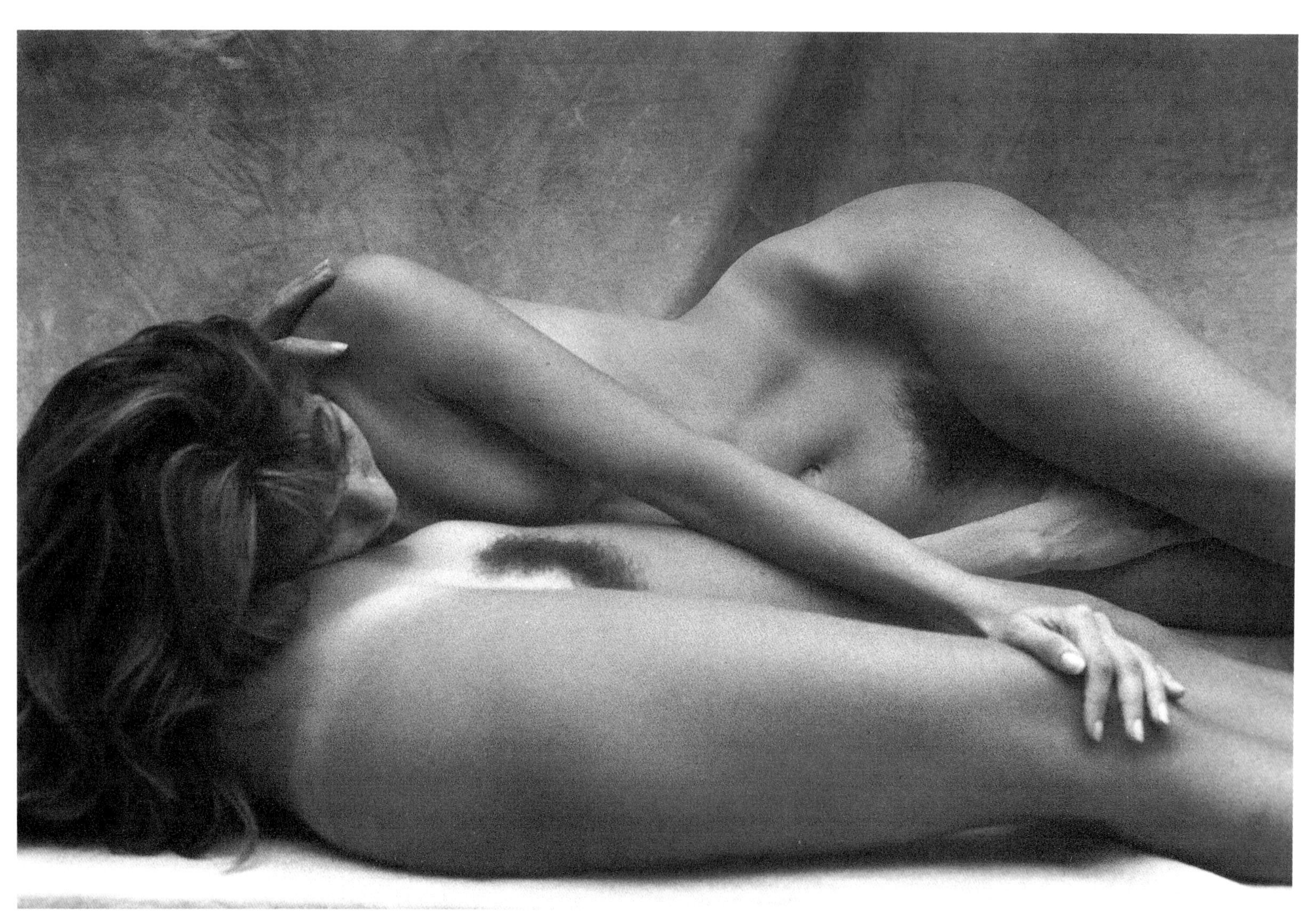

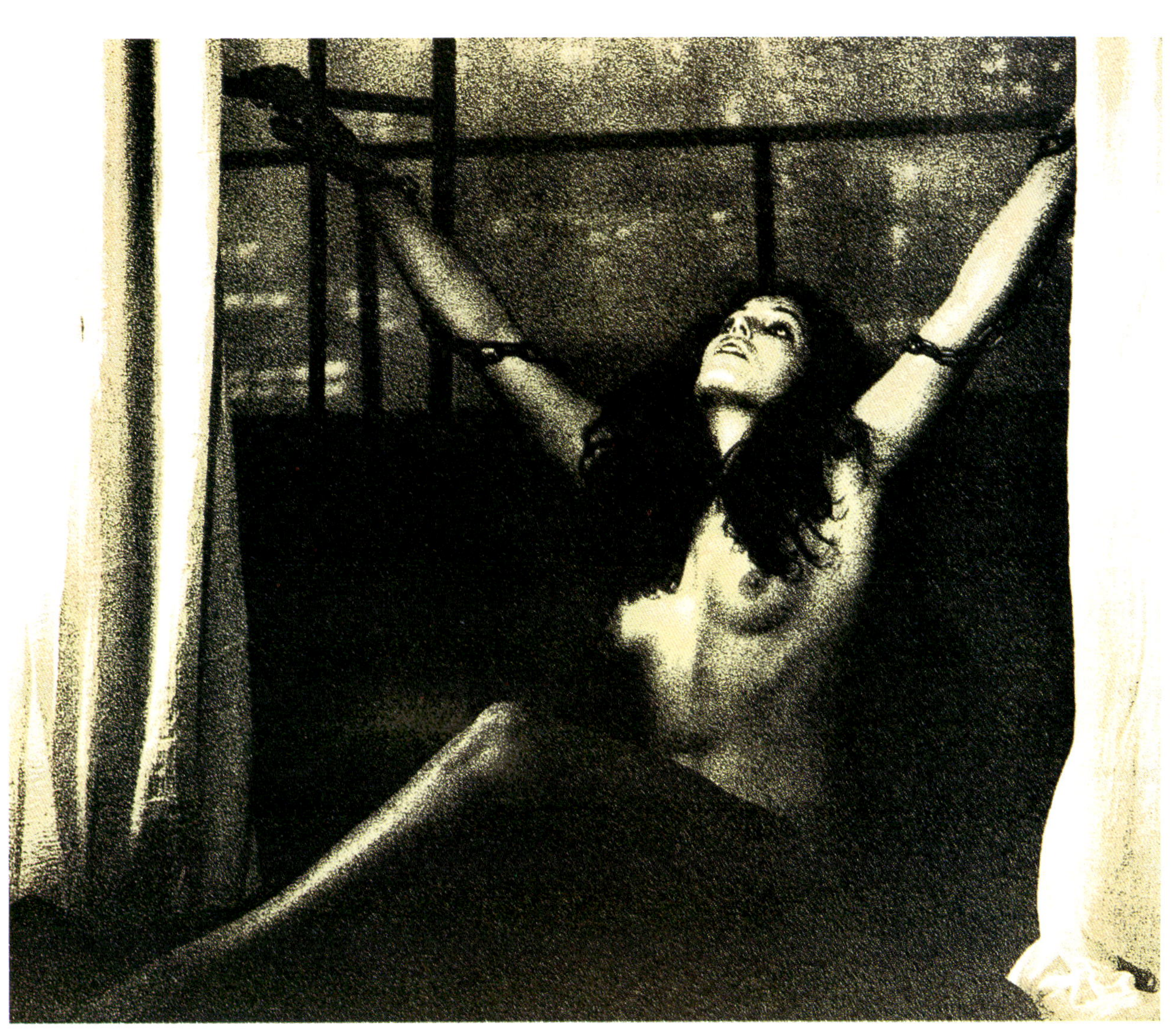

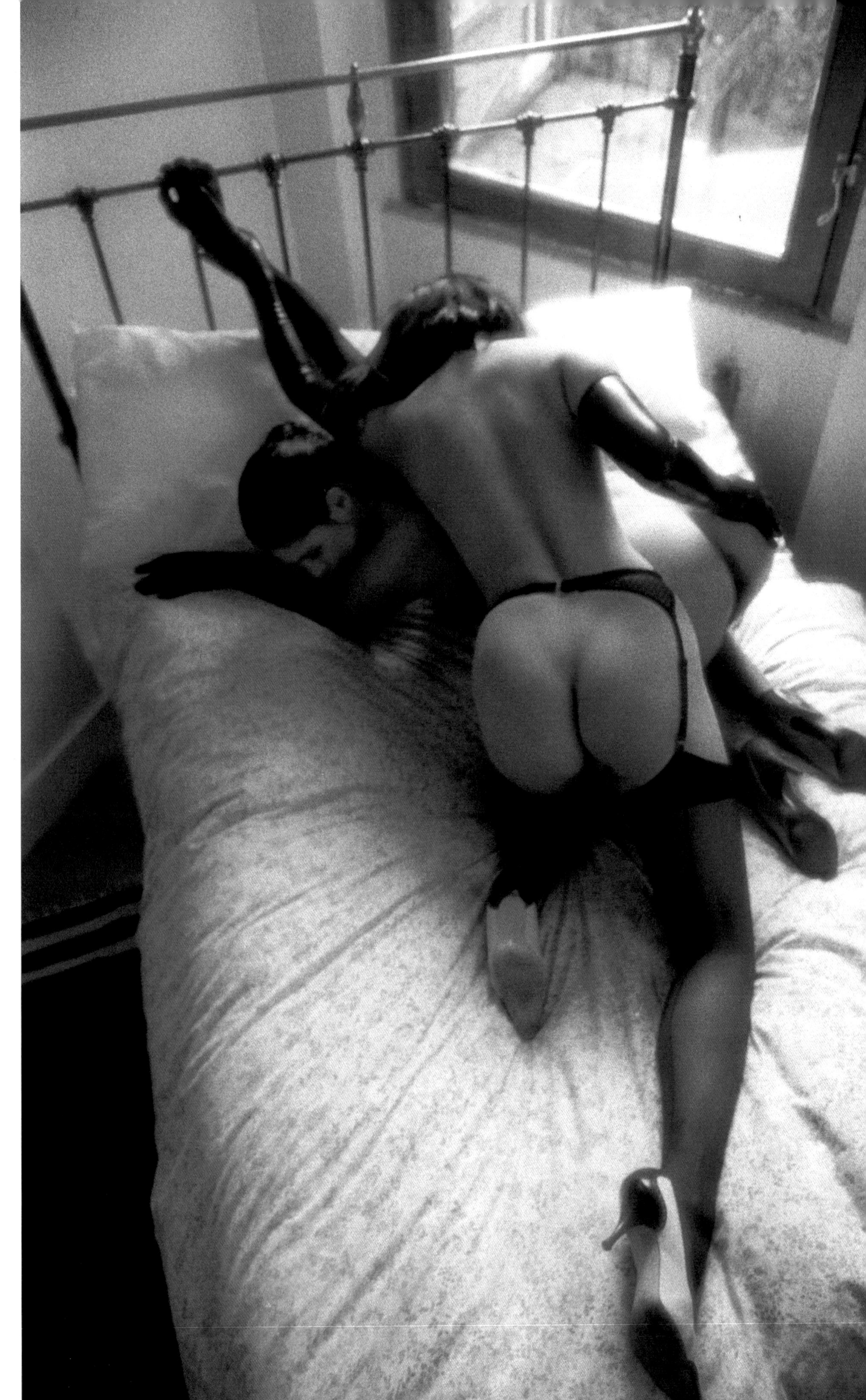

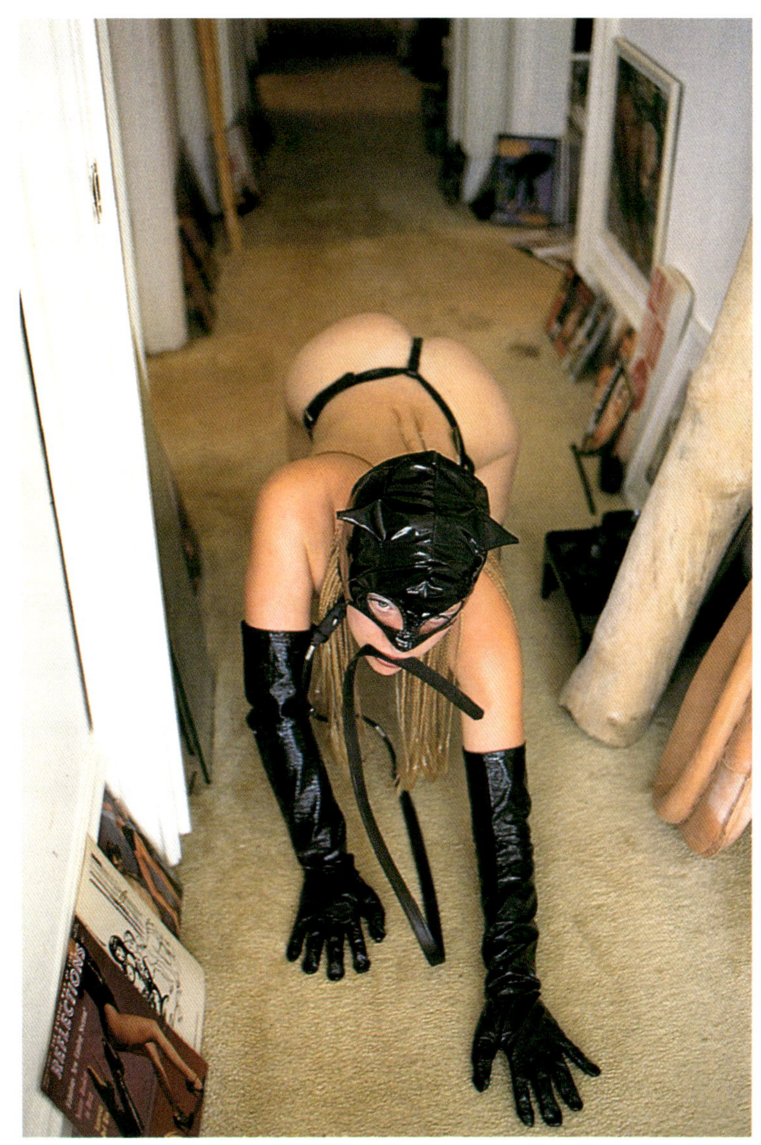

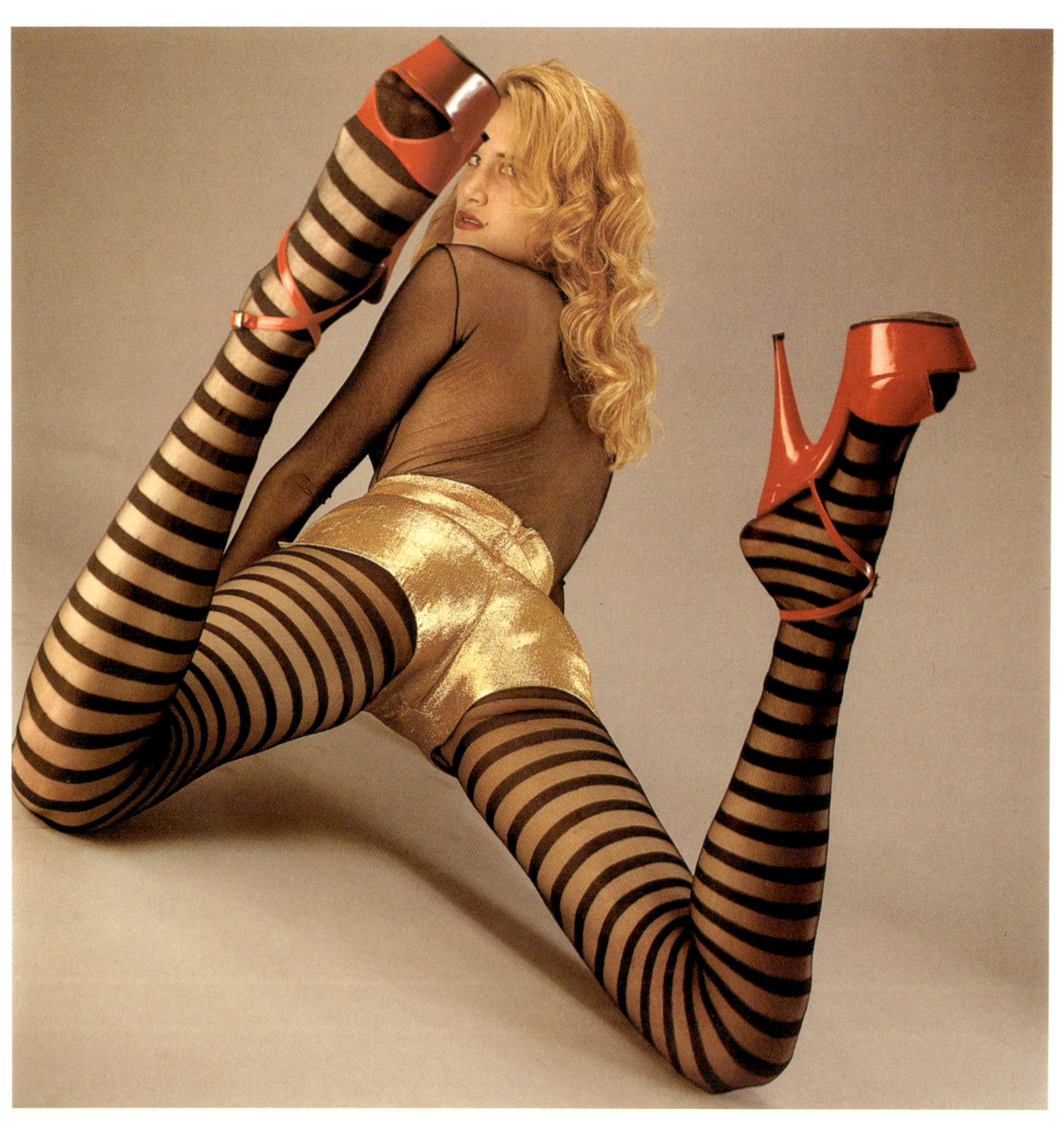

JEFF DUNAS 1990

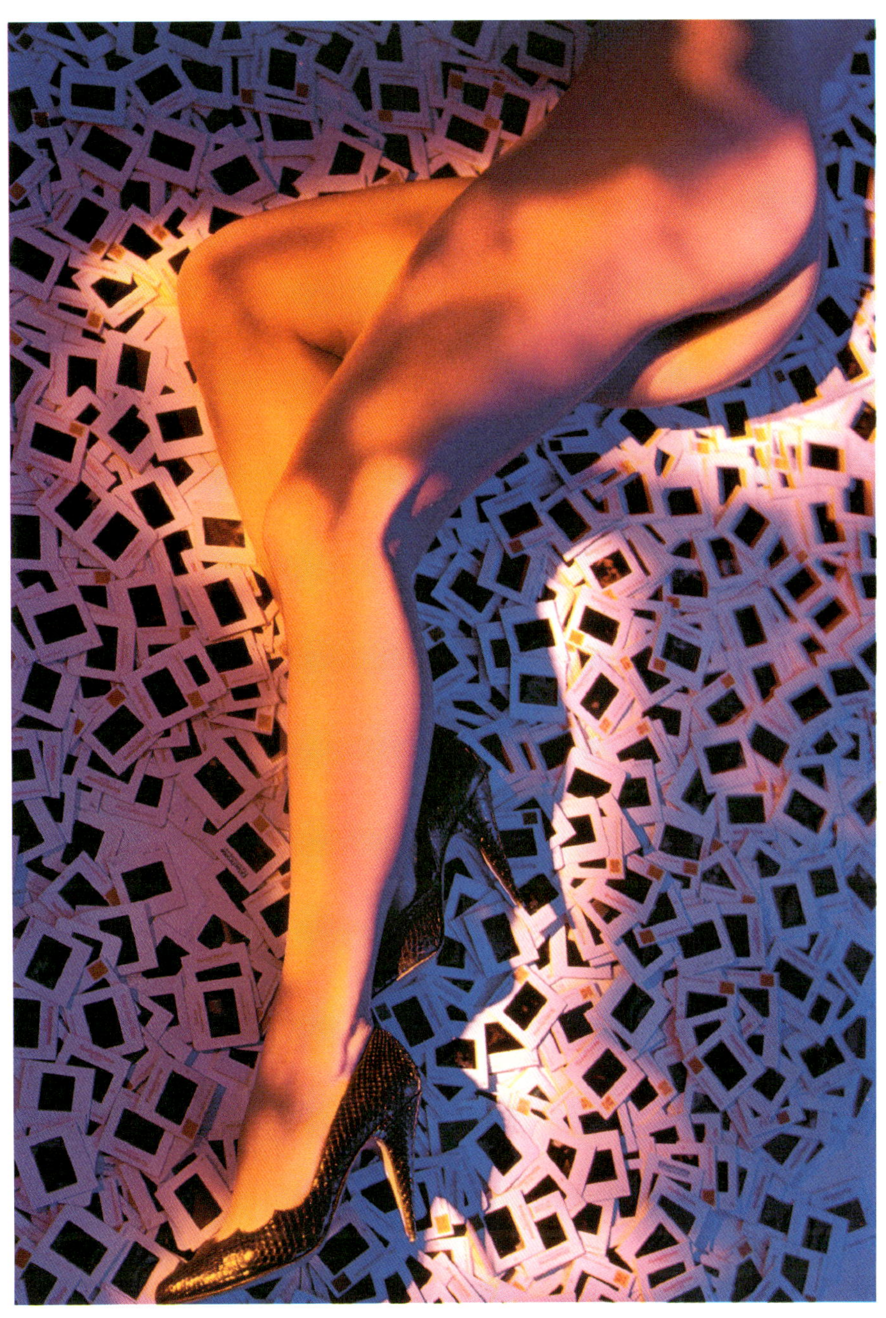

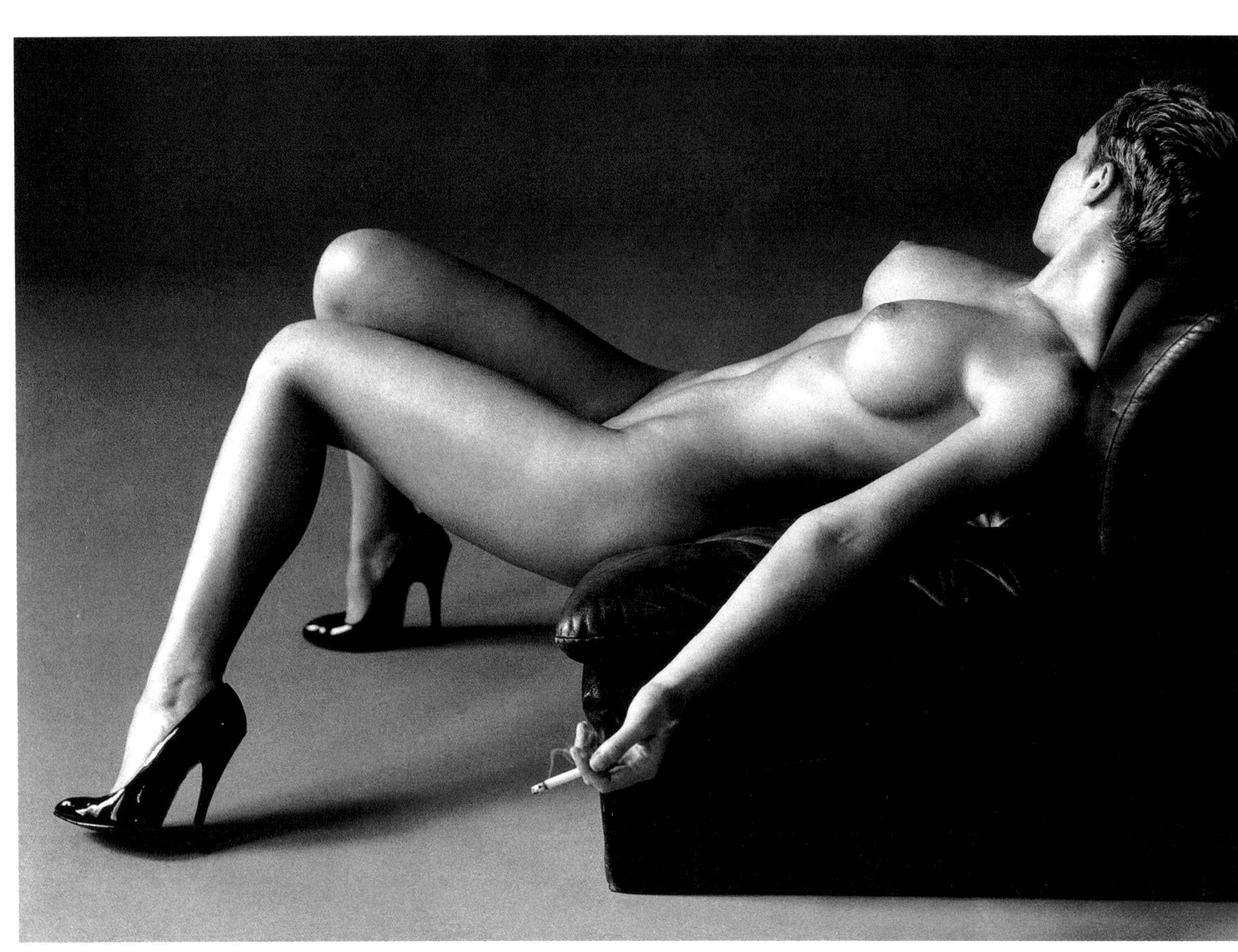

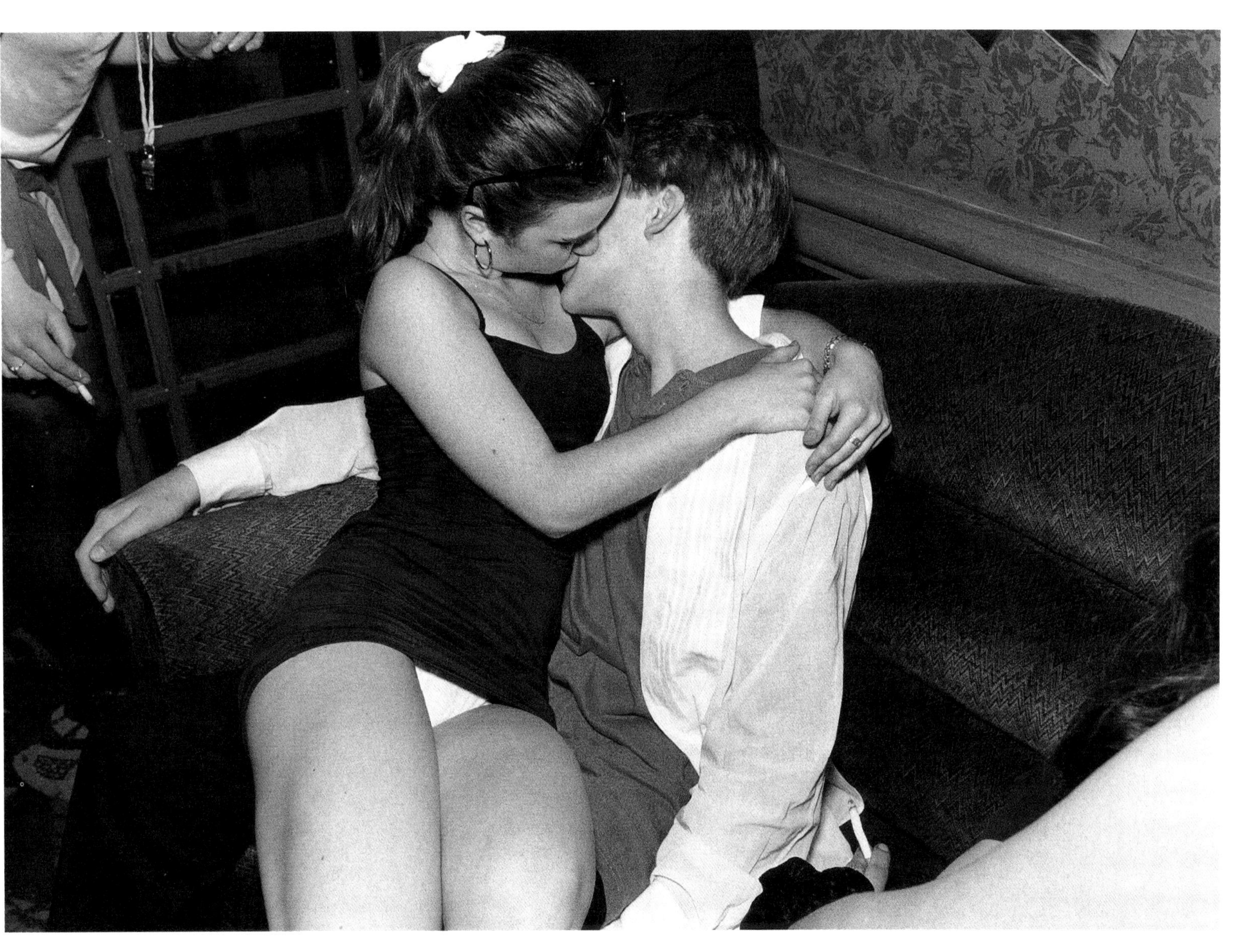

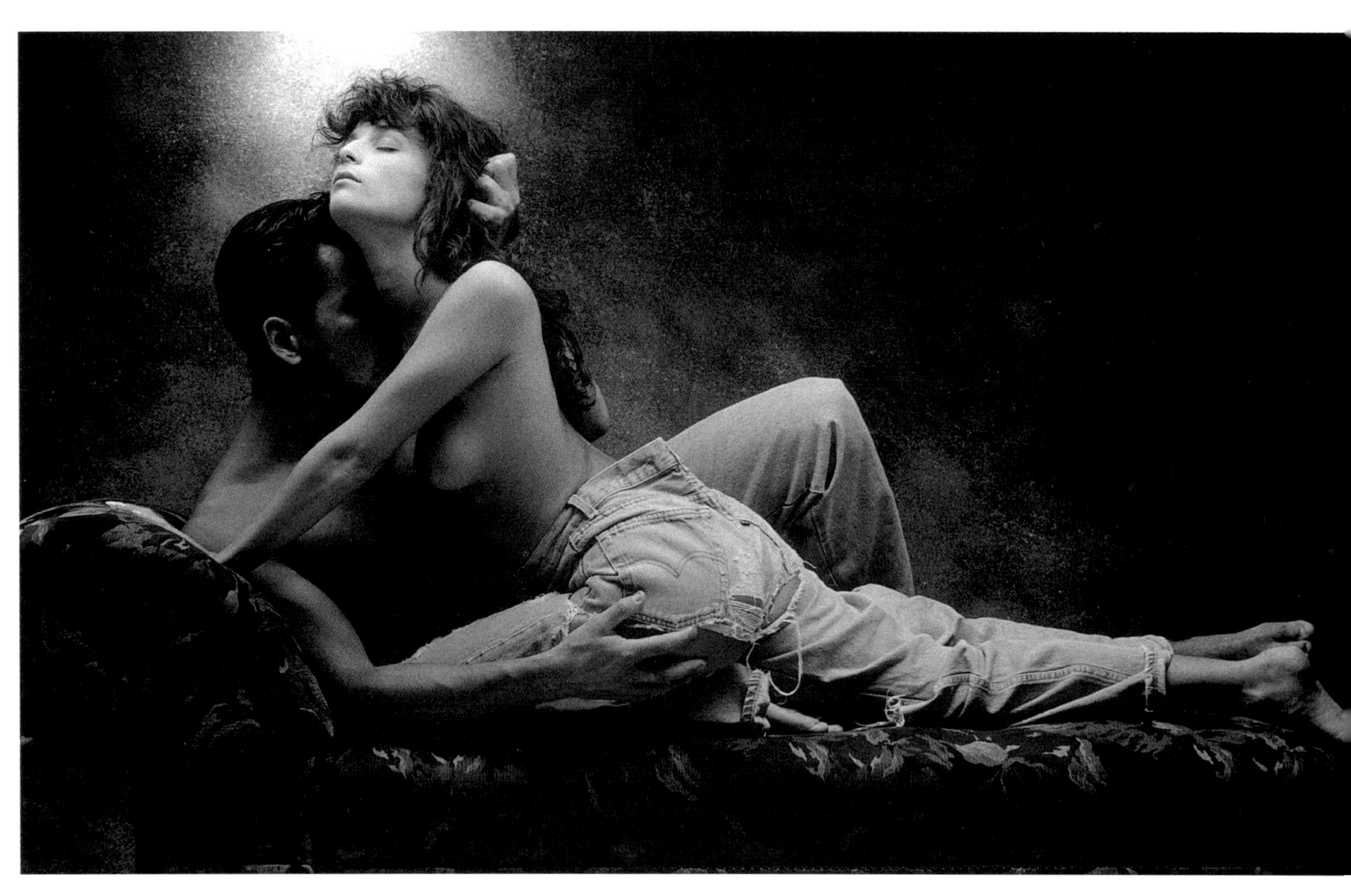

 ROD ASHFORD 1991

(right) **DAVID PENPRASE** 1996

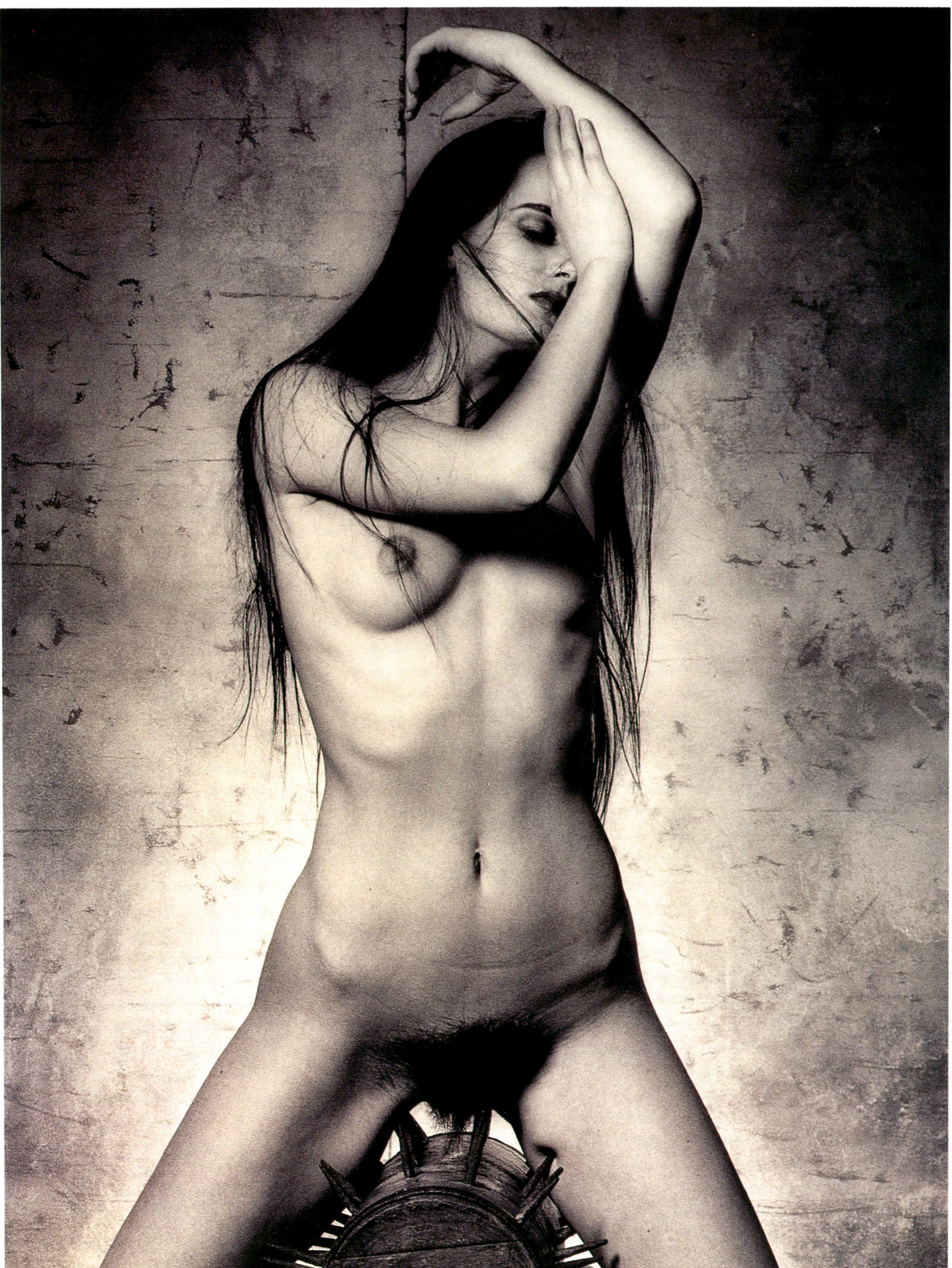

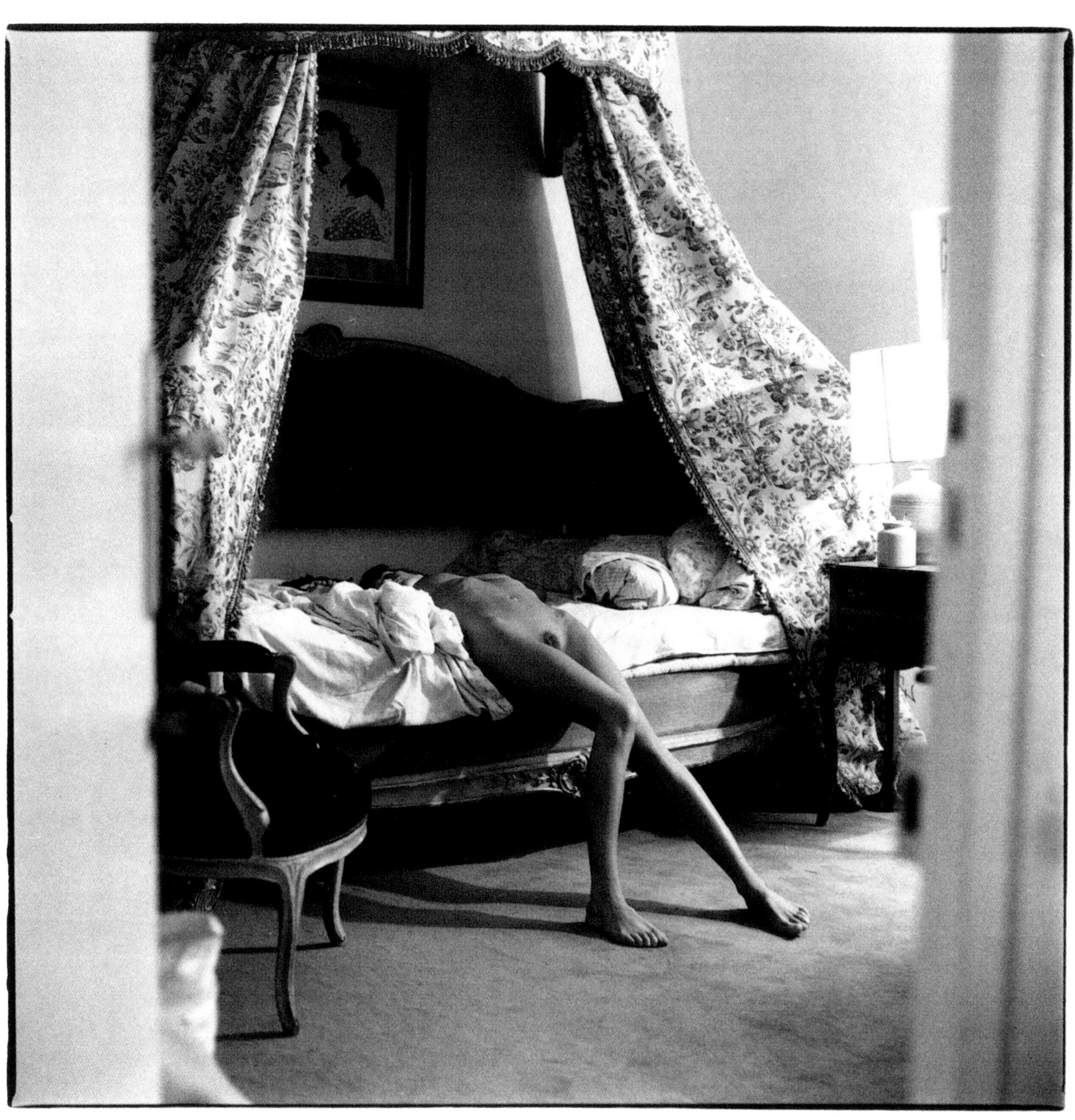

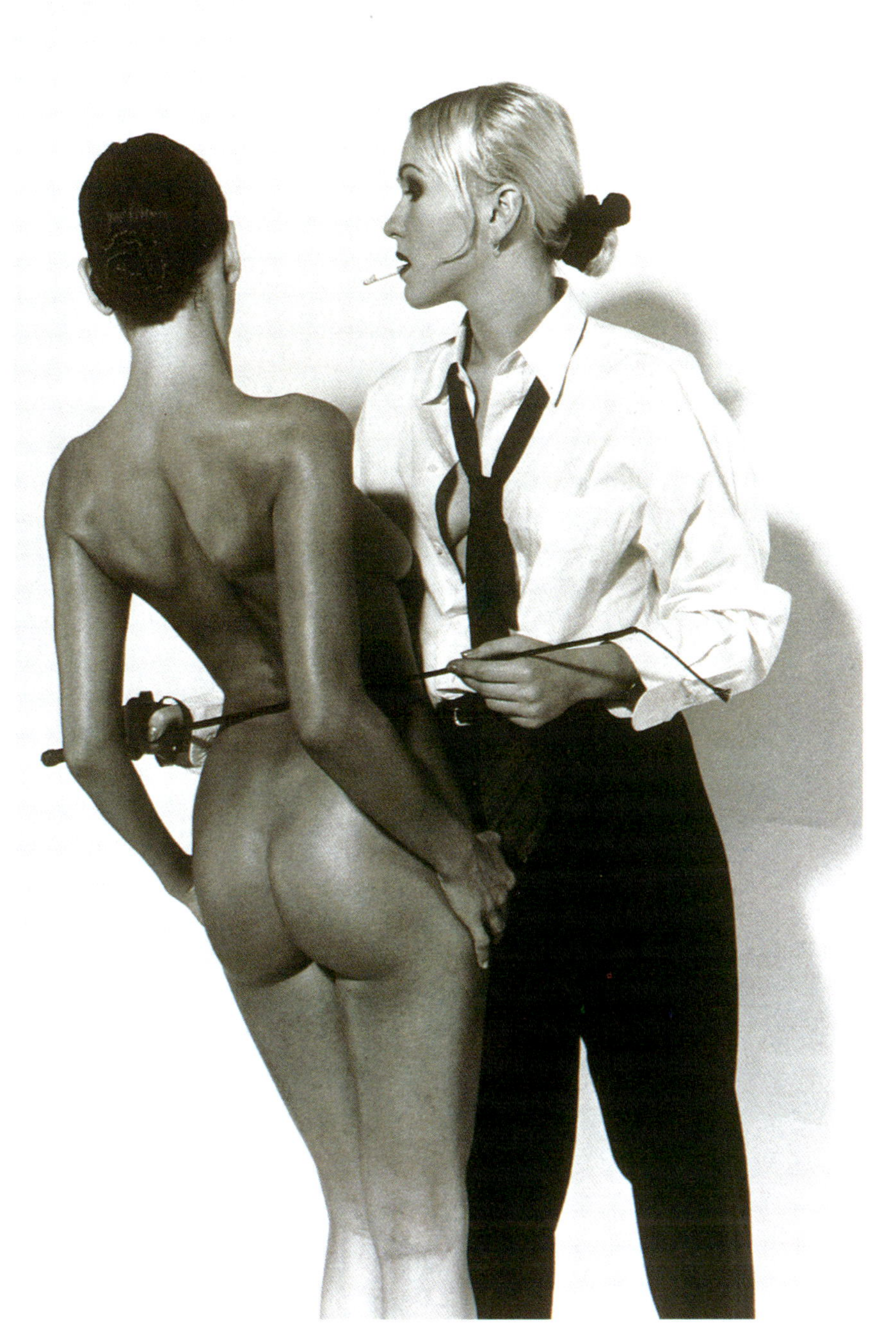

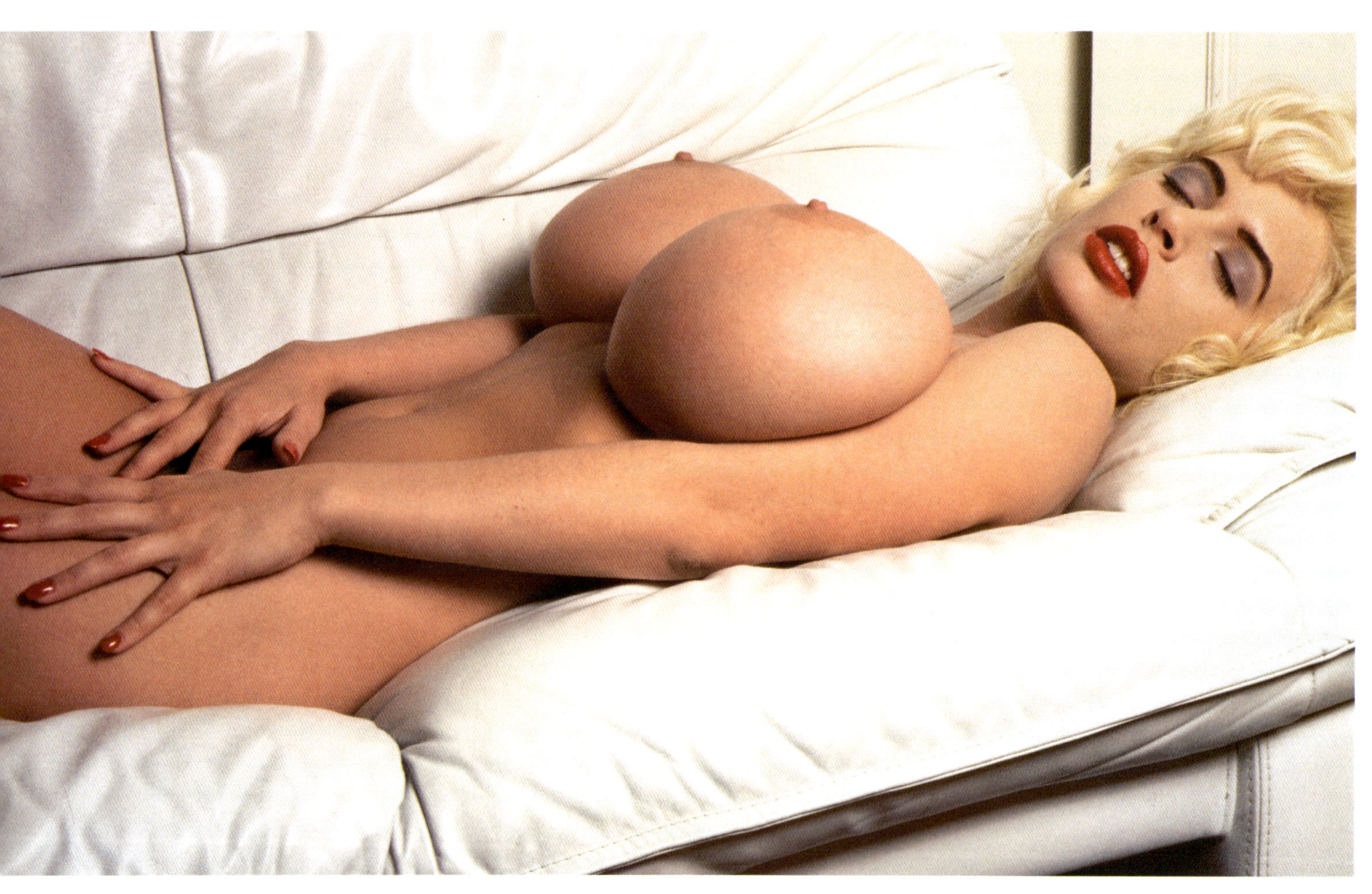

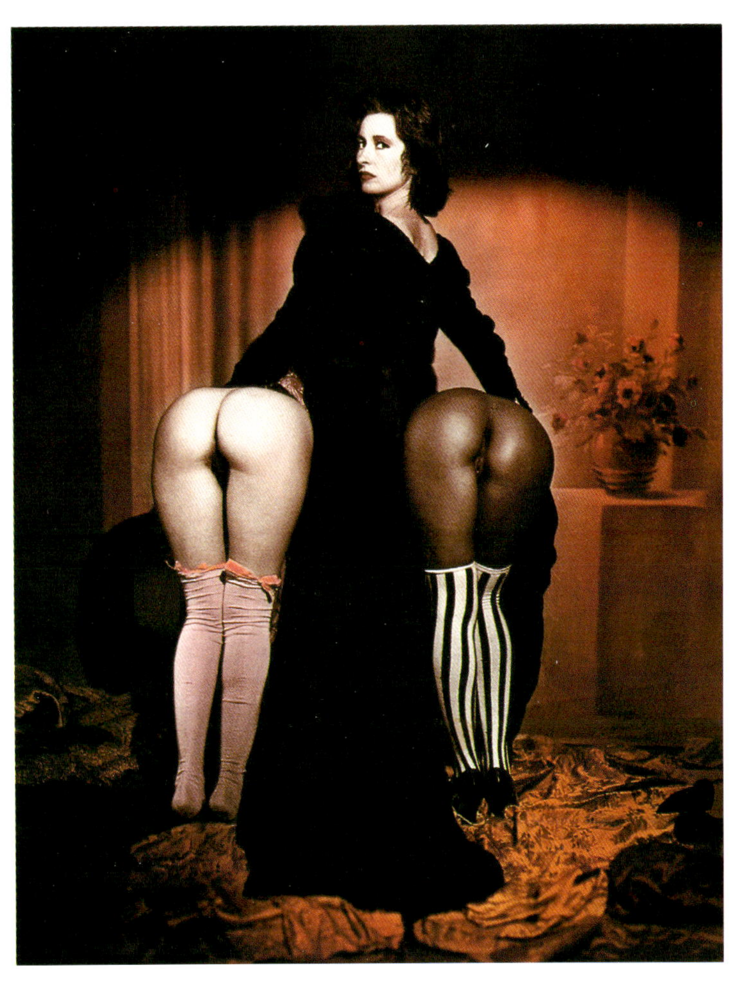

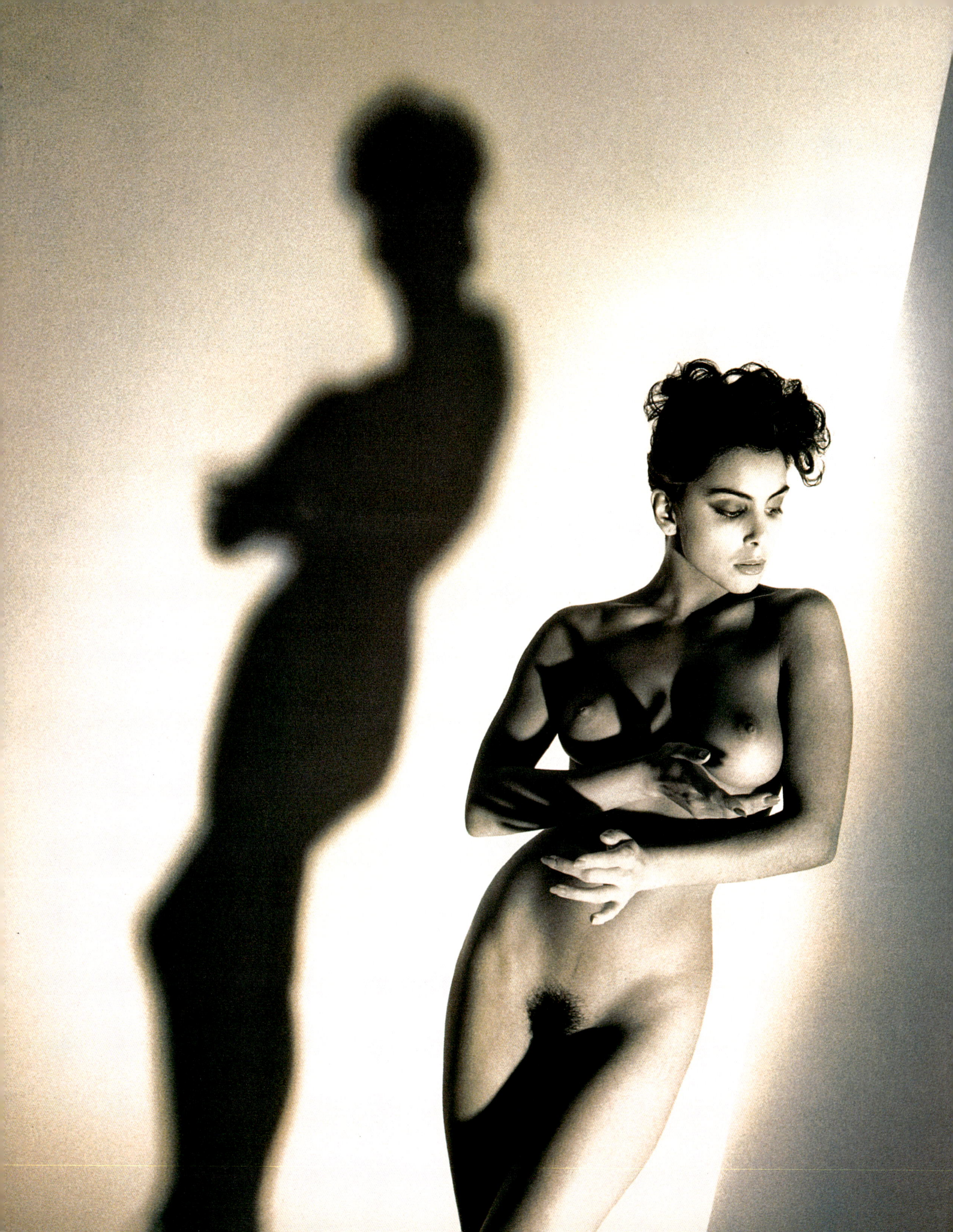

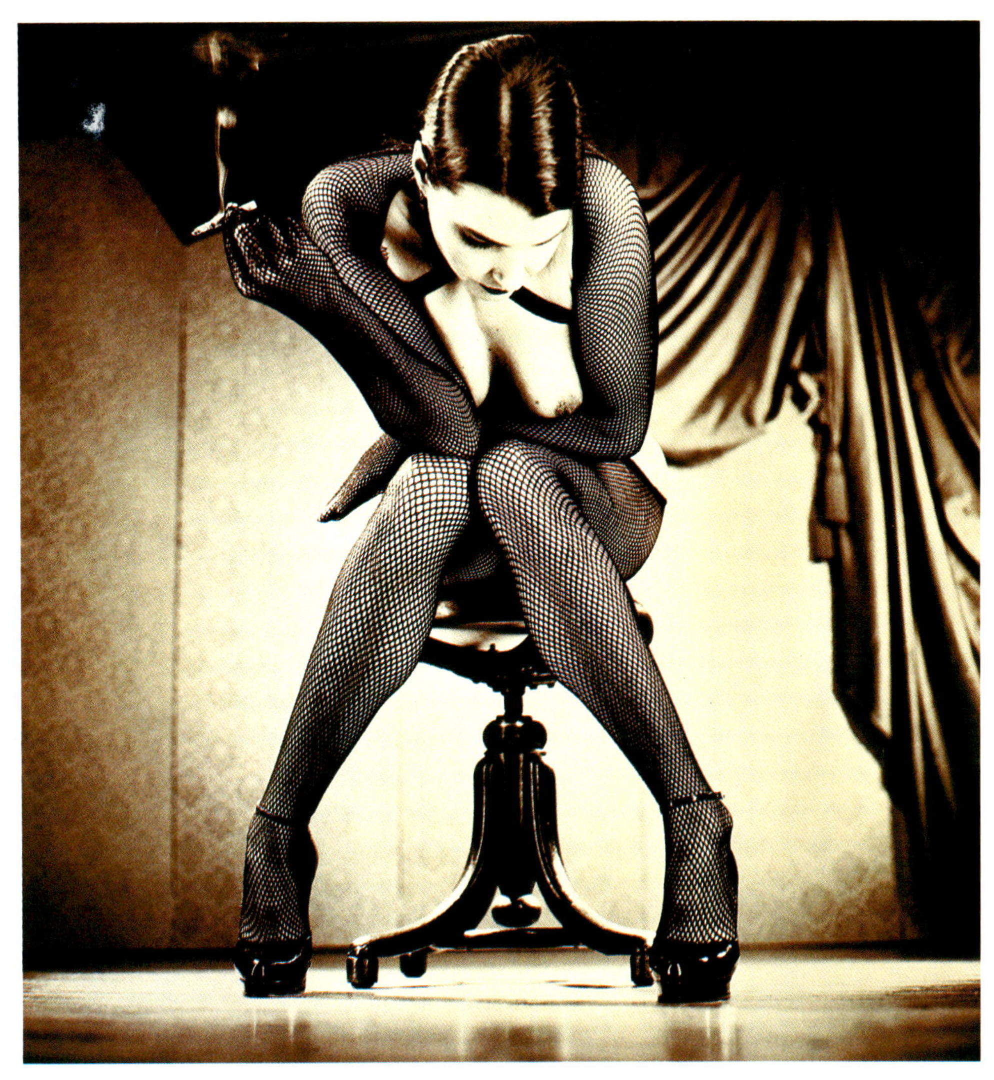

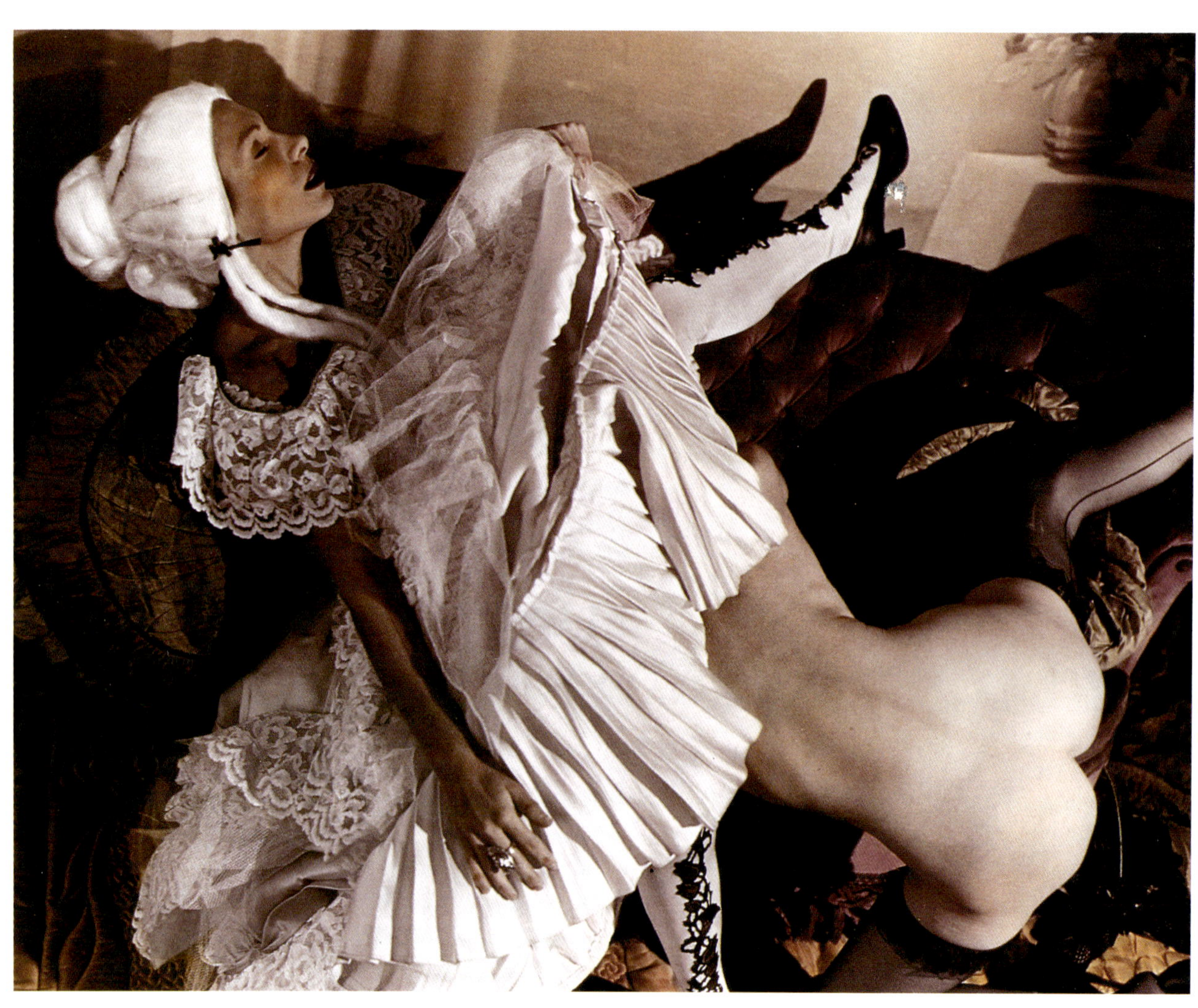

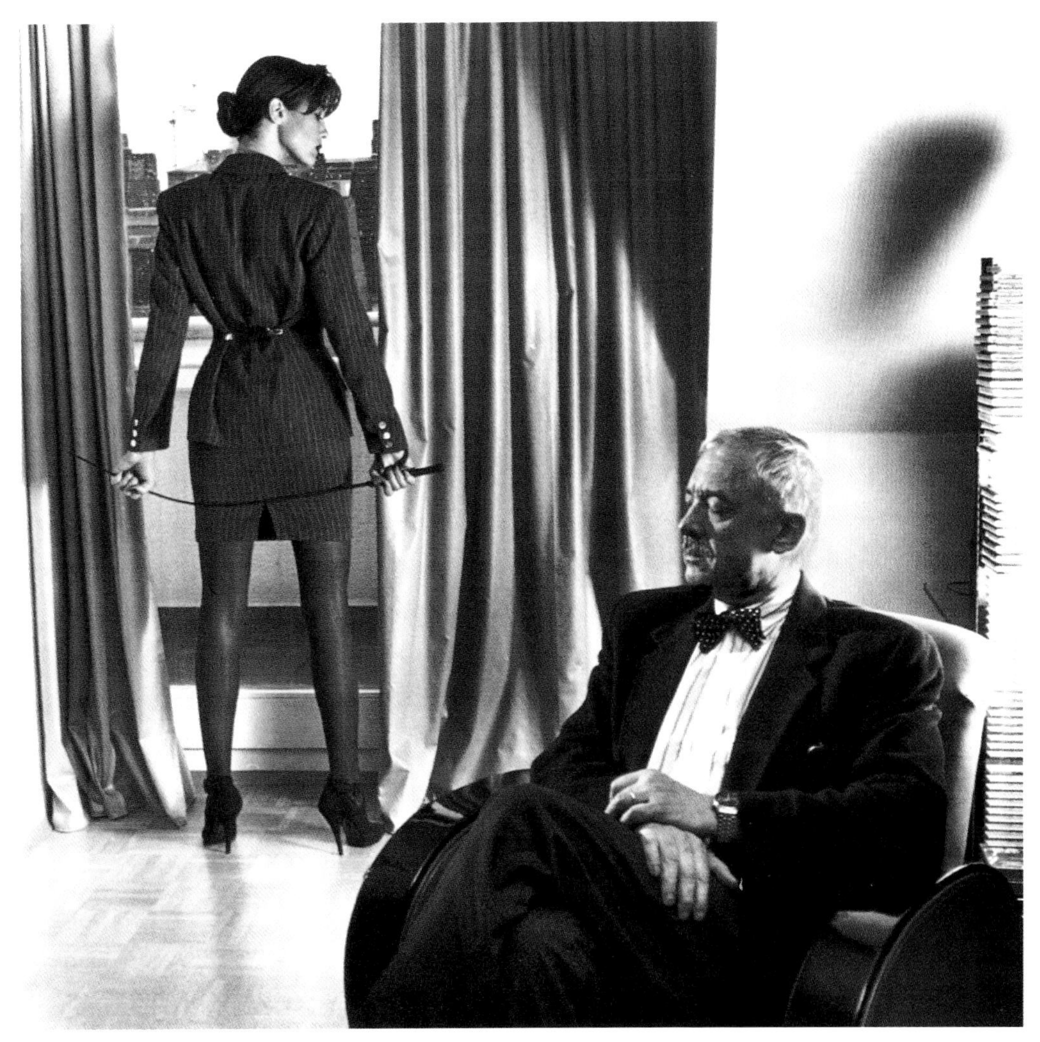

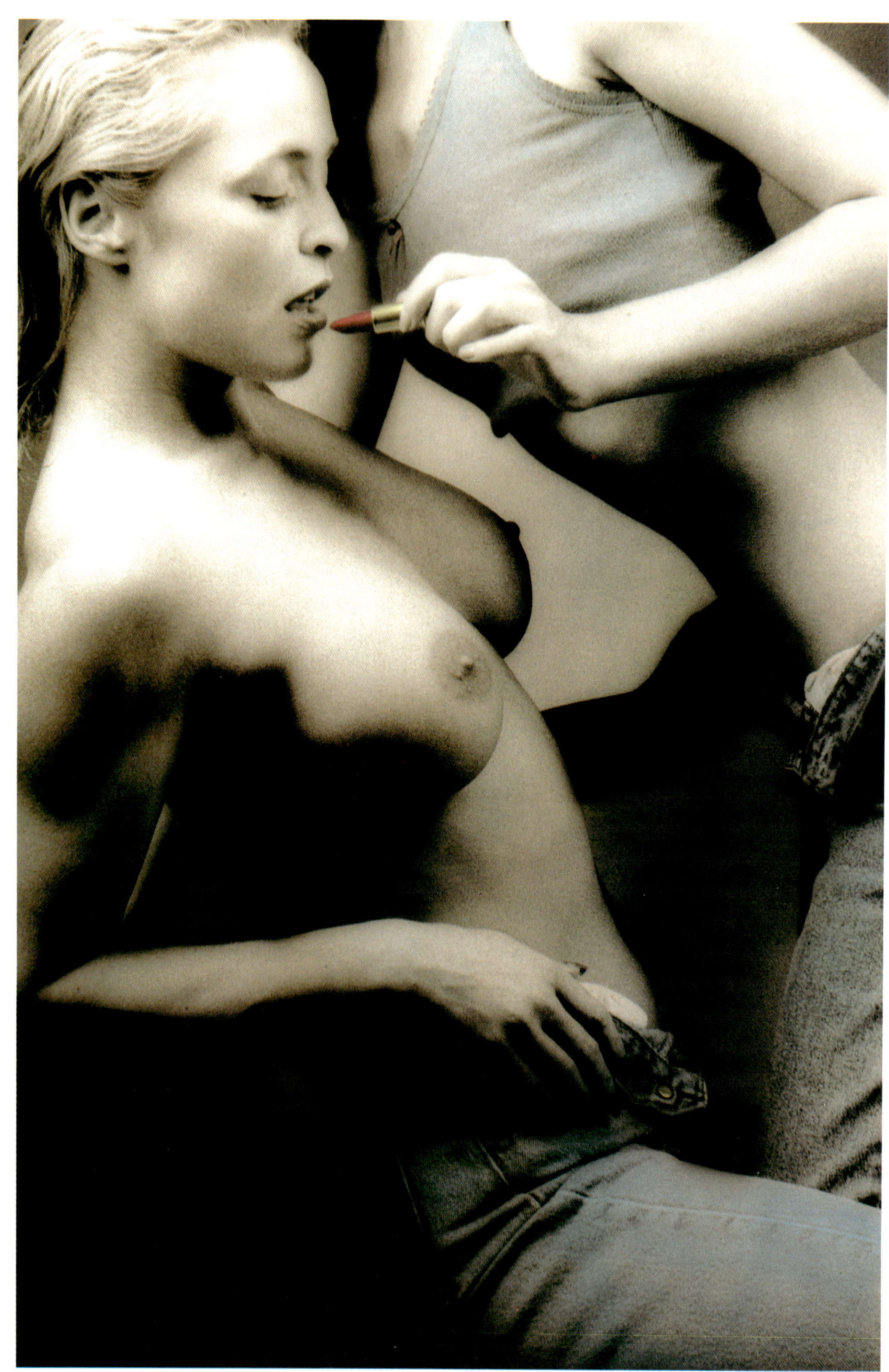

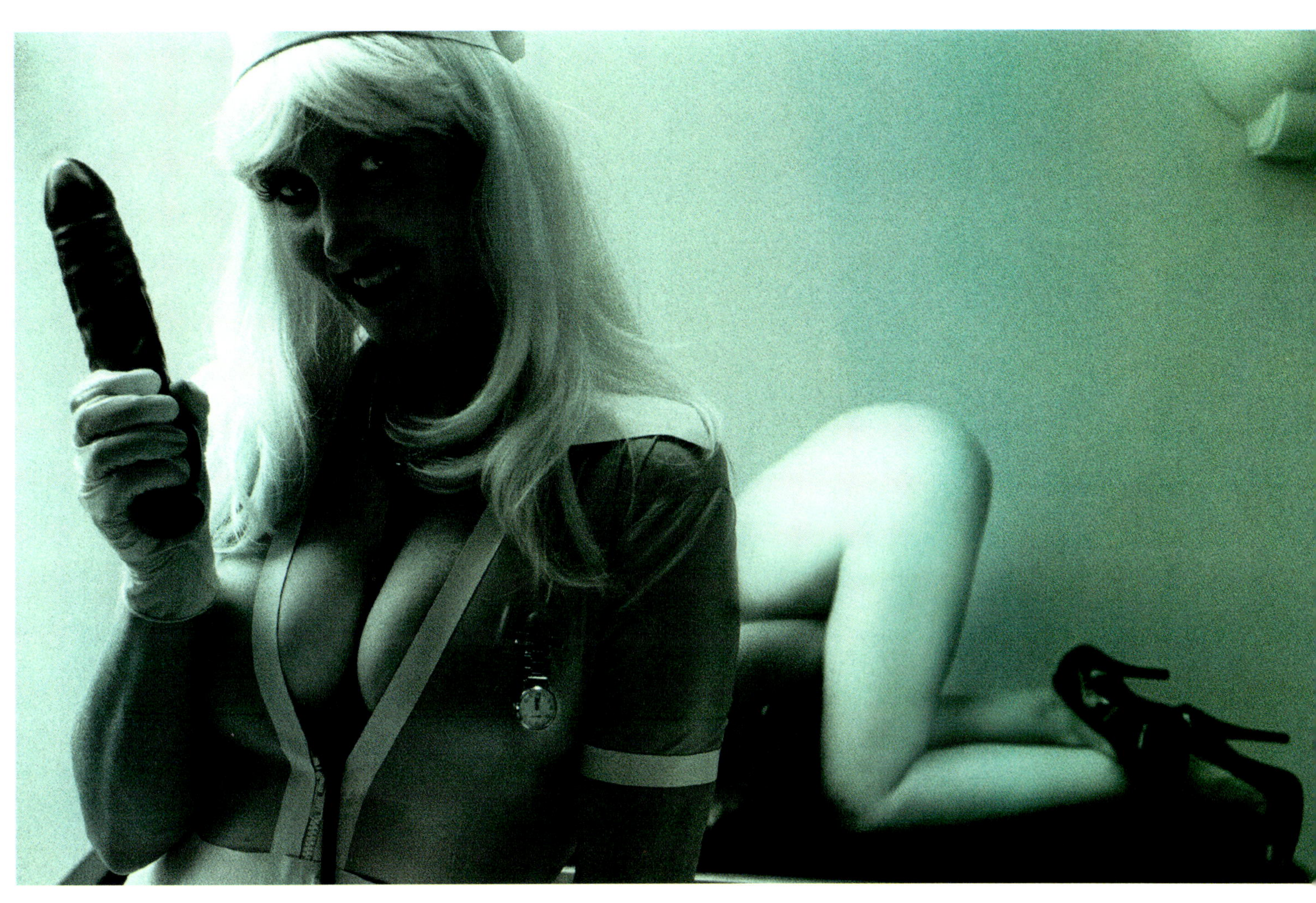

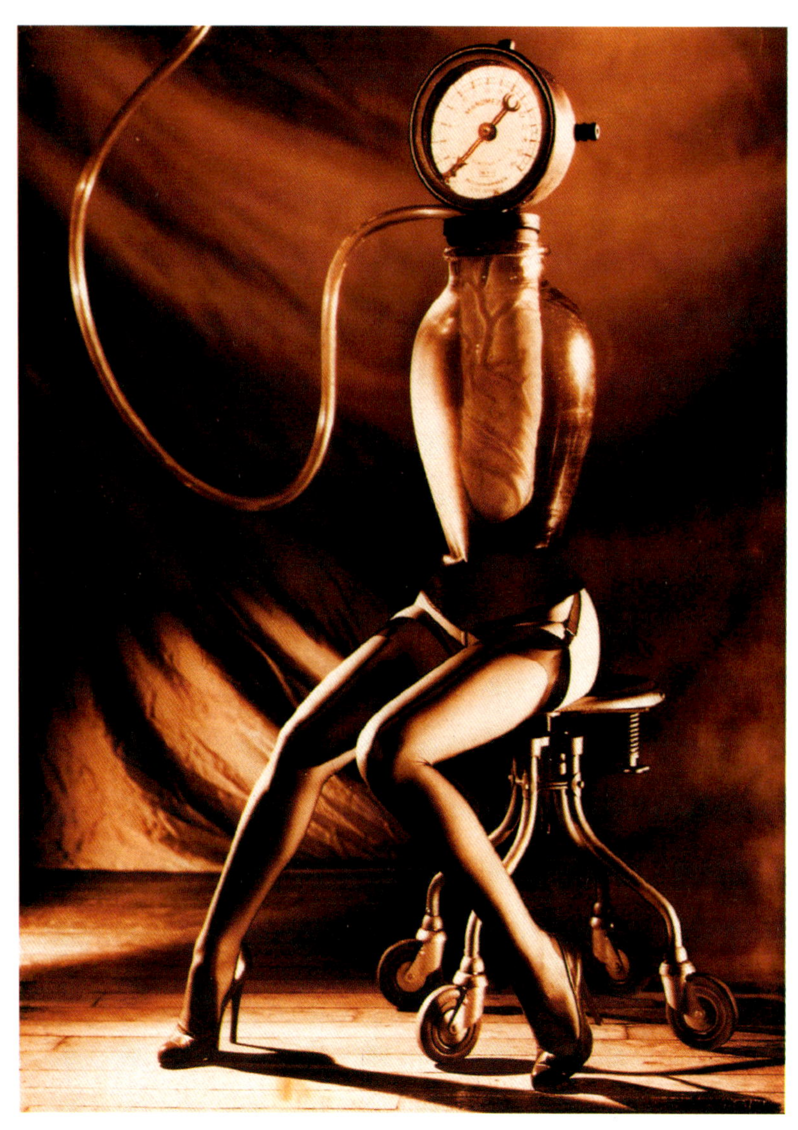

INDEX

A

After Lunch (Lichfield) 100
Agelou, E. 28, 29, 30
ambrotype 9
Anonymous (1855) 20
Anonymous (1855) 21
Anonymous (1880) 23
Anonymous (1885) 24
Anonymous (1890) 25
Anonymous (1900) 27
Anonymous (1910) 31
Anonymous (1910), Two lovely breasts round and full 32
Anonymous (1911), Bertram Park 33
Anonymous (1920) 34
Anonymous (1920) 35
Anonymous (1920) 36
Anonymous (1930) 41
Arizona Sunset (Eichler) 149
Ashford, Rod 141, 198, 208
- Handcuffs 92
- Layla 173
- Lipstick 218

Aubergine I (Blum) 123
August - Pirelli (Parkinson) 76

B

Barnack, Oscar 12
Berquet, Gilles 116, 152, 176, 215
- Brèue histoire de l'oeil 155
- Dans la Serre 128
- Grand Phalène, prince des ténèbres 175
- Morceau en Forme de Poire 109
- Sainte 131
- Sans Plomb 98 220

Bertram Park (Anonymous) 33
Black is My True Love's Heart (Clarke) 83
black-and-white photography, modern use of 17–18
Blonde on White Leather (Elliott) 212
Blum, Gunter
- Aubergine I 123
- Gotischer Torso 164
- Herztorso I 122
- Netztorso III 119
- Strumpfhalter 118
- Tanja Mit Rad 195
- Techno Torso 106

Boulevard Flandrin, Paris I (Dunas) 86
Brandt, Bill
- Nude Campden Hill London 63
- Nude London 59, 62
- Nude London 61 Theatre Girl 60

Brève histoire de l'oeil (Berquet) 155
Brewster, Sir David 9
Bubblegum (Eichler) 168
Burnished Blondes (Dietrich) 77

C

calotype 8–9
camera obscura 7–8
cameras, design 11–12
Carmen (Karsten) 135
cartes-de-visites 16
Central Park, NYC (Lichfield) 110
Chambre Rue la Condamine (Roff) 210
Château de Breteuil, Vallé de Chevreuse (Dunas) 70
Chevi '62 (Roff) 71
Chippy (McKell) 6, 145
Clarke, Bob Carlos
- Black is My True Love's Heart 83
- Faithful Unto Death 97
- Furka 139
- Hammersmith Palais 207
- Nell 206
- The Punishment of Luxury 96
- Twisted 138

Clergue, Lucien
- Diana Lake of Garda 115
- Nude at the Beach, Camargue 159
- Nude in the Lighthouse, Camargue 101

collodion 9
colour photography 10–11
Composition (Muray) 44
computers 13
Contemplation of the Eternal (C. Hamilton) 121
context 6–7
Conversation While Undressing (C. Hamilton) 120
Cornfield (McKell) 140
Couple entwined (Swannell) 127
Curto, Paolo, Nude woman throwing hair out of pool 142
Cynthia and the Motorbikes (Mourthé) 143

D

Daguerre, Louis 8
daguerreotype 11, 14–15
Dans la Serre (Berquet) 128
Davis, Roger 16–17
The Deep Devotion of Ida (Saudek) 114
Diana Lake of Garda (Clergue) 115
Die Chauffeurin (Dietrich) 78
Dietrich, John
- Burnished Blondes 77
- Die Chauffeurin 78
- Laughing Domina 148
- Pink Rubber 165
- Replicant 87

digital photography 13
Disdéri, André 16
Diszipline über Alles (Saudek) 150
The Dressing Room (Wedge) 80
Dunas, Jeff
- Boulevard Flandrin, Paris I 86
- Château de Breteuil, Vallé de Chevreuse 70
- Grayhall Mansion, Beverley Hills III 102
- Homage to Kodachrome 205
- Les Essarts-le-Roi, France 66
- Nude no.3, Los Angeles Studio 214
- Pasadena, California 94
- Rue Marbeus, Paris 68

Dupouy, Alexandre
- Intèrieur parisien 132
- L'éducation de Scarlett 196
- Les Jeux de la Comtesse B. 213
- Un après-midi chez la marquise 216

E

Eastman, George 10
Eat Soup (McKell) 163
Egg (McKell) 117
Eichler, Wolfgang
- Arizona Sunset 149
- Bubblegum 168
- Madlen and Conny 211
- Nadine and Madlen at home 187
- Nylon Nightmares 154
- Once Upon a Time in the West 171
- Unlocked 104
- The Visiter 217

Elliott, James
- Blonde on White Leather 212
- Hungerlust Capitalism 181
- Red Velvet Gloves 89
- Streetwalker Blues 88

F

Faithful Unto Death (Clarke) 97
Farber, Robert, Nude by pillar 178
Feigning innocence, South of France (D. Hamilton) 74
ferrotype 9
fetishism 18
film stars 16
First Nude (Parkinson) 58
Flippers, Barbados (Lategan) 98
Flying Nude-Bare Naked Out the Window (Roff) 64
Fox Talbot, William Henry 8, 15
Fundamental Practice (C. Hamilton) 192
Furka (Clarke) 139

G

Girl in Dressing Room (Wedge) 81
Good Morning America (Lichfield) 130
Gotischer Torso (Blum) 164
Grand Phalène, prince des ténèbres (Berquet) 175
Grayhall Mansion, Beverley Hills III (Dunas) 102

H

Hamilton, China
- Contemplation of the Eternal 121
- Conversation While Undressing 120
- Fundamental Practice 192

Hamilton, David
- Feigning innocence, South of France 74
- Monica, Saint-Tropez 84
- Provocation, South of France 85

Hammersmith Palais (Clarke) 207
Handcuffs (Ashford) 92
Herschel, Sir John 8
Herztorso I (Blum) 122
Hesser, Edwin Bauer, Jean Harlow 50
Homage to Great Vincent (Saudek) 99
Homage to Kodachrome (Dunas) 205
The Hook (Lichfield) 93
Horst, Horst P.
- Lisa on Silk 49
- Odalisque III, NY 52

Hungerlust Capitalism (Elliott) 181

I

Intèrieur parisien (Dupouy) 132

J

Jarrae (Morey) 161
Jean Harlow (Hesser) 50
Julia Campion (Mourthé) 189

K

Kampert, Klaus 194
Karsten, Thomas
- Carmen 135
- Katharina 146, 147
- Yvette 160

Katharina (Karsten) 146, 147
Kodak 10
Koppitz, Rudolf, Study of Motion 43
Kroll, Eric 203
- M.M. 204
- Musette Minx 156
- Susan in the Country 103
- Susan Smith on her Back 184

L

Laid Back (Marchant) 188
Lategan, Barry
- Flippers, Barbados 98
- Mary 69

Latex by Cynthia (Mourthé) 199

Laughing Domina (Dietrich) 148
Les Essarts-le-Roi, France (Dunas) 66
Layla (Ashford) 173
L'éducation de Scarlett (Dupouy) 196
lenses, design 11–12
Lerebours, N. P. 14
Les Essarts-le-Roi, France (Dunas) 66
Les Jeux de la Comtesse B. (Dupouy) 213
Lichfield
- After Lunch 100
- Central Park, NYC 110
- Good Morning America 130
- The Hook 93
- Moscow Underground 82
- Piano Keys 157
- Provence 95
- Studio June 1993 113

lighting 11
Lipstick (Ashford) 218
Lisa on Silk (Horst) 49
Lujia Campion (Mourthé) 193

M

McKell, Iain 6
- Chippy 145
- Cornfield 140
- Eat Soup 163
- Egg 117
- Moulin Rouge, Vivienne Westwood, Spring 1997 197
- Three in a Boat 137

Maddox, Richard 9
Madlen and Conny (Eichler) 211
Maingot, Rosalind, Poise 48
Manassé 45, 46
Mantlepiece (Roff) 72
Marchant, Nic 124
- Laid Back 188
- Pigalle 136

Marconi, Guglielmo 22
Marks, George Harrison 17, 54, 55, 56, 57
Marlene Attacks (Mourthé) 170
Mary (Lategan) 69
M.M. (Kroll) 204
Monica, Saint-Tropez (D. Hamilton) 84
Morceau en Forme de Poire (Berquet) 109
Morey, Craig
- Jarrae 161
- Natalie 177
- Raven 112

Moscow Underground (Lichfield) 82
Moulin Rouge, Vivienne Westwood, Spring 1997 (McKell) 197
Mourthé, Christophe
- Cynthia and the Motorbikes 143
- Julia Campion 189
- Latex by Cynthia 199
- Lujia Campion 193
- Marlene Attacks 170
- No Milk Today 186
- Sandre and the Hook 133
- Sandre, Paris 129
- Smoking no Smoking 111

Muray, Nickolas, Composition 44
Musette Minx (Kroll) 156

N

Nadine and Madlen at home (Eichler) 187
narrative 6
Natalie (Morey) 177
naturism 16
Neith With Tumbleweed (Ritts) 90
Nell (Clarke) 206
Netztorso III (Blum) 119
Niépce, Joseph Nicéphore 8
No Milk Today (Mourthé) 186
Nude (Weston) 47
Nude at the Beach, Camargue (Clergue) 159
Nude Campden Hill London (Brandt) 63
Nude in the Lighthouse, Camargue (Clergue) 101
Nude London (Brandt) 59, 62
Nude London 61 Theatre Girl (Brandt) 60
Nude no.3, Los Angeles Studio (Dunas) 214
Nude by pillar (Farber) 178
Nude woman throwing hair out of pool (Curto) 142
nudes, attitudes to 6, 14, 16, 17
Nylon Nightmares (Eichler) 154

O

Obscene Publications Acts 15, 16–17
Odalisque III, NY (Horst) 52
Once Upon a Time in the West (Eichler) 171

P

Pandora (Park) 37
Pasadena, California (Dunas) 94
Park, Yvonne, Pandora 37
Parkinson, Norman
- August - Pirelli 76
- First Nude 58

Penprase, David 107, 151, 158, 172, 180, 209
Petzval, Josef 8
Piano Keys (Lichfield) 157
picture postcards 16
Pigalle (Marchant) 136
Pink Rubber (Dietrich) 165
Pirelli calendar 17
Poise (Maingot) 48
Polaroid 10
Portrait of Young Girl (Roff) 167
The Prayer (Ray) 42
Provence (Lichfield) 95
Provocation, South of France (D. Hamilton) 85
The Punishment of Luxury (Clarke) 96

R

Raven (Morey) 112
Ray, Man 16
- The Prayer 42
- Violon d'Ingres 39

Reclining Nude (Swannell) 182
Red Velvet Gloves (Elliot) 89
reflex cameras 12–13
Replicant (Dietrich) 87
Reutlinger, Léopold 26
Riebicke, Gerhard 40
Ritts, Herb
- Neith With Tumbleweed 90
- Tatjana II 91

Robl, Monika 166, 191
- Sappho 162, 179, 185

Roff, Charles 6, 18
- Chambre Rue la Condamine 210
- Chevi '62 71
- Flying Nude-Bare Naked Out the Window 64
- Mantlepiece 72
- Portrait of Young Girl 167
- Sisters Metallic Shoot 200
- Stockings Rue la Condamine 183
- Where's the Soap 190

Rue Marbeus, Paris (Dunas) 68

S

Sainte (Berquet) 131
Sandre and the Hook (Mourthé) 133
Sandre, Paris (Mourthé) 129
Sans Plomb 98 (Berquet) 220
Sappho (Robl) 162, 179, 185
Saudek, Jan
- The Deep Devotion of Ida 114
- Diszipline über Alles 150
- Homage to Great Vincent 99
- Walkman 75

Schulze, Johann 8
Scott Archer, Frederick 9
Sisters Metallic Shoot (Roff) 200
Smoking no Smoking (Mourthé) 111
The Society for the Suppression of Vice 15
stereoscope 9, 11–12, 15
Stockings Rue la Condamine (Roff) 6, 183
Streetwalker Blues (Elliot) 88
Strumpfhalter (Blum) 118
Studio June 1993 (Lichfield) 113
Study of Motion (Koppitz) 43
Susan in the Country (Kroll) 103
Susan Smith on her Back (Kroll) 184
Swannell, John 134
- Couple entwined 127
- Reclining Nude 182

T

Tanja Mit Rad (Blum) 195
Tarrant, Jon 201
Tatjana II (Ritts) 91
Techno Torso (Blum) 106
Theatre Girl (Wedge) 67
Three in a Boat (McKell) 137
Tina on the Azotea (Weston) 38
tintype 9
Twisted (Clarke) 138
Two lovely breasts round and full (Anonymous) 32

U

Un après-midi chez la marquise (Dupouy) 216
Unlocked (Eichler) 104

V

Violon d'Ingres (Ray) 39
The Visiter (Eichler) 217

W

Walkman (Saudek) 75
Watson, Trevor 18, 108, 125, 126, 144, 153, 169, 174, 202, 219
Wedge, James 17, 61, 65, 79
- The Dressing Room 80
- Girl in Dressing Room 81
- Theatre Girl 67

Wedgewood, Thomas 8
Weston, Edward
- Nude 47
- Tina on the Azotea 38

Wheatstone, Sir Charles 9
Where's the Soap (Roff) 190
Wlassies, Olga and Adorian 51
Wog (Olga and Adorian Wlassies) 51

Y

Yvette (Karsten) 160

LIST OF PICTURE TITLES

All pictures untitled except the following:

32 Two lovely breasts round and full
33 Bertram Park
37 Pandora
38 Tina on the Azotea
39 Violon d'Ingres
42 The Prayer
43 Study of Motion
44 Composition
47 Nude
48 Poise
49 Lisa on Silk
50 Jean Harlow
52 Odalisque III, NY
58 First Nude
59 Nude London
60 Nude London 61 Theatre Girl
62 Nude London
63 Nude Campden Hill London
64 Flying Nude-Bare Naked Out the Window
66 Les Essarts-le-Roi, France
67 Theatre Girl
68 Rue Marbeus, Paris
69 Mary
70 Château de Breteuil, Vallée de Chevreuse
71 Chevi '62
72 Mantlepiece
74 Feigning innocence, South of France
75 Walkman
76 August - Pirelli
77 Burnished Blondes
78 Die Chauffeurin
80 The Dressing Room
81 Girl in Dressing Room
82 Moscow Underground
83 Black is My True Love's Heart
84 Monica, Saint-Tropez
85 Provocation, South of France
86 Boulevard Flandrin, Paris I
87 Replicant
88 Streetwalker Blues
89 Red Velvet Gloves
90 Neith With Tumbleweed
91 Tatjana II
92 Handcuffs
93 The Hook
94 Pasadena, California
95 Provence
96 The Punishment of Luxury
97 Faithful Unto Death
98 Flippers, Barbados
99 Homage to Great Vincent
100 After Lunch
101 Nude in the Lighthouse, Camargue
102 Grayhall Mansion, Beverley Hills III
103 Susan in the Country
104 Unlocked
106 Techno Torso
109 Morceau en Forme de Poire
110 Central Park, NYC
111 Smoking no Smoking
112 Raven
113 Studio June 1993
114 The Deep Devotion of Ida
115 Diana Lake of Garda
117 Egg
118 Strumpfhalter
119 Netztorso III
120 Conversation While Undressing
121 Contemplation of the Eternal
122 Herztorso I
123 Aubergine I
127 Couple entwined
128 Dans la Serre
129 Sandre, Paris
130 Good Morning America
131 Sainte
132 Intèrieur parisien
133 Sandre and the Hook
134 Horse Series 1
135 Carmen
136 Pigalle
137 Three in a Boat
138 Twisted
139 Furka
140 Cornfield
142 Nude woman throwing hair out of pool
143 Cynthia and the Motorbikes
145 Chippy
146 Katharina
147 Katharina
148 Laughing Domina
149 Arizona Sunset
150 Diszipline über Alles
154 Nylon Nightmares
155 Brèue histoire de l'oeil
156 Musette Minx
157 Piano Keys
159 Nude at the Beach, Camargue
160 Yvette
161 Jarrae
162 Sappho
163 Eat Soup
164 Gotischer Torso
165 Pink Rubber
167 Portrait of Young Girl
168 Bubblegum
170 Marlene Attacks
171 Once Upon a Time in the West
173 Layla
175 Grand Phalène, prince des ténèbres
177 Natalie
178 Nude by pillar
179 Sappho
181 Hungerlust Capitalism
182 Reclining Nude
183 Stockings Rue la Condamine
184 Susan Smith on her Back
185 Sappho
186 No Milk Today
187 Nadine and Madlen at home
188 Laid Back
189 Julia Campion
190 Where's the Soap
192 Fundamental Practice
193 Lujia Campion
195 Tanja Mit Rad
196 L'éducation de Scarlett
197 Moulin Rouge. Vivienne Westwood, Spring 1997
199 Latex by Cynthia
200 Sisters Metallic Shoot
204 M.M.
205 Homage to Kodachrome
206 Nell
207 Hammersmith Palais
210 Chambre Rue la Condamine
211 Madlen and Conny
212 Blonde on White Leather
213 Les Jeux de la Comtesse B.
214 Nude no.3, Los Angeles Studio
216 Un après-midi chez la marquise
217 The Visiter
218 Lipstick
220 Sans Plomb 98

ACKNOWLEDGEMENTS & PICTURE CREDITS

The publishers would like to thank the following sources/photographers for their kind permission to reproduce the photographs in this book:

All photographs supplied by the photographers, and:
Sylvie Blum-Neubauer Art-Reprasentanz 106, 118, 119, 122, 123, 164, 195
©Bill Brandt Archive Ltd. 59, 60, 62, 63
©1981 Center for Creative Photography, Arizona Board of Regents 38, 47
Courtesy Jean Pierre Faur Editeur, Paris 109, 116, 131, 152, 155, 175, 215, 220
Hamiltons Photographers Limited, London 49, 52, 58, 76
The Image Bank 142, 178
Kobal Collection 50
Eric Kroll ©EK http://www.fetish-usa.com 102, 103, 156, 203, 204
Robert Montgomery & Partners 184, 202
Nostalgia Publications Ltd. 1 Victoria Street, off Nunnery Lane, York, YO2 1LZ, England. http://www.demon.co.uk/nospub/ 54-57
Courtesy Persona Films 176
© Man Ray Trust Paris, France 39, 42
© Herb Ritts, Courtesy Fahey/Klein Gallery, Los Angeles 90, 91
The Royal Photographic Society Collection, Bath, England 33, 37, 44, 48
Uwe Scheid Collection 20-32, 34-36, 39-43, 45, 46, 51
by courtesy of Unipart Group of Companies 82, 95, 100, 110, 113, 130, 157
by courtesy of United Distillers 93

Every effort has been made to acknowledge correctly and contact the source and/copyright holder of each picture, and Carlton Books Limited apologises for any unintentional errors or omissions which will be corrected in future editions of this book.

Carlton Books Ltd. would like to extend a special thank you to all the photographers for their help and co-operation in this project.
Thank you also to: Jacques Dupouy, Sarah Jarrett @ John Swannell Studios Ltd., Peter Kain & Penny Daly @ Lichfield Studios, Jean Paul Kernot, Natalia Puchalt @ Fahey/Klein Gallery, Tatiana Robbins & Jo Noon @ Hamiltons Photographers Limited, Sarah Saudek, Uwe Scheid & Frau Schmidt, Bo Steer & Elaine Ashton @ Robert Montgomery & Partners, Bettina Tetens @ Studio Klaus Kampert, Trudi @ Center for Creative Photography Arizona, Amanda Wedge.